AUSTRALIA

Publisher:	Aileen Lau
Project Editors:	Amanda Curtin, Tim Griggs, Vivien Kim, Aileen Lau, Bina Maniar & Dee Reesik
Design/DTP:	Sares Kanapathy
Illustrations:	Karen Leong
Cover Artwork:	Susan Harmer
Maps:	Superskill Graphics

Published in the United States by
PRENTICE HALL GENERAL REFERENCE
15 Columbus Circle
New York, New York, 10023

ISBN 0-671-87912-X

Titles in the series:
Alaska - American Southwest - Australia - Bali - California - Canada - Caribbean - China - England - Florida - France - Germany - Greece - Hawaii - India - Indonesia - Italy - Ireland - Japan - Kenya - Malaysia - Mexico - Nepal - New England - New York - Pacific Northwest USA - Singapore - Spain - Thailand - Turkey - Vietnam

USA MAINLAND SPECIAL SALES
Bulk purchases (10+copies) of the Travel Bugs series are available at special discounts for corporate use. The publishers can produce custom publications for corporate clients to be used as premiums or for sales promotion. Copies can be produced with custom cover imprints. For more information write to Special Sales, Prentice Hall Travel, Paramount Communications Building, 15th floor, 15 Columbus Circle, New York, NY 10023.

Printed in Singapore

AUSTRALIA

Text by Geoffrey Somers

With contributions from:
Amanda Curtin
Tim Griggs
Morten Strange

Project Editors
Amanda Curtin
Tim Griggs
Vivien Kim
Aileen Lau
Bina Maniar
Dee Reesik

Prentice Hall Travel

New York   London   Toronto   Sydney   Tokyo   Singapore

C O N T E N T S

C O N T E N T S

C O N T E N T S

C O N T E N T S

Outdoorsy oz, land of plenty .... and

plenty of land, where life is full

leisure, pleasure and sunshine.

f wholesome

Cars and trucks and things that go .... any which way to travel across this vast continent, an island of

desert, farmland and ranches,

outback, bush,

world. A stunning array

Born free... on the largest island in the

of flora, wildlife and marine life

proliferate from the deserts to the seas.

to span the rivers and horizons,

Buildings, bridges and blimps

far beyond the imagination and

dreams of Bligh and Cook.

Your first impressions of Australia will be of clear blue skies, huge horizons, lots of space, and the sense of freedom all this brings. It is a sort of freedom of the spirit that seems to grow with every breath of fresh air you take. The whole atmosphere seems pleasant and somehow calming. You feel you have arrived somewhere really different, somewhere nice, somewhere inviting.

Blue skies, huge horizons and an inviting sense of freedom.

Your first experience of the Australian people will be at the airport's immigration and customs desks. Here you will be confronted by burly six-footers whose intimidating appearance vanishes at once with their broad and genuine smiles of welcome. Courtesy and helpfulness, smiles and friendliness – these, too, are part of the es-

Introduction

1

Australian 'traffic' as protected by roadsigns.

sence of a country that will begin to grow on you within hours of your arrival.

Australians do not recognise class distinctions and there is no false pride about them (although they are certainly proud of their country, often intensely so!). They will take you at face value, even make allowances since you are a visitor. And providing you return smile for smile and respond naturally, you will soon be enjoying the outgoing and engaging nature of the average Australian.

Of course you've come to sightsee, so let's turn to some unique Australians that will captivate you, starting with the country's very own KKK – the Koala, Kangaroo and Kookaburra club. They have lots of delightful mates such as the platypus, wombat, frill-necked lizard, dingo, lyre bird, fairy penguin and black swan, and many others that are less delightful and so are best seen behind glass at the zoo. And then there's the flora: kangaroo paws, banksias, spider and donkey orchids, blackboys and gorgeous wild flowers that are as unusual as they are colourful.

City Sights

Then, of course, there are the man-made sights – the cities. Sydney is big, beautiful and brash. Its crown is a harbour of immense beauty; the jewel in that crown the curiously attractive Op-

Experience the friendliness of folk in the cities and out in the towns.

much a reason to visit Down Under. Australia's national poet, Banjo Paterson, penned these two magnificent lines about "the bush":

"And he saw the vision splendid of the sunlit plains extended"

Splendid indeed. Picture rolling green pastures that are turned into checkerboards of colour by mobs of grazing sheep, cattle or horses; vast fields of wheat, a million sheaves bowing their heads as they are rippled by a balmy wind; paddocks of corn, maize and other crops stretching as far as the eye can see; trees of immense grandeur standing guard over billabongs; and further, on the horizon, the forbidding mountain ranges that etch a stark picture beneath blue skies punctuated with cottonballs of pure white cloud.

The bush has many secrets. Listen to the parakeets, galahs and other brilliantly plumaged birds as they cackle an angry warning at your approach, or to the curious laugh of the kookaburra. Catch a glimpse of a big boomer kangaroo as he bounds into the protection of the bush in fear of your imagined shotgun, or the flushed hare as it flees into its burrow.

Look out for a koala, perched far from your reach in the crook of a eucalyptus tree, munching a pawful of tender, aromatic leaf tips while showering droppings on to anyone who might venture below. Sense your innards freeze as you stumble on a slow-moving goanna with flashing blue tongue and chilling hiss. Observe the proud bearing of the dingo, seemingly a delightful dog, but a cunning killer which cannot be domesticated; and the smirk of the cane toad, the bane of Queensland.

Then there is the delight you will experience as you spot quaint country road signs such as "Koalas cross here at night", "Kangaroos next 15 km" or "Wombats cross here".

And the dismay you will feel as you see by the roadside the broken carcass of a spiny ant-eater that was not nimble enough to escape the wheels of a thundering truck, a jet black crow that strutted too close to the edge, or a magnificent 'roo that stood half a second too long on the road, mesmerized by the approaching headlights. Possibly, you'll feel less sympathy for the large snakes whose ribbon-like remains bear testimony to the excellent aim of some passing motorist.

Yes, these are all persuasive reasons to visit Australia and they are only a sample from Australia's enormous welcoming table. The many other attractions such as beaches, rivers, resorts, food, adventure trips, national parks, Aboriginal cave paintings, the outback, the Red Centre, Bondi Beach and Ayers Rock are described in the chapters that follow.

But hopefully your appetite has been whetted and you have a taste for the feast of sights and experiences that await the visitor to Australia.

Welcome to warm colourful Oz!

For most of its geographical history, the Australian land mass was part of the super-continent. With the cooling of the earth's crust, the super-continent broke up, and over millions of years the pieces drifted apart to form the continents as we know them today. To illustrate the changes wrought by this movement, the Nullarbor Plain linking both sides of Australia was once sea floor. The Ice Age also left its mark, one example being Sydney Harbour, which is actually a "drowned" valley.

About 50 million years ago, the joined land mass of Australia and New Guinea separated from Asia in the north-west and Antarctica in the south. Thirty-five million years later, New Guinea broke away, making Australia the world's largest island and her smallest continent. After the last Ice Age, 2 million years ago, gi-

'roo and 'mu crested and perched on Parliament House, Canberra.

ant animals and birds roamed the then green land until 15,000 years ago, when the climate dried up and the mega-fauna died out. Ten thousand years ago, sea levels rose to form the Bass Strait, separating Tasmania from southern Australia. Volcanoes were still erupting 6,000 years ago and the seas had risen to their present levels.

Australia is the lowest and flattest of all the continents, as well as the driest. Totalling 7,682,300 square km, it is almost as large as the United States (excluding Alaska), and 50 percent larger than Continental Europe (taking the USSR as the border).

Australia's western shores are washed by the Indian Ocean and its east coast by the Pacific. Its nearest land masses are Southern Africa to the west and South America to the east, with Irian Jaya/Papua New Guinea to the north and Antarctica to the south.

"Native Lords of the Soil"

Aborigines moving down from Southeast Asia at least 40,000 years ago became the first inhabitants of Australia. The sea level then was much lower, and chains of islands provided stepping stones south. Nevertheless, voyages of 60 km and more had to be made across water – arguably the world's first waterborne migration. Though black-skinned, the Aborigines are not a negroid race but of Aryan extraction. (They do not "throw back". Today, blonde hair and

blue eyes are not uncommon among oft-diluted descendants).

Twenty thousand years ago, settlements were well established, albeit sparsely, across the country. The Aborigines led a nomadic life, following the movement of wildlife with seasonal changes. The menfolk were hunter-gatherers who fashioned weapons and tools from stone, wood, bone and shell. The hunters required cunning, stealth and accuracy to stalk sharp-eared game such as kangaroos. Campfires were made by furiously rubbing the point of one stick into a hole in another, or by striking granite stones together to produce sparks. The women grubbed for insects, roots and seeds. Life was as harsh as the conditions they had to endure. It was customary for childbirth to take place by the wayside with minimal fuss. Within minutes, the mother would place the infant to the breast and move after the tribe, sustained by a handful or two of placenta. Mobility was the key to survival; crippled babies were killed instantly, and the aged were put to death on becoming an impediment. When a group had many young men and few maidens, or a long drought brought near-starvation, a crude operation performed on the youths with a sharp stick or stone ensured that there would be no unwanted mouths to feed.

Arrival of the White Man

When the first white settlers arrived in

Australia just over 200 years ago, there were at least 300,000 Aborigines. But steadily the numbers dwindled as white-introduced factors devastated tribes. With no natural immunity to western disease, many were killed by small-pox, tuberculosis, measles, whooping cough and in-fluenza. Prime coastal hunting and fishing grounds were lost. Spears were no de-fence against guns, and the Aborigines were driven onto peripheral scrub-land or near-desert. A few were shot: some for hunting sheep or cattle on former tribal land, oth-ers because they were con-sidered untrustworthy and a danger to the whites. As the naturalist Charles Darwin wrote: "Wher-ever the European has trod, Death seems to pursue the aboriginal. [In] the Ameri-cas, Polynesia, the Cape of Good Hope and Australia... we find the same re-sult."

Outside the cities, where little law prevailed, Aboriginal people were occa-sionally murdered for sport; a shot through the head of a native or a kan-garoo made little difference to the hard-ened pioneers of the era. But the cruel-ties inflicted on mainland Aborigines pale when compared with Tasmania's drive to rid the island of some 5,000 native people.

There, in 1830, the whites joined hands in a huge human dragnet to trap the Aborigines like animals, but the bush-wise quarry slipped through to safety. Feelings against them rose to a fury: "The natives have been very troublesome and treacherous, spearing and murdering all they find.... The only alternative...is to annihilate them at once", wrote one settler. But the "an-nihilation" of the Tasmanian Abo-rigines was not to be swift. Instead, they were searched out in small groups and coerced into going to the bleak, virtually gameless islands in Bass Strait, north of Tasmania, where it was planned to "Europeanise" them. By 1875, the race had completely died out.

The last Tasmanian full-blood was the purported beauty, Truganini. Hers was a tragic story. Her sister had been kidnapped by a sealer, her mother stabbed to death, her uncle shot, and her tribal husband's hands cut off be-fore he was flung into the sea to drown. She died after a life of hardship and misery on Flinders Island, but even in death there was no dignity for Truganini. Her embalmed head was sent to London as a scientific curiosity, and only in

Plight of the Aborigines in Australia's early history.

1990 was it returned to Australia and given to an Aboriginal rights group for proper burial – 115 years after her death.

On the mainland, the Aborigines rapidly lost their hunting skills, their pride and much of their identity. A Polish explorer, Count Paul de Strzelecki, summed up their plight: "Degraded, subdued, confused and distrustful, ill concealing emotions of anger, scorn or revenge, emaciated and covered with rags, these native lords of the soil, more like spectres of the past than living men, are dragging on a melancholy existence to a yet more melancholy doom".

Suddenly their world had collapsed. They had no hunting grounds, no rights, no possessions and no place in the white man's world. A keen-eyed few were called on in emergencies as "black-trackers" to guide search parties hunting down fugitives and lost children. Others worked as stockmen, labourers and domestic servants on the great pastoral stations. However, the great majority had to eke out an existence as beggars or, for the gins (women), as prostitutes.

Today's Aborigines are entitled to social welfare payments, but sadly, in some cases, much of this money is spent on alcohol. Aboriginal land rights and compensation are an ongoing issue on Australia's political agenda. In recent years, some tribal lands have been returned to Aboriginal ownership, the most notable example being the magnificent Ayers Rock, again known by its Aboriginal name, "Uluru".

The "Great South Land"

The ancient Greeks postulated that a "Great South Land" must exist to balance the earth on its axis. Such reasoning was crushed in the Middle Ages with the emergence of the flat-earth dogma, but by the 15th century visionaries such as Prince Henry the Navigator of Portugal were again debating the existence of "Terra Australis Incognita" (Unknown Southern Land). The Portuguese were the first Europeans to find Australia's west coast, but having carved up the New World with Spain by Papal decree and believing this to be out of bounds to them, they tried to keep their discovery a secret. (Of course, the navigators first made certain that the rocky coastline hid no immediately accessible Peruvian-style El Dorado).

The Dutch were the next to visit Australia's rocky coast, with the help of stolen maps bought from the Portuguese. They called it "New Holland". In 1642, the Dutchman Abel Tasman found another large land mass further south than had previously been explored, which he named "Van Diemen's Land" after the Governor-General of the Dutch East Indies, Anthony van Diemen. Tasman's discovery was Australia's biggest island, now named Tasmania after the intrepid explorer.

On some old maps, Australia was described as "Terra Australis" or "Continens Australis". In 1605, the Spaniard de Quiros named what he thought was the Great South Land "Austrialia del Espiritu Santo" (Southern Land of the Holy Spirit), but actually he was about 1500 km east, in the New Hebrides.

Well into the 19th century, the continent was variously known as New Holland, New South Wales or Botany Bay, but eventually, on the common-sense recommendation of the English navigator Captain Matthew Flinders, it was named Australia.

The coast is dotted with many names that remind us of those who sought the country's secrets. Examples include

Torres Strait, named after the Portuguese Luiz Vaez de Torres; Dirk Hartog Island after a Dutchman of the same name; Cape Leeuwin and Arnhem Land after two Dutch ships; and Pelsart Islands after Francois Pelsaert, commander of the Dutch ship *Batavia*, which was wrecked there in 1629. With the arrival of English adventurers, other names appeared on the map, like Dampier Archipelago after the English buccaneer-turned-explorer William Dampier. Evidence of explorations by the French are many: the Monte Bello Islands, Geographe Bay, Capes Naturaliste, Leveque, Buffon and Adieux, the Bonaparte and Recherche Archipelagos, D'Entrecasteaux Channel and Point, Rivoli and Lacepede Bays.

Explorer Extraordinary

Australia became particularly attractive to England following the loss of the American Colonies in 1783. England needed somewhere to transport her convicts, and reports by Lieutenant James Cook suggested that Australia offered great promise. Cook, a brilliant young navigator, had been chosen to captain the 368-ton barge *Endeavour* on a voyage along the east coast of Australia in 1770. The main purpose of the expedition was purportedly to allow scientists to observe over the Pacific the passage of Venus between the earth and sun.

His sealed orders, however, were to investigate the worth or otherwise of

Raising the Union Jack in the new colonial outposts.

what was then called New Holland. After circumnavigating New Zealand's two main islands, Cook sailed west to make his first landfall in what he called Botany Bay because the nearby bushland yielded many interesting plants, shrubs and trees. On 21 April 1770, Cook raised the British flag and formally took possession of the eastern coast of New Holland, naming it New South Wales.

Cook, promoted to the rank of Captain, made two more voyages to the Pacific, in 1772–1775 and 1776–1779. On the second of these, he was killed in a clash in the Hawaiian Islands by a large force of natives armed with spears.

Cook left his cartographic stamp along much of the east coast of Australia, with names like Bass Strait, Bateman, Byron, Jervis, Rockingham, Wide and Broken Bays, Breaksea Spit, Broadsound and Cleveland; Capes Hawke, Moreton and Howe; Point Danger and Eddystone Rocks; and such islands as Broughton, Dunk, Fitzroy, Gloucester, Northumberland and Prince of Wales. Towards the end of his voyage along the Great Barrier Reef, Cook's nomenclature became tinged with irony when he chose the name Cape Tribulation for a place where, as he later recorded, "began all our Troubles". The following day, the *Endeavour* crunched into what he named Endeavour Reef.

Cook's successor was the equally intrepid explorer Captain Matthew Flinders, who circumnavigated Australia and Tasmania in his voyages of 1795–1799 and 1801–1803, filling in most of the remaining blanks on the map.

The Golden Fleece

On Cook's recommendation but not at the exact place he had chosen, a white settlement began on the shores of the future Sydney in January 1788, with the arrival of the First Fleet. In command was the man chosen to be the colony's first governor, Arthur Phillip, a superannuated captain in the Royal Navy of whom historians noted: "He was sent out to found a convict settlement (but instead) laid the foundations of a great dominion". The ships landed 548 male prisoners and 188 women, plus the 280 officers sent out to guard them or to help organise the construction of simple dwellings and the planting of crops.

Transportation was a cruel, harsh punishment, and it was sometimes meted out for the most trifling of offences, such as stealing a loaf of bread. Conditions on the convict ships were appalling, and 48 prisoners died on the long journey. However, in the settlement's first few years of failed crops and near-starvation, it seemed at times that these were the fortunate ones.

Two years later, the Second Fleet arrived carrying the venal officers of the New South Wales Corps, the perpetrators of the Rum Rebellion of 1808 (see page 20), and in 1791 the Third Fleet brought another load of felons, some harlots, as well as a number of forgers and a few Irish political agitators.

The Eureka Stockade, Ballarat.

In 1792, the first trading ship, the *Philadelphia*, dropped anchor in Sydney Harbour, finding it to be one of the safest and most magnificent in the world. Within a year, the first free immigrants stepped ashore in Sydney. Life was hard for the new settlers. They had to grapple with previously unknown extremes of weather, scurvy, crime and shortages of food, clothing and skilled labour.

Ten years after the first landing, two events took place that were to have a tremendous impact on the future of the country – the first Merino sheep were imported from the Cape of Good Hope (on the southern tip of Africa) and coal was found near Newcastle. In 1803, the first samples of Australian wool, coarse though they were, were hailed in Eng-

land, where the mills were suffering a shortage of supplies from Spain because of the Napoleonic Wars. The settler who brought the samples was the fiery, duel-fighting John Macarthur, who had come to Australia as a Major in the New South Wales Corps. Macarthur arranged for better-class Merinos to be sent to Sydney, as well as rams and ewes from the Royal flock at Kew. He then returned himself on the appropriately named *Argo* with a grant for 5,000 acres of fine pasture land. Through Macarthur's efforts, the country became the land of the Golden Fleece, and the first shipment of saleable wool was exported to England within four years. Meanwhile, the enormous coal deposits that had been discovered in the Newcastle district were the impetus for the beginnings of industrial development in New South Wales, and soon steamships began plying the eastern seaboard.

In 1804, Tasmania's capital, Hobart, was founded. Perth, capital of Western Australia and set on the banks of the Swan River, was founded in 1829, 132 years after the Dutchman Wilhem de Vlamingh first visited it. Melbourne, probably the most conservative of Australia's state capitals, and second in size only to Sydney, surprisingly had its birth as late as 1835, only a year before Adelaide in South Australia.

Australia's states were already becoming sensitive to the presence of convicts and selective about their inhabitants. The fledgling settlement in Queensland's Moreton Bay asked, unsuccessfully at first, for free men, but Sydney's cry was heard first, and transportation of convicts to New South Wales ended in 1840. Perth was settled as a free colony, but convicts were introduced in 1850 at the request of the settlers, who were suffering from a crippling shortage of labour and external capital. Transportation ceased in 1850 on Australia's eastern shores, and in 1868 in the west. Australia could now raise its eyes from the spectre of the ball-and-chain gangs working on the roads to higher dreams.

The original squatters were an early example of the Australian people's famous "cheek". The name described those settlers who ran sheep and built pastoral empires on land to which they had no legal title, although gradually it came

to be used to refer to pastoralists and graziers in general.

The practice of squatting resulted from the conflict between the government's desire to concentrate settlement around designated centres and the settlers' desire to make use of the vast areas of pasture lands suitable for grazing sheep. It was a conflict that was resolved – to the benefit of the squatters – in 1847 after lobbying by the newly formed Pastoralist Association. Squatters were granted 14-year leases on the land they occupied, with options to purchase.

The "legal" squatters became men of enormous affluence. They built elaborate houses and lived as fine gentleman – as far as that was possible in Australia's harsh country. Indeed, some lost their entire fortunes through sheer extravagance. However, most went on to

HE FOREST CREEK DIGGINGS, MOUNT ALEXANDER, PORT PHILLIP.

By the last decade of the colonial era, Australia moved from prison to paradise, and opportunists rushed in for wool, crops, coal and gold.

found the great stations that have been immortalised in Australian literature.

The First Gold Rush

In the 1850s, "Gold!" became the cry on everybody's lips. Thousands of hopefuls had boarded ship from Sydney for the United States to join the "Forty-niners" in the great Californian gold rush. Only two years later, in 1851, news spread faster than a bushfire that gold had been found near Bathurst, in New South Wales, and soon afterwards strikes were reported in Victoria. Back flocked the diggers from San Francisco, joined by hundreds of thousands of fortune-seekers from Britain, Europe and China.

The existence of gold was known to the government well before 1851, but the news had been suppressed to protect the fragile, convict-based economy. It has been argued that the authorities' concern over the loss of so much young blood to the Californian goldfields could have been behind the announcement of the Bathurst and Victorian finds. By law, all gold and silver found in the ground was the property of the Crown. However, the law did not cover alluvial (surface) gold, as the experienced diggers from California announced with a "whoop" – and at first, all finds were alluvial. In any case, gold brought people and prosperity, so the authorities soon changed the law.

Professionals, sly grog sellers,

Rum Rebellion

Australians have a reputation for being convivial people: they like a drink from time to time.

Nor is it altogether an undeserved reputation. Some would say this is not just because Australia produces some of the world's best wine and beer. Australian drinking also has historical roots that go very deep.

In the very early days of the settlement, New South Wales was a lonely and desperate place. The population of Sydney was made up almost entirely of convicts and their guards of the New South Wales Corps: each group was as hard-bitten as the other. It was not surprising that men and women alike found their solace in booze – most of it imported rum. It served both as an anaesthetic and currency.

It is easy to imagine the euphoria when word got around one day in 1793 that 7500 gallons of rum had arrived in Sydney Harbour on the aptly-named American trading ship *Hope*. The *Hope* carried other vital cargo too, but the skipper was a businessman. He insisted the colony had to buy the entire cargo of rum first.

John Macarthur, later to become a legendary figure in the early settlement of New South Wales, was at this time regimental paymaster of the New South Wales Corps. Ever a man with a visionary eye for business, Macarthur pledged the regiment's money and bought the rum for himself and his fellow officers. They then sold it to the other settlers.

This was more than just a good bargain. It put into the grasp of the New South Wales Corps (thereafter known as the "Rum Corps") a virtual monopoly of the settlement's premier trading commodity – grog.

Building on this for many years afterwards the Corps, quite unconstitutionally, moved from strength to strength, controlling trade in a wide variety of goods.

Officers of the Corps didn't simply get rich through rum. They became all-powerful for a time in their remote outpost.

The early Governors of New South Wales were mostly naval men, despised by the officers of the Rum Corps, and government attempts to rein in the Corps were flaunted more and more openly.

Things came to an extraordinary pass on 26 January 1808, exactly 20 years after the first settlement. It was on that day that the officers of the Corps decided they had had enough of their latest reforming naval Governor and over-threw him. The irrepressible Macarthur organised the coup from prison, and had the pleasure of regaining his liberty and seeing the Governor

preachers and newspapermen made their homes in the many towns which sprang up around the major strikes. Bendigo, Ballarat and Castlemaine became thriving centres, while Melbourne was transformed into a booming commercial capital.

Fuelled by the surge of diggers, Australia's population reached 1 million in 1858. But not everybody was as welcome as his neighbour. The frugality, patience and tirelessness of the Chinese gold-seekers angered many miners, and differences were exacerbated by language problems. There were fights, then riots, and finally restrictions on Chinese immigration – and the "White Australia" policy was born.

By the time Australia entered the last decades of the colonial era, it had changed from a prison to a paradise, thanks to wool, gold, coal, sugar, wheat and other crops. The sugar industry in Queensland was growing so fast that the White Australia policy had to be relaxed to allow the importation of cane-cutters from Asia as a source of cheap labour, a scheme that at times smacked

himself confined.

This particular Governor, incidentally, had extraordinary bad luck with mutinies. He was none other than William Bligh, whose ship the *Bounty* had been taken from him a few years earlier in perhaps the most famous maritime hijack of all time.

Such was the Rum Rebellion of New South Wales. Nor was it simply a case of rash action by a handful of disgruntled officers. It was a full-scale coup, and after it the Rum Corps ran the new colony as a military junta for two years, to all intents and purposes out of the control of London.

So powerful were the perpetrators, and so vital to the prosperity of the colony, that the Rum Rebellion went virtually unpunished. Once again William Bligh, freed now by the new Governor Macquarie from the clutches of this latest band of mutineers, was to be cheated of the revenge he demanded.

At the time there was not much amusement about the colony's addiction to alcohol, and nothing very attractive about the corrupt army officers who trafficked in it.

Nevertheless, perhaps it's only in Australia that a military putsch could have been fuelled entirely by…rum.

of near-slavery. It had taken 70 years for the population to reach 1 million, but in just 19 years it had doubled, then it reached 3 million in 1889, just 101 years after the first landing.

However, it was not all smooth sailing for the colonists. An unprecedented land boom in Victoria in the 1880s culminated in an almighty crash that saw banks fail and a wave of bankruptcies. Then the maritime industry became embroiled in an industrial dispute that lasted five years and involved not only the waterside workers, but shearers and

miners as well. Eventually, the workers realised that their voices would only be heard if they entered the political arena, and as a result the Australian Labor Party was born.

Out of the gloom of financial failure and strikes came a new ray of hope. In 1892, gold was discovered in the West: first at Coolgardie and soon after at Kalgoorlie. Huge numbers of gold-seekers from all walks of life invaded what became known as the "Golden Mile", and gold transformed the fortunes of another colony, Perth, just as it had Melbourne decades before.

The Birth of a Nation

In 1901, Australia's colonial era came to an end when the self-governing colonies of New South Wales, Victoria, Queensland, Tasmania, South Australia and Western Australia federated to become the six states of the Commonwealth of Australia. There had been many years of cooperation between colonies on such issues as the cessation of transportation, although there were also areas of conflict, such as free trade versus protectionism, which impeded the progress towards nationhood. The recognition of the need to defend Australia's shores played a major role in the colonies' decision to unite.

A Federal Constitution was drawn up, and the British Westminster System of Parliament adopted. Edmund Barton was made the country's first Prime Min-

Early settlements.

ister, the head of the Federal Government, and each state elected a premier to govern its own legislature. A federal governor-general and state governors represented the new nation's colonial links with Britain, but their functions were mainly ceremonial. Key operational areas like defence, foreign affairs and trade, customs, immigration and quarantine were placed under federal control, while the states were allocated jurisdiction over law and order, education, health, primary industries and forests, roads, mines, harbours, roads and railways, water supplies, public works and community services.

The first Federal Parliament was opened in Melbourne, which, helped by the wealth from its goldfields, had leap-frogged Sydney to become Australia's premier city.

The Warring Spirit

Australia had already begun repaying its debt to its founding fathers in faraway Westminster. A popular song of the day proclaimed "Australia Will Be There", and she was. Contingents were sent to help British troops in the Sudan in 1885, the Boer War in 1899 and China in 1900. However, it was in the Great War of 1914–1918 that Australia's greatest sacrifice yet was made.

Packed troop ships sailed regularly as Australia threw its all behind "King and Country". Never-ending casualty

The Kelly Legend

Australian folklore often features the exploits of the bushrangers, outlaws on horseback who enjoyed strong public sympathy and support because of the almost universal hatred of the police and authority which prevailed at the time. Bushrangers counted on that support and cultivated it by taking pains to rob only from the rich and by avoiding unnecessary violence. And while they rarely gave to the poor, they were sometimes generous with the rum they had stolen. In return, they found a ready supply of accomplices, and the police were faced with a shortage of informants. Many bushrangers achieved fame, such as Ben Hall, Jack Donohoe (The Wild Colonial Boy) and Moondyne Joe, but the most famous of all was Ned Kelly.

Edward Kelly was born in Victoria in 1854, the son of an Irish convict. He started his criminal career modestly, stealing cattle and horses, but soon gained notoriety after shooting a constable who was in the act of arresting Ned's brother, Dan. The Kelly brothers fled to New South Wales and joined up with Joseph Byrne and Stephen Hart to form the Kelly gang. Despite the large rewards offered for their arrest, they roamed the countryside for several years, robbing banks and small towns. Kelly's infamy soared after he killed three constables in one particular battle with the police.

It was in the Victorian town of Glenrowan that Kelly made his last stand. The gang was ambushed by the police in the local hotel, and all but Ned were slain. After being tried for his crimes and found guilty, he was hanged in November 1880, just 26 years old.

Ned Kelly has been the subject of three major films (with Mick Jagger playing the lead in one), a rock opera, several plays, a ballet, paintings, sculptures, ballads and reenactments. Criminal he may have been, but Kelly was a hero to the working classes of his time and his legend has fascinated generations ever since.

lists in the newspapers unfolded the disaster that befell the Australian and New Zealand Army Corps forces at Gallipoli in 1915, giving birth to the legend of the fighting ANZAC spirit. Severe losses to bullets and deadly gas were subsequently to occur in the French trenches. Eventually, the war claimed 60,000 Australian lives, with 325,000 casualties, all from a total population of less than 5 million.

Back in Australia, the country surged ahead in kangaroo-like leaps and bounds, overcoming the occasional disasters such as bushfires, floods and droughts that plagued the country – and still do. In 1917, the transcontinental railway opened to link the eastern capitals with Perth and the "Golden West".

Captain Ross Smith and Lieutenant Keith Smith flew from England to Australia in 1919, while other aviators such as Charles Kingsford Smith and Charles Thomas Ulm crossed the Pacific to pioneer international routes. In the dusty outback of northern Australia, the Queensland and Northern Territory Aerial Services began operations in 1920, offering joyrides and charter flights. Today, under the acronym Qantas, it is Australia's national airline and enjoys the reputation of being the safest airline in the world.

In 1927, the squabbling between Melbourne and Sydney over which should be the national capital was ended by moving the Federal Parliament to

Canberra, well inland and roughly equidistant from the two.

As a result of the expansion of domestic radio services, the Royal Flying Doctor Service was formed in 1928, providing the vast, sparsely populated outback areas with a centralised medical service, as well as a social communication network.

The 1920s, a decade of relative prosperity, slid into the 1930s, a decade of disaster. The worldwide Great Depression struck Australia, and it was a time of declining export prices, rising taxes, massive retrenchments, wage cuts for those lucky enough to have a job and sustenance work for those who weren't so lucky. The average Australian, who had grown accustomed to a high standard of living, was suddenly faced with making do and going without – and it was a bitter pill to swallow.

For Sydney, the highlight of the decade was the opening of its magnificent Harbour Bridge in 1932. In an astonishing manifestation of the anti-establishment stance so often seen in Australia, a galloping major named de Groote pushed by the VIPs on his charger "opened" the bridge by hacking through the obligatory ribbon with his sword. Six million Australians guffawed at the upstaging of the politicians.

War Again

Until 1939, Australia was a land of 7 million people who thought of themselves as rugged individualists. At the same time, they took pride in looking at the map and seeing their country as the largest red blob of the British Empire in the southern hemisphere. Britain was the "Old Country" that everybody looked up to. The advertising slogan of the time – "Buy British, Buy Best!" – was considered not a catchcry but a statement of faith. British workmanship was accepted as the best in the world. By contrast, every Australian was convinced that the Japanese produced "cheap and shoddy" exports, and their planes and tanks were "made of tin". That dream ended with a bang on 8 December 1941. Pearl Harbour and its aftermath jolted Australia into bloody reality.

Australia had proudly been among the first to go to Britain's aid when war was declared in September 1939. One army division after another sailed off to serve "King and Country". Australian pilots flew in the Battle of Britain, while the navy helped sink an Italian light cruiser in the Mediterranean and a marauding German battleship in the Atlantic.

These were stirring deeds indeed, but a high price was paid – and not only from casualties. Many Australian troops were taken prisoner in Greece and Crete, and the surrender of Singapore put many more into the cruel Japanese POW camps.

Its forces critically weakened, Australia was left to defend itself to a large extent. Its northern cities and towns were bombed regularly, and Japanese

After the pioneer years a federal government prevails. The Southern Cross and the Union Jack unite on the flag.

troops and warships formed a menacing crescent in the north. Enemy air and naval bases extended from Timor and Java in the west to New Britain and the Solomons in the east. Two midget submarines even got into Sydney Harbour and hit a ferry.

With Churchill intent on defeating Nazi Germany and its European ally, Italy, Australian Prime Minister John Curtin had no choice but to turn to "Uncle Sam" for military help. General Douglas MacArthur and the American forces he commanded, initially from Melbourne and later from Brisbane, became Australia's saviours. The country was the springboard from which the Allied forces gradually won back control of the Pacific. But it was a painful coming of age for Australia.

Post-War Immigration

The lessons of World War II had taught Australia that she had to look after herself. Peace-time saw the country jerked from cosy pre-war isolationism into international *realpolitik*. Australia had to find its own place in the family of nations, but for many years that place, unrealistically, was not seen in an Asian context.

When the cry went up that Australia must "Populate or perish", it was automatically assumed that the newcomers would be white.

Immigration reached near-frenzy

when a concerted campaign to attract English settlers first began. Ex-servicemen and their families were offered free passage (funded by the British Government), while other families could make the voyage for 10 pounds per adult, with children travelling free. The prospect of a new life "Down Under" attracted such interest that even before the scheme began in 1947, there were three-quarters of a million enquiries at Australia House in London.

Apart from Britons disenchanted with the lifestyle of the immediate post-war years, a far larger pool of possible migrants lay at hand in Europe. Twelve million people had been displaced by the war, and 170,000 of them chose to emigrate to Australia. Wartime differences were forgotten, and migrants flocked in from Italy, Germany, Austria, Greece and the eastern European countries. The immigration net was extended to Egypt, Lebanon and Turkey, and then to Chile, Argentina, Brazil and Peru. Between 1945 and 1963, over 1.5 million people emigrated to Australia, changing the country's racial composition forever.

The White Australia policy was totally disbanded in the 1970s, a decade that saw significant emigration from Asia, including large numbers of Vietnamese refugees.

Government of the Nation

The Federal Government in Canberra

Aboriginal art from early times.

carries out its functions through two elected houses: the lower house (the House of Representatives) and the upper house (the Senate). There are 148 members of the lower house and 76 senators, with seats apportioned on a per capita basis throughout the country's six states and two territories. The lower house, where most legislation originates, debates an average of 200 bills each year, which subsequently go to the Senate for ratification. After passing to the Governor-General for Vice-Regal assent, they become law.

The peppery daily session called "Question Time" gives back-bench politicians the chance to question the Prime Minister and cabinet ministers about the Government's stance on the issues of the day. Through constant media coverage and broadcasting of parliamentary proceedings, the government is kept accountable to the nation for its actions and attitudes, particularly on controversial subjects.

The Senate provides a system of checks and balances against the lower house, and is itself subject to counterbalances: it cannot amend bills dealing with national finances, or increase any proposed charge on the public.

The National Parliament usually has two main sessions each year: the first from February to June and the second from August to December. While the cumulative total of the legislators' "working days" in Canberra is seldom more than two-and-a-half months a year, they return to their respective constituencies between sittings to deal with voters' problems at the grassroots level.

The Prime Minister and inner members of the cabinet live in and work from Canberra, where they are responsible for hands-on decision-making on international and domestic issues.

Australia's parliamentary system works on a party basis, the two main parties being Labor (broadly representing the working and lower middle classes) and the National or Liberal Parties (broadly representing business interests and the middle and upper classes). States with an agriculture-based economy have a strong Country Party machine to represent rural interests.

The most dramatic event in Australia's post-war history was in November 1975, when the Governor-General, Sir John Kerr, dismissed the Federal Government led by Labor leader Gough Whitlam. Australia's economy was falling into recession, and Whitlam's government was facing opposition in the Liberal-controlled Senate. When the Senate blocked supply and demanded an immediate election, the Governor-General exercised never-before-used powers provided for in the Constitution and sacked the government. Liberal leader Malcolm Fraser was appointed as interim Prime Minister until new elections could be held.

Labor supporters throughout the country were outraged by the Governor-General's actions and took to the streets in protest, but to no avail. The subsequent elections one month later saw Fraser lead the conservatives to a landslide victory. The Labor Party came into power in Canberra, led by a former Rhodes scholar and trade union arbitrator Bob Hawke. The Governor-General is the man Hawke displaced as head of the Labor Party, Bill Hayden, who had happily accepted his new non-political role. The Liberal Party suffered its third successive defeat by Labor in the 1990 Federal Elections. However, Hawke was replaced by Paul Keating the new Prime Minister of the Federal Ministry on 27 December, 1991.

Fierce leadership battles and squabbling within and between the parties feature heavily in Australia's politics and despite their serious implications, rarely fail to entertain.

Australians call their homeland the "Lucky Country" – and for good reason. Australia is blessed with a multitude of natural assets and is one of the world's great larders. But the people of Australia are a happy-go-lucky lot, and in recent years have grossly overspent on luxury imports, tipping the balance sheet into the red. In 1988–1989, the deficit totalled almost A$3,500 million, causing the country's Treasurer to warn seriously that Australia was in danger of becoming a "banana republic". That caused a bit of a laugh among free-spending Aussies – but the recession that began in 1991 sent the economy into a nose-dive and unemployment became widespread. The Prime Minister decreed that Australians could no longer rely on the natural resources of the "Lucky Country" and instead must strive to use her intellectual and entrepreneurial resources to become the "Clever Country".

The image most people have of Australia is of a country rich from its exports of wheat, wool and meat. Indeed, these are important entries on Austral-

Economy

Farming carrots in Victoria.

29

Open-cut coal mining in the "Lucky Country".

ia's balance sheet, but much more of Australia's wealth now comes out of the ground. Mineral sales to overseas countries bring in A$16,000 million a year, the most valuable export being coal, worth an annual A$5,045 million.

Although it is not widely known, Australia is the world's largest producer of diamonds. Of the 30 million carats mined from the Argyle fields in the north, 6 percent are pure, high-quality gemstones, 39 percent are cheap gemstones and the balance are industrial-grade diamonds.

Australian opals are world famous.

Golden Sands

Australia is also the world's largest source of mineral sands, which are used as alloying elements in both ferrous and non-ferrous metallurgy. These sands are found in igneous rock and are carried by river from the hills of the interior to the coastal beaches where, being heavier than beach sand, they become concentrated by wave and tidal action. Each year, bulk carriers sail away with 1,349,500 tonnes of ilmenite, 465,000 tonnes of zircon, 249,200 tonnes of rutile and 12,000 tonnes of monazite.

Nickel, iron ore and steel are also major exports. Australia is the world's third largest source of nickel and the fourth largest producer of iron ore. Exports of iron ore, mainly to Japan and China, are worth A$1,685 million per annum, while yearly production of steel ingots is valued at A$6,651 million.

Though the fabulous gold boom days are over, Australia remains the western world's fourth biggest producer of gold, and also smelts 1,100 tonnes of silver a year. Zinc mines produce 753,000 tonnes and lead mines 486,000 tonnes. Alumina and aluminium bring in a combined $A2,000 million each year.

Nature's bounty extends to fuel oil and natural gas. Australia's oilfields produce 29.5 million cubic metres of crude oil per year, and natural gas output totals 14,751 gigalitres. The annual production of uranium, which averages 4,450 tonnes, sells at A$40.70 per pound

Minerals, minerals everywhere...

The ultimate "Golden Fleece"!

– truly "enriched uranium"!

The thrust of Australia's export trade is no longer directed at Britain and Commonwealth countries but at Asia. Japan is Australia's biggest trading partner, with an annual turnover in excess of A\$18 billion. Japan buys coal, copper, gold, iron ore, lead, alumina, aluminium and mineral sands. Two-way trade with the People's Republic of China is worth more than A\$2 billion, while Singapore has become Australia's fifth largest export market. Australia's recognition of Asia's place in its new-found perception of the world is reflected in the fact that 536,000 people born in various Asian countries – mainly Taiwan, Hong Kong and mainland China, but also Vietnam, India and Japan – now live in the "Lucky Country". This represents over 3 percent of the total population.

Man vs Sheep

For nearly 200 years, Australia has profited greatly from agriculture, but the tide has turned abruptly. The country is currently experiencing a rural crisis fuelled by high interest rates and falling world prices for wool and wheat. Nevertheless, agriculture is still a vital contributor to Australia's economic wealth. Sheep farming brings in A \$3,338 million from wool each year, plus a bonus of A\$720 million from lamb and mutton sales. Strangely, the number of sheep seems to rise roughly in accordance with

Some of the best steaks are delivered from the cattle ranches and beef sales contribute significantly to the economy.

the population. In 1861, there were 1.5 million people and 20 million sheep; in 1901 there were 3.5 million people and 71 million sheep; and now that the population has almost reached 17 million people there are 150 million sheep!

Beef sales from Australia's 22 million cattle are worth about A$2,820 million, while dairy products, mainly butter and cheese, make a relatively small contribution to trade since most is sold on the domestic market. Statistics concerning the sales of cheese are revealing. Of 177,000 tonnes produced each year, domestic sales account for 111,000 tonnes, with 66,000 tonnes sold overseas – but Australia now imports 18,000 tonnes of "exotic" cheeses.

There is a healthy trade in pork and poultry, and the fast-growing fishing industry is worth A$850 million a year. Wine exports are forming an increasing share of the annual output of 371 million litres, thanks to the development of good quality wine sold inexpensively in 4 litre casks with spigots. Honey now contributes A$16 million in annual revenue as South American "killer bees" attack and decimate domestic swarms in the United States. Almost half of Australia's production goes to the United States and other overseas markets.

The yearly wheat harvest is worth A$2,700 million. New South Wales grows the largest share, followed by Western Australia and Victoria. However, the gross area of land under wheat has decreased since the mid-1980s.

"The Clever Country?"

The "Clever Country" concept is a pet initiative of ex-Prime Minister Hawke.

The argument is that Australia can only break out of its boom-and-bust economic cycle, caused by dependence on selling commodities overseas, if it can add value to its exports. The PM's prescription is to add brainpower to Australian exports – hence the "Clever Country".

In fact, while Australians have never had a large manufacturing base, they are very good at specialised high-tech, and have had some significant wins in niche markets. Many of these come as a surprise to people who think the country produces only wool and wheat.

AWA Defence Industries, for instance, sells millions of dollars worth of air navigation equipment – radar and direction-finders – and is emerging as a prime regional supplier with sales to China, India, Vietnam, New Zealand, Indonesia, Papua New Guinea and many others. The company also sells advanced communications systems and key components of weapons systems. A host of Australian companies are involved in the US$5 billion ANZAC Frigate project, to build ten ships for the Australian and New Zealand Navies, and in a sister project, which is only slightly smaller, to build six conventional submarines in Australia. The Australian firms work on such key elements as electro-optics, radar, communications and control systems, and sonar. Well over half the value of these huge projects is spent in Australia, and the country now has the biggest industrial defence base in the southern hemisphere.

A Melbourne company, ASTA, builds all-composite rudder assemblies for the new Boeing 757, and other components for the Airbus A330/340 series. Australian firms also build US-designed F/A-18 tactical fighters under licence, and make components as disparate as wiring looms, fault-analysis packages and boron-patching devices.

More Success Stories

Australian Telecom ranks with the very best such organisations in the world, and contributed something like US$6 billion to Australian GDP in 1988/89 alone. Telecom will have a US$320 million national fibre optic network completed by the mid 1990s. It is working with Pacific Dunlop on big telecommunications contracts in Pakistan, Saudi Arabia, India and Vietnam, and across the Pacific, using Australian-made fibre-optic cabling. Telecom is working on a multi-million dollar deal to prime-contract a revolutionary Over-the-Horizon radar network to watch Australia's northern approaches. The project will take several years and will most certainly be extended. Telecom and other Australian concerns also build and design satellite dishes and ground-stations for international users.

Australia has also had some success with automobile and automotive component exports. Mitsubishi Motors Australia won a deal worth US$7.2 million annually to manufacture 12-valve cylinder heads for the Japanese-built 1991 model Lancer. In late 1990 the Australian company announced an even bigger export success to Japan – a US$24 million deal to manufacture and supply more than 35 components for the new Sigma and Diamante models. The Japanese integrate the Australian components into the vehicles and export them worldwide. Meanwhile Nissan Australia claims to be Australia's largest exporter of manufactured aluminium products. The company sells US$20 to 24 million worth of manifolds, induction chambers and cylinder heads to Japan for incorporation into Nissan models.

The list is almost endless. Perth alone boasts two highly successful engine technology companies now contracted to the motor giants. Textile companies use advanced high-tech equipment to capitalise on Australia's wealth of natural fibres, especially wool – and sell their products in large quantities to Japan. Australian biotechnology firms are among the world's leaders for genetic engineering of crops and livestock and are about to break into the world's US$10 billion-a-year market for citric acid. Several firms design and make top-flight laboratory equipment and medical supplies, including pacemakers, which sell all over the world...

All of which is a lot cleverer than just selling wool and wheat.

New South Wales grows the most wheat followed by Western Australia and Victoria.

Various other crops such as oats, sorghum, cotton, rice, peanuts, maize and barley are worth an aggregate of A\$1,293 million, and A\$920 million worth of vegetables are grown each year. A relatively new industry that has shown promise is oilseed production.

The "Sunshine State" of Queensland weighs in with 24 million tonnes of sugar cane, worth A\$586 million, and also makes a considerable contribution to the A\$168 million fruit export trade (fresh, chilled, canned or bottled). Of the 65,000 tonnes of dried fruits processed yearly, 57,000 tonnes are exported.

Mighty Tourism

Tourism is one of Australia's biggest industries. When a strike by domestic pilots in 1989 put this industry at risk, the two main domestic airlines brought in overseas pilots and leased overseas planes with crew to ensure that services, though restricted, kept operating. Even Australian Air Force transport planes were called in to augment domestic flights. Met with an unbending government stance, the strike failed, but the flow-on effects to the economy were incalculable. Hotels and resorts, particularly in Sydney and the tourist areas of Queensland, laid off many staff. Japanese and other tourists chose alternative destinations. Restaurants and tourist service industries were badly hit. Then, just as the tourism industry was recovering, the 1991 recession sent visitor arrivals plummeting again.

Despite all of these, the estimated 2.3 million overseas visitors in 1990 spent a massive A$6.6 billion and tourism managed to remain the nation's biggest foreign dollar earner, accounting for 9 percent of its total export earnings. In recognition of the value that this industry provides to the Australian economy competition for the tourist dollar continues unabated.

The 1990-1991 Budget allocated A$40 million for the Australian Tourist Commission to provide for the overseas marketing of Australia as an international tourist destination. With the government's commitment to overseas marketing, the continuous upgrading of facilities and the abundance of travel and accommodation deals available, there has never been a better time to visit Australia.

Sydney Harbour is one of the biggest and safest ports in the world. It was thanks to the acumen of the indefatigable explorer James Cook that the first settlement began on its shores. The fact that Australia had such a magnificent port from the outset gave it a flying start in the growth and development of its trade and contact with the world.

Australia is a "Lucky Country" indeed to be so extravagantly endowed, but its success was – and still is – lubricated by the honest sweat of generations of farmers, miners and other toilers whose trademark is a sunburnt face, with sunburnt arms and legs protruding from T-shirt and shorts.

Don't Worry, Be Happy

The result today, notwithstanding the recession, is a stunning national success story probably not duplicated in any other country in the world. Of course, such a sweeping claim invites argument. Certainly, Australia lacks the pyramiding economies and industrial dynamism of Japan or Taiwan, or the enormous financial cushion of Switzerland. But Japan and Taiwan have no

Stock 'buzz' in Sydney.

36-hour working week or outdoor life-style, no magnificent beaches, and extremely limited sports facilities, and the Japanese code of regimented behaviour is the antithesis of Australia's easygoing ways. The Swiss undeniably have the money, but they prefer to count it, not spend it.

Australians share in their country's prosperity and enjoy what it provides. Although today's economic climate has forced a tightening of belts across all sectors of the community, most families have their own homes fitted with all the standard modern conveniences, a swimming pool and two cars, and some also have a caravan for holiday trips. The fact that the house is on mortgage and everything else on hire-purchase does not prevent them from living life to the full. An indication of the almost too easygoing lifestyle of the Australians is that they have to be forced by law to vote in federal and state elections. If they do not exercise this right – a right many people elsewhere in the world have died for – they are fined.

The Australian way of life is all the more astonishing when it is remembered that a little over 200 years ago, the country was nothing but sheer desolation – rocky harbours, rugged terrain, strange animals, noxious insects and not one cleared field. Six or seven generations – leavened with one infusion of fresh blood after another – have wrought from its once-harsh soil what many have called a paradise on earth.

Australia is a very big place. Visitors frequently fail to appreciate at first just how big it is. They tend to think that Sydney and Melbourne must be at least *fairly* close together, like maybe London and Manchester. In fact they are over 1000 km apart. Others imagine that if they are staying in Sydney, it's a small matter to drop in on the Great Barrier Reef. But that's well over 2000 km away.

Australia is about the size of the continental United States, excluding Alaska. It's approximately 7.6 million sq km, or about half as big again as Europe. New South Wales alone, not the biggest state, is 75 percent the size of Western Europe. Australia is almost 3200 km from north to south, and 4000 km from east to west, and its coastline measures some 37,000 km – more than the circumference of the earth.

Perth on the western coast is about as far from Sydney in the east as Lon-

The physical landscape ranges all the way from lush to arid.

Geography & Climate

The natural wonders never cease.

don is from Damascus. If you are staying in one, and want to visit the other, it is a bit like visiting San Francisco from Boston. It's a trip that most locals don't make in their lifetime.

This huge continent embraces half-a-dozen climatic zones. Much of the northern third is tropical, with the northern seaboard almost touching Indonesia and with monsoonal climatic conditions to match. The far south of Tasmania is cool temperate, and some islands out in the Southern Ocean are nudging Antarctic conditions.

The Great Dividing Range, Victoria.

In between is every gradation of climate, with the effects of the winds and the oceans largely unobstructed by the continent's low profile. The settled southeast and southwestern coastlands enjoy for the most part a warm temperate climate, shading into subtropical to the north. Most of Australia's major cities enjoy extraordinarily pleasant weather, broadly Mediterranean or Californian in nature. As a result, many migrants from Britain and Northern Europe cite the climate as the main reason for staying!

High and Dry

It's a different story in the interior, of course. The Great Dividing Range runs roughly parallel to the east coast and a few miles inland for the entire breadth of the continent.

Most settlement takes place on the seaboard side of these mountains. Beyond them – and they took the early settlers 30 years to cross from Sydney – the land slopes down to a vast and increasingly arid centre.

Here in the driest places, rainfall is only about 100 mm per annum, and for huge areas of Central Australia it isn't much more than that. In some years the rain disappears altogether in these regions, and then returns with a vengeance.

The little settlement of Whim Creek in Western Australia, for example, reg-

Cattle country that depends on the blessedness of sufficient waters and good weather.

istered a microscopic 4 mm in 1924 – but on another occasion had 747 mm in a single day.

Temperatures vary just as dramatically. Near Marble Bar in Western Australia the average summer temperature is 41°C, often for weeks.

At Charlotte Pass in New South Wales it hit -22°C in the winter of 1947, while the town of Bourke in the same state got within a whisker of 53°C one day in far-off 1877 (and comes close these days too!).

Australians like to quote the harsh-

vast majority of Australia's cities are pleasant, sunny comfortable places to live.

Temperatures in every mainland state capital except Darwin reach a summer average in the upper 20°C, and it virtually never freezes in Sydney, Perth, Brisbane or Adelaide even in winter.

Living in Sydney, from the climatic point of view, is a bit like living in the South of France or Hawaii. Perth, Adelaide and Brisbane aren't much different. Melbourne is a little cooler, Hobart more so (though it's still on a par with Rome), and Darwin positively steamy.

To Begin With...

How did it all begin? How did this vast landmass get there, so far away in the middle of the South Pacific Ocean that it is only in the last 200 years that white men were even sure it was here? One thing's for sure: It's been here a long time. Even the earliest observers could see that Australia had a characteristic weather-beaten look.

The continent's highest mountain, Mt Kosciusko in the south of the Dividing Range, is only 2228 m high, or about one-quarter the height of Everest. The early geologists reasoned that it had been worn down from something much higher.

They were right to think the place was ancient. Australia's present topography is older than that of any landmass on earth.

ness of their climate, the ferocity of their cyclones, heatwaves, bushfires and floods. It's true that for many country dwellers the climate does affect them more dramatically than, say, the average European.

But it's worth remembering that nearly all Australians are city-dwellers (around 90 percent of them, in fact). The

The art of nature at Cathedral Gorge, Bungles.

It is now generally accepted that it once formed part of Gondwanaland, the supercontinent that was made up of Africa, India, Antarctica, Papua New Guinea, South America, New Zealand and Australia.

There is evidence of this in the geology of the areas concerned, but also in the discovery of the fossilised leaves of a kind of fern, preserved in the coalseams of all these landmasses except for those of North America, Europe or northern Asia.

Gondwanaland is thought to have formed about 200 million years ago. Much later it began to break up, and around 65 million years ago Australia began to break off and drift north. In fact it's still drifting, moving towards Southeast Asia at 5 cm a year – as one observer puts it, about the rate at which your fingernails grow.

It was this separation which marooned so many of the bizarre animal and plant species which are native to the continent and which are not found anywhere else. At various times, depending on the sea levels, Papua New Guinea, Tasmania and Kangaroo Island off South Australia would all have been part of the main landmass, which allowed at least some of the peculiar native flora and fauna to spread to these areas.

But Australia as a whole was separated forever from the rest of the world, and the native creatures protected from the rest of the world's predators – until 1788.

Sand dunes beside a lake at Fraser Island.

Only man seems to have been able to cross the gulf. Probably during one of the most recent Ice Ages, Aboriginal people crossed the gulf between what is now Timor and the northern coast of Australia.

The Ice Age bound up water in the ice caps, and this lowered sea-levels, narrowing the channel that the Aboriginals had to cross. They would have found the centre of Australia wetter, lusher and more hospitable than it is today. In it they found and hunted some extraordinary creatures, including a three-metre kangaroo, a giant frog, various carnivorous marsupials and a wombat the size of a rhino.

Although the last of these became extinct only 6000 years ago (an eye-blink on such a timescale) the Aboriginals still remember them in their stories.

But back to the present. Australia's enormous size, the variety of its climatic zones, and the effects of water and wind over uncountable millennia, have produced a variety of landforms unparalleled anywhere else. The early explorers, approaching always from the sea, noted in particular the grandeur of Australia's endless coastline.

South-bound

To the south, the Great Australian Bight is dominated by sheer limestone cliffs up to 100 m high, against which the Southern Ocean dashes. In places along

The unbelievable turquoise of the Great Barrier Reef, Queensland.

the southern coast of Western Australia the sea has broken these ramparts down into fantastic rugged shapes, as along the shores of the D'Entrecasteaux National Park.

By contrast, 700 km north of Perth is Shark Bay, the finest natural harbour on the west coast of the continent. It features vast banks of sand and seagrass sustaining huge populations of *dugongs*.

At the northern tip of Queensland there are great mobile dunefields, murky salt swamps and mangroves, while moving south down the east coast of the continent are endless beaches of white sand fringing sandstone bluffs.

One of the strangest features of this coast is Fraser Island. Fraser is the largest sand island in the world, 123 km long and 22 km wide. Richly timbered, it has sparkling clear lakes which hold water only because of the thin membrane of fallen leaves which lines them. The tallest dunes reach 240 metres above the sea, and the sand continues below sea level for another 600 metres. It seems that currents from the south carried the sand north, and deposited it here against volcanic outcrops on the "corner" of the continent.

The formation of the sand island is probably responsible for an even greater wonder just to the north: the Great Barrier Reef itself.

Moving south, the coastline breaks here and there to allow the valleys behind to be drowned by the sea, and to form magnificent natural harbours.

The Olgas of the Northern Territories.

Sydney Harbour is an obvious example of this, hundreds of metres deep, and sheltered on all sides. It is an indication of how deceptive the surf-beaten coast can be – Captair. Cook, who landed a few kilometres south in Botany Bay, had entirely failed to spot Sydney Harbour as he sailed past.

Volcanic activity is responsible for fang-like Balls Pyramid, a cone of bare rock which juts from the sea 700 km east of Sydney near windswept Lord Howe Island. With no beach, Balls Pyramid is the haunt of enormous gannets and of

screwpines like giant triffids, standing on stilt-like above-ground roots several metres long.

Australia is not immune from volcanic activity today. In 1990 a dozen people were killed in the New South Wales city of Newcastle when an earthquake hit the town. One of Australia's youngest volcanoes is Mt Gambier in South Australia.

The city of Mt Gambier sits right on top of it, and draws its drinking water from the Blue Lake in the crater itself. The volcano may be extinct, but no-one knows for sure.

Rock Formations

Many of Australia's most striking rock forms are the result of weathering of sandstone, often on a massive scale. In the southeast Kimberley region of Western Australia, for example, is the Bungle Bungle massif.

Here an ancient mountain range has been ground down by sandbearing winds to molar-like domes of 300 m high.

Water and wind together have hollowed out stone, pitting and tunnelling it into weird sculptures which the Aboriginal people have marked with their paintings.

South of Perth, Wave Rock shows how wind alone can sculpt stone – in this case into a curving 15 m breaker of stone, frozen in time.

Something similar has happened

the occasional intrepid climber, who must swim ashore before attempting the climb. Lord Howe itself is thought to have been formed by the same volcanic activity.

Today it is a subtropical jewel in the South Pacific, lonely and storm-battered, but hauntingly beautiful and with its own strange flora and fauna, including

Lasseter's Reef: It's Australian for "Dream"

The Red Centre of Australia has seen many men's dreams wither in the heat.

Very often the men themselves have withered alongside those dreams. Instead of taking gold and riches from this harsh country, they have left their own bones to bleach there.

One such man was Harold Bell Lasseter. His ship of dreams struck a reef in 1931 – it was a reef of gold seven miles long: Lasseter's Reef.

The story, simply told, goes like this. One day in 1930, a man called Lasseter revealed to a small group of Sydney businessmen that 30 years before he had stumbled upon a gold reef about 300 miles (480 km) west of Alice Springs. He could find it again, he said, if backed by a properly equipped expedition.

Lasseter checked out. Though he lived in suburban Sydney, he had been born in Victoria, and his father had been a prospector just as he claimed. There was nothing unusual about young men at the turn-of-the-century trying their luck looking for gold in the unexplored wastes of Central Australia. There were indeed stories of gold finds in the area he described.

Perhaps the dream factor was at work already. Australia was in the grip of the Depression, the economy on its knees. There was a dreadful drought which had lasted for three years. In the cities men were out of work and hungry, and on the land settlers saw their farms blow away in twisters of red dust. Seven miles of gold would make a big difference. They backed him.

His expedition, led by experienced bushman Fred Blakeley, left Alice Springs in July 1930. It was a small but modern expedition, with motor trucks and even a plane. But Lasseter couldn't find his gold. He and his companions spent months looking for the fabled reef until Blakeley decided that Lasseter was a crank or a fool or a con man, and took the party back to Alice Springs.

All except Lasseter himself. He insisted on carrying on. The party had met a young dingo-hunter in their search, a man called Paul Johns, and Blakelely could not dissuade Lasseter from contracting Johns and his camels for one last try. What happened after that is a matter of conjecture. Eventually Lasseter sent Johns back to the Alice with letters in which he claimed to have found his reef at last, though he never showed it to Johns. He then went on alone. It seems that on this last leg Lasseter's camels bolted, and he was rescued by the local Aboriginals. He stayed with them for some weeks, and finally, in January 1931, sick and weak, he made a desperate bid to reach help on foot. He died in the attempt and the Aboriginals buried him in a shallow grave. His body was exhumed in 1957, and reburied in Alice Springs.

Was there a reef? Is there one still? Blakeley remained convinced Lasseter was a con man, though it was not clear what Lasseter could hope to gain. Nor could anyone say why Lasseter should give his life looking for a reef he did not believe was there. And others of his party remained certain that Lasseter was speaking the truth.

The pilot of the expedition's plane (a respectable and experienced journalist) actually claimed to have spotted the reef from the air, but was unable to get an accurate fix on its position. But if it was there, why couldn't Lasseter find it? His son Robert has now organised multiple expeditions to Central Australia to try to vindicate his father, but he too has failed to find the reef. The Australian Army goes looking for it every year as a rough-terrain exercise, but they haven't found it yet either.

Well, Australia's a big country! Finding a strip of gold-bearing rock just seven miles long and a few feet thick, in timbered country, in the harshest and hottest terrain on earth, is not so very easy. Especially if for some reason the local Aboriginal people don't want you to find it. And the area is, after all, sacred to them...

Whatever the truth of it, it was a story which everyone wanted to believe in the depressed 1930s.

In the conservative 1990s, when there seems little left to explore, it is a saga which has lost none of its old romance. Within the last five years this writer has met a man who claims to have seen Lasseter's Reef, and all it would take to get there would be...

But you wouldn't be interested.

The Three Sisters in the Blue Mountains.

at Uluru and Kata Tjuta (Ayers Rock and the Olgas), about 500 km from Alice Springs.

Here vast masses of sandstone have been worn into the great red sandstone formations we know today as Australia's most famous natural landmarks. It is not surprising that the Aboriginals here regarded the bulbous and grotesque shapes as possessed of magic – as perhaps they are.

Meteorite impact is responsible for one other extraordinary formation, the 50-metre-deep crater at Wolf Creek in

The Healing Trees

All around the world, vast acreages of rainforest are going up in smoke every year.

In fact today Australia is one of the few developed nations of earth with any significant reserves of rainforest left, which is one reason why the logging issue is so contentious here.

Unfortunately there are plenty of good reasons for chopping down trees. For many people in the world they are the only source of fuel. For others they provide construction timber for their homes. These are measurable benefits, though they will only last as long as the forests last. Only recently have we come to see that we also need the biological diversity of our forests. But the importance of the genepool is a difficult one to sell.

It is necessary to look for tangible worth from the forests if we are to get an impression of the immense potential wealth of the world's forests.

It's not hard to find examples. The pharmaceutical industry, that most sophisticated producer of pills and potions, depends heavily on wild plant sources for its drugs. Many of these derive directly from rainforest flora. The monetary value of this industry even as it exists today certainly runs into the billions. How much it would be worth if properly developed is anybody's guess – but it certainly beats logging.

Several thousand plants worldwide are known to have anti-cancer properties, and about three-quarters of these are rainforest species. At least one Australian species, the *Tylophora* vine, has come under scrutiny. It produces the drug Tylocrebrine which has proved effective against lymphoid leukemia.

Corkwood is another Australian success story. An alert Brisbane doctor, Joseph Bancroft, noticed that Aborigines used this small rainforest tree as a narcotic, and also to drug fish. He found that it caused dilation of the eyes, and could be of great help in treating certain eye conditions and in eye surgery.

We now know that corkwood produces the alkaloid hyoscine. It found other uses during wartime for treating shell-shock and motion-

Prison boab tree in Western Australia is as its name suggests!

sickness, and is today grown commercially in Queensland.

Everybody but we Australians, it seems, have seen the commercial advantages of another native drug-producer, the *kangaroo apple*. Russia has enormous plantations of these Australian rainforest shrubs, and there are research programmes under way in countries as diverse as Cuba and Egypt.

Why all the fuss? The leaves of this bush produce compounds called salasodines, plant steroids which are chemically very similar to human hormones. These can be refined to produce synthetic human hormones whose most dramatic use is as contraceptives. They form the basis of that most revolutionary medication – the Pill. They are also used to mimic other sex hormones for the treatment of a variety of human ills.

Plant steroids of this kind, once refined, also yield cortisones and hydrocortisones, and these are invaluable in the treatment of arthritis, allergies and a range of skin diseases. Strangely, the *kangaroo apple* industry in Australasia has never been developed, despite calls by anguished Australian and New Zealand chemists.

The list does not stop here. Overall, it is estimated that there is a 25 percent chance that any medication you take owes its origin to the world's rainforests.

The problem is that once these forests are gone, they are gone for good. Or, in this case, for bad. They won't grow back like weeds in the backyard. They would take hundreds of years to regenerate – some individual Australian trees have been around since the Norman Conquest of England in 1066. Many species are undoubtedly already lost forever.

The loss of the forests also seems certain to have a catastrophic effect on climate, since forests are the lungs of the planet, sucking up carbon dioxide and giving back oxygen. The loss of their huge water-holding capacity will also have a calamitous effect on the salination of the top-soil, on erosion and on rainfall patterns.

Besides, rainforests are full of beauty, and we need as much of that as we can get. Preserving them sure beats bartering our birthright for poor pasture and plywood.

remote Western Australia. Nearly a km across, the Wolf Creek crater is thought to have been caused by a meteorite weighing several tonnes, striking the earth at 10 km/second. Nearly a tonne of meteoric iron has been picked up in and around the crater.

The diversity of Australia's vegetation is as startling as the variety of its landforms. Once the entire continent was covered by forest, and even today large tracts of tropical rainforest – in continuous existence for millions of years – survive in Queensland and northern New South Wales.

The more typical forest cover is eucalyptus. These gumtrees come in a bewildering variety of shapes and sizes. In some eastern areas there are towering and majestic stands of ancient eucalyptus forest; further south the uniform pelt of gumtrees over the mountains west of Sydney gives them a striking azure hue and caused them to be called the Blue Mountains. Further south still, snowgums clothe the icebound crags of the Victorian Alps.

Inland, the country gives way to golden plains, sloping away for hundreds of kilometres to the saltbush and spinifex of near-desert, biscuit dry and red as brick dust.

Australia is, by anyone's reckoning, an extraordinary country. Part of its thrill is that very few people live there, comparatively speaking, and very few of those live in the great open lands inland of the fertile coastal plain.

There is much still to be discovered.

Flora & Fauna

Terra Australis, the mysterious southern continent, exerted a magnetic pull on the minds of Europeans even before they were sure it was there.

From the early Middle Ages, the imagined inhabitants of a great southern land beyond the seas fascinated sailors and armchair explorers alike. Even in those days people were mesmerised by stories of the weird and wonderful, the grotesque and gigantic. Where they didn't exist, they were invented. Spielberg would have made a fortune then too.

Sunshine beams through the rainforest.

The French geographer Andre Thevet in the 1570s gave what he claimed were eyewitness accounts of a beast with the head and foreparts of a man, and the rear end of a lion. One hundred and fifty years later a British spy working in the Netherlands – Louis Renard – published a book with hundreds of illustrations of creatures from the seas around Terra Australis. Among them is a colour picture of a mermaid, looking understandably miserable, and accompanied by the note: "It lived on shore in a tub for four days and seven hours. It occasionally uttered cries like that of a mouse."

When Europeans began to explore the coastline of the southern continent in fact rather than in fantasy they had no reason to feel let down by the real inhabitants of Australia. These were at least as bizarre as squeaking mermaids and man-headed lions. In 1696, the Dutch voyager de Vlamingh found on the west coast of the continent: "a large number of bush rats, nearly as big as cats, which had a pouch below their throats into which one could put one's hand, without being able to understand to what end nature had created an animal like this."

If he had stayed longer, or put his hand into more of the pouches, de Vlamingh might have come to understand Nature's purpose in creating marsupials like the ones he observed. The pouch, we now know, protects the tiny and near-embryonic young of the marsupial while it develops.

One big advantage, in evolutionary terms, is that birth is less hazardous and exhausting, because marsupial young leave the mother's body while still extremely small. They can also be protected for longer inside the mother's pouch, coming to terms more gradually with the hostile outside world than the

young of placental mammals. Kangaroo *joeys*, for example, emerge from the womb when just a few centimetres long, but will still be found sneaking a ride in the pouch when they have reached a strapping size, some months later.

Like de Vlamingh, European visitors today still think of marsupials as uniquely Australian. Koalas, wombats, possums, wallabies and kangaroos are about as Australian as the boomerang. The kangaroo even has a place in the country's coat-of-arms, and on the logo of two major Australian airlines. In fact marsupials aren't, quite, unique to Australia. They do exist in other countries. But the mistake is understandable. Two-thirds of all the world's marsupial species are to be found in Australia.

The early seafarers found genuine sea-monsters too: The great white shark reaches six metres in length, and the Dutch sailor Jan Carstenz reported seeing them in Australian waters as far back as 1623. Six years later another Dutch-sponsored navigator, Pelsaert, reported an equally familiar threat from the Australian pantheon when he went ashore to get water after a shipwreck. The place was hot and barren, he reported, with nothing worth recording except: "We found much multitude of flies here, which perched on our mouths

The flora ranges from hardy cacti to delicate drops of flowers.

Perhaps Captain Cook's expedition, though not the first to Australian shores, was the first to recognize the flora and fauna of Australia as worth examining for its own sake. That was why the botanist Joseph Banks (later Sir Joseph) was sent along to record what they found.

It was well worth recording. The early explorers and settlers found the eucalyptus forests raucous with gaudy birds – cockatoos, galahs, lorikeets. The bush was alive with timid creatures the size of deer, with hare-like heads and long thick tails, which bounded away in leaps of several yards using their back legs. Stranger still, they kept their young in bags under their bellies.

Goannas, six-foot lizards like miniature dragons, inhabited the dry forests and would take food from around the campfire as soon as they became accustomed to the sight and sound of Europeans. If startled, they would run up the nearest tree – or up the nearest tall man if there was no tree available!

Everything seemed unfamiliar. The hills around the first settlement – now Sydney Harbour – had the look almost of an English parkland, yet bathed in a harsh Mediterranean light. In the trees hung grey bear-like creatures which the locals called koalas, comatose most of the time because of the two pounds of narcotic eucalyptus leaves they ate every day. On the ground blundered eighty-pound animals – wombats, the Aborigi-

and crept into our eyes, that we could not keep them off our persons."

Anyone who has spent time in the Australian bush will know how Pelsaert felt on that fleeting visit nearly 400 years ago. He was wrong about a couple of important things, though: The country was neither barren nor useless, nor populated entirely by flies. It was in fact teeming with life. There were strange creatures, marooned millions of years ago when Australia drifted away from the rest of the world as part of the supercontinent of Gondwanaland. There were forests of trees quite unknown anywhere else, forests so vast that they seemed to cover the ancient land like the pelt of some huge animal. All this was waiting for someone to discover.

A saltwater crocodile in Kakadu National Park.

nals called them – which dug tunnels like small mines in the sandy soil. At night, between the gumtrees, creatures like squirrels soared and swooped on furry membranes, living off nectar, and clouds of fruitbats flapped on leather wings over the harbour as if to a nightly Dracula convention.

Joseph Banks and the long line of naturalists who came after him were to discover even more wonders as, during the late years of the 1700s and the early days of the 19th century, settlers penetrated further into this continent.

They found a duck-like creature with webbed feet and a beak. It laid eggs like a bird, swam like a fish – yet was fur-covered and unmistakably a mammal. Equally weird was the other egg-laying

mammal, now known as the echidna, which carried its eggs in a belly-pouch and fed on ants gathered on a sticky tongue as long as its own body.

The pioneers as a rule put a low priority on the cute and cuddly. They were more interested in survival than conservation, and in cases this was just as well. For not all the new creatures they found were to prove friendly.

In the north they saw crocodiles nine metres long capable of running down and devouring a horse. They found deadly snakes on land and in the sea, fish among the coral which would kill a man who stepped on them and jelly-fish which would paralyse him while swimming. In the gardens of the newly founded colonies were spiders like the

Sealion in Kangaroo Island,
South Australia.

funnel-web and the redback, so venomous that no antidote was known. Worse, they particularly favoured the corners of man's stone houses as their own homes (they still do).

Wild Wonders

Australian wildlife was in fact sealed in a timecapsule, protected by its remoteness. The Aboriginal people who inhabited the great island continent lived in balance with it, and made no devastating impact on the land. Australia was unknown and untouched, its human inhabitants living as they had done in the Stone Age and many of its creatures and plants stalled at some midpoint of

evolution, and its isolation protecting it not only from man but from competition with other more efficient or predatory animals which had evolved elsewhere in the world.

Generally speaking, native Australian animals seem to have survived the early threat posed by man and his best friend – the Aboriginals and his dogs. The really dramatic changes have occurred since the arrival of the Europeans. He brought more than the odd hunting dog. With him came the gun, the plough, and a whole retinue of four-footed friends from Europe: cattle, sheep, goats, rabbits, foxes and cats.

So it was inevitable that much of Australia's protected heritage would be swept away as the place galloped in seven generations from *Dreamtime* to

... sings on the old gum tree.

Flames of the forest.

the computer age. Some of the destruction was wanton. Settlers shot the furry koalas out of the trees for sport, and slaughtered populations of *mutton-birds* on offshore islands more or less for fun.

Some was accidental. Eleven pairs of rabbits kept as pets by a settler family in Adelaide escaped and populated the entire continent in a few decades, multiplying to plague proportions. Pet cats turned feral and made easy meat of native birds and rodents. Foxes, introduced for sport, preferred hunting to being hunted. Starlings, pigeons and mynahs were introduced and competed aggressively and successfully with native bird species. Much more damage was commercial. The bush, which once clothed the whole of the eastern sea-board from Cape York to the Great Australian Bight, was cleared for sheep and cattle and crops, and the high forest was felled for cedar ("red gold") and for dozens of other commercial timbers.

At sea, the whales, which used the Southern Ocean as their last refuge and whose breeding grounds off Tasmania were so crowded that it was dangerous to take a boat across, were hunted to near extinction for oil to lubricate the high-speed machinery of the Industrial Revolution. Harmless *dugongs* went the same way. Twenty Australian mammal species have become extinct since the first European settlement just 200 years ago – several of them in the last 30 years. That represents a third of all mammal species to become extinct anywhere in the last 500 years and is a rate of extinction greater than anywhere else on earth. Most Australians are unaware of that and are appalled when they find out.

The Green Movement

It's easy to sympathise with Britain's Prince Philip, International President of the World Wide Fund for Nature (WWF), who lamented on a recent trip to Australia: "It's like swimming against the stream. As fast as you achieve something you have another disaster on your hands. You save one species from extinction while two more head for the endangered list."

The picture is not all gloom and

doom. Despite the damaging impact of European man in Australia, many modern Australians are among the most conservation-minded people in the world. The "green" factor in Australian politics is a key to votes and power. It does not simply reflect some vague anti-establishment sentiment among the young, but a straightforward desire to stop any further degradation of the bush – even if it costs money. Green activists, for example, have stopped the vast Franklin Dam in Tasmania, have severely limited mining in and around the Kakadu National Park, and have modified logging practices across the country.

At least one marsupial - the grey kangaroo - is still common enough to be a real pest. Others are being bred in captivity and re-introduced to the wild. The WWF, meanwhile, has launched a number of projects to save particular threatened Australian species, and has mobilised its 30,000 Australian members to back the effort.

Not all these projects concern creatures which are cute and cuddly. In Perth, the WWF and Perth Zoo have initiated a captive breeding scheme and a management programme for the western swamp tortoise, of which there were just 30 creatures left in the world before a captive female boosted the population by 33 percent a few weeks ago.

Near Alice Springs in the Red Centre of Australia, the WWF is reintroducing the bilby to the wild. The bilby definitely is cute and cuddly, with grey-blue silky fur, rabbit-like ears and a

Beauty alone is sufficient reason to support the green cause.

Tasmanian Devil!

large furry tail. It could have been invented by Tolkien. Reintroduced bilbies are now breeding successfully. Also bred in captivity and reintroduced to the wild is the numbat, a long-nosed marsupial about the size of a squirrel. Numbats were everywhere when Captain Cook arrived, but they seem to have been decimated by foxes. Numbats add variety to the fox's diet, and are totally vulnerable. Conservationists are fighting a holding action with fox-poisons and captive numbats breeding schemes until a permanent solution can be found.

Animal Migrants

Before the coming of the Europeans, perhaps one million Aboriginal people lived very well on what Australia had to offer. They were hunter-gatherers and lived off roots, berries, and insects, and the meat of the mammals, fish and reptiles around them.

Yet of the thousands of nutritious species of Australian plants and animals, virtually none has been taken over as a food source by the white man. Not a single native land-dwelling vertebrate has been commercially harvested, and of all the forest fruits eaten by the Aboriginals only the macadamia nut has been farmed.

Instead, the Europeans brought their own crops and animals. Many of these proved stunningly successful from the economic point of view, adapting to their new environment and thriving in it. Today virtually all of Australia's agricultural cornucopia has been introduced, and is now exported to the rest of the world: wheat, barley, beef and dairy cattle, fruit, vegetables… and sheep. There are 150 million sheep in Australia today, ten for every two-legged Australian and 12 percent the world's total. They are worth over US$4.5 billion in exported wool in a good year, not to mention lamb and mutton meat exports.

There are between one and two million feral goats in Australia today. They were introduced with the First Fleet in 1788, and adapted much more quickly than the humans did. Later they were imported on a large scale for farming ventures, which almost all failed. Only now, at long last, is some profitable attempt being made to harvest them from the wild and even to re-domesticate them. In 1988/89 goat meat (or "chevon") was exported to the tune of US$10 million. Probably an equal amount was generated by the sale of goat fibres like mohair and cashmere. Meanwhile the vast majority of Australian goats run free, feeding on mulga and saltbush and looking remarkably well for it.

It's a similar story with camels. The first few were introduced in 1840 as "beasts of burden" for pioneers, and over the next forty years they were imported in growing numbers for work in the Western Australian goldfields. Latterly they helped build the Ghan Railway from Adelaide to Alice Springs, so named after the Afghan drivers who were imported with them.

There was an Australian Camel Corps in World War I, and the last police camel patrol swayed off across the desert as recently as 1952. Now there are thousands of them, thriving in Australian deserts. A few are domesticated for tourist safari purposes, some are even exported to Arabia. A few dozen are raced yearly in Alice Springs. The rest make up the largest wild herd of camels anywhere in the world, and are numerous enough to appear on road signs in the outback, warning drivers to look out for them.

A Bee-Line for Honey

Every time you see a honey bee in Australia, sucking at a wattle or eucalypt blossom, remember that even these insects are imports. There are native bees, but the ones which produce Australia's excellent honey all spring from colonies brought in from Italy, central Europe or Spain. Now the descendants of these migrant bees are exports too, finding markets all over the world. A particularly big bee market is about to open up in the formerly protected United States, whose own bees are being threatened by "Africanised killer bees" spreading up through Mexico.

The list does not stop there. Australian horseflesh is among the most highly regarded in the world, and great herds of wild horses – *brumbies* – roam the high country of the Dividing Range. This is where the horsey flick "*The Man from Snowy River*" was set. But there was not so much as a hoofprint here before the European settlement.

Wild buffalo roam the semi-arid lands of the north. Imported and escaped rainbow trout leap in the mountain streams. Indian mynah birds, like English starlings, flock in every Sydney suburban garden.

Some of these newcomers have multiplied so successfully in Australia that they have become a real nuisance. Some, like the rabbit, the fox and the cat, have been an unmitigated disaster for native wildlife. Man has not proved to be a quick learner when it comes to the import of the wrong species.

Way back at the start of the 19th century, the British introduced to Australia the cochineal beetle, from which was made the dye for the British soldiers' famous red coats. Unfortunately, the British also introduced the beetle's foodplant,

the prickly pear cactus. The beetle didn't much like Australia, but the cactus did. By the early years of this century it had spread over vast areas of the eastern seaboard, defying all attempts to slow its progress. It took yet another migrant, the aptly-named *Cactoblastis* moth to spell doom for the prickly pear in one of the world's most dramatic examples of biological control.

But perhaps the most famous migrant of them all is one that even many Australians don't realise is an import – the dingo. This elegant, intelligent hunting dog is thought to have been originally brought in by Aboriginal people before it set out on an independent career. In fact the word "dingo", though taken over by the Europeans to mean "wild dog", actually means "domesticated dog" in the Aboriginal language.

The dingo might be a migrant, but admittedly he and his masters did arrive about 60,000 years ago. That puts both Aboriginal and dingo a rung or two above us blow-ins in terms of Australian seniority.

About 60,000 years ago an imported domestic, now an independent "wild dog".

Bird-Watching

Among globe-trotting birdwatchers Australia has got the reputation as one of the best place around! In Australia you can enjoy beautiful parrot species that will come right up to you and feed; you can sight huge flocks of waders and waterfowl in the wetlands; and for the more serious ornithologist there are rarer birds which you can study in remote parts of the bush.

There are about 700 different bird species in Australia, including the original population of native residents and natural migrants; including introduced species and the latest list of rare vagrants. Geographically, Australia is part of the Australasian Region which includes the island of New Guinea, the adjacent islands in the eastern Indonesian archipelago and New Zealand. Only about 10,000 years ago you could still walk from Australia to New Guinea, thus the fauna in these two places have much in common – including whole families of spectacular forest birds like; birds of paradise, bowerbirds and lyrebirds.

Other characteristic Australian bird families include a diverse range of parrots, and cocka-toos which only occur in this habitat. Less colourful but just as fascinating are; whistles, butcherbirds, tree-creepers, mould-builders, pardalotes, wattlebirds and many other region-endemic families, and honey-eaters (66 different honey-eaters in Australia), each occupying its own special niche within the environment – which look and behave like bulbuls. Starlings and sunbirds which are so numerous in the nearby Oriental region are poorly represented in Australia. Other major bird families common in other regions that you should not waste your time looking for in Australia include hornbills, woodpeckers, shrikes, nuthatches and buntings!

There are great differences in the nature of the habitat and the associated avifauna across the continent, since most of the landscape is rather flat, altitude does not play much of a role but latitude and rainfall patterns do!

Up north, tropical rainfall is a contributing factor and most of the precipitation falls on a narrow brim along the northern east coast - Queensland is the place to go if rainforest birds are what you are after. So far, 400 diffferent birds have been recorded in Brisbane alone,

Left: Rainbow Lorikeet
Right: Brown Honey-Eater

more than half of all the species occuring in the whole country, including members of special-ised rainforest families and genera-like fruit-pigeons, pittas, bowerbirds and scrubwrens. Check out the city parks and the D'Aguilar Range a bit further afield for resident birds, Moreton Bay is an important site for migratory wetland visitors during the summer.

Further north along the Gold Coast the rainfall sometimes exceeds 3,000 mm creating patches of lush, lowland rainforest. It is worth seeking out some of the protected areas, they are usually great for birds and have visitor's facilities and a local checklist available; unless you have a lot of time on your hands it is also a good idea to engage the services of a guide as birdwatching in the forest is not easy and you are going to see and learn so much more this way – you will also be supporting the local environmental efforts in the same time!

Eungella National Park is famous; near Townsville, Paluma Range has honey-eaters, flycatchers, catbirds and also the elusive Aus-tralian Cassowary, one of Australia's flightless birds in the Ostrich family that only occurs here and north to Cairns and the Cape Continent; a third species, the Dwarf Emu, is extinct now, (although many Australian birds have declined in numbers due to hunting and habitat loss this is the only one to disappear completely since the Europeans arrived). The terrain around and north of Cairns is tropical wilderness containing some of Australia's largest National Parks, Lakefield, Staaten River and others; offshore lies the famous Great Barrier Reef that among other things supports large colonies of tropical seabirds; terns, boobies and frigatebirds.

Also in the north Darwin is the jump-off point to Northern Territories birding locations – avoid the period Dec-March when the heat and humidity is oppressive! The region has no real rainforest and is better known as a rare birds habitat with many records of vagrant visitors from the north. It also has some great wetland sites — most notably the giant Kakadu National Park located east of Darwin; the park has massive congregations of herons, egrets, storks and ducks but also many good bush birds. Katherine and Victoria River are less known but well worth a visit.

The town of Alice Springs which is also part of the Northern Territories, located 1200 km inland in the heart of the dry and barren interior, is a good base for seeing some unique Australian bush birds, the Uluru National Park being nearby. Many species like the Budgerygah and Zebra Finch have survived well in captivity but you can see them in the wild in their true surroundings. Look out also for Wedge-tailed Eagle, Rainbow Bee-eater, Yellow-throated Miner, Mistletoebird and some interesting pigeons, warblers and others that have made this seemingly inhospitable place their home.

In Western Australia rainfall drops falls sharply, and in many places it is less than 300 mm per annum creating the typical Australian landscape of grassland and low scrub forest. Perth is the capital of this huge state and has many good parks and lakes with birds typical of the region, nearby Rottnest Island is a much-visited destination that is relatively easy to "cover" for a birdwatcher. North of Perth the wetlands around Broome are becoming the centre of some intensive wader studies; to the south the South-West Corner has some magnificent landscapes and a number of national parks good for birds; treecreepers, parrots and flycatchers often come close in, note the large kingfisher species; the Laughing Kookaburra which is very conspicuous in this area and one of Australia's many endemic birds. Advanced birders can go looking for shrike-tits, fairy-wrens, emu-wrens and firetails in the surrounding vegetation.

In the southern Australian states of Victoria, South Australia and New South Wales the land-

scape is slightly wetter again, especially in the eastern parts. The landscape is characterised by humid woodlands turning semi-arid and arid further inland. These parts are also more densely inhabited but there are always city parks and nearby protected areas worth visiting. On Phillip Island not too far from Melbourne in Victoria the nightly return of Little Penguins onto the beach has been turned into a major tourist attraction! Even Sydney, the big city, is well known for its wild birdlife with about 400 species recorded within a 50 km radius – in thanks partly to an enthusiastic resident group of active birders working hard to spot so many ... NSW is also where you find the highest mountains in Australia, the Snowy Mountains protected inside the Kosciusko National Park, obviously a good area to see the relatively few montane and alpine bird species on the continent.

Otherwise seabirds are one of the main attractions of the south coast area, you are getting closer to the fertile seas surrounding the Antarctic. The New South Wales Ornithologists Club organises boat trips out of Sydney Harbour where you are sure to see many species of albatross, petrels, cormorants, shearwaters and other impressive offshore birds like Australian Gannet and Great Skua. Continuing south across the sea you will reach Tasmania, where spectacular trails will take you to remoter parts of the state.

Most of the 11 bird species endemic to this island can be seen in the near vicinity of the capital Hobart; parrots, thornbills, wattlebirds, honey-eaters, pardalotes and currawongs - all absolutely unique birds, you will find nothing quite like them anywhere else in the world.

For identifying Australian birds in the field any of the two main guides available will do well: G. Pizzey's **A Field Guide to the Birds of Australia** , Collins, 1980, and P. & P. & R. Slater's **The Slater Field Guide to Australian Birds**, Rigby, 1986. For practical advice on birding in all the states get John Bransbury's **Where to find Birds in Australia**. Several other more general books are avialable, for in-depth information on all the species occuring on the continent get **Reader's Digest Complete Book of Australian Birds**.

Refreshing white-petalled daisies rise to brighten the grass.

Australia is in the middle of an identity crisis.

Take a stroll through Sydney and you can hear, see and feel it at every turn. Drop into a milk bar and there's a fair chance the proprietor will be speaking Arabic, if not the more familiar Italian or Greek. Up in Chinatown the streetnames and even the names of the Australian businesses are in Chinese characters. Your taxidriver will ask your destination in English (though not always fluently) but you may notice that he comes from Korea, Kampuchea or even Kenya.

For Sydney and Melbourne, Australia's two major state capitals, have become two of the most multicultural cities on earth, and Australia's smaller towns reflect the same cultural cocktail on a reduced scale. One estimate states that of the 3.5 million residents of Sydney, 40 percent speak a language other than English as their first language, or have at least one parent who does so.

There are mosques and Buddhist temples in the

Young Australians today.

69

An afternoon with matrons and bowls.

city. There is a thriving Indian settlement on the NSW north coast which maintains the Hindu tradition throughout an entire community. There are churches of every Christian sect and denomination from Coptic to Catholic (lots of *those*), and in many the services are given in the language of a distant homeland.

Australian schools now routinely teach Japanese, Indonesian, Cantonese and Mandarin among many other languages, and the children seem to take to them with a good deal of enthusiasm. They can see the point of learning Indonesian, for example: they have 160 million close neighbours who speak it. Teachers can hardly advance the same argument for French. There is an excel-

lent multicultural television station (arguably the best TV channel of the lot). At odd times of the day and night you can catch radio and TV broadcasts in Dutch, Vietnamese, Thai, Serbo-Croat...

The Australian Spread

Glance at the "Restaurants" section of the Yellow Pages. It lists eating houses offering the cuisines of Greece, Lebanon, Africa, Sri Lanka, India, China, Malaysia, Indonesia, Italy, France, Japan, the Netherlands, Singapore, Thailand, Korea... and Australia. Just what Australian cuisine actually is is a matter of some debate, but you can find restaurants which will serve you witchetty

It's a great life on a family outing.

grubs and goanna (lizard) steaks, if you really want to do the thing properly.

All this is, perhaps, no more than you would expect of a major international city. But a mere 20 years ago, no-one would have expected it of an Australian city. For the pace of change in Australian society has been truly extraordinary. And while there are tensions, what is surprising is that the country is not having a much more difficult and divisive time than it is.

White Australia

Picture the country in the 1950s and 1960s. It had a population of 12 million or so and rising. The rise was split roughly 50/50 between natural increase and immigration. Australia had learned from World War II that it needed a bigger population both for defence and economic development, and it knew that immigration was the only way to boost numbers quickly enough. Without immigration, and with mid-century declining birthrates, the Australian population would actually have declined over time.

But migrants in those days came overwhelmingly from Great Britain and Ireland, with some from other countries of Europe. The newcomers were virtually all Caucasian. If they didn't speak English, they were expected to learn it pretty quickly. Commented then Minister for Immigration and later Liberal

As much his land too!!

Party leader Billy Snedden:

"I am quite determined we should have a monoculture with everyone living the same way, understanding each other, and sharing the same aspirations. We don't want pluralism."

While the terms of reference for immigration were steadily loosened up, post-war planners still confidently expected a ten-to-one ratio in favour of newcomers from the British Isles.

As that sort of attitude implies, Australia was a deeply conservative, Eurocentric (indeed, Anglocentric) nation. It did have a small Chinese population, with roots going back to the goldrush days of the 19th century, and of course significant numbers of Aboriginal people. But both groups were small and had negligible impact on the dominating Anglo-Celtic culture of the country. The White Australia policy was firmly in place, and it meant just what it said. Australia was one of the few countries on earth which enshrined racism in official policy. And it was easy to maintain. As many as half-a-million British people were listed as applicants for migration at any one time, and in 1953 nearly 2 million Italians declared themselves prepared to emigrate.

With Australia looking for only about 100,000 migrants yearly, there was no need to turn to Asia and in fact there was plenty of prejudice against doing so. After all, the Japanese had been implacable enemies in World War II and had come close to invading Australia. Thousands of Australians had

Fun times!!

died or suffered terribly in prisoner-of-war camps. Australians of the old school had a solid contempt for Asian people, a contempt mixed with fear of the "yellow peril" to the north. Then quite suddenly in the late 1960s it all changed. Britain faded as Australia's major trading partner and began to look towards a rejuvenated and united Europe. Australia in turn was forced to look elsewhere for trade. For the first time Australia began to consider itself actively a part of the Asian region, and not simply an outpost of Europe. That meant a shift in attitude towards Asian people too.

In 1973 the Whitlam Labor Government finally dismantled the crumbling White Australia policy. While the number of migrants didn't change much

Strine, the Oz Language

"G'day, mite, 'owjabee?" Put simply, this means "Good-day, my friend, how are you today?" Inevitably, you will encounter on your travels such near-incomprehensible examples of Australian slang, delivered in an accent that doubles your confusion. What is universally known as "Strine" – a combination of Aussie accent and lazy pronunciation for "Australian" – has evolved over more than 200 years, partly from Cockney rhyming slang and Irish cheekiness, but also from the rigours of life on the land and from linguistic laziness.

You might think "Emma Chissit" and "Emma Charthay" are two ladies encountered in shops all over Australia. Slowly turn the words over on your tongue and you'll realise they're not ladies at all, but that the speaker is asking "How much is it?" and "How much are they?" Shockinginnit?

Everyday words that get the "treatment" include Sinny (Sydney); Arberbrij (Harbour Bridge); Opraous (Opera House); a couple more ladies named Laura Norda (law and order) and Gloria Soames (glorious homes), and the strangulated days of the week: Mundee, Chewsdee, Wennsdee, Thirstee, Frydee, Sadddee-n-Sunndee. The month of Janree is followed by Febbree, Marje, Ayepril, Mye, Chewn, Chewlie, Orgis and so on. And don't forget those fatal words to-die (today) and yes-to-die (yesterday).

Here is a brief traveller's guide to Strine:

Acca (academic); aggro (aggravation); arvo (afternoon).

Bickies, big bickies (money, lots of money); bitser (mongrel dog; something made of disparate parts, bits of this and bits of that); barra (barramundi, a succulent species of fish); blowie (blow-fish; puffer-fish); bodgie (a person or item that is suspect); bottle-o (rag and bone man); bushie (countryman); boatie (keen yachtsman or weekend sailor); boof (a simpleton); bombo (cheap raw wine, also fourpenny dark); big-noter or bullduster (braggart); bakker beyond (back of beyond; somewhere in the vast outback); bonzer (highly satisfactory).

Chalkie (teacher); cocky (farmer); coldie (cold can of beer); compo (compensation).

Dero (a derelict; a hobo); drongo (a dullard, a buffoon); dinkie-die (100 percent correct, perfect); demon (a policeman); daks (men's trousers, also strides or tweeds); docco (documentary film).

Ekka (Brisbane's exhibition grounds).

Fisho (fisherman); the fisho's (a fish-and-chip shop); flake out (to fall asleep, especially after over-indulgence).

Garbo (garbage collector); greenie (conservationist); galah (a foolish fellow as silly as the bird of the same name).

Hostie (air hostess); hottie (hot-water bottle); hoop (jockey).

Kark it (to die); kero (kerosene); kindie (kindergarten).

Metho (methylated spirits; also, a dero who drinks metho); milk-o (milkman); mossie (mosquito); mushie (mushroom); muddie (mud crab); myxo (myxomatosis, a man-made disease that kills wild rabbits); mulga (the countryside).

Oz (Australia); Okker (a true-blue Aussie; an Australian); okko (an octopus).

Pigs! (expression of disgust or disbelief; abbreviation for pigs' ear); pollie (politician); pokies (poker machines); possie (position); punisher (an ear-basher; a bore); plonk (cheap wine).

Reffo (refugee); rego (registration); rellies (relatives); Rotto (the Western Australian island of Rottnest); rozzer (policeman).

Salvo (member of the Salvation Army); sanger (sandwich); shrewdie (shrewd person); smoke-o (tea-break); spasso (foolish or lazy person, therefore a spastic); speedo (speedometer); surfie (indolent youth whose life is spent surfing); stubby (short, squat bottle of beer); swaggie (swagman); swiftie (a swift confidence trick); shouse (lavatory, toilet).

Tassie (Tasmania); tinnie (tin of beer); trammie (tramwayman); trannie (transistor radio); truckie (truck driver); tweeds (trousers); turps (turpentine); troppo (suffering from permanent sunstroke).

Uni (university); upter (when things are "up to mud" or no good); ute (utility truck).

Wino (alcoholic wine-drinker); wharfie (waterside worker); whinger ('erson who constantly complains); wowser (strict non-drinker and non-gambler); whacko! (expression of great jubilation); wanker, whacker (foolish day-dreamer).

Yachtie (keen yachtsman); yabbie (type of

small freshwater lobster); yakker, hard yakker (work; hard work); yike (fist-fight); yobbo (oaf).

Expressions

An everyday salutation: Owyergoinmite (How are you going, mate), to which the customary response is Karnkomplainkannya (Can't complain, can you?).

Derisory: He couldn't knock the dags off a sick canary; couldn't go two rounds with a revolving door; couldn't get a kick in a stampede; wouldn't work in an iron lung; couldn't blow the froth off a beer.

Caddish behaviour: To come the raw prawn.

Ill fortune: If it was raining hundred-dollar bills I'd be hit on the head with a dunny door; I've copped the wrong end of the pineapple.

Good fortune: You wouldn't be dead for quids, wouldya?

Hardworking: Busy as a one-armed bill-poster in a gale.

Related to birds: May your chooks turn into emus and kick down your dunny door; has the eagle shat? (have we received our pay-cheque yet?).

Related to boots: Put in the boot (to kick a man when he's down); chewy on your boot (to wish somebody bad luck – derived from the hope that an opposition footballer kicking for goal has chewing-gum on his boot, and so mis-kicks).

Ironic: Happy as a bastard on Father's Day.

Worthless: As useless as an ashtray on a motorbike; as a hip-pocket in a singlet; as a glass door on a dunny; not worth a brass razoo.

Demonstrative: Flash as a rat with a gold tooth; all dressed up like a pox-doctor's clerk.

Item in short supply: Scarce as rocking-horse manure.

Drought conditions: The country's as dry as a Pommy's bathmat.

Cold: as the hairs on a polar bear's bum.

To hurry: Go like a cut snake (which is somewhat faster than a rat up a drainpipe); off like a bride's nightie; flat out like a lizard drinking; first cab off the rank.

To dip into the till: Tickle the Peter.

Hungry: So hungry I could eat a horse and chase the jockey; I could eat the leg off a skinny priest.

Announce meal-times: Rattle the pig-bucket.

Badly cooked food: This would kill a brown dog!

To be exhausted or finished: Done like a dinner.

When preparations are satisfactory: Set like a jelly; all teed up.

Mean chap: Wouldn't shout (buy his round of drinks) if a shark bit him; has death adders in his pocket; lower than a snake's belly.

Abandoned: Left like a shag on a rock.

Self-deprecatory terms used by a generous host: No worries, a mere bag of shells; just Mintie wrappers.

When a driver suddenly does a U-turn: Chuck a U-ie.

Extra-healthy: Fitter than a Mallee bull.

Gambler: Victim of the punt.

Off-colour: Crook as Rookwood (name of an old Sydney cemetery).

To dispute a point: Have a blue.

To possess prior knowledge: Have the wood on.

To express dismay or dejection: Stone the crows!

Absolutely correct: Ridgie didge.

Very good: Crash-hot, extra grouse.

Extra good: Beauddiful (beautiful).

Sensationally good: Beauddy!

Scared: Packing 'em.

Stupid fellow: A chop short of a barbecue.

Smelly: On the nose; on the bugle.

To cease work or some other activity: Stack your cue in the rack.

Slyness: Cunning as a latrine rodent.

Pregnant: In the pudding club.

To give birth: Drop a joey (a baby kangaroo).

Toilet: Dunny.

Drunk: To have a neckful or a gutsful; to be Molly the monk (drunk); to be absolutely blind or mortal.

Hung-over: To have hot pipes and a mouth like the bottom of a cocky's cage.

Hang-over cure: A hair of the dog (another drink).

...Strine, the Oz Language

Being by nature a corner-cutter, time-shaver and lover of nicknames, the average Aussie will truncate names as readily as words, so don't be surprised to hear the Prime Minister, Bob Hawke, referred to as "Hawkie", or local actor Stuart Wagstaff called "Waggers", and anyone with a surname like McDonald is bound to be known as "Macca".

Three words in common coinage among men are mate, bloody and bastard. In addressing a stranger, the word mate will be added purely as an honorific: thus "Gotta match, mate?" Bloody and bastard very rarely have a negative connotation as they do in more traditional English. There is an everyday application for both words in thousands of contexts. For example, it might rain all bloody day, in which case the weather would be a bit of a bastard. On the other hand, there mightn't be any rain at all, and an anxious farmer would certainly describe such a situation as a real bastard. A fellow might get a bloody rocket from the boss at work, in which case it would be a bastard of a day for him. Conversely, some lucky bastard might win a fortune on the pools and turn it on for the mob (shout free drinks for everybody in the pub), in which case a bloody good time would be had by all!

Nearly every Aussie is conscious of his or her accent and often will pronounce again, syllable by syllable, a remark that has obviously baffled a visitor. Such obliging help often concludes with the salutation "Have a nice day" – even if it sounds like "Avvanice die".

– generally still around 100,000 every year – there was now no special treatment for the British or Europeans. If you qualified to come to Australia (you needed specific skills and a reasonable grasp of English, among other things), the Immigration Department didn't care whether you were from London or Lesotho, Sheffield or Shanghai.

In less than two decades, the transformation of Australian society has been dramatic. The 121,000 permanent migrants who arrived in 1989/90, for example, came from 100 different countries. Rather more than 30 percent came from Asia, half as much again as the total from Britain and Ireland.

Asian Migrants

Nearly 4 million Australian residents

were born overseas – that's just shy of a quarter of the total population. No fewer than one in three native-born Austral-

Young man and a baby.

Rock, pop and the outdoors.

ians has at least one parent who immigrated to the country. While l.2 million overseas-born Australian residents come from Britain and Ireland, some 600,000 are Asian-born, and obviously that proportion will grow as the rate of Asian immigration continues to accelerate.

These changes have brought some friction. You will still find die-hards who lament the passing of the White Australia policy. Quite a lot of white native-English-speaking Australians will use the term "Australian" as if it only applied to them: "it was spot-the-Australian downtown today…".

Some problems are more serious. There are new and sinister forms of crimes, and a certain amount of feuding between and within ethnic groups. Strifes overseas, for instance in Yugoslavia, are sometimes echoed – if faintly – in Australia. The police, overwhelmingly white Anglo-Celts, have trouble penetrating some close ethnic communities and gaining their trust. There are occasional religious tensions too. Ignorant attitudes surfaced against Muslims, (who now make up the second largest religious group in Australia), during the Gulf War in early 1991.

There is also some real hardship among ethnic minorities, particularly when the economy turns down. Prejudice exists here as everywhere else. Migrants have trouble getting their qualifications recognised, overcoming cultural hurdles which go far beyond the language barrier, and understanding

Muddy fun.

Australia's complex and at times bureaucratic processes. Especially in times of recession, there are inevitable cases of migrants tempted to Australia as a land of opportunity, only to find themselves unemployed and far from home.

While all of this is true, the problems seem predominantly to be those of adjustment, and no wonder. Less than a generation ago Australia was – despite traditional anti-British rivalry – in some ways more British than Britain. It was arguably more conservative, and it was certainly whiter.

Yet by 1988, when Australia celebrated its Bicentennial, all that had irrevocably changed. Monoculturalism was so dead that it now seems laughable. Nobody seriously expects the ap-

proximately 100,000 Vietnamese and 25,000 Kampucheans and Laotians who have arrived in the last few years to start talking like Crocodile Dundee.

Policy Reversal

Multiculturalism is now the widely accepted creed, and the firmly stated policy of the government.

The diversity of cultures within Australia is seen as an enrichment of the local scene. Imaginative state-funded education programs seek not simply to teach migrants English, but to teach English-speaking management how to communicate more effectively with their increasingly multicultural workforces.

Aussie cowboys in Alice Springs.

The Governor General and former Foreign Affairs Minister Bill Hayden has stated quite openly that he expects Australia to become a Eurasian country, and that he hopes it does. That sort of a comment would have been political suicide less than a generation ago, but when Hayden made it in the 1980s it passed almost unnoticed. On the other hand, when respected historian Geoffrey Blainey dared to suggest that too many Asian migrants were arriving he became the target of an extraordinary outburst of anti-racist feeling. Blainey's modest enough argument was drowned in the clamour, but the fact that it attracted such vilification is itself an indication of how far things have moved.

Racism is of course specifically leg-islated against in Australia, and very recently five violent racist leaders were convicted and jailed in Western Australia. The arson campaign which they had conducted against the businesses of Asian migrants in and around Perth is probably the worst outbreak of racist feeling in Australia in recent years.

It is virtually without precedent, and commanded no support from the community except from a few cranks. Nearly 30 percent of Western Australia's residents were born outside Australia, and WA recently became the second state after NSW to ban racist literature by law.

As a multicultural society Australia has so far worked extraordinarily well. It seems to have so far avoided the kinds

Australians take sun, sea and swimming very seriously.

Taking a friendly break.

of racist turmoil which Britain and the United States have had to endure. It seems very unlikely to have those kinds of problems in the future either, possibly because Australia has embarked on the multicultural road so much later. It has no legacy of bitterness festering in an oppressed underclass which has had to fight for its equality.

Undoubtedly there will be continuing problems. There is intense debate as to the eventual size Australia's population should be allowed to reach.

There will certainly be a bunfight over whether or not Australia should become a republic. While the issue is hardly important in practical terms it seems absurd to expect Ethiopians and Koreans and Peruvians to dedicate them-selves to the service of Queen Elizabeth II of England, even if she is Queen of Australia too.

In the main, though, it all seems to be working remarkably smoothly. Certainly many born-and-bred Australians find the changes disconcertingly rapid, and mourn the passing of what they regarded as traditional Aussie values. Despite this, only the most dyed-in-the-wool conservatives would argue that the changes are not inevitable. And almost everyone, conservative or otherwise, will admit to a thrill of anticipation about the future facing Australia.

Whatever else may be said about it, multiculturalism has made Australia an intensely colourful and exciting place to be.

The Aboriginals

Captain Cook did not discover Australia in 1770. It was already discovered.

Nor, when Captain Arthur Phillip arrived leading the First Fleet in 1788, did he bring with him the first Australians. Only the newest ones.

The latest research estimates that 1 million people already lived on the Australian landmass when Phillip first landed here. As many as one tenth of these may have occupied what is now New South Wales. Certainly they lived all around Captain Phillip's new settlement. They saw his ships sail into Botany Bay, and watched in uncanny silence. They showed so little sign of surprise that they did not even trouble to stop fishing. The shock caused by his ships, easily the biggest mechanisms of any kind ever seen by Aboriginal people, probably put them beyond the range of human reaction.

The first Aboriginal word noted by Phillip and his people is supposed to have been "warra!", shouted to them a little later from the shores of what is now

Aboriginals, the original settlers, form only a fractional percentage of the population today.

83

Aboriginal "creole" is used for instruction in schools.

Sydney Harbour as they sailed in. It means, with prophetic irony, "Go away!" Soon enough, the Aboriginal people had good cause to wish Captain Phillip had indeed gone away and never returned.

Strange Encounters

It is hard to blame him, his marines and his settlers for much of what happened. Rarely have two cultures clashed so completely. They failed to mesh at any level. To the white settlers, rough enough men and women themselves, the Aboriginals seemed only a step up from wild beasts. They had no cities, no metals, no armies, no wheel, no written language.

The settlers hardly had time to dis-

cover that Aboriginals did indeed have a complex and effective social organisation, and had evolved it over uncounted generations. Nor that they had a vivid spiritual life, rich and magical artistic talents, and an extraordinary understanding of the land. The Europeans could have learned much. They might profitably have asked themselves, for example, how the land supported thousands of Aboriginal people while they themelves had to send ships to Cape Town to avoid starvation.

But they had no time to learn these things, even if they had overcome their prejudices. For almost at once they passed on to the Aboriginal inhabitants a deadly cocktail of diseases against which the Aboriginals had no immu-

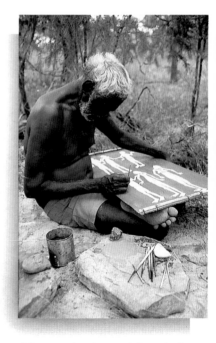

Meeting the demand for tribal art.

Primitive Aboriginal art is still to be found on rock and in caverns and provide inspiration for modern art.

nity: smallpox, tuberculosis, influenza, venereal disease, leprosy and hookworm among them.

Aboriginal society effectively collapsed around the areas of white settlement, and the complex tapestry of their existence frayed and then disintegrated. There was plenty of outright violence on the part of the settlers, especially later when Aboriginals developed a taste for sheep. There was more than one instance of groups of white men, helped by the police, actively hunting Aboriginals. In Tasmania they were utterly exterminated. As recently as 1928 there was an infamous massacre of dozens of Aboriginals at Coniston Station in the Northern Territory.

There was little need for such bru-

tality. Unlike the Maoris of New Zealand, Australian Aborigines were not especially warlike and in most areas they mounted no effective opposition. They were destroyed by the white man's diseases and displaced by his technology and his livestock, rather than decimated by his firepower.

Well into living memory, Aboriginal people were shunted onto reserves, separated from their children, refused the right to education in their own languages, and forced to become Christian.

Diet, despair and drink killed them in thousands. The population sank to 150,000 by the early part of this century – about an eighth of the figure 150 years earlier. Today there has been something of a resurgence, and in the 1986

Aboriginal dance performance.

census about 278,000 people, or 1.5 percent of the Australian population, identified themselves as Aboriginals.

Roots

No-one knows exactly where the Aboriginals came from, nor when they came. Recent archaeological studies by the Australian National University have rewritten the textbooks and shown that settlement by Aboriginals probably took place at least 60,000 years ago. They almost certainly crossed from the Asian landmass. The fossil record shows that they did not originate in Australia, which has never had any primate life of its own. In anthropological terms 60,000 years is a very long time indeed, and once the newcomers dispersed across the landmass they developed in very different ways.

There never was, and is not today, one Aboriginal culture nor one Aboriginal nation.

It is estimated that by 1788 there were between 600 and 700 "tribe-nations", speaking between 200 and 250 quite distinct languages and a large number of dialects. There are known to have been eight or more separate languages spoken in Tasmania alone, which had probably been cut off from any contact with the mainland since the Bass Strait was submerged after the last Ice Age about 10,000 years ago.

Though there is a case for claiming

some level of interrelationship between native Australian languages, no such connection has yet been shown to exist between Australian languages and other tongues spoken elsewhere in the world.

In most cases, we shall now never know. Tasmanian languages vanished with the people who spoke them. Fifty or so others on the mainland are now lost, and as many as 100 others are spoken by elderly people only and seem doomed to extinction. The only bright spots are that bilingual education is now encouraged, and, in a strange twist, two new Australian languages have emerged. Both are "creoles", mixing English and Aboriginal words, but both are now recognised as distinct languages, widely accepted as mediums for education.

Mixed Feelings

Against this generally sombre background it is hardly surprising that when Australia celebrated its 200th birthday in 1988, there were strains of discord to be heard.

The year-long Bicentennial extravaganza involved the expenditure of mil-lions of dollars and man-centuries of work on a range of cultural and not-so-cultural activities across the island continent. Most towns had a facelift. Bicentennial sporting events took place in every conceivable competitive activity from air-races to toad-races. There were fireworks displays, parades, speeches, dances, Royal Visits, fly-pasts and the spectacular arrival from all over the globe of the greatest fleet of antique sailing ships ever seen.

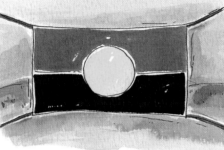

Seen from another point of view, however, the Bicentennial actually marked the 200th anniversary of a European invasion. Small but vocal groups of Aboriginal people designated 26 January 1988 as just that – Invasion Day. Elders of their people mourned on Sydney's waterfront as the recreation of Captain Phillip's landing went ahead. Noisy protest marches took place, in which Aboriginal people were joined by a large number of whites who sympathised with their stance.

Since then the entire issue of Aboriginal rights, and particularly land rights, has been gathering strength. There is now an Aboriginal flag.

There are Aboriginal protests at most occasions where the issues are even vaguely relevant. Calls for compensa-

Ayers Rock or Uluru was returned as a sacred site to the Aboriginals in 1985, as a genuine gesture of recognition of Aboriginal rights.

tion over the seizure of sacred or traditional Aboriginal land have become routine.

There is a good deal of what Australians call "ratbaggery" in all of this: deliberate stirring by activists (usually thought of as leftwingers) for political ends.

Aboriginal people are not oppressed in the sense that, for example, African blacks are oppressed.

Despite vigorous attempts to enlist the support of Nelson Mandela during a recent visit, the African leader was clearly unsure of what, in political terms at least, Australian Aboriginals were complaining about.

Australian Aboriginals have the same rights under Australian law as anyone else. They have the vote (though

Aborigines have the same rights as others under Australian law.

only since the 1960s). They cannot be barred from any position in the land, any more than any other people can be barred on the basis of race.

Despite all that, there can be little doubt that Aboriginals as a race and a culture could find little to celebrate in the coming of the white man. Notwithstanding their technically equal rights, the figures show beyond all doubt that the system in place up to now has – somehow – disadvantaged them.

Aboriginals are imprisoned 15 times more frequently than non-Aboriginals on a per capita basis. Their average lifespan is 22 years shorter. Their infant mortality rate is twice that of the rest of Australians. The incidence of disease, alcoholism and domestic violence is

Younger generations are naturally better off than their forebears.

Aboriginal warriors in the rainforest.

much higher than in the rest of the community.

There is no Aboriginal in a top management position with an Australian company, nor in the senior ranks of the Defence Forces, despite a long and illustrious history of military service by Aboriginals.

Making Peace

Obviously Australia has a long way to go in dealing with the issue of its own Aboriginal people.

But that isn't to say it has made no progress. The policy of assimilation, which dominated post-war Australian attitudes towards Aboriginals until 20 years ago, now seems laughable. It is impossible to imagine an Australian politician saying today, as the architect of assimilation did then: "in the course of time it is expected that all persons of Aboriginal or mixed blood will live like white Australians do."

Gough Whitlam's Labor Government in 1972 replaced this doctrine with one of self-determination. This was defined as "Aboriginal communities deciding the pace and nature of their future development as significant components within a diverse Australia." That Government also recognised the reality of land rights for Aboriginals.

The return of land to Aboriginal people is much more than a token gesture. It has moved ahead with particu-

Aboriginal Myths

For thousands of years before the coming of the Europeans, Australian aboriginals inhabited a world of the spirit more personal and immediate than anything the white man had to offer.

This web of belief was intimately associated with the land itself. The Aboriginal's entire physical world was created during the *Dreamtime* by spirit beings who fought, loved and hunted over the earth.

Some were fabulous creatures, like the splendid Rainbow Serpent, who left tracks across the face of the land as river-valleys and gorges and caves. Others manifested themselves in lightning and storm.

Many more were less exalted beings who lived in tribal groups like mortals. They were frequently associated with particular creatures or plants, with which they shared identity. At the same time spirit beings like these were the first ancestors of men, and Aboriginal people considered themselves their direct heirs. They kept alive their ancestors' deeds and the lessons they taught in ritual and ceremony – but also as an inseparable part of everyday life. They were able to link topographical features precisely with *Dreamtime* events. This track marks the trail of blood left by a wounded warrior, that cavern is the womb of a tribal mother, these rocks were the eggs of the Rainbow Serpent.

While everyone played a part in this spiritual landscape, within the Aboriginal community there would be men born with special powers. After suitable initiation these individuals were believed uniquely able to interpret messages from the spirit beings all around. They were also thought capable of acts we would consider magical. They could heal sickness, or intercede with the gods to bring on rain, or travel huge distances in impossibly short times. Or kill, for Aboriginal magic was far from always benign. It is interesting that the deadly power of "pointing the bone", and paranormal skills such as telepathy, became fully accepted even by many hard-headed western observers.

An Aboriginal art style has emerged and become very commercial.

The new settlers were scornful that Aboriginals had no ordered "religion" as white men understood it. Certainly they had no churches or temples. Yet what the newcomers failed to understand was that the Aboriginal lived, in effect, within one vast open-air cathedral. Every stone and plant, bird and lizard had a spiritual significance. When the Aboriginal went "walkabout" – sometimes for weeks on end – he was not trying to avoid work. In fact he was on a pilgrimage, renewing his spiritual knowledge through contact with the land. It is one of the tragedies of white settlement that the European and the Aboriginal ways of life proved to be mutually exclusive. White settlers entirely failed to acknowledge the spiritual landscape that overlay the physical one for Aboriginal people. Instead, they broke up Aboriginal communities and forced Christianity on the people.

Worst of all, they took the land as their own. To the Aboriginal (and incidentally to many other non-European peoples) the concept of owning land was an absurdity, like owning air. When the white men settled the country, fenced it and farmed it, they destroyed the economic and the spiritual base for Aboriginal life.

There is some hope. Traditional Aboriginal communities do survive here and there. At least one school has been set up to teach young people the traditional Aboriginal ways.

Aboriginal studies courses are common in universities, and Aboriginal art is in vogue. In an age when westerners themselves are becoming aware of the limitations of materialism, more and more people are begining to wonder if Aboriginal beliefs have something to teach the 20th century. Probably at no time has the Aboriginal heritage been treated with as much respect in Australia as it is now. It remains to be seen whether this is too little, too late.

lar speed in the Northern Territory, which, being a territory and not a state, is controlled directly from Canberra for many key issues. The Northern Territory is also home to a much higher proportion (22 percent) of Aboriginal people among its population than any other state or territory, though the absolute numbers are not high.

Today some 33 percent of the land of the Northern Territory has been returned to Aboriginal hands, and it is estimated that by the time the claim process is complete about half of the Territory's land area will belong to Aboriginal people.

The famous central Australian landmark of Ayers Rock (Uluru) was returned to Aboriginal ownership as a sacred site in 1985, and Katherine Gorge National Park (Nitmiluk in the Aboriginal language of the region) was returned in 1989. Far from being wasteland, both sites are major tourist venues, and their Aboriginal owners have permitted their continued use as such.

The same legislation has also set up the machinery for returning a proportion of the royalties from mining to Aboriginal communities on whose land the mining takes place. The money is distributed by an all-Aboriginal Advisory Committee for a variety of cultural and economic activities.

The communities today invest in major hotels and tourist developments, in garages, shopping centres and cattlestations.

"Reconciliation" is the current buzz word, with the entire community being asked to comment on an initiative taken by the Hawke Government, but supported by virtually everyone, to bring the two cultures closer together.

Better late than never.

Culture

Unpicking the strands which make up the cultural tapestry of any nation is a risky business – especially in the case of a young country like Australia.

Modern Australia has been around for just 200 years. Yet the mainly European cultural traditions upon which its painters, playwrights and performers have drawn goes back a great deal further than that. Shakespeare and Mozart were pretty evidently not Australians, but modern Australian creative artists can claim them as their ancestors with as much justice as the Europeans.

Australian's art is considered young, but full of vigour, its inspirations often drawn from European culture.

95

At the same time, migrants are arriving yearly in their tens of thousands from every part of the globe, bringing with them vibrant artistic traditions of their own. You end up with a cultural cocktail which is kaleidoscopic, bewildering and virtually impossible to characterise.

Stereotypes

Perhaps as a result, there's no doubt about the vigour of the arts in Australia today. It is ironic in the extreme that

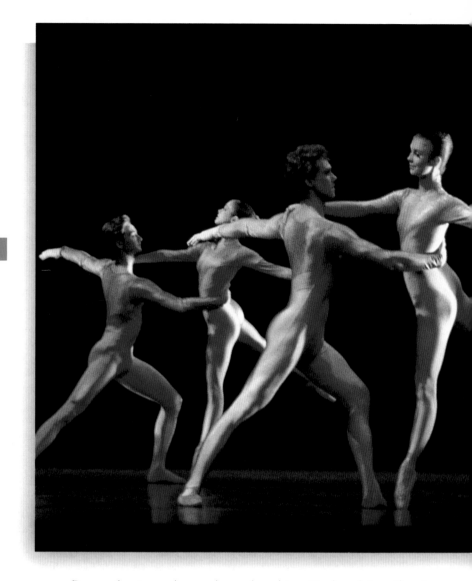

Dance, theatre and opera have played to critical acclaim with not
a few world class performers rising to great fame.

the stereotype Australians of comedy
are loudmouthed beer-swilling men and
appallingly snobbish women, all of
whom think that a theatre is somewhere you go for an operation. More
than one Australian comedian has become famous by creating characters like
these, and has become unpopular with
many compatriots in the process. Australians are understandably uneasy with
such caricatures, especially when they
are so avidly seized upon overseas. A
Japanese critic once commented on the
quality of the film *Crocodile Dundee*

very high proportion of its population is within reach of big city art galleries, museums, concert halls and theatres. Its city-state demography also accounts for the vigour of Australia's various companies of performers, which have fiercely loyal followers in their own cities and increasingly global reputation.

International Fame

The Australian Ballet Company is a good example. Based in Melbourne, the Ballet gives up to 186 performances every year and raises 80 percent of its own funding from box office receipts and sponsorships. Since annual operating costs top A$14 million, that is no small feat. The Company is now 30 years old, and in 1987/88 made a hugely successful tour of the USSR, Greece and the United Kingdom, where the Queen saw their performance at Covent Garden and personally congratulated many of the cast. In 1989 the Company made a spectacular Asian tour and in 1990 made appearances in the United States to rapturous audiences at some of the country's premier venues.

In its repertoire the Australian Ballet Company numbers classical and modern pieces, including occasional Australian works. A recent one featured the music of Australian composer Peter Sculthorpe, whose innovative and very Australian work is becoming widely known to international audiences.

The Sydney Dance Company best

(hardly an intellectual triumph in itself), saying that the film was a surprise, coming from the Australians who were generally considered uncultured yokels. As so often with national generalisations, the opposite is true.

Australian are among the world's most avid opera buffs and theatregoers. Being such a highly urbanised society, a

represents Australia's contribution to contemporary dance. Hugely popular, the Company has performed to some half-million people across Australia in the last five years, and has toured all over the word. It has an especially loyal audience in the United States. Charismatic artistic director Graeme Murphy is something of an Australian legend (at just over 40) with a prodigious output of original material and an impressive background as a dancer in his own right. Under his guidance the Sydney Dance Company is unquestionably one of the premier contemporary dance companies in the world.

The Australian Opera also has a strong record of success and popularity. In the summer season of 1991 alone, for example, the Opera performed to over 69,000 people, with 95 percent of seats sold. In total during 1991 it has presented 215 performances of 17 operas in at least three cities. It regularly presents national simulcasts of complete operas through the Australian Broadcasting Corporation, and these are extremely popular among the listening public.

The Australian Opera is a truly international company and its leading light for many years, that Australian Dame Joan Sutherland, was one of the world's great postwar sopranos until her retirement. But it is interesting to note from the Company's programme the depth of Australian talent upon which it can draw. In its repertoire, for instance, is Gounod's *"Romeo and Juliette"*, which is based on the original

famous production of one of Australia's best-loved artistic talents, the late Sir Robert Helpmann. The Opera has also presented two works by the Australian composer Richard Meale and author/librettist David Malouf, one of which was based on an original novel by the late Patrick White.

Who's Who

Australian musicians and composers number among them several other outstanding figures. One example is Malcolm Williamson, who in the mid-70s was appointed to no less a post than Master of the Queen's Musick. Another is the international concert pianist Roger Woodward. And a third is the dearly-loved conductor of the Sydney Symphony Orchestra, Stuart Challender.

Partick White was probably the best-known Australian man of letters since the war, and commanded an international reputation. In 1973 he became the first Australian to win the Nobel Prize for Literature. In fact Australia has produced many excellent writers, especially writers of popular fiction (or at least of fiction more popular that White's: his books are notoriously difficult to read). Peter Carey (**Bliss**, **Oscar and Lucinda**) recently won the international Booker Prize. He follows in the footsteps of another fine Australian writer Tom Keneally (**Schindlers Ark**). David Malouf, mentioned above as a librettist, is also an award-winning au-

Aboriginal dance, a part of the culture.

thor. Morris West has been vastly popular all over the world for three decades or more for his prolific output of novels, yet many people don't realise that he is Australian, C J Koch's "*The Year of Living Dangerously*" is a minor classic and became a successful film in the 1980s.

Among current Australian poets, Les A Murray is gaining increasing recognition for his work.

The country has also produced some excellent historians. The recently deceased Professor Manning Clark wrote the definitive independent history of

Banjo Paterson

Be careful what you say if, on your first visit to Australia, you should stumble across the poems of "Banjo" Paterson.

Are they sentimental? Often. Naive? Childish? They can certainly look that way. Is the rhyme a little forced and are the bush life caricatures overdone? Maybe they are.

But don't say so. Banjo Paterson is very nearly the patron saint of Australia. Through his poetry, his ballads and his other writings he crystallised a uniquely Australian way of life. He managed to do so at just the point in history – the turn of the century – when Australians were achieving national Federation and effective independence from Britain.

It is fully appropriate that the words to Australia's unofficial national anthem, "Waltzing Matilda", sprang from the pen of Banjo Paterson in 1895. Many Australians still think it should be the official anthem.

Banjo Paterson captured the harshness and the humour of bush life. He evoked all of its natural grandeur, its human warmth, and its tragedy. It is little wonder that in this context his poetry was so stunningly successful.

Yet until he published **The Man from Snowy River and Other Verses** in 1895 Paterson was almost unknown. He was just a young solicitor who had written a couple of notable ballads under the pen-name "The Banjo".

But after the publication he rocketed to a position of fame occupied only by superstars today. More than 100000 copies of this book were eventually sold, 10000 of them in the first year alone. Within months the obscure solicitor whom no-one outside Australia had heard of commanded a reading public wider than any other living writer in English except Kipling.

Paterson had a lot in common with the great Kipling. The Englishman also wrote of the common people with passion and with compassion – soldiers and traders and travellers and workers.

Kipling too recreated the ballad as a poetic form, a form which incidentally dated back to the Middle Ages. And Paterson shared another key characteristic with Kipling: he was not of the same stamp as the people he wrote about.

Paterson did indeed grow up on a country property, Illalong near Orange in western New South Wales. He certainly did know a thing or two about country life, about horses and gambling and the laconic outback wit of the people. But he was not one of them. While not wealthy, Andrew Barton Paterson's people were genteel, educated and cultured. The young Andrew spent half his time in Sydney, was schooled at Sydney Grammar, and easily moved into the professional classes.

In some circles at the time he was bitterly attacked for idealising bush life, particularly by rival writer Henry Lawson, and the feud between the two stimulated some of the best work either of them produced.

Paterson did not rest on his literary laurels. He gave up legal practice in 1899 when he was 35, and must have astonished his circle of lionisers by signing up as war correspondent for the Sydney *Morning Herald* and sailing away to cover the Boer War. Hardly had he returned to Sydney when he left again to cover the fighting associated with the Boxer Rebellion in China (though he missed it).

Paterson, by then married with a family, settled for a while. But he seemed unable to shake the wanderlust. When World War I broke out in 1914 he immediately went to England hoping to get work as a war correspondent again. When that didn't work out, though he was then fifty years old, he signed up for active service as an ambulance driver in the mud and blood of France.

By 1916 he was a major with the Australian Forces in Cairo, and did not return to Australia for another three years.

Banjo Paterson lived to see another war start, and died in 1941 before he knew it was won. But he did live to see himself become the Australian bard, a position he still holds today. It is interesting that while Kipling's books today are hard to find outside a reference library, Paterson's work is read and memorised by thousands of Australians.

Children read him in school, his ballads inspire hugely successful films, and at smart dinner parties in the very best suburbs someone will end up reciting "Saltbush Bill" or "The First Engineer".

Sydney Opera House, symbol of cultural activities and landmark of Australia.

Australia (a must for any serious student of the country). On a more popular level, but no less informative, is the work of Australian art critic and journalist Robert Hughes, who has won international bestseller status with **The Fatal Shore**, a gripping history of the birth of the nation. Be warned – this book is unputdownable. If you buy it when you land in Australia, you won't see anything for the first week.

Painted Works

The very uniqueness of Australia and of its flora and fauna has probably had more of an effect upon its painters than on any other creative group. Some of the most delightful illustrative work inspired by first contact with Terra Incognita is in the form of botanical drawings like those of Banks and his collaborators who voyaged with Cook in the late 18th century. A little later, John Gould achieved extraordinary fame by publishing his magnificent "*The Birds of Australia*". These illustrations, mostly the work of his sadly exploited wife Elizabeth, won him fame even above that of his American ornithologist counterpart John Audubon. Even today, Gould reproductions hang on more Australian walls than the work of any other artist, though frequently unacknowledged.

But this was illustration rather than art in the creative sense. The earliest Australian artists were born in Europe

The Australian Film Industry

The Australian climate is almost ideal for filmmaking, with long hours of sunlight and weather patterns which are generally predictable. Add to this a multitude of scenic and wilderness locations, from surf beaches to picturesque outback towns, from modern coastal cities to red sand deserts, and it is easy to see why Australians have been involved in film production almost from the moment the motion picture was invented.

Some believe that *Soldiers of the Cross*, made in Australia about the turn of the century, was the world's very first feature film.

The earliest authenticated Australian feature was produced in 1906. Its subject was folk-hero Ned Kelly, leader of a gang of daring robbers called "bushrangers". Such themes were favourites with the audiences of the day. By 1914 over eighty feature films had been produced, many of them based on successful stage productions.

The industry flourished until after World War

I, most of the films continuing to focus on aspects of history or traditional rural life. But audiences were discovering exciting new attractions.

In the 1920s, as in many other parts of the world, American films and film stars soared to overwhelming popularity in Australia. United States distributors gained a stranglehold on cinemas. Local film production declined and the industry was threatened with extinction.

The arrival of sound films and the Great Depression in the 1930s saw an even further decline. Sydney-based Cinesound Studios and Melbourne's Eftee continued the struggle to produce features, as did a handful of courageous producer-directors, but local production has almost died by the 1950s. Newsreel production, however, flourished. Fox Movietone News and Cinesound Review remained, until the arrival of television, virtually the only productions on the screen in which Australians could see aspects of their own country.

Pop and rock groups have been highly successful as have movie stars.

though it is, is in the English tradition and he himself acknowledged his debt to Turner. Hughes suggests that only with the vibrant watercolours of S T Gill, depicting the tumultuous days of the 1850s Victorian goldrush, did something truly indigenous begin to happen, though Gill himself was English-born.

Something certainly had to happen sooner or later. Well into the 1850s Australia was philistine country indeed, and young Australian artists had hardly any access to the work of painters abroad. They had to develop their own styles. Besides, Australia was not Europe. Its birds and beasts and plants simply refused to fit into European artistic moulds. The whole atmosphere of the place was dramatically un-Northern, and the very light had a harsh, super-Mediterranean quality about it.

In the early 1880s a group of young artists, inspired by the French Impressionist movement, established themselves at a farmhouse in the outer Melbourne settlement of Heidelberg. Key figures in what became known as the Heidelberg School, active from 1885-96, were four names which became internationally famous. These were Tom Roberts, Arthur Streeton, Frederick McCubbin and Charles Conder. *"Shearing the Rams"* and *"Bailed Up"* by Roberts are paintings which many people would recognise instantly, even it they were unacquainted with Australian art and had never heard of the artist. The same is true of McCubbin's romantic paintings of pioneering life, and Streeton's

---

Documentary filmmaking in Australia has a long and prolific record and many fine productions have emerged. Pioneer cinematographer Frank Hurley's *The Home of the Blizzard* and *In the Grip of the Polar Ice* showed the rigours of expeditions to Antarctica in 1913 and 1917. Damien Parer's *Kokoda Front line*, a daring eye witness account of World War II in Papua New Guinea, won for Australia its first Hollywood Academy Award.

Australian documentaries, drama mini-series and feature movies are regularly played on the television networks.

The 1970s and 80s were the most prolific period of film production in Australia.

Encouraged by government support in the form of generous taxation allowance, investors turned to film production eagerly. A number of notable feature films like *Picnic at Hanging Rock, My Brilliant Career, Crocodile Dundee* and the widely successful *Mad Max* films were produced.

---

and brought European traditions of painting with them. States art critic and historian Robert Hughes: "the idea of an 'Australian' culture was unthinkable: a resident colonel in Calcutta would have soon have called himself an Indian."

So for many years, at least up until the middle of the 19th century, it is virtually impossible to detect anything uniquely Australian about painting produced here. The bush is stylised to look like Buckinghamshire parkland, kangaroos look something like deer, and Aboriginals become part of the Noble Savage tradition. Conrad Martens, who arrived in Sydney in 1835, probably occupies the highest rank of colonial watercolourists. But his work, fine

brilliant harshly lit landscapes. Conder returned to England after a disappointing reception in Australia and became a figure in the European art establishment, a close friend of Oscar Wilde and Toulouse Lautrec. But his paintings too are now much sought-after in Australia.

Around the turn of the century there was a tendency to populate Australian bush scenes with art nouveau nymphs and satyrs. Sydney Long's *"Pan"* (1898) may be the most familiar of this period to a modern audience. Not long after came the passionate, vigorous and controversial figure of Norman Lindsay, riotously mixing classical motifs and influences from different traditions, and always flirting on the edge of what was then thought of as pornography.

Hamburg–born but Australian–raised Hans Heysen was active through the early and middle years of this century and his work is still immensely popular. He settled in Adelaide and many of his detailed landscapes depict South Australia, where a long walking trail is named in his honour. He was knighted in 1959. Like another fine Australian landscape painter, Lloyd Rees, he tends to link the art of the 1920s with current movements, but without truly belonging to either period.

A contemporary of Rees, and working at his peak during the 1940s, was perhaps Australia's most famous artist of the middle years of the century, Sidney Nolan. He is best known for his childlike series of paintings of the Ned Kelly legend, which are displayed in the Austral-

ian National Gallery in Canberra, along with some of the innovative portraiture of Arthur Boyd. If you are visiting the National Gallery, it is a good opportunity to spend some time in the fine Sculpture Garden there, which features among the work of many other artists that of contemporary Australian sculptor Robert Klippel.

Art Collections

Most of the Australian state galleries have collections of paintings by the big names from Australia's art history – the Heidelberg School, Heysen and Nolan, for example. Most also have significant international collections, too, particularly the National Gallery in Canberra. But try the Art Gallery of NSW for collec-

![A mosaic mural at a Melbourne fire station.]

A mosaic mural at a Melbourne fire station.

tions of two of Australia's finest women painters from earlier in this century, Grace Cossington-Smith and Margaret Preston.

On the current scene are a number of Australian painters who have achieved considerable fame overseas, among them Colin Lancely, Tim Storrier, and Brett Whiteley.

On the popular end of the spectrum is the exuberant work of Pro Hart, and the hugely sought-after child-visions of Sydney Harbour, sails and the Opera House created by Ken Done, whose work appears on every imaginable piece of Australia as well as on the walls of homes and galleries.

Aboriginal art is in vogue right now and commands sky-high prices in Eu-rope and New York – a timely recognition of the vibrance of Aboriginal art forms. But recognition has come too late for one Aboriginal artist whose star rose too soon. Albert Namatjira developed an extraordinary talent for using watercolours, in the white man's tradition, late in the 1930s.

For 20 years he commanded super-star status in Australia for his vivid landscapes of the harsh country around Alice Springs where he grew up. But he was torn between two cultures. As an Aboriginal, Namatjira was for many years not even a citizen of the nation which feted him. He died a broken-hearted man in 1958 after a brief term in prison for supplying alcohol to his own people.

ARAF

TIMOR SEA

DARWIN

N

0   200   400

KILOMETRES

INDIAN

OCEAN

NORTHERN
TERRITORY

WESTERN AUSTRALIA

SOUTH AUS

KALGOOLIE

INDIAN

OCEAN

PERTH
FREMANTLE

GREAT
AUSTRALIAN
BIGHT

A

ALBANY

SOUTHERN OCEAN

GULF
OF
CARPENTARIA

AUSTRALIA

CAIRNS

TOWNSVILLE

MACKAY

AUSTRALIA

ROCKHAMPTON

SOUTH

PACIFIC

OCEAN

QUEENSLAND

TOOWOMBA   BRISBANE

NEW SOUTH WALES

TASMANIA

WOLLONGONG   SYDNEY

CANBERRA

HOBART

TASMAN
SEA

VICTORIA

BALLARAT

MELBOURNE

GEELONG

Sydney is the oldest and largest city in Australia, and it is a city of many faces. It is at once gracefully old and traditional, but also chromium new. It is staunchly Australian, but at the same time comprises an overflowing ethnic cocktail. Visitors report either that its inhabitants are cold and unresponsive to the point of xenophobia, or outgoing and helpful, depending upon whom they have met. Through it all, however, one thing is consistently true: Sydney is vibrantly alive and exciting. It gives everyone a buzz.

The big-city thrill begins when your jetliner slides in from the Pacific, and descends over the parade-ground orderliness of the outer suburbs. Then you catch the first glimpse of a magnificent blue-green harbour with creamy white bays. Next perhaps you will spot the Harbour

Sydney/NSW

■ ■ ■ ■ ■ ■

Seagulls and Sydney Tower.

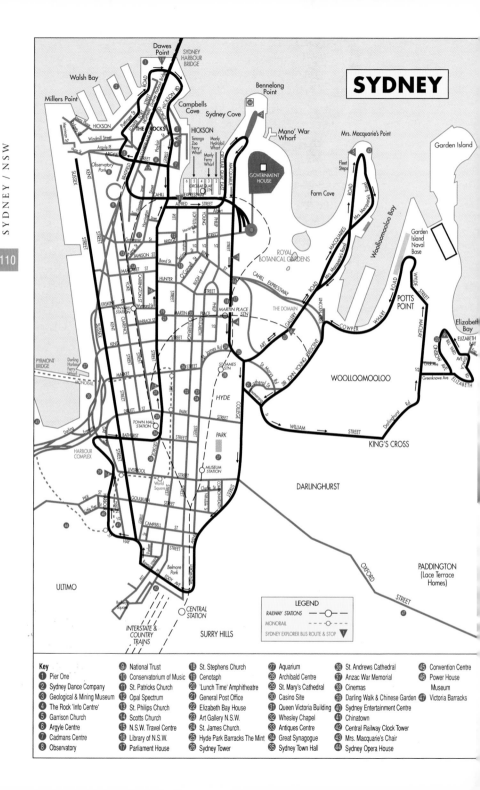

SYDNEY

LEGEND
RAILWAY STATIONS ——○——
MONORAIL – – –○– – –
SYDNEY EXPLORER BUS ROUTE & STOP ▼

Key

1 Pier One
2 Sydney Dance Company
3 Geological & Mining Museum
4 The Rock 'Info Centre'
5 Garrison Church
6 Argyle Centre
7 Cadmans Centre
8 Observatory
9 National Trust
10 Conservatorium of Music
11 St. Patricks Church
12 Opal Spectrum
13 St. Philips Church
14 Scotts Church
15 N.S.W. Travel Centre
16 Library of N.S.W.
17 Parliament House
18 St. Stephens Church
19 Cenotaph
20 'Lunch Time' Amphitheatre
21 General Post Office
22 Elizabeth Bay House
23 Art Gallery N.S.W.
24 St. James Church.
25 Hyde Park Barracks The Mint
26 Sydney Tower
27 Aquarium
28 Archibald Centre
29 St. Mary's Cathedral
30 Casino Site
31 Queen Victoria Building
32 Whesley Chapel
33 Antiques Centre
34 Great Synagogue
35 Sydney Town Hall
36 St. Andrews Cathedral
37 Anzac War Memorial
38 Cinemas
39 Darling Walk & Chinese Garden
40 Sydney Entertainment Centre
41 Chinatown
42 Central Railway Clock Tower
43 Mrs. Macquarie's Chair
44 Sydney Opera House
45 Convention Centre
46 Power House Museum
47 Victoria Barracks

The spectacular skylit roof of Darling Harbour Arcade.

Bridge, the enormous silver-grey coat-hanger that has been Sydney's landmark for more than 60 years. Beside it like a nest of ceramic sails, the Opera House juts proudly into the harbour, the only building that can rival the great bridge as the very signature of Sydney.

The airport and other entry points to Sydney are well supplied with visitor data. Nevertheless, an early stop for the serious visitor should be the **New South Wales Travel Centre** on the corner of Pitt and Spring Streets, in the city, open Mondays to Fridays from 9 am to 5 pm. (tel: 02-231-4444). If you are starting your Australian tour from outside New South Wales, there are branch offices in Melbourne at 353 Little Collins Street (tel 03-670-7461); in Brisbane at the corner of Queen and Edward Streets (tel: 07-229-8833); and in Adelaide at 7/F, Australian Airlines Building, 144 North Terrace (tel: 08-231-3167). From any one of these, armed with as many pamphlets, brochures and maps as take your fancy, you will be well equipped to begin your tour.

Getting Around the City

In Sydney there is no easier way to take in alot in a short time than to catch the red **Sydney Explorer** bus. For A$10 for adults, A$5 for children and A$25 for a family, you can hop on and off the buses all day as they run every 15 minutes between 9.30 am and 5 pm, getting

The metropolis by night.

off for a closer inspection of whatever catches your fancy. Wander around for as long as you like, then jump back on to the next bus, and so on. You can buy tickets when you board the bus or from the Travel Centre.

Let's take a closer look at some of the key places, bearing in mind that if you are feeling energetic you can walk around most of them. A good place to start is the waterfront at **Circular Quay**.

It is served by a railway station, bus and cab ranks, and a dozen or more piers sending ferries and pleasure boats out across the harbour and beyond.

Several of Sydney's great hotels, including the **Intercontinental** on the east and the **Regent** on the west, are located at Circular Quay, and it has

always been the focus of the city's life. Like worker ants scurrying to and fro, cross-harbour ferries and other craft, including the occasional hydrofoil to Manly, glide in and out of Circular Quay carrying endless hordes of commuters and sightseers.

The scene enchanted Joseph Conrad, who wrote in 1906: "From the heart of the fair city down the vista of important streets could be seen the wool-clippers lying at the Circular Quay, no walled prison-house of a dock that, but the integral part of the finest, most beautiful, vast, and safe bay the sun ever shone upon".

Today the quayside is a gathering place, especially at weekends, for entertaining buskers and hawkers who sell

The Opera House against the bridge has become one of the most distinctive landmarks in the world.

all manner of trinkets. Among the guitarists and *didjeridoo* puffers a bearded optimist lethargically rattles two short sticks on an upturned treacle tin, hoping to elicit a coin from passers-by for his rhythmic pretensions.

Some Sydney Signatures

While here, you are unlikely to be able to resist a visit to the **Opera House**, which rears its white sails away to your right. It is a stunning monument to Sydney's highly regarded world of performing arts. It is itself peculiarly Australian in some of the best ways – aggressive, unconventional and optimistic. It's not too cynical to say that its very

Australian in other ways too: like Canberra, it was designed by a foreigner, and it ran over budget by a factor of about ten. No matter what you think, however, it is almost impossible not to be impressed by it. Much of it is built on different levels with steps and stairs going every whichway. It may be a little complicated to find your way about, or even just to get out, so you may wish to take a guided tour of this unusual venue.

If you are interested in the performing arts, choose from the copious programmes available and attend an art exhibition, a concert, a film, a play, the ballet or the opera. Many of these run at the same time at the Opera House, a world-class venue where world-class performers appear regularly. There are

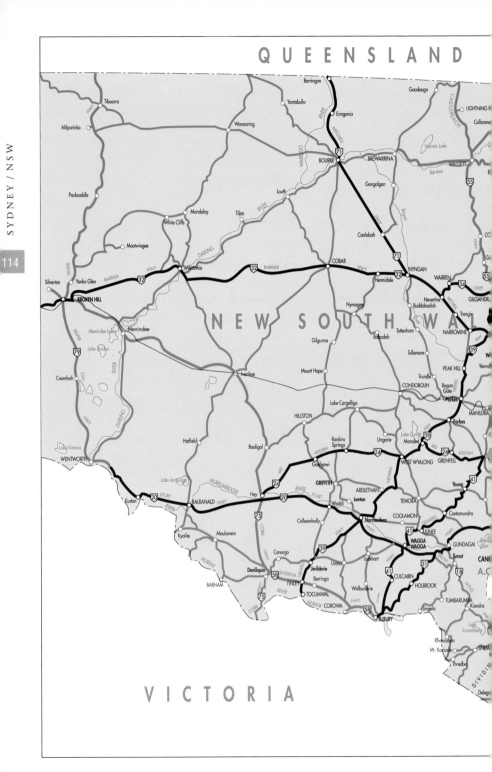

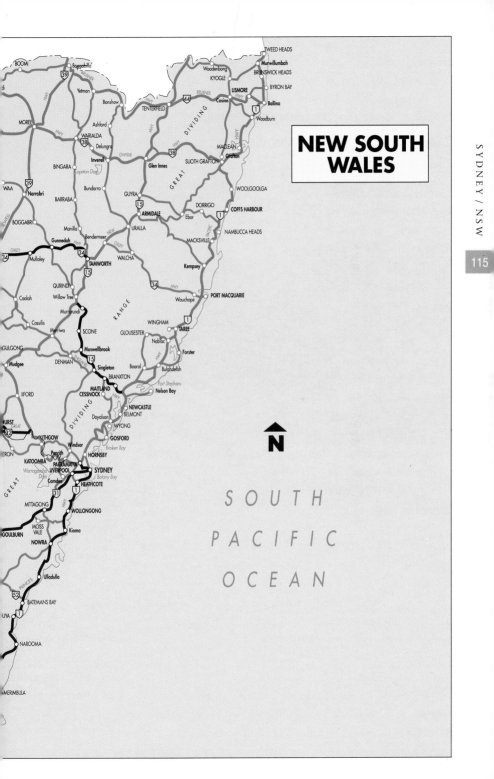

NEW SOUTH WALES

N

SOUTH

PACIFIC

OCEAN

BOOM!
Boggabilla
39
Yetman
MOREE
Ashford
WARIALDA
38
Delungra
BINGARA
Inverell
GWYDIR
39
WAA
Narrabri
Bundarra
BARRABA
BOGGABRI
Manilla
Bendermeer
Gunnedah
OXLEY
34
Mullaley
TAMWORTH
15
QUIRINDI
Coolah
Willow Tree
Murrurundi
Cassilis
Merriwa
SCONE
GULGONG
Muswellbrook
Mudgee
DENMAN
15
Singleton
BRANXTON
ILFORD
MAITLAND
CESSNOCK
HURST
32
Doyalson
ERON
LITHGOW
WYONG
Windsor
GOSFORD
Penrith
HORNSBY
KATOOMBA
PARRAMATTA
Warragamba
LIVERPOOL
SYDNEY
Dam
Camden
HEATHCOTE
MITTAGONG
31
WOLLONGONG
GOULBURN
MOSS
VALE
Kiama
NOWRA
Ulladulla
52
BATEMANS BAY
UYA
NAROOMA
MERIMBULA

TWEED HEADS
Murwillumbah
Woodenbong
BRUNSWICK HEADS
KYOGLE
LISMORE
BYRON BAY
Casino
BRUXNER
Bonshaw
TENTERFIELD
Ballina
44
Woodburn
DIVIDING
MACLEAN
Glen Innes
SUOTH GRAFTON
Grafton
GREAT
GUYRA
WOOLGOOLGA
15
DORRIGO
ARMIDALE
COFFS HARBOUR
Ebor
URALLA
NAMBUCCA HEADS
MACKSVILLE
WALCHA
Kempsey
34
PORT MACQUARIE
Wauchope
RANGE
WINGHAM
GLOUESTER
TAREE
Nabiac
Booral
Forster
Bulahdelah
Port Stephens
Nelson Bay
NEWCASTLE
BELMONT
Broken Bay
Botany Bay

five theatres, a cinema, an exhibition hall, two restaurants and six bars. Sadly it lacks a public parking area, although it is within walking distance of public transport. For cut-rate tickets to various entertainments and performances, not only at the Opera House but at all venues, try the **Halftix Booth** at the top of Martin Place in the city centre, about a kilometre south up Pitt or George Streets. Wait until the afternoon of the performance when unsold tickets become available at very reasonable prices.

To the left of the Opera House, if you are looking out over the water, there is a gusty promenade leading to the harbour's edge for a fine view back towards Circular Quay.

The panorama takes in the bridge and the passing parade of hundreds of different vessels. Sit on the water's edge and savour the beauty of this scene or have a drink or a light meal at one of the restaurants that overlook the water. Some have outdoor terraces too. It is at once obvious that **Sydney Harbour** is an attraction in itself, and its importance can never be overestimated by anyone trying to capture the soul of Sydney. A visitor who has not walked beside or sailed over the harbour and given it his or her undivided attention for a while at least has really not seen Sydney. It is a glorious expanse of water that deserves the magnificent city that is built on its shores (and strangely enough, missed entirely by Captain Cook). How it must have brought tears to the eyes of many an old salt as his storm-battered barque heaved through the Heads to safety, eight weeks or more out of Portsmouth or London!

Before you recommence your tour, take a look out into mid-harbour to your right, where you will see a rocky outcrop crowned with a squat fortress-like building. This is **Pinchgut**, more formally known as **Fort Denison**. Built as a fort to protect Sydney against the non-existent Russian invaders of the last century, it got its name of Pinchgut because to its narrow, slimy, freezing cells were sent the most recalcitrant of the early convicts to be starved into submission, thus the resulting pinched gut. Or so the story goes. Since transportation had stopped by the time Pinchgut was built, there may be some romance to the tale.

Now look left across to the far side of Circular Quay, under the southern end of the bridge. This is where the historic area known as **The Rocks** is clustered along the waterfront. This harbourside area was Sydney's original commercial and maritime quarter in the years following the first settlement in 1788. It is now being restored.

Fort Denison – Pinchgut Island in the harbour.

In the old days, The Rocks did not have an enviable reputation. More than a 100 years ago, as gin palaces and doss-houses spread everywhere, it became the lair of old lags and other thugs who formed a gang known as "the Push". They were hard-core criminals, outside whatever law there was, who preyed on drunken Jack Tars and on one another. Today, many of the original old buildings of The Rocks have been authentically restored and you can take a walk back into Australia's early history. You aren't likely to get cornered by the Push any longer, but it's still possible to get robbed, and you should watch out for inflated tourist prices in the small shops here.

Take a close look at **Sergeant Ma-** **jors Row** which was the colony's first street. **Cadman's Cottage** was built in 1815 – the year of Waterloo – and is the area's oldest building, and one of the oldest in the country. The **Hero of Waterloo Hotel** clearly echoes that same far-off event. Here, as a protest against the glass tax of the day, some of the windows were just painted on the building, and these paintings still remain. The **Garrison Church** dates from the 1840s and is well worth a visit. You will also see **Bligh House**, named after Captain Bligh of "Mutiny on the Bounty" fame, who later became Governor of New South Wales. The **Argyle Stores** is now a tourist complex with some offices too.

Note the rows of narrow terraced

Where urban and surburban blend into each other.

houses as high as they are long and quite reminiscent of the English houses they were modelled on, though in many ways quite unsuitable for this much warmer climate. Victorian terraces of this kind are quite a common sight in many areas of Sydney, and in some districts have become extremely fashionable.

Horse-drawn coaches add to the atmosphere of the Rocks, and if it's a weekend or evening and you hear music, it will be coming from one of several lovely old pubs with roomy bars and deep cellars where dinky-di Oz singalongs are a real experience. Everyone is welcome at these events. Just grab a beer and join in. At the top of one of these quaint streets the observant visitor

may detect an old-fashioned stand-up loo which gives a view of the head of its user. It seems somehow typical of the robust informality of the area.

There are some fine restaurants here too, and cheaper cafes. But don't overlook the pubs. They **are** often the cheapest and best places at which to eat, here as elsewhere in Australia. For the big spenders there are arcades of good quality souvenirs, jewellery and arts and craft shops, many operated by Japanese and Chinese people who are doing a roaring trade with their countrymen.

Stargazing and a Waterfront Lunch

Sydney Observatory is not far to the west of here on the other side of the feeder roads to the bridge and on top of **Observatory Hill**. An impressive old pile flanked by cannon, it affords wonderful views of the harbour and gives out loads of information on astral matters, some of which is a bit high-powered for ordinary mortals. It is open Mondays to Fridays from 2 pm to 5 pm, and on weekends from 10 am to 5 pm and entrance is free. However, you can wander up the green hill and picnic there virtually any time. Purists wishing to scan the heavens at night should phone (02)-241-2478 to establish *bona fides* and get a booking.

Looking back south from the top of Observatory Hill, you cannot fail to see the glittering expanse of **Darling Har-**

bour, all steel-framed structures, banners and promenades. The name is misleading as it is a sort of convention/shopping/eating complex rather than a harbour proper.

A series of soaring, ultra-modern, glass, concrete and steel buildings of aircraft hangar proportions is set on grounds where concrete is king, grass comes a poor second and shady trees are a virtual no-no, at least until they have a chance to grow. The complex was built in time (more or less) for Australia's Bicentennial celebrations in 1988, and is still shiny-new.

Visitors are often interested in the knick-knack shopping, the monorail that whooshes overhead, the waterfront restaurants, the **Sydney Aquarium** and the **Chinese Gardens**.

Try a superb lunch within metres of the crowded water scene. An alfresco lunch at Darling Harbour with a glass or two of Australian Chardonnay is a very "Sydney" thing to do, but then track down some of the old sections in this area. It's great fun to see the two sides of the old **Pyrmont Road-Bridge** raised so that the funnels of tugs and the masts of yachts can pass below. Following a warning signal the gates swing closed railway-crossing style on pedestrians, up goes the roadway in two halves and everyone must wait until the boats have passed, the road-bridge is lowered and the gates re-opened.

The **Pumphouse Pub** is also at Darling Harbour and well worth a look-in, not just to to see the massive pumps, boilers and other mechanical parapher-

The whole harbour is converted into a watery playground by enthusiasts especially during weekends.

Lively and imaginative art shows are part of the Sydney scene.

nalia that once moved thousands of tons of water to and fro. It is tastefully transformed into a charming tavern where, of course, you'll also stop for a beer pulled in old-fashioned style by the barman.

While you are in this area of town, you could consider a short cab ride (or hop back on the Sydney Explorer) to the nearby suburb of **Ultimo** to visit the **Powerhouse Museum**. It's a highly innovative museum that brings together science, technology, social history, art and design, plus objects from Austral-

The Monorail zooms into the Sydney skyline.

ians' everyday life.

It is a world-class museum of its type, a very long way from the dusty mahogany cabinets we associate with the word "museum", and is an excellent way of getting an insight into exactly what makes Australians different. Since the aim of the place is to present non-thematic exhibitions representing revolutions in thinking, be prepared for the unconventional. To categorise a few of the exhibits could be misleading since none is representational of the whole.

However, there is a NASA space station, the state's first locomotive, a 1920s suburban kitchen, a 1930s suburban cinema, three centuries of stylish objects... and so much more. As you might imagine, the design of this ultra-mod facility is in line with its philosophy. It's a place you'll either love or loathe. The Powerhouse Museum is open daily from 10 am to 5 pm and entrance is free. After that, retrace your steps to Darling Harbour to continue with the tour.

The Centre of Things

Head into the centre of town now, a few hundred metres on foot or just a couple of stops on the controversial **monorail**. A special way of viewing Sydney is from on high, aboard this very quiet "people mover" which does a 3.6 km loop across Darling Harbour, down to the Haymarket on the fringes of Chinatown and

Downtown Chinatown.

back into the heart of the city above Pitt and Market Streets. It costs only A$2 per passenger but unlike the Red Explorer Bus, if you get off at any stop you must pay again to get back on.

If you choose this method of getting about, you might feel like making a stop at **Chinatown**. It is one of Sydney's most colourful areas, reflecting the long involvement the Chinese have had with Australia. It features the expected variety of eating outlets, and one of the favourite pastimes for Sydneysiders is a Sunday morning *yum-cha* (morning tea, Chinese style) at one of these places. In the backstreets (the streetnames are in Chinese script) you will find unpretentious Chinese stores selling spices, medicines, woks and porcelain, and in many of them you won't hear a word of English spoken. The area of Chinatown stretches up from the edge of Darling Harbour southwards towards Sydney Central Station. Its central thoroughfare is Dixon Street, and while you are wandering up that little piece of Asia in Australia, bear in mind that you are almost next door to the vast new **Entertainment Centre** and quite near several other major theatre venues. That makes Chinatown a fine place to eat at if you plan to take in a show. Now, hop back on the monorail, or walk a couple of blocks north down George Street, past all the cinema centres.

If you aim for **Town Hall** you will find yourself close to the splendid **Queen Victoria Building**. An elegant structure, superbly restored, this is "the most beautiful shopping centre in the world" according to fashion doyen Pierre Cardin. Originally built in the 1890s in the style of a Byzantine palace to mark the enduring reign of Queen Victoria, it slowly fell into disrepair and disuse. Thankfully, a Malaysian Chinese company saw beneath the dirt and tacky renovations the grace and charm of its former glory and saved it from the wrecker's ball. Three years' work resulted in its restoration into a building to which the visitor is irresistibly drawn again and again. Visit it just once and you too will fall under its spell. Just around the corner from the Queen Victoria Building is the **Strand Arcade**, off Pitt Street, much smaller, but equally charming and elegant and as full of excellent shops.

In fact this whole area of the city centre bulges with speciality shops, surprising arcades and outlets for everything from haute couture fashions to bargain-basement bins. The two main department stores are **David Jones** and **Grace Brothers**, both of which rival their European counterparts. The elegant, swanky David Jones Emporium immodestly describes itself as "the most beautiful store in the world". But there are scores of others, and for the traveller a good supply of duty free shops too.

Another landmark you might have noticed during your plane's final approach is an enormous metal spire with a gold fingernail sprouting amid the high-rise buildings surrounding it. This is **Sydney Tower** in the heart of the city

Victorian grandeur at QVB.

and not more than 300 m towards the water from the Queen Victoria Building. Here at Sydney Tower high-speed lifts whisk you up to the observation deck for breathtaking views of Sydney and its suburbs. Or you can dine in the revolving restaurant overlooking this beautiful city and drink in the scenic panorama at greater leisure. This is a spectacular way to see Sydney by night but hours can change, so check by phoning (02) 229-7444. You can call in any time for a snack in the revolving self-serve restaurant and coffee shop.

The Old Eastern Flank

Go back to Town Hall, cross George

Hyde Park, not in London.

Street and then walk eastwards along Park Street, across the junction with Pitt (parallel to George and Sydney's other main street) and across Castlereagh and then Elizabeth. Park Street becomes William Street at this point, as it crosses **Hyde Park**. This park has some pleas-

ant gardens, and up to your right you will see the art-deco **ANZAC War Memorial**, which has a display of letters and other objects and is worth a visit.

You might make a detour here, if you are into inner city sophistication, not to say decadence. Take a stroll down

Street theatre in the park.

Oxford Street, which starts at the south-eastern corner of Hyde Park, not far from the ANZAC Memorial. This is a place of ethnic restaurants, antique shops, avant-garde bookshops, sleazy cinemas and some very old pubs and leads you into **Paddington**.

This trendy suburb, usually called "Paddo" has crooked streets of terraced homes with pretty, lacey, wrought-iron work. At the far end of Oxford Street is **Victoria Barracks**. Plenty of ceremony can be witnessed at the **Changing of the Guard** between 10 and 10.30 am every Tuesday, followed by guided tour. It is the largest barracks block in the Empire of old and took convict builders seven years to complete – from 1841 to 1848. It is still in use by the military.

Returning to William Street and continuing east, you will emerge from Hyde Park at an intersection and see the **Australian Museum** on the opposite corner. Collections concentrate on natural science, anthropology and ethnology and exhibits are changed regularly from the stock of over 8 million items. There is a snack bar to fortify you on your rounds which can begin at 10 am, must end by 5 pm daily, and are free.

Just behind the museum, by the way, is **Sydney Grammar School**, still in use and probably the oldest surviving educational establishment in the country.

If you look straight up William Street to the east, you will see the **Hyatt Kingsgate Hotel**, and **Kings Cross** – Sydney's red-light district – clustered around it (see box story, page 127). Though it is only about a kilometre from where you stand, turn aside from these temptations for the moment and head left down College Street beside Hyde Park, follow it as it bears left at the foot of the park, and cross over into Macquarie Street. You will find a series of Sydney's finest buildings, mostly in ochre sandstone, ranked down this splendid thoroughfare as it strikes north towards Circular Quay and the Opera House.

Hyde Park Barracks was built in 1819, designed by convict architect Francis Greenway, among whose other surviving works are **St James Church** in Sydney and **St Matthews** in the outer township of **Windsor**.

Greenway had been sentenced to death, commuted to transportation for life, for forging a building contract in Bristol. His elegant Barracks building has been put to many uses, the latest being, most appropriately, a museum of New South Wales social history.

There is also a fine restaurant in the courtyard. Next door **The Mint** is one of Sydney's oldest buildings. Originally it was the "Rum Hospital", having been built in 1816 in exchange for the exclusive rights to import rum into the colony (see box story, page 20).

Today it houses one of the country's best collections of colonial decorative arts and is open daily from 10 am to 5 pm except on Wednesdays when it only opens at noon. **Parliament House**, a little further down, is the distinguished building from which New South Wales

Victoriana in the dome at the QVB shopping arcade.

Kings Cross

Every city has a Kings Cross: the place where you can watch people let their hair down and where you can join in the fun if you like.

Like its counterparts in other cosmopolitan cities around the world, Kings Cross does not officially exist. Sydney's centre for late-night "entertainment" is in the suburb called **Potts Point** – but don't try telling that to anyone on the hyperactive streets near the **Alamein Fountain** on a Saturday night, they will just think you are mad.

Some people would say you were mad to be there at that time anyway, as the Cross has a "reputation". It is now the centre of sleaze, the Soho of Sydney, where ladies in impossibly tight skirts have been a regular feature for over thirty years.

Before that it was the Bohemian quarter where the artists (and their models) created Australia's first real café society. And to this day it is here in the Cross that you will find the best cup of coffee in Sydney.

That's the other side of The Cross – it's hardly ever called Kings Cross by the locals – it is a local residential area with a high population density of people who live their lives in a convenient and leafy suburb less than a mile from the centre of downtown Sydney.

And it is more than convenient: it is vibrant, colourful and diverse, a uniquely Australian space where the raffish and Bohemian past continues its activities next-door to apartment buildings, fashionable restaurants, Italian cafes, offices and bookstores – although some of these have curtains on the doors... to protect the innocent.

Kings Cross was not always like this, of course. In fact, the district was known as **Woolloomooloo Heights** in the last century when the skyline was dominated by windmills, now replaced by luxury hotels and trendy apart-

Larking about.

ment buildings.

Here too were the country houses of the successful merchants who preferred not to live too close to their thriving businesses in **The Rocks**, the teeming and unsavoury area which grew up around the docks of the new settlement. Right through to the mid-1950's, The Cross was the entry point to Sydney for country folk who liked the genteel and slightly Bohemian flavour of the residential suburb with its small, comfortable hotels in the quiet tree-lined streets close to the downtown shops and business district.

And they are still coming to The Cross. Only now they come from all over Australia, the Asia-Pacific region and the rest of the world. Kings Cross is the focal point of Sydney for visitors who want to see the colourful part of this vibrant city in all its night-time glory and bustle. It is the place they remember, for its diversity, its street theatre, its tree-lined streets, its bars, strip-shows, cafes and gourmet restaurants – all the glitter and glamour that makes what could be a sleazy quarter a tourist centre for safe, sophisticated and quality entertainment.

has been governed since 1827. It is open 9 am to 4.30 pm from Monday to Friday.

Through Civic Pride to Greenery

All these buildings and others are grouped down the righthand side of Macquarie Street as you walk north towards the water. But if the civic pride is beginning to weigh heavy upon you, cut through between a couple of them and walk across the green expanse of the **Domain**, which you will find spread out behind them. This ancient piece of parkland is where Sydney's "Symphony Under the Stars" and "Opera in the Park" are held during festival season in January. They are among the biggest open-air events in the world, and if you are there at the right time, drop in for the experience alone.

Crossing the Domain, you have to keep south of the canyon in which the Cahill Expressway runs, and this will inevitably bring you out on the far side of the greenery at the **Art Gallery of New South Wales**. Its collections range from early artworks of Australia to contemporary works, plus British and European works including paintings by Rembrandt and Picasso. It also has a good restaurant, and you will incidentally find another of these opposite the front door. If you turn right, towards the water, as you step out of the Gallery you cross the Cahill Expressway and walk down Mrs Macquaries Road, which

brings you past the **Royal Botanical Gardens** after a few metres on your left. Laid out in 1810 on the water's edge, it is one of the oldest gardens in the country and well worth a visit, not only to enjoy the beautiful walks, but also because it provides a superb view of the harbour. It also contains the **National Herbarium**, a visitors centre and a shop and is open from 8 am to sunset. There is a delightful walk from here, down to the water (there's another fine restaurant in the middle of the park) and along the waterfront to the Opera House.

Since this brings you back to your starting point, you might feel like resting your tired legs and having a closer look at that famous harbour. Sydney is a grand sight from the water. *Harbour Explorer* cruises show you different aspects of The Rocks, Opera House, Darling Harbour, Watsons Bay with its great seafood and even Taronga Park Zoo. This is a water-borne version of the Explorer Bus, so it's a hop-on, hop-off arrangement allowing one-hour stopovers between boats and costs A$15 for adults and A$8 for children. A very comprehensive trip is offered by State Transit's two-and-a-half-hour **Harbour History Cruise** where the gangplank goes up at 10 am from Circular Quay. Then it's off to Fort Denison (Pinchgut), Shark Island, Clarke Island, under the bridge and in and out of several bays to the Parramatta and Lane Cove Rivers, Goat, Cockatoo and Spectacle Islands and finally back past Darling Harbour – all for the fee of A$10 for adults and

Hot summer days.

A$5 for children and pensioners.

Getting on the Right Track

Sydney is home to four racecourses. The best track is **Royal Randwick** which dates back to 1833 and is close to the city. **Canterbury** and **Rosehill** are further out and **Warwick Farm** has a semi-country atmosphere and is very popular with picnickers. There is racing at one of these venues every Saturday and Wednesday afternoon, as well as on almost every public holiday afternoon with big fields, top horses, famous jockeys, keen racing and bookmakers as well as the tote. Admission costs A$5. Harness racing meetings are held every Tuesday and Friday evening at **Harold Park** in the inner suburb of **Glebe**. It is exciting action under a "ribbon of light" system and admission costs A$5. You can catch a greyhound race or two any Saturday and Monday night at **Wentworth Park,** also in Glebe.

Outside of the City Centre

Built in 1803 in Wentworth Road, in the now exclusive eastern suburb of **Vaucluse, Vaucluse House** was richly decorated with colonial furniture and fittings, and illustrates the sumptuous lifestyle enjoyed by the wealthy as less fortunate settlers struggled to eke out a living from the harsh land. There are

Taking it all in at the beach.

tearooms for lunch or tea and scones. It is open Tuesdays to Sundays from 10 am to 4.30 pm. Entry costs adults A$4.

At the other end of today's social scale, yet not more than three or four kilometres away to the south, is **Bondi Beach.** This once-famous ocean-beach suburb is now taken over by greasy-spoon restaurants and boarding houses. It may have fallen on hard times, but many still consider it the most dramatic Pacific beach in Sydney. If you're interested in taking a swim or just seeing some more magnificent beaches, Sydney has 34 ocean beaches, some of the best along the northern coastline beyond Manly. There are sensational views from the road overlooking **Dee Why Beach** in this area.

Manly is itself a worthwhile half-day trip – many Sydneysiders do it at weekends. Catch the hydrofoil which takes 20 minutes and costs A$4, or the ferry for a 35-minute A$3 ride from Circular Quay. Some people take the ferry across and back in their lunch break, and it's certainly the cheapest way of seeing the harbour.

Manly has a seven-day-a-week holiday atmosphere with swinging pubs, clean beaches, fine restaurants, snack bars, shops that stay open until late and an oceanarium with more fish and cold-eyed sharks than you ever thought the sea could contain, prowling inches from your eyes.

Cabramatta is not really thought of as a tourist destination, but it is well worth a visit as it is Sydney's "Little Asia" where many of the non-millionaire Asian immigrants live. It's less organized, less expensive, and less exclusively Chinese than the "official" Chinatown in the Haymarket. Enjoy street after street of Thai, Vietnamese and Malaysian shops, stores and restaurants. It is only about an hour by train from Sydney. Get out at Cabramatta Station, cross the bridge to the shopping district and, presto, you're in Singapore, Bangkok, Hongkong, Kuala Lumpur or Saigon.

Go West, Young Man

Allow the best part of the day to visit **Parramatta** a few kilometres to the west of the city proper, and today the demographic centre of Sydney. It's most easily reached by train from Central, but a ferry service is opening soon to the Harbour. Parramatta reeks of early history. It is Australia's second oldest settlement and still contains the nation's oldest house, **Elizabeth Farm House** (1793), the home of argumentative wool baron John Macarthur. The simple home contains some of the family's original possessions and the outbuildings some of the earliest examples of convict-made farming implements. Note the dripstone to supply simply purified water. Here you will also see the bedroom where Macarthur, under restraint because of increasing madness, lived out his last few years. Other historic buildings include **Experimental Farm Cottage**, built in 1793 on the colony's first land grant, and **Government House** where William Bligh, among others, lived. Inside Government House, later used as a boys' school, are displayed many furnishings of the early colonial days, all brought by sailing ship from England.

.On the heart of Parramatta are several historic buildings, in particular **St John's Anglican Church** built in 1855.

As a diversion for the kids, go north from Parramatta on the Castle Hill Road to West Pennant Hills and **Koala Park**, where you will find koalas, kangaroos, wombats, dingoes and other indigenous animals and birds. The park also boasts Australia's first koala hospital. It is open daily from 9 am to 5 pm. If you are not

Parramatta, an old site.

The Blue Mountains.

driving, take the train to Pennant Hills Station via Strathfield, then Bus No 655 to Koala Park.

About an hour's trip by road from central Sydney (67 km) and not far beyond Parramatta brings you to **Warragamba**, also the location of a very large dam. Here you can find a genuine safari park, with free range lions, tigers and bears as well as a leaping dolphin show, a parrot circus, pets' corner, kangaroos and snakes. Motorists absolutely must remain in their vehicles behind locked doors. The need for this quickly becomes apparent as lions licking their chops approach one vehicle after another. There is a restaurant, a children's playground, and a picnic ground with barbecue pits. The park is open Wednesdays to Sundays and on public holidays. Coach tours can be arranged through Newmans, (tel: 02-225-8061) among other operators. Not far away is **Australiana Pioneer Village**, an example of olde New South Wales complete with smithy's forge, coach rides, genuine bush tucker (food), an old-style general store, 'roos, emus and an entertainment programme. It's an hour from Sydney and just 5 km from **Windsor**. The village is open from 10 am to 5 pm five days a week, but closed on Mondays and Fridays. Windsor itself must be visited: a picturesque settlement with a particular reputation for its antique shops.

Also on this side of Sydney, and just beyond Parramatta, is Australia's **Wonderland** at **Minchinbury**, 45 minutes from the city centre. It is Australia's biggest theme park. It features giant rollercoaster rides and other attractions, which offer tons of fun for children and grown-ups alike. It is only open on Saturdays, Sundays and public holidays, from 10 am to 5 pm. And before you reach the Blue Mountains, out in the same direction is a colonial-style sheep farm re-created at **Gledswood Homestead** in the **Camden Valley**. Enjoy a sheep-shearing demonstration, boomerang-throwing, wine-tasting and an Oz barbecue lunch. The flies come free! Coach tours depart daily from Sydney.

The Blue Mountains

Further west still, the **Blue Mountains** mark the beginnings of the Great Dividing Range, though in reality they are more like steep hills, reaching only 1000 m at the top. Most of the area is now national park, and, yes, the eucalypt-clothed mountainsides really are blue. It's a traditional holiday area for Sydneysiders, and professional people started coming up here in the late 1800s, as soon as the railway went in. The region retains much of the atmosphere of those days. Although the top of the Mountains is fully 100 km out of Sydney centre, and about half of that even from Parramatta, there are plenty of people who commute from the Mountains into town. One reason is the excellent train service, which goes from Sydney Central to the very top of the Mountains via

Old world charm in the Blue Mountains.

Parramatta in a couple of hours. Virtually all the main settlements are grouped around this rail line and the road which follows it.

Coach tours to the Blue Mountains often include **Featherdale Wildlife Park,** which is literally alive with native animals, and then go on to **Katoomba,** the area's main town, right at the top. It has a skyway, a funicular-style railway, an 1881 hotel, and – in common with most of the settlements in the Upper Mountains – breathtaking mountain scenery, with fascinating rock formations and superb bushwalking. The whole area evokes the 1890s, when it first became popular, and there is a thriving trade in antiques and local crafts. Further west still, the **Jenolan**

Limestone Caves give you a view of what the mountain scenery is like from the inside. On the way there is the **Zig Zag Railway**. To enjoy a steam train ride that takes you over one of the most exciting stretches of railway ever built, put a day aside and head for the **Lithgow** district on the far side of the Mountains. Remember as you chug along the edge of the gorge that this used to be the only way over the Mountains to the rolling plains of the Golden West.

Head North for History and Wine

Old Sydney Town not far from **Gosford** on the coast north of Sydney is an ex-

Surfin' Australia.

tremely well presented re-creation of life in colonial Sydney. Theatricals include a pistol duel and an escaped convict run to earth by soldiers and given a flogging. Bullock-cart rides, an old-style tavern and street theatre add to the charm. Everyone is in period costume, and they all seem to enjoy it. Coach tours can be arranged daily and return via the beautiful **Hawkesbury River**. By the way, there are some wonderful cruises to be had on the Hawkesbury, and it is possible to hire a houseboat of your own.

About an hour's drive north of Sydney, near Gosford and in the same general vicinity as Old Sydney Town is another kind of attraction: **Reptile Park**. If it crawls, creeps and bites, you'll find it here. Watch alligators being hand-fed,

hold a friendly snake, see spiders and snakes milked of their venom and share lunch with the kangaroos and wallabies. Or take a walk in the adjoining **Forest of Tranquillity** which has beautiful cliffs, palms, bubbling waterfalls and nature walks. The reptile park is open daily from 9 am to 5 pm and can be visited on a coach tour.

Further north still is New South Wales' wine country. Best known among the main wine-producing areas in this region is the **Hunter Valley** around Pokolbin and Cessnock or, further north, at Muswellbrook and Denman. Day tours can be arranged as can stopovers of a few days to a winery which include accommodation, meals and a bottle or two. What an intoxicating idea!

Too Much of a Good Thing

The above describes only a circuit of a few hours travel out of Sydney, and mentions only a few of the attractions even within those limits. And it may well be all you have time to do if you are based in Sydney, and visiting for less than a matter of weeks.

It is worth remembering, however, that New South Wales is almost as big as the whole of Western Europe. Because it is the most populous state (with around 6 million inhabitants) it offers more variety in terms of places to visit and tourist attractions than any other state. It would be impossible to cover more than a fraction of them. If you are the adventurous type though, and have the time, try travelling to the **Golden West**, beyond the Blue Mountains, for rolling wheatlands and sheep country, giving way to the arid lands around **Broken Hill**. Or maybe southwest to the alpine districts of the **Snowy Mountains** on the border with Victoria, a haven for skiers in winter and walkers in summer.

A journey to the far north of the state will take you after a journey of 1000 km to the **Border Ranges** not far south of Brisbane in Queensland, and to some of the finest national parks in the country. Throughout all these areas you can sense that the state is getting its tourist act together. Farm holidays and farmhouse overnight accommodation is now easily arranged, and the NSW Travel Service will have details of hundreds of serene country hideaways if you want the quiet life.

Many offer riding, walking and sports facilities. Some are very exclusive indeed, and many more are at the other end of the scale. And don't forget the coastline which is spectacular, and for most of its length free of the box-jelly-fish problem that Queensland has in the summer. The whole littoral is dotted with campsites, hotels, and resorts – but long stretches are preserved forever as national park. But, if you are the city type, it's possible you will never get out of Sydney. It's a big city, one of the biggest in area anywhere in the world, and unquestionably one of the great cities of the world. Sophisticated, historic, vibrant and increasingly multicultural, it's hard to believe that one of its many faces won't smile at you.

Melbourne has the feel of a Victorian city: not just a city in the state of Victoria, that is, but a city from the Victorian age. It is aloof, somewhat old-fashioned, and dignified. There is a touch of the dowager about Melbourne. Melbourne is Old Money. It is conservative with a capital "C".

The people of Melbourne are said to look down their noses at Sydney, regarding Australia's biggest city as pretentious and "fast". Certainly there are significant contrasts between the two. Sydney somehow does seem to be more aggressive, and Melbourne more respectable. This is hard to justify rationally. Sydney is, after all, the older of the two.

Probably the rivalry goes back to the days of Federation when both cities wanted to be

European – inspired Princess Theatre.

139

Melbourne / Victoria

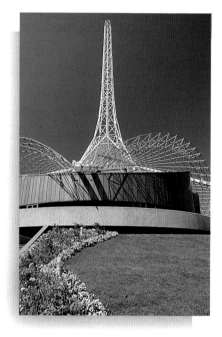

The Arts Centre.

reminiscent of the Eiffel Tower.

There are other touches of France too, like the long, tree-lined boulevards, the fine restaurants, the chic and fashionable shops. The elegant city arcades, mostly off Bourke and Collins Streets, are another reflection of Melbourne's prosperous history. One of them by the way has statues of Gog and Magog at one end. There is a plethora of cultural venues too. In one recent month sampled at random, the city staged (among many other cultural attractions) a Picasso exhibition, the Melbourne Film Festival, a Cole Porter revival, a Mozart series by the Melbourne Symphony, performances by the Australian Ballet, and Shakespeare on stage. Melbourne is – or manages to seem – intensely civilized. At weekends, Melburnians go to church and then look in the newspaper to see where that day's pleasant Sunday afternoon entertainments are to take place. That is at least the way it feels!

Victoria itself is the smallest of the mainland states and so all of its tourist attractions are within a day's drive of Melbourne. While it comprises only 3 percent of Australia's total land area, Victoria boasts one-third of the country's national parks – 33 in all. Its smallness is only relative – it is several times the size of Great Britain – and geographically it is a state of vivid contrasts. Inland are the vast wheatlands of the Mallee District. In winter, snow mantles the mountain ridges. In summer, the beaches are nearly Mediterranean in their warmth and colour. Everywhere

the national capital. But there does seem to be a different atmosphere about Melbourne. Maybe it's the weather. While Sydney is sunny more-or-less year round, Melbourne has a cooler climate and is quite cold in the winter. In Melbourne it seems to rain a good deal (an illusion: Sydney actually has the higher rainfall).

Comparisons with Sydney aside, Melbourne has a style missing from every other Australian city. Maybe it's something to do with the quaint but comprehensive tram system, rattling through the heart of the city. Or the pavement cafés and the theatres. The place is just a little like Paris. It is no accident that the lattice-like spire over the Victorian Arts Centre is distinctly

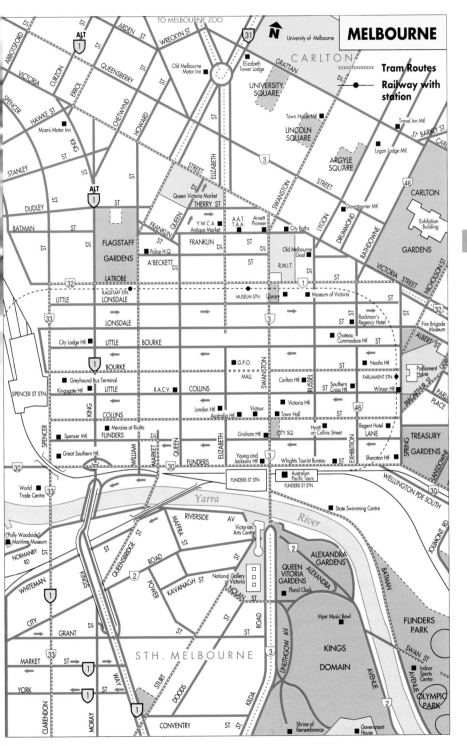

MELBOURNE / VICTORIA

there are beautiful private as well as public gardens: the climate ensures this is a "green thumb" state.

Walking Melbourne

Actually you don't have to walk, thanks to those stately green and cream trams which ply Melbourne's remarkably wide and tree-lined main streets. The trams, along with the city's trains and buses, are operated by the transport authority everyone calls "the Met". You can get all kinds of information from the Met by calling their Information Centre on (03) 617-0900, or by going along to **The Met Shop** at 103 Elizabeth Street in the heart of the city. However, let's assume you are the energetic type, and have just got off the train at **Spencer Street Railway Station** on the western edge of the city centre. There's a tourist information bureau here too.

Leave the station behind you, and turn right along Spencer Street until you reach **Collins Street**, leading off to your left. You'll recognize it because just a block down Collins is the glittering **Menzies at Rialto Complex**, with its twin towers of glass and steel lording it over the other buildings. Nowhere does Melbourne flaunt her style more effectively than in Collins Street, one of the most impressive thoroughfares in Australia. Here, under the trees, nestle the most exclusive fashion outlets, elegant tea-shops, the blue-stocking **Melbourne Club**, many buildings of elegant design and a few historic churches, including **Scots Church**, the **Uniting Church** and, just a few steps down Swanston Street off Collins to the right, **St Paul's Cathedral**. This little group is all within a block or so of the junction of Collins and Bourke, in many ways the premier crossroads of the city. It is on this intersection too that you will find the **Town Hall**, an exercise in pomp and circumstance in stone. Opposite is **City Square**.

The "Paris End"

Sad to say, beyond this point and heading east on Collins, a couple of multistorey interlopers have taken away some of the charm and exclusivity of what old-timers call the "Paris end" of Collins Street. Many would say that the **Hyatt** on **Collins** complex is a worthy architectural successor to old-world grandeur, and it does at least house the stylish **Billich Gallery** with a fine collection of cityscape artworks. On the other hand, **Nauru House** is a large office block which towers uneasily over these once-revered neo-Parisian precincts. It is an investment for the future financial security of the people of Nauru against the day when their island's stocks of guano fertilizer are finally exhausted. (With typical drollery, Australians immediately dubbed the structure

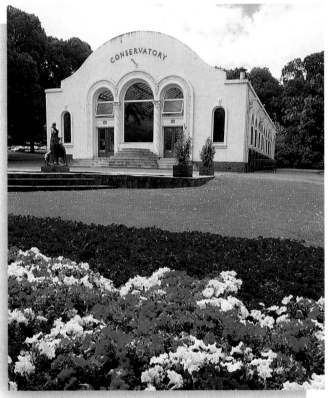

The Conservatory in Fitzroy Gardens.

Birdshit House, and, like the product, the name has stuck). A few more steps, past the **Regent Hotel** on your right, and you will emerge on Spring Street, running north-south. Here you will find yourself facing the splendid **Treasury Buildings.**

This is a particularly interesting area of the city, with several important buildings and other sights clustered in superb gardens on the far side of Spring Street. To the right of the Treasury are the **Treasury Gardens**, and to the left is **Parliament House**, with its classical lines set off by Doric columns. Behind

that is the magnificent **St Patrick's Cathedral**, looking onto MacArthur Street. This is the largest cathedral in Australia. The ornateness and grandeur of the interior are awesome. Behind the cathedral **Fitzroy Gardens** open out into an expanse of greenery and trees, and here you will find one extraordinary little building, **Captain Cook's Cottage.** In his voyages to Australia Cook never touched the coast of Victoria, but the humble home where the navigator grew up was brought from England and re-erected stone by stone here in the Fitzroy Gardens. Judging by

MILDURA
RED CLIFFS
STURT HWY
20
Murray River
CALDER HWY
79
ROBINVALE
Hattah
16
MURRAY
VALLEY
River
Manangatang
Piangil
Walpeup
OUYEN HWY
OUYEN
12
79
SWAN HILL
HWY
16
Patchewollock
Speed
Sea Lake
Ultima
MURRAY
Lascelles
CALDER
Culgoa
BARHAM
Lake Tyrrell
SUNRAYSIA
Hopetoun
Quambatook
KERANG
COHUNA
Beulah
Birchip
Dumosa
WHYCHEPROOF
IONDON HWY
Rainbow
Lake Hindmarsh
Boort
MURRAY
16
ECHUCA
Lake Buloke
CHARLTON
ROCHESTER
75
VALLEY
Jeparit
HWY
79
SHEP
WARRACKNABEAL
Litchfield
Wedderburn
Serpentine
Stanhope
Lake Warong
WESTERN
NHILL
BORUNG
DONALD
HWY
Elmore
Rushworth
Kaniva
8
HENTY HWY
Rupanyup
ST ARNAUD
MIDLAND
Murchison Eas
DIMBOOLA
HWY
Bridgewater
VALLEY HWY
NORTHERN
39
Gymbowen
Dunolly
BENDIGO
HWY
WIMMERA
Natimuk
HORSHAM
79
Lake
Eppalock
Apsley
Halls
Gap
Stawell
AVOCA
Maryborough
CASTLEMAINE
HEATHCOTE
HWY
Edenhope
THE GRAMPIANS
KYNETON
75
Harrow
8
KILMORE
Ararat
WESTERN
MIDLAND
DAYLESFORD
WOODEND
Rocklands
Res.
Balmoral
GLENELG
BEAUFORT
HUME
Cavendish
BALLARAT
HWY
CASTERTON
River
Dunkeld
Lake Bolac
Skipton
Ballan
V   I   C
COLERAINE
GLENELG
Hamilton
HAMILTON HWY
BACCHUS
MARSH
8
79
31
Li
Dartmoor
Penhurst
MIDLAND HWY
Meredith
PRINCES HWY
HENTY HWY
Nelson
Lismore
Cressy
PORT
PHILLIP
BAY
DANDENON
HEYWOOD
MORTLAKE
GEELONG
FRANKSTON
DISCOVERY
BAY
CAMPER DOWN
Lake
Corangamite
Winchelsea
QUEENSCLIFF
Port Sea
Portland
PORTLAND
BAY
TERANG
HWY
TORQUAY
COWF
Port Fairy
WARRNAMBOOL
COLAC
Anglesea
Phillips Is
1
Port Campbell
Lavers Hill
Lorne
Apollo Bay
Cape Otway

BASS

Cape Wickam

King
Island

VIC

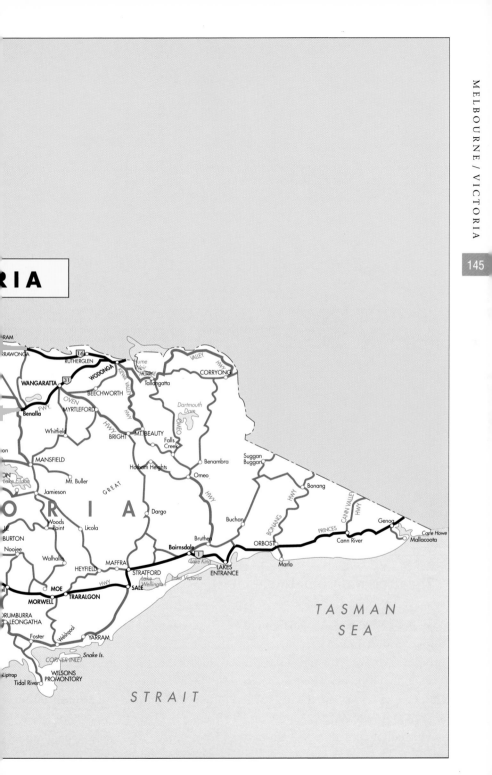

RIA

ARAM
RRAWONGA
16
RUTHERGLEN
WANGARATTA
31
WODONGA
Hume
Weir
Tallangatta
CORRYONG
BEECHWORTH
Benalla
OVEN
MYRTLEFORD
FWY.
KIEWA VALLEY
OMEO HWY
Dartmouth
Dam
Whitfield
BRIGHT
MT. BEAUTY
Falls
Creek
MANSFIELD
Benambra
Suggan
Buggan
Mt. Buller
Hotham Heights
ON
Lake Eildon
GREAT
Omeo
Bonang
Jamieson
HWY
Woods
Point
Dargo
CANN VALLEY HWY
ORIA
Licola
Buchan
BONANG HWY
Genoa
BURTON
Bruthen
Cape Howe
Noojee
Bairnsdale
PRINCES
Mallacoota
1
Walhalla
ORBOST
Cann River
HEYFIELD
MAFFRA
Lake King
Marlo
STRATFORD
LAKES
ENTRANCE
Lake
MOE
SALE
Wellington
Lake Victoria
MORWELL
TRARALGON
HWY
RUMBURRA
LEONGATHA
TASMAN
Foster
Welshpool
YARRAM
SEA
Snake Is.
CORNER INLET
Liptrap
WILSONS
Tidal River
PROMONTORY
STRAIT

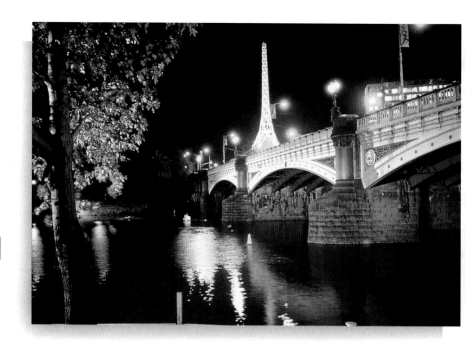

Evenings in Melbourne.

the way most people must stoop to enter the cramped rooms, the people of Cook's day (1728-79) were very short. Besides the cottage, Fitzroy Gardens contains a miniature scale model of an **English Tudor Village** and the **Arts Path** decorated with over 10,000 ceramic tiles.

Theatres and Chinatown

Make your way back to **Parliament House**, so that you are facing across Spring Street towards the city. Just to the right of the **Princess Theatre** opens Little Bourke Street. The theatre itself, restored to its original 1923 glory and convincingly haunted, is well worth a visit.

Walk along Little Bourke Street for a few hundred metres. This is Melbourne's theatre district, with the **Comedy Theatre** and **Her Majesty's Theatre** on the right side of the street, and a cluster of cinema centres fronting onto Bourke Street, off to the left.

As you proceed along this stretch of Little Bourke you will find yourself in Melbourne's exotic **Chinatown**. The Chinese have a long history in Victoria, and especially on the Victorian goldfields. Their story is almost as long as that of the Europeans, and their culture is well established here. There is a **Museum of Chinese Australian History** along here, housing Melbourne's very own dragon, Dai Loong ("big dragon" in Cantonese). Needless to say, the culi-

The shimmer of glass and steel, indelible marks of modern Melbourne.

Caring and sharing – Melbourne lifestyle.

nary options are numerous in the area.

Turn off right from Little Bourke Street into Russell Street. Not far down here you will find the **Old Melbourne Gaol**. One cell block of this grim bluestone building remains as a reminder of the days of transportation of convicts and the harsh system of justice under which they suffered. One hundred and four condemned men were hanged here, the most notable being the bushranger Ned Kelly, whose much publicized armour is now on show. The Gaol is open daily from 9.30 am to 4.30 pm. Almost opposite is the back of the **National Museum and Library**, whose main entrance is on Swanston Street. Not only is it a graceful building, but it also contains splendid old cars, swords,

armour, guns, dioramas, a planetarium, dinosaurs, pterodactyls, and hands-on scientific exhibits that fascinate children and adults alike. It is open daily from 10 am to 5 pm, and entry is free.

This may be the time to make a small detour, taking a tram from outside the National Museum along Latrobe Street eastwards for a couple of blocks. This will drop you at **Carlton Gardens**, and set back in the grounds you will see the stately **Royal Exhibition Building**. This structure sent a gasp of amazement around the whole country when it was the venue of the Great Exhibition of 1880.

Today, more than 110 years later, the 60-metre dome still its proud centrepiece, it remains a most remarkable

The Botanical Gardens is always a restful respite.

building and is regularly used for exhibitions. The opening of Federal Parliament took place here in 1901.

At this point you are not too far from the fine old **Royal Melbourne Zoo**, which is a little to the north on Elliot Avenue, and on the tram route. It is set in **Royal Park**, Melbourne's largest park, which covers an astonishing 180 hectares. The Zoo has an especially fine Butterfly House. After that, find your way back towards the city to **Queen Victoria Market** on the northern edge of town, abutting Victoria Street and Elizabeth Street. The Market is just the place to go on a Sunday from about 9 am to 4 pm as there are about 500 stalls offering almost anything imaginable for sale. If you then walk south up Eliza-

beth, Queen or William Streets (the latter brings you past the Old Mint) you will emerge once again in Bourke Street, and looking down it to your right you will see Spencer Street Station, where you started from.

You can finish your walk (though by now it will be getting lengthy) by continuing south up Spencer Street to the Spencer Street Bridge. The trams run up this way too. On your right you will see the imposing **World Trade Centre** and the **World Congress Centre**, reminders both of Melbourne's significance as a modern business capital among the greatest in the Southern Hemisphere, and in Australia second only to Sydney.

Cross the bridge, and from it you

will see the good ship "**Polly Woodside**" a genuine windjammer with a rich history. Built of riveted iron in 1885, she is now the centrepiece of a maritime display just over the Spencer Street Bridge at the corner of Normanby and Phayer Streets, South Melbourne. The display is open daily from 10 am to 4 pm.

If even this doesn't seem like enough, turn left over the bridge and carry on eastwards along the south bank of the Yarra to the Princes Bridge, or you could hire a bike for this stretch. Bikes are readily available for hire along scores of tracks in Melbourne, and especially up the banks of the Yarra. Alternatively, you can recross Spencer Street Bridge and take a ferry from the World Trade Centre to Princess Wharf.

Let us assume you've reached the north bank end of the Princes Bridge. You will see **Flinders Street Station** off to your left on the far side of the river – a structure which looks more like a national theatre than a station. Built in 1910, it reflects the wealth and civic pride of Melbourne at the turn of the century, when it was one of the world's foremost cities. (It still is, but today there are more of them!)

On your side of the water, the continuation of the Princes Bridge going south is St Kilda Road. From here that you can see Melbourne's Eiffel Tower clone: the tower above the **Arts Centre**, just on the south side of the Princes Bridge in St Kilda Road.

The Arts Centre itself is a culture lover's paradise as the **Melbourne Con-** cert Hall, three theatres, the **National Gallery of Victoria** and the **Performing Arts Museum** are all grouped here. The Gallery houses one of Australia's finest collections of European, Australian and Oriental Art.

There are also several restaurants and bars, including **The Vic Restaurant** which ranks among the city's best appointed with its classical decor. Though this is beginning to get a little too far to walk with comfort, the **Shrine of Remembrance** is to be found along St Kilda Road: at exactly 11 am on the anniversary of Armistice Day, November 11, a shaft of light illuminates the Stone of Remembrance.

To the left of St Kilda Road are a cluster of fine gardens grouped along the Yarra. The most spectacular of these must be the **Royal Botanical Gardens**, covering 36 hectares, and with 7 km of footpaths. Full of birds and plants, the Gardens also feature the **Separation Tree**, where citizens of Melbourne gathered to celebrate their split with New South Wales in 1851. Adjoining the Gardens is the **Kings Domain**, with the outdoor **Sidney Myer Music Bowl**. There is also another building of great historical interest here. This is **La Trobe's Cottage**, another authentic English home brought to Melbourne like Captain Cook's Cottage. In this case the house was moved by its owner, Charles La Trobe, initially superintendent and later lieutenant-governor of Victoria. Thus this simple cottage became the state's **First Government House**, by which al-

Old terrace houses converted into smart and fashionable restaurants.

ternative name it is also known. Restored to its period with many of the original furnishings, it is open six days a week from 11 am to 4 pm, but is closed on Fridays.

On the Outskirts

Among many graceful old buildings to be found within range of Melbourne are two outstanding residences. **Como** in Como Avenue, South Yarra, and to the south of the city centre, is the epitome of colonial grace and was built about 1855. It is set in six acres of garden and furnished with period pieces by the National Trust. It is open daily from 10 am to 5 pm. **Ripponlea** (192 Hotham Street,

Elsternwick) is another 19th-century mansion with 33 rooms set in 13 acres of exquisite gardens. It is open daily from 10 am to 5 pm. Morning tea is available.

In the same suburb is the grim Jewish **Holocaust Museum**, at 13 Selwyn Street, Elsternwick, with audio-visuals, films, and displays. There is no charge for entry. Still on a Jewish theme, there is also the **Jewish Museum of Australia**, on the corner of Toorak Road and Arnold Streets, South Yarra, which places emphasis on the Australian experiences of Jewish people. Not far away is the classy shopping suburb of **Toorak** (pronounced "T'rack" by the "In Crowd"). Here trendy boutiques, elegant antique shops, exclusive milliners and *twee* coffee shops daintily rub shoulders.

Cricket, an age-old passion.

In the same general direction, but just over the Yarra River from the Botanical Gardens, is the **National Tennis Centre**, with its computerized roof which opens or closes to shade the courts. The Australian Tennis Open is fought out here in January, but it is open to the public at other times of the year. Also to the south of the city is **Luna Park Amusement Park** at St Kilda, with heart-stopping rides in a carnival atmosphere. It is open Friday nights, Saturday afternoons and nights, and Sunday afternoons. A little further down the shore of Port Phillip Bay is the port suburb of Williamstown. Here you can inspect the fine **Maritime Museum** with its museum ship and nautical relics, which is open Saturdays and Sundays

from noon to 6 pm. Also in Williamstown is the **Railway Museum**, featuring restored locomotives, carriages and wagons. It is open on Saturdays and Sundays from 1 pm to 5 pm.

Moving round to the western side of the city, the **Fire Brigade Museum** is to be found in Victoria Parade, West Melbourne. This is great fun for boys of any age, with everything from classic fire engines to gleaming brass helmets. It is open on Fridays from 9 am to 3 pm and Sundays from 10 am to 4 pm. Diagonally opposite, and about 2 km out of the city centre to the east is **Melbourne Cricket Ground** with its **Gallery of Sport** – Australia's first multi-sport museum. It features displays of sports memorabilia, videos, and souvenirs and is open

Tuesdays to Sundays from 10 am to 4 pm. The cricket ground itself is well worth inspection as it has an enormous amphitheatre with seating for almost 100000, originally used as the main venue for the 1956 Olympics. After its summer use for cricket, it draws equally large crowds for Australian Rules football matches in winter.

Don't be misled by the name **Meat Market Craft Centre** at 42 Courtney Street, North Melbourne. It was originally just that, but now it is an arts and crafts centre brimming with original pieces.

The Melbourne Cup

In the same general direction is the famous **Flemington Racecourse**, best known as the venue for Australia's most glamorous horse race, the Melbourne Cup, on the first Tuesday of every November. If you plan to attend the Cup, be sure to arrange bookings well in advance! The city and the racecourse is jam-packed with visitors at this time. On the big day (a public holiday in Victoria) the whole city is motionless, even the traffic, as everybody stops to listen to the race. In fact this fanatical interest is not exclusive to Melbourne – all Australia takes a keen interest in this premier event. The Cup is part of the **Spring Carnival**, a wonderful time to be in Melbourne, but the Flemington course is used year-round for lesser meetings. Apart from Flemington, the city

boasts three other splendid tracks, **Caulfield**, **Moonee Valley** and **Sandown**. Racing takes place at one of these every Saturday and Wednesday and on holidays. There is horse-racing daily, except Sundays, at various provincial racecourses, and there are exciting trotting events at Moonee Valley on Saturday nights.

For followers of the greyhounds, there are mid-week fixtures at night at **Olympic Park** and Sandown. While on the subject of sports, it's worth noting that there are more than 30 public golf courses in and around Melbourne. The best way to contact them is to consult the Yellow Pages.

The High Street in suburban **Armidale** is a treasure-house of fine antique shops and ultra-modern fashion outlets set amid elegant Edwardian and Victorian buildings. There are also gift shops, art and jewellery shops, antiquarian bookshops and stylish restaurants and cafes. Most are open daily. Browse and be tempted! Trains from the city run direct to Armidale Station or take tram number 6 from Swanston Street (alight between stops 34 and 40).

The Dandenongs and the Yarra Valley

The **Dandenong Ranges** is virtually an outer suburb, just an hour or so out of Melbourne to the east. Lookouts high up in the hills provide wonderful views of Melbourne and Port Phillip Bay. The area totals 25,000 hectares of national park and forest, mile upon mile of natural beauty, with walking trails and tourist drives.

The region is dotted with small townships offering snacks, souvenirs and antiques. Many of these settlements are picturesque to the extreme, and have long roots back into Victoria's history. Dame Nellie Melba lived in **Coldstream**, and is buried at **Lilydale**, where the historical museum displays a changing exhibition on the great singer on Wednesdays and Thursdays.

While here make a point of going to **Belgrave**, a few kilometres due south of Lilydale, to take a ride on the **Puffing Billy**. This narrow-gauge train chuffs through 13 km of spectacular mountain scenery between Belgrave and Emerald Lake. Closed only on Christmas Day, it operates 364 days a year. At Emerald Lake there is a fine country resort with 200 acres of lakes and gardens and golf courses, and nearby the world's largest small-scale working model railway. The area has a long history of steam transport, originally to carry out the timber which has always been a mainstay of the economy.

In the late 19th century more timber was hauled out of Yarra Junction than from any other place on earth except Seattle. If you have the time, call in at the **Upper Yarra Historical Museum** at the Junction, open on Sundays, to get the feel of life here in the last century.

In fact the existing Puffing Billy first chugged its way up into the Ranges in 1900, not as a timber train but carrying passengers to guesthouses in **Warburton** and **Healesville** (65 km east of the capital and beyond the Dandenongs proper). Another railroad, the **Yarra Valley Railway**, runs from Healesville to **Yarra Glen** taking visitors by trolley through a 150-metre bricklined tunnel, but only on Sundays from 11 am to 4.30 pm. Today these settlements are even more picturesque – and much better serviced – than in the old days. At Yarra Glen the original house of Edward Henty, the state's first white settler, is now the **Grand Hotel** and demands a visit.

If you get as far as Healesville a trip to the **Healesville Sanctuary** is a must. The Sanctuary is home to many of Australia's endangered animals like the platypus, as well as more common ones such as kangaroos, emus and wallabies. For humans – 350,000 of them a year and there's room for more – it is a favourite place to picnic, or to go bushwalking. Among other attractions in the area is one of Victoria's oldest farmsteads at **Gulf Station**, Yarra Glen, open from Wednesday to Sunday as a working farm from the old days, with butchery, dairy and schoolhouse and all the animals. Call in too at **William Ricketts' Sanctuary**, set up in the 1930s by naturalist, musician and sculptor William Ricketts. His particular forte was interpreting Aboriginal myth, and his work can be seen in the Sanctuary on Mt Dandenong Tourist Road.

The Yarra Valley is one of the birth-

Vineyards in the Yarra Valley wine district.

places of the Australian wine industry. Victoria's first Lieutenant Governor, La Trobe, was so enthusiastic about the grape-growing potential of the state that he not only planted vines in the gardens of Government House but helped persuade some of the winemakers of Neuchatel in Switzerland to come to Victoria in 1837 to start vineyards. He may have been influenced by his wife, who was herself Swiss.

French growers also arrived to help start the industry, which now flourishes. There are today 37 wineries and 82 vineyards all across the Valley and the Dandenong, and many of them will welcome a visit from an enthusiastic sampler – but if you're driving, only sample in strict moderation: the Aus-

tralian anti-drink-driving laws are fierce, and rightly so.

Gold Fever

In the 1850s gold was discovered at **Clunes** near **Ballarat** around 110 km west of Melbourne, and the new city virtually emptied itself of its population in the ensuing goldrush. Forty of the 42 Melbourne police officers resigned, for example, and their departure was symbolic of the collapse of normal life. Settlers abandoned their farms to go to the diggings, Chinese miners arrived in droves, and there was social and economic upheaval. Much of this colourful time has been re-created for those who take the trouble to drive out for a couple of hours on the Western Highway. You'll be heading for Ballarat, the heart of it all, but if you're travelling with children look out for **Kryal Castle** 9 km before you get there. This isn't much to do with Victoria's Wild West, but it's great fun. It's a medieval English castle with drawbridge, dungeons, battlements, maze, armour and a chopping block for executions. Don't miss the live shows! It's open daily 9.30 am to 5 pm. Then on into **Ballarat**.

Here you must not miss **Sovereign Hill Gold Mining Township**, a superb re-creation of those frenetic goldrush days in Victoria, complete with rebuilt main street, stagecoaches, underground mine workings, and people in traditional dress everywhere. Sovereign Hill

A gold-miner's room in Ballarat.

has a worldwide reputation, and sports all kinds of *olde-worlde shoppes* and hotels (even a licensed theatre restaurant). You'll spend hours here and enjoy every minute.

Ballarat itself is the scene of the goldminers' historic rebellion at the **Eureka Stockade**, in 1854 (see box story, page 158) and it is possible to visit the actual site. Ballarat's **Gold Museum** is open daily 9.30 am to 5.20 pm and there is also a military museum.

Take a trip on the paddle cruiser *Sarah George* for a different perspective on things, or wander around town to see the lovely old buildings. Many of them are pubs – it seems the miners were a thirsty lot! The ornate bar of the **Royal Hotel** is a must. There is also the **Ballarat Wildlife Park**, with free-roaming native wildlife and a particularly good reptile house. As added attractions Ballarat offers **Golda's World of Dolls**, incongruously enough, an **Antique Toy Gallery**, and vintage trams to ride on. Also in the area are a number of vineyards, and some pretty lakes and dams (like **Lake Wendouree**).

However, among the one-time tent cities of miners nothing can equal **Bendigo**, and for this you will have to detour for about 100 km northeast up the Midland Highway out of Ballarat. The route there takes you through some particularly lovely country, with historic buildings and pubs at **Castlemaine**, and boating and fishing on **Jubilee Lake** and **Lake Daylesford**. There are fine walking trails in the region of the lakes,

The solid protrusions of The Grampians.

and near Daylesford are the **Wombat Hills Botanic Gardens**. At its height, Bendigo was one of the wealthiest cities in the world. Many elegant buildings testify to its good old days, but today it is booming again, thanks to tourism and such attractions as the **Deborah Goldmine** in the main street, and its **Tram Museum** which houses trams from as far away as the United States. There are also antique shops, the **Joss House**, the **Wax Museum**, and the **Bendigo Pottery Works**, which has a showroom full of temptations.

Return to Ballarat, and instead of going straight back into Melbourne, turn right up the Western Highway. Within a few kilometres you reach another gold-rush town, **Ararat**, which has a good art

gallery and a collection of woolcraft. Among the many historic buildings in Ararat look for the timber building where **Miners' Rights** (licences) were issued – a constant source of friction and eventually of violence among miners. A little further west still is **Stawell**, another briefly prosperous mining town and site of the Stawell Gift Footrace every Easter. **Mini World** here is a big attraction for the kids. Once again, several vineyards offer distraction for the adults.

Wild Country

Turn off left at Stawell for the spectacular **Grampians National Park**, one of the loveliest in the state and only 26 km

Eureka Stockade

Every nation has its Eureka Stockade.

The French have the Bastille, the Americans the Boston Tea Party, the British the Magna Carta. Usually the historical incident bears little relationship to the myth which has grown up around it – but it remains vitally important in the national consciousness all the same.

Rarely, though, has revolt been as completely fictionalised as the skirmish at the Eureka Stockade in the Victorian goldmining town of Ballarat on 2 December 1854. Partisans have claimed it as an echo of Irish rebellion against the "foreign tyrant" Queen Victoria, which it wasn't. Only some of the participants were Irish. Karl Marx saw it as a Victorian workers' revolution, though nearly all the men involved were landowners. More than one prominent modern politician has claimed that Australian democracy was born at Eureka, which is absurd.

What actually happened shows it to have been an unglamorous and rather tragic little affair. With the Australian goldrush of the early 1850s thousands of hopeful gold-diggers from all over the world came to the Victorian diggings to try their luck. Conditions were harsh, the men rough and tough, and heartbreak much more common than fortune. The Government of Victoria, then a separate colony, taxed the miners by way of a heavy licence fee. The diggers objected, especially when the new and inexperienced Governor Sir Charles Hotham attempted to have licence inspections carried out twice weekly. They argued that they were treated as second-class citizens – miners were not entitled to vote – while Victoria grew wealthy on the fruit of their labours. The licence inspectors were arrogant bullies who used their power to harrass and exploit the diggers.

In October 1854 there was a series of ugly incidents after a digger was killed in a brawl with the publican of the Eureka Hotel, a man with an evil reputation who was neverthless acquitted. Miners burned the hotel and stoned troopers sent to keep order. Late in November, miners burned their licences in protest: the authorities promptly and provocatively ordered a licence check, and when they tried to enforce it, shooting broke out.

The diggers, now in open revolt, chose a young man named Peter Lalor as their spokesman. Lalor was Irish, as were many diggers, and from a strongly Irish nationalist family. But he seems to have been chosen not as a firebrand revolutionary but ironically because he was well-educated and articulate. Indeed, Lalor was a conservative and a believer in aristocratic principles – not the stuff of workers' revolutions. He went on to be a prominent Victorian MP and leading figure of the establishment.

He got no chance to use his gifts on the authorities. He and the diggers had chosen and fortified a knoll and built a barrier round it: this was the Eureka Stockade. For just a day or two the little protest movement did look like a real

off the main road. It is also the state's largest, at 167,000 hectares. Here there are high sandstone ridges teeming with wildlife, strange rock formations, waterfalls, wildflowers and Aboriginal paintings – and a good information centre at **Halls Gap**. If national parks are your particular interest, you could cross the park onto the Henty Highway and strike north through Horsham towards the **Little Desert National Park**, which gives a unique view of the untouched native mallee scrub, embraces a salt lake and – despite its name – boasts a profusion of spectacular wildflowers. **Horsham** itself has a special claim to fame: it hosts Australia's richest inland fishing contest every year on the banks of the **Wimmera River**.

The other alternative after emerging from the Grampians onto the Henty Highway is to turn left – south – towards

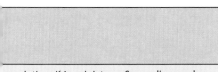

revolution, if in miniature. Some diggers drew up a Declaration of Independence, though it's hard to see how this could have been made to mean anything in the middle of Victoria. Some reinforcement diggers arrived, singing the Marseillaise, but they rapidly melted away when they saw the futility of the exercise. Lalor designed a flag, blue with the Southern Cross in the form of a star.

During the first night, on 1 December, theatricals gave way to reality. All but about 150 of the original 900 or so diggers drifted away from the stockade. If the authorities had simply waited, the whole incident would probably have fizzled out. But they did not wait. They stormed the stockade, losing half-a-dozen of their own men and killing 22 diggers.

Thereafter commonsense prevailed. The captured "rebels" were acquitted by sympathetic juries. The goldfields administration was reformed and the heavy licence fees abolished. The parliamentary system was adopted in Victoria, and the diggers got the vote.

It's arguable that none of these reforms was attributable to the Eureka Stockade. All were in train before the bloody dawn of 2 December. But for Australians the legend of the Eureka Stockade was born, to be dusted off and paraded, along with Lalor's fiery flag, whenever there is a stand against bone-headed authority.

To do so may not have much to do with historical accuracy. But it is very Australian.

the coastal town of **Portland** and the sea. On the way you will pass through **Hamilton**, which claims for itself the title of the wool capital of the world, and is the location of **Summit Park**, a working sheep farm open to the public. Then drive on to the coast at Portland. Once here, you are within range of **Mt Richmond National Park**, which is in and around an extinct volcano and has some excellent walking tracks and good fish-

ing. Just a little inland again is the **Lower Glenelg National Park**, which has as central feature the 60-km **Glenelg River Gorge**. Victoria's first white settler, Edward Henty, founded a permanent settlement at Portland in 1834, and in its **Historical Museum**, you can see the very plough he used to turn Victoria's first furrow. His retirement home of **Burswood** was built here too in the 1850s, and is today still in fine condition. If you feel more active than that, and haven't had much luck with the Wimmera's fish, Portland stages a gamefishing contest, and local fishermen will take you out all year round.

The Great Ocean Road

Portland is on the **Great Ocean Road** and a drive of around 350 km back to Melbourne faces you if you head west. However, it is among the most scenic coastal roads in the world, mainly built between 1916 and 1932, and is an attraction in its own right.

The first stretch of 100 km will take you to **Warrnambool**, where the whales come close enough inshore during the calving season to be spotted from the road. Another 70 km or so brings you to **Port Campbell National Park**, a park that has spectacular rock formations carved by wind and sea, with names like the Twelve Apostles, London Bridge and the Arch. Take time to visit **Loch Ard Gorge** where the only two survivors of the "Loch Ard" were swept ashore in

Breathtaking rock formations along the great Ocean Road, Victoria.

violent seas in 1878, while 48 others died. Just a little further and almost adjoining is another national park around **Cape Otway**, with eucalyptus forest, fern gullies, and wonderful fishing, swimming, snorkelling and surfing. But be careful: this is a wild coast and has claimed many lives.

Instead of turning off inland for Geelong, you should stick to the coast and drive the extra 40 km down to **Queenscliff** and **Point Lonsdale**. A fort of considerable proportions protected the insignificant settlement of Queenscliff from the (imagined) Russian threat. Point Lonsdale is where an escaped convict, William Buckley, lived with the Aboriginals for 32 years in the early years of Victorian settlement. Known as the "Wild White Man", he eventually came in from the cold and gained a pardon. You can see the cave where he lived. He is the origin of the common Australian phrase "Buckley's chance" – in other words, no chance at all. Geelong itself is an interesting port. You need not retrace your path but can cut straight across from Queenscliff in about half an hour. Enjoy a pub lunch in the nautical atmosphere, and then pay a visit to Victoria's oldest wooden building, the **Customs House**, in the **Botanical Gardens**. The **Wool Museum** with its speciality boutiques and exhibits is also worth inspection. From Geelong you can visit Port Phillip Heads and look out over the infamous **Rip**.

On the main road back to Mel-

Weeribee Park.

bourne is **Werribee Park**, at **Werribee**, a 60-room Italianate mansion illustrates the grand lifestyle of its pastoralist owners more than 100 years ago. It has a superb rose garden, lake, grotto, safari zoo, restaurant, and gift shop, and is open daily from 10 am to 4.30 pm. Aviation buffs may want to make a detour at this stage to the **Air Force Museum**, in the RAAF Base, Point Cook.

The range of planes starts with a Sopwith Pup and a Richtofen-style Fokker triplane, and leads up to a Vampire and a Sabre jet. All sorts of weapons, uniforms and memorabilia are on show. It is only a little over an hour's drive out of Melbourne and is open Sundays to Thursdays from 10 am to 4 pm. Entry is free.

Going Eastwards

The traditional holiday area for Melburnians is in fact out to the east, following the curve of the coast round **Port Phillip Bay**. Though quite densely populated, the area is well worth a visit and is within easy reach of the capital. **Tynong** is not a bad place to make the first stop. Call in at the **Victorian Farm Shed** there, on the Princes Highway. It is just past the township of Nar Nar Goon, which is an Aboriginal way of saying "koala bear" and it features livestock parades, sheepdogs in action, shearing, wool-classing, and hand-milking displays. Shows are staged at 10.30 am and 2 pm. Also at Tynong is **Gumbuya Park**.

The twelve apostles of Victoria rising from the waters.

Adventure playgrounds, merry-go-rounds, toboggan slides, indoor bowls, a water-slide, mini-cars, and indoor golf are open daily.

Heading east you can either branch down the Nepean Highway to the shores of Port Phillip, or turn down the Bass Highway towards one of Victoria's greatest attractions, Phillip Island. Before you get there, though, call in at **Coal Creek Historical Village** at Korrumburra. This is a 1890s railway town come to life again. There are some 40 buildings, a mine, blacksmith and sawmill. Combine this visit with an almost obligatory look at the fairy penguins at Phillip Island. At dusk every evening these delightful penguins troop ashore to Summerland Beach to rest and feed their young. Sometimes the number can be disappointingly low, so don't get your hopes up too high, but many thousands have not been disappointed. Phillip Island's fairy penguins are one of the best known tourist sights in Australia, and it is astonishing to find such an attraction so close to Melbourne. There is a good deal more here than penguins. Seals bask on the rocks, there are native animals including koalas living wild in a nearby park, and **Churchill Island** – closed for many years – is now open to visitors under the Victorian Government Trust. There are boat trips to early convict settlements at **Seal Rocks** and **French Island** too. Following the Bass Highway east for another 100 km or so will bring you to **Wilsons Promontory**, another much loved tourist destination,

Waves froth over the shores of Angle sea.

Port Campbell cliffs.

known locally as "the Prom". It is especially famous among scuba divers. It is a good area for walkers too, and has plenty of parkland set aside from tourist development. Yet another 150 km will bring the determined visitor to **Lakes Entrance,** the key point of access for the fascinating **Gippsland Lakes.** These superb saltwater lakes and channels cover over 400 sq km and form the country's largest system of inland waterways. At **Sperm Whale Head** there is the **Lakes National Park,** with a large population of wild kangaroos and more than 140 native bird species. It is possible to camp there, or to stay at the nearby **Rotamah Island Bird Observatory.**

Striking back towards the capital on the inland route, the Princes Highway has the advantage of putting you within range of the **Baw Baw National Park,** about 60 km north of the highway from **Moe** (itself about 80 km from Melbourne). The plateau is high timber and snow country, with excellent bushwalking in summer and cross-country skiing in winter. About the same distance to the south of the main road are the **Strzelecki Ranges,** the "Heartbreak Hills". They were deforested through the ignorance of the early settlers, and are now being replanted. Today they make a patchwork of small farms, forest and gullies. A visit to the nearby **Tarra Valley** and **Bulga National Parks** will show you what it looked like in the old days.

Canberra was custom-built as Australia's national capital. It was an artificially created city conceived somewhat on the same lines as Brasilia, though the architects were not permitted the total extravagance of its Brazilian counterpart. Australia's capital is four hours' drive from Sydney and eight hours' drive from Melbourne, but commuter jet services and tourist coaches run constantly to and from those cities. There are train services too, but one of the Australian capital's most obvious disadvantages for visitors is the lack of a regular fast train connection to Sydney. There is talk of putting that right, though.

Canberra grew out of the bitter rivalry between Sydney and Melbourne as to which should become the new nation's capital after the Federation of the Australian states in 1901. Its location reflects the subsequent compromise – it keeps its distance geographically from both cities – but its inhabitants must pay the penalty of its

Canberra

167

The thoroughly modern stainless steel flagpole atop Parliament House, the ultimate in flag-flying.

inland position. It is in fact the only major Australian city which is also not a port. Away from the sea, Canberra's summers are scorching and in winter the nights are often freezing – and sometimes the days are too. On the other hand, to see Canberra in springtime under a sea of blossom or to breathe its sharp clean air on a bright winter's morning is a delight, especially to visitors with European tastes. Originally the area was known as **Limestone Plains** because of the large deposits of limestone, slate, sandstone and granite in the district. Local stone and slate were used to construct some early buildings in the days when it was still a sheep and general farming area. Few of these survive in the modern Canberra of today.

International Competition

The transformation from farmland to national capital began a few years after the Yass-Canberra district was chosen in 1908 as the site for the Australian Capital Territory. One condition had been that the new capital city should be in New South Wales and if possible "within 100 miles of Sydney". The site is actually 288 km from Sydney and 750 km from Melbourne. Canberra itself was hatched in the incubator of an international planning competition launched in 1911. It grew from blueprints for a city of 25,000 which was expected eventually to treble in population. Today, instead of housing 75,000 people, it is

home to over 300,000.

Unlike any normal city, Canberra did not develop on the banks of a river or under the protection of a mountain range. It conformed to its blueprint and even its graceful lake is man-made. Although the city long ago outgrew its original design, the general concepts have been reserved and extended by modern planners. There are those who say that, as a totally 20th-century city, Canberra lacks soul. Others harp that it is laid out on too large a scale, as it

Canberra enjoys its share of domestic as well as foreign tourists.

designed more for cars than people. But to still others it has a light and airy style, which blends with enhanced natural features to create a city unique in Australia and perhaps in the world. Certainly people born and brought up in Canberra – as well as many of the newcomers who have settled there in the last few years – are fiercely loyal to it. Some of Canberra's attributes are beyond argument. It is beautifully green and beautifully clean. That 80-year-old scheme has produced results that not only delight town-planners and architects, but, far more importantly, have created a garden city, or as some residents say "*a city in a garden*". Some of the country's greatest thinkers and intellectuals are concentrated within its 2368 sq km, as well as many leading public servants, and it follows that Canberra's lifestyle has developed a spirit, style and charac-

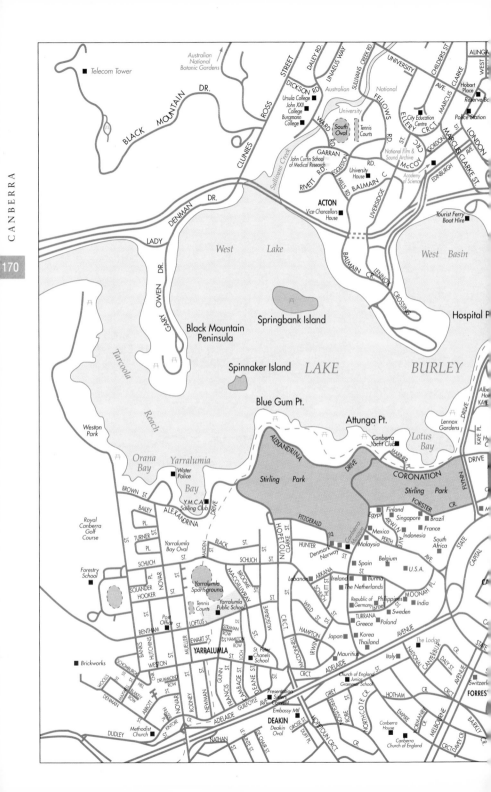

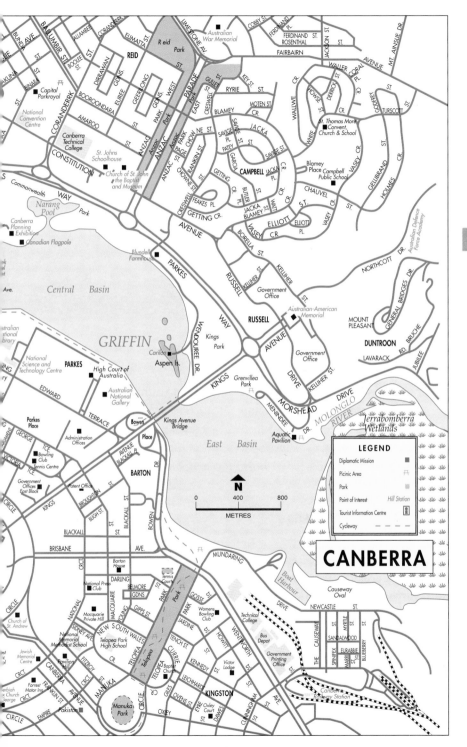

CANBERRA

Custom-built capital, hatched out of an international planning competition in 1911.

ter all of its own. It has more restaurants per capita than any other Australian city, for example. As befits a city which hosts diplomats from all over the world, nearly every type of cuisine is available.

From Flies To Files

At the time of Canberra's conception, Australians, ever irreverent of authority and particularly so of politicians, lampooned the whole idea, suggesting the proposed capital should be called "Gonebroke" or "Swindlesville". Already it had too many flies, they said. Now it would have too many civil servants with their files and red tape.

Criticism was rekindled when it was

a non-Australian, Chicago landscape architect Walter Burley Griffin, who won the design competition. Though his creation turned out to be a city of brilliant imagination (if initially a little austere) that did not protect him from attacks by Australian critics. In those days, so soon after Federation, Australians were even more fiercely nationalistic than they are now (which is saying something) and it rankled that their capital should be designed by a foreigner – especially an American.

However, thanks to the Aborigines, Canberra does have an indigenous flavour, at least to its name. The native name, Kanberra, is said to be derived from the peaks of its surroundings, Mt Ainslie and Black Mountain, and means

"Woman's Breasts" – perhaps an appropriate image for the young country's mother city. The story of Canberra's conception and birth is told at the **National Capital Planning Exhibition** at Regatta Point on the north shore of Lake Burley Griffin, and within walking distance of most north side hotels.

Check the Weather

The people of Canberra long ago became inured to the extremes of its seasons. Perhaps in the old days the privileged few found the climate compensated for by the occasional invitation to a swish diplomatic reception at Government House, or to the Prime Minister's residence for dinner. In Canberra it starts getting cool from April onwards with an average maximum temperature of 19.7°C in that month. This drops to 15.1°C in May, 12°C in June, 11.1°C in July, then improves slightly to 12.8°C in August and 15.9°C in September. If it's any compensation, residents say their winter is "very healthy".

Certainly Canberra has a profusion of trees, very little industry, and thus no big-city smells or pollution. The air is stunningly fresh, and, on winter mornings, delightfully crisp. Bursts of sunshine highlight the snow in June and July to create alpine picture-postcard scenes, but of course there is no white Christmas here. By October the sudden turn-around to summer has begun and occasional days can become blow-torch hot, especially in January and February when blistering temperatures of up to 42°C have been recorded.

Advance Advice

Some of Canberra's places of interest are bunched together in the same vicinity, but many others are spread higgledy-piggledy around the city. And in area it *is* a big city, so that you won't be able to cover much of it on foot. If you're on a set tour there'll be no problem. If you're an independent soul, burn the midnight oil over your map and carefully work out each day's itinerary, otherwise you'll criss-cross your tracks constantly. Even then you may find it confusing because of the circular-style road pattern. It has been said that in Canberra the shortest distance between two points is not a straight line – because the city's design did not allow for straight lines. Not for nothing did former Prime Minister, Malcolm Fraser, decide after half a lifetime in Canberra that – in his famous phrase – "life wasn't meant to be easy". Canberra does boast a super-efficient Tourism Commission and advice is both free and helpful.

If you're in Sydney or Melbourne, and Canberra is the next stop on your itinerary, cut a few corners by getting the advice of the branch offices of the Canberra Tourism Commission in those cities. They'll smooth the way by suggesting itineraries and making travel and accommodation arrangements to

Autumnal leafy gold beautifies the Canberra landscape.

fit your budget. The Sydney office is at 64 Castlereagh Street (tel: 02-233-3666; fax: 02-231-6714) and is open Mondays to Fridays, 9 am to 5 pm. The Melbourne branch is at 102 Elizabeth Street (tel: 03-654-5088; fax: 03-650-1441) with the same opening hours. If you're driving into Canberra from Sydney, you'll come in along Federal Highway 23, which becomes Northbourne Avenue as you enter the built-up areas. On your way through the suburb of Dickson pull in at the well signposted Visitor Information Centre on the left and collect any maps and brochures you need. It's open Mondays to Fridays, 9 am to 5 pm, and on weekends from 8.30 am to 5 pm.

Getting Around

A good bet to get a feel for the city is to take a **Canberra Explorer** coach from the **Jolimont Centre**, Northbourne Avenue. If you did not collect the usual brochures and maps on arrival, pick them up at the Tourism Commission here, at the corner of Alinga Street and Northbourne Avenue – open from 8.30 am to 5.15 pm on Mondays to Fridays, 9 am to 5 pm on Saturdays and 9 am to 1.30 pm on Sundays (tel: 06-245-6464).

In case you're wondering, the Commission's logo is a stylization of the four-legged flag-mount over Parliament House. While you're there, walk along Alinga Street to the adjoining **Post Office** and spend an engrossing half-hour or so examining the first-floor exhibition of stamps and other postal items. It will give you an immediate idea of the care Canberra takes in mounting the highest quality exhibitions and displays to show Australia at its very best. Note that the post office is closed on Saturdays and Sundays.

Buses from the Jolimont Centre leave every hour from 10.15 am and make 20 stops during a one-hour trip around the major attractions. You can stay on board to see all 20 at one time then decide which ones you wish to spend time visiting. Alternatively, get off at a location that catches your fancy, inspect it, then get back on the next bus. Or do it yourself by public bus. Besides the Tourism Commission, route maps, timetables and discount sightseeing tickets are also available from all Action bus interchanges.

Trips by tourist coach (as opposed to public bus) cover not only Canberra and its attractions, but push well into the countryside to visit the neighbouring snow country, sheep stations and dinky-di Oz outdoor barbecues. This can be quite an adventure, but you need two things – time and money. The atmosphere on such trips is very easy-going. It's common for the coach driver to point out local wildlife, and not unknown for him to stop suddenly to let a koala make its slow way across the road.

Chauffeured tours by limousine are available but are not inexpensive. For most a more realistic option is to hire a car, and this is a good way to see the place once you've worked out the circu-

lar road system. Make sure you get a copy of the five detailed tourist drives from the Tourism Commission, or from the Visitor Information Centre, Northbourne Avenue in the suburb of Dickson.

There are more exotic ways of getting around too. You can hire a light plane or a helicopter, or even step into the wicker basket of a hot-air balloon, to get an overview of things. Another less offbeat (and less costly) way of seeing Canberra is by bicycle. The main city attractions are linked by cycling paths; the Tourism Commission issues a map of these as well as advice on where to hire a bike. You can also hire a launch for a cool chug around Lake Burley Griffin on a hot day, and there are boat trips on the lake for those who prefer not to have to drive themselves.

Where to Stay

There are few cities in Australia more purpose-built to handle tourists than Canberra. Since it is the nation's showplace, it has been attracting visitors since its formative years. Most tourists will be there on a package deal that includes accommodation, but Canberra also provides rooms for all independent travellers from the well-heeled to those on a low budget.

There are serviced executive apartments, furnished holiday flats, hotels (from five-star to cheap pub-style rooms), and private hotels. These are cheaper than ordinary hotels, but unlicensed.

The Science Institute in space-age style architecture.

Further down the scale are hostels such as the various residential houses of the National University and the YMCA, and a little away from the town centre are self-contained cabins with cooking facilities and on-site caravans.

Motorists have still more choice of places to stay than other travellers. There were 55 motels and motor lodges at the last count, rated on a scale of four diamonds downwards. For those who bring their own houses with them, there are caravan sites where the driver can unhitch the van, plug the electric and plumbing entrails into the site's master supplies, then hop into the car for a spot of sightseeing. Those who wish to rough it in comfort can try farmhouse stays which include three meals a day, all mod cons and plenty of fresh country air

only faintly tinged by cow dung. For those who really want to do it tough there are more basic campsites in the wide-open countryside around the capital. Make sure you wear your thermal underwear in winter. Good luck!

City Centre

If you've been told that Canberra lacks a city centre, your informant is 15 years behind the times. It is true that a hotchpotch of shops and the not-very-glamorous Canberra Rex Hotel once seemed to pose as its hub, but no longer. A redevelopment scheme has given Canberra a bustling city centre with department stores – one of the smarter ones features a pianist on a Steinway – ar-

The War Memorial pays tribute to Australia's valiant and loyal participation in the last war, in which many lives were lost in major conflicts.

cades, markets, travel agents, carparks and all the other trappings of a modern up-market mini-metropolis. Because Canberra once had very little of a centre, emphasis was originally placed on developing shopping and other facilities in the residential suburbs.

Today, busy shopping centres seem to be dotted everywhere, one of the largest being close to Parliament House in **Manuka**.Canberra long ago outlived the capital's original *raison d'être* – as a site for Australia's Houses of Parliament and ancillary government departments, and a home for politicians and departmental staffers.

The Canberra of old was envisaged as a place that would run robot-like on the engine of Australia's bureaucracy,

fuelled, presumably, by the hot air of its political masters. Happily, progress has taken the steam out of both the argument and the engine. It's a sign of the times that today cosmopolitan Canberra has a full-blown sex industry (try the escort services that are advertised in the hand-outs) and is the distribution centre for Australia's pornographic videotape trade (plain brown wrappers used!). These developments may not have been in the original plans, but they certainly add to the local colour and vitality of the place.

After World War II, when Canberra became established in its role, many of Australia's biggest enterprises set up office here in order to be at the hub of national decision-making. As a result banks, insurance companies and investment houses today take their place along with the headquarters of dozens of federal government departments and other government institutions. Besides a plethora of civil servants, its 300,000 inhabitants include hard-nosed businessmen, property developers, entrepreneurs, restaurateurs, journalists, academics and many other men and women of talent and artistic bent.

"Pokies" and Fine Food

Australians are great clubmen. Not the stuffy leather-and-mahogany types of clubs favoured by the British, of course. That would be far too formal for easy-going Aussies. Instead they go for sporting clubs, servicemen's clubs, informal businessmen's clubs – and often these are the best and cheapest places to eat and drink, even if you are not a member. Canberra is particularly well-supplied with such institutions. If you like to defy the odds, many Canberra clubs offer batteries of "pokies" for poker-machine addicts. These machines are set by law to return 87 percent of the money invested – but the operative question is, of course, "when"? Guest membership of such clubs is provided at reception, which means most are effectively open to visitors whether they are members or not. That's worth knowing because even if you aren't the gambling kind many of these clubs also have splendid restaurants serving fine food.

The **West Belconnen Leagues Club** has a museum of fascinating old "pokies" for the real connoisseur of one-armed bandits, though the outer suburb of **West Belconnen** is a fair way out, unless you are driving. The **Tradesmen's Club** also has an odd museum – for bicycles, including a penny farthing. For the serious punter, Canberra has two racecourses where occasional Sunday races take place as well as the customary Saturday ones.

Parliament House – A Talking Point

Visitors to Canberra are by no means all tourists. They include jet-setting politicians and diplomats, government mandarins, lobbying businessmen, and architects and planners keen to see one of their professions' masterpieces. Tourists comprise the largest percentage of its visitors, but they are not all from overseas. Many Australians want to see the political Golconda into which their taxes have been poured since Federal Parliament moved here in 1929. Most particularly they want to see for themselves its latest grandiloquent gesture, the new **Parliament House**. Students arrive by the coachload for on-the-spot lessons in civics and teams of escorts run endless free guided tours of the new building. Many Australians leave fired with national pride and patriotism, but more than a few are numbed at the extravagance of this flamboyant new billion-dollar talk-shop for politicians.

Like Canberra's master plan, the design for the new building came from the United States. The exciting concept from an American company, Mitchell Giurgola, was judged best out of 329 worldwide entries. Australian patriotic feelings were once again ruffled by this choice, but then were smoothed somewhat by the knowledge that locally-born architect, Richard Thorp, had a hand in the blueprint. Critics who have gone there to scoff at the end product have been left bedazzled at its magnificence and the dominating presence it imposes over the city.

Sited in splendour on **Capital Hill** – you'll see it from anywhere in the city – the new Parliament House was opened by Queen Elizabeth II in 1988. An Australian flag the size of a double-decker bus tries bravely to flutter atop the new building, but a near-gale is required to billow it out to its fullest span. It flies from no common flagstaff, but from a truly Space Age structure that surges symmetrically skyward on four enormous shiny struts. Almost overnight this startling structure with its huge flag became Canberra's central landmark. This is the ultimate in flag-waving! At 81 m high the four-legged flagmast is the world's largest stainless steel structure. Technicians dizzily ride a miniature cable car up one of the legs to oversee the raising and lowering of the flag. Confident in the talents of their successors, the politicians insisted that the entire building have a life of at least

200 years. It took eight years to complete and the 300,000 cubic metres of concrete that went into its construction look likely to ensure its permanence for many generations. While the building's remarkable flagstaff is the icing on the cake, the building's interior is also full of surprises. The foyer features 48 marble columns intended to create the impres-

Cockington Green, English country life in miniature.

sion of a native eucalyptus forest. The foyer is complemented by marble staircases at either end and the Great Hall features timber from all over Australia as well as black ebony from Papua New Guinea. The backdrop to the Great Hall is a tapestry of a bush scene measuring 20 m by 9 m. (The loom on which it was made took two years to build).

The building is staffed with a seemingly limitless number of cheerful guides whose services are free. So is entry and the use of the 2000-vehicle carpark beneath the building. Visitors are escorted to the public galleries of the House of Representatives at the western end of the building and to the Senate. Tours take about an hour and cover many of the building's other treasures. These include one of only four originals of the Magna Carta which is preserved in argon gas in an oak case.

Other exhibits include some of the 70 works of art commissioned for the building and the 3800 paintings, sculptures, pictures, photographs and ceramics purchased for decoration. Among the portraits of self-important Prime Ministers, one stands out – that of a shirt-sleeved John Gorton, a wartime fighter pilot short on protocol and long on informality. That's a particularly Australian combination, even among politicians. The new Parliament House is an irresistible drawcard – enthusiasts say that a million visitors a year can't be wrong. Facilities include a post office, cafeteria, theatre, exhibition area and a terrace with sweeping views of Canberra and surroundings. It is open daily from 9 am to 5 pm (except on Christmas Day) and is as good a place as any to start seeing the sights.

Canberra is bisected by **Lake Burley Griffin**, named in honour of its American designer. Like so many features of the nation's capital, it is also man-made. Even the fish are re-stocked yearly. Canberra's flat, featureless limestone plains of 80 years ago now burst with a variety of trees. Millions have been planted since the city's foundation, though the planting rate has now dropped to about

15,000 a year. If you didn't know how much of Canberra was artificial, it is unlikely you'd ever guess, for the enhancements have been carried out with skill and flair.

Now, slap in the middle of Canberra, Lake Burley Griffin affords delightful walks and bike-rides along its 35 km of foreshores, dotted with picnic and barbecue areas and places for fishing and boating, as well as its own ferry terminal for pleasure cruises.

A Monumental Drawcard

Besides being a national shrine to the country's war dead, the **Australian War Memorial** is one of the world's finest war museums. It's a must for visitors, whether military-minded or not, and is just a few minutes in a taxi. (Canberra isn't really made for walkers when it comes to sightseeing, but the energetic can make the War Memorial on foot from north side hotels and motels). The Memorial contains superb models and displays of the nine major conflicts in which 102,000 Australians have fallen over the years. The whole museum is of such excellence it is hard to single out any particular section or display. Taken together, the exhibits make the Memorial one of the most popular tourist destinations in Australia, as well as a centre of serious academic research. On a purely visual scale alone it makes a monumental statement about man's monumental folly – war.

Australia has one of the finest war museums.

Relics range from a World War II Lancaster bomber (G for George) to remnants of the Fokker triplane of the Red Baron, Manfred von Richtofen, reputedly shot down by groundfire from ANZAC diggers (although that's a contentious point). There are tanks, artillery pieces, captured weapons, uniforms – even two halves of a Japanese midget submarine that got into Sydney Harbour during World War II and caused some death and destruction. To visit the museum is to step briefly on to the shores of Anzac Cove, Gallipoli, or into the trenches on the Western Front. It is to plod over the Kokoda Trail in New Guinea or to ponder again the fate of the cruiser *HMS Sydney*, lost with all hands, off the West Australian coast in World War II.

The visitor joins the diggers behind the perimeter at Tobruk, shares the experience of grim captivity in a German stalag, and glimpses the dreadful privations of life as a prisoner of the Japanese working on the Burma Railway. At each turn there is another fascinating surprise about some less well-known chapter of Australia's military history – relics of the struggle against the fanatical Bannermen in Imperial China, for example. Moving closer in time there is a section devoted to the Vietnam War, in which over 400 Australians died, and which divided opinion in Australia as it did in the United States. The War Memorial has a well stocked bookshop, and is open daily from 9 am to 4.45 pm. Like Parliament House, entry to it is free.

Afterwards, make a slow passage

along **Anzac Parade**, a further tribute to Australian sacrifices in war. This leads from the War Memorial to the lake and is lined on either side with bluegums, while flowering native shrubs beautify the median strip. It was planned as Canberra's "processional way", and while it makes a lengthy walk it gives the visitor a fine sense of the Australian capital's essential dignity.

More Militaria

An unusual military monument is the **Australian-American Memorial** – a soaring 79 m aluminium tower topped by a 3.5 tonne eagle astride a globe. About 2 km south of the War Memorial in the district of **Russell** and on a line with the **Kings Avenue Bridge**. With typical Australian irreverence the emblem is locally nicknamed Bugs Bunny. However, the Memorial was built by public subscription to pay tribute to America's military help to Australia in its darkest hours of 1942. It's a sincere tribute: Australians are keenly aware that without American help, invasion by Japan was only a matter of time. The Memorial boasts a carillon and there are recitals on Sundays, Wednesdays and public holidays.

Those whose interest in Australian militaria is not exhausted by now may like to add another visit to their list, though it will take them a little out of town, over the eastern side of Mt Pleasant, the **Royal Military College**, Dun-

troon (see box story, page 186) occupies the site of "Duntroon", a grand mansion built by the settler Robert Campbell in 1825 and named after the family castle in Scotland. Geographically it's not far from the Australian-American monument, but you would need to take a taxi. Retaining the name of Duntroon, the home and outbuildings were expanded to form the country's original military academy from 1911 onwards. Tours of the grounds can be made every weekday afternoon from 2.30 pm, except on public holidays and between November and March. The starting point for tours is **Starkey Park** in Jubilee Avenue. Also worth a visit, though perhaps more out of curiosity than reverence, is the **Prime Minister's Lodge** on the corner of Adelaide Avenue and National Circuit, in the shadow of Capital Hill. It's been the seat of Australian Prime Ministers since 1927, but can be viewed only from the outside. **Government House** (the house is called Yarralumla) is the official residence of the Governor-General, and was formerly the homestead of a large sheep station. It stands on the south shore of Lake Burley Griffin. But it is also closed to the public and it is best seen from the lake.

Foot-slogging around the "Nationals"

For those hardy types doing as much of their sightseeing on foot as possible, the Science and Technology Centre, Na-

The Snowy Mountains.

tional Library, High Court and National Gallery are all within walking distance of each other along Parkes Place, facing Lake Burley Griffin on the Capital Hill (south) side.

The **National Science and Technology Centre** (also known as the **Questacon**) has over 200 hands-on scientific exhibits and is particularly fascinating for children. They can operate a hand-powered hovercraft, for example, or observe an active bee-hive at work. The centre has a shop where you can make small purchases, and there is a caféteria. The Centre is open daily from 10 am to 5 pm. Apart from 6 million books, newspapers and periodicals, tapes, films, and music scores, the **National Library** has extensive print-re-

lated exhibition areas, sculptures, stained-glass windows and a print shop. The Library is stunning as a piece of architecture too. It is open daily from 9 am to 4.45 pm, except Good Friday and Christmas Day (tel: 06-262-1279). At the nearby **High Court**, dramatic murals depict its history and functions. It is open daily from 10 am to 4 pm and three courtrooms are open for viewing. Tours are free and the restaurant is licensed.

The **National Gallery** is for many people Canberra's pride, and for quite a few Australians it is the principal reason for visiting the capital. It contains eleven galleries of art, changing exhibitions and a sculpture garden, as well as a shop, restaurant and snack bar. Its Abo-

Duntroon – Australia's West Point

Federation in 1901 was the signal for a sudden uprush of patriotic feeling in Australia.

The union of all six Australian states under one Government meant that the new country became effectively independent, though still a Dominion of the British Crown.

Among other assets transferred to the Commonwealth of Australia from its component states were 29,000 troops. Their first Commander, General Sir Edward Hutton, at once saw the need for Australia to have its own training academy for officers, and he campaigned to have one founded along the lines of Canada's Royal Military College. He soon got an important ally. Field Marshal Lord Kitchener of Britain visited Australia in 1910 and recommended that Hutton's suggestion be taken up.

It very soon was. Colonel William Throsby Bridges was commissioned by the Australian Government to look into the idea, and he travelled widely to see just how Britain, the United States and Canada structured their military colleges. Before the end of that same year, 1910, he made his report and was asked by the Government to set up the Royal Military College (RMC) of Australia. Bridges was to be its first commandant, a post he enthusiastically accepted.

He chose Duntroon, a former sheep station which had been taken up by the Sydney merchant Robert Campbell in 1825. It was one of the few considerable estates near the proposed new Federal capital of Canberra. The Government at first leased and later bought Duntroon House and 370 acres of property. With astonishing speed, the Royal Military College of Australia – the RMC – was officially opened on 27 June 1911 and received its first intake of 32 Australian and 10 New Zealand officer cadets.

To this point the whole project seems to have gone unbelievably well. There is even something a little precocious about it all. It was as if Duntroon were a toy college producing toy soldiers, impossibly far away from the world's hotspots and existing mainly to allow Australia to claim that it really did have a military tradition of its own.

How quickly all that was to change!

WW I broke out in August 1914. Of 117 Australians who graduated during the war, 40 died before the end of it in 1918. At Gallipoli alone, that disastrous landing which forged the ANZAC spirit, 17 RMC graduates died along with 8000 of their countrymen. It was at Gallipoli too that General Bridges, the RMC's founding commandant, was shot by a Turkish sniper and died a little later. He was 54. His body was brought back to Australia and buried on a hillside overlooking the college he did so much to found. Current Turkish legend still has it that his horse was buried with him, but this is certainly a myth.

Horse or no horse, General Bridges initiated the RMC's authentic heroic tradition. Since

riginal displays are a must, and its collections of modern art (including Jackson Pollack's famous and controversial "Blue Poles") are world-class. The Gallery opens daily from 10 am to 5 pm, and though an entrance fee is charged, once inside, tours of the Gallery are free. Among the other "nationals" in Canberra is the **National Sound and Film Archive** on McCoy Circuit, Acton, just five minutes by cab from the centre of town and on the north side of the lake. The Museum here has re-runs of voices and faces of Australian stage, screen and radio stars. Many people don't realize that Australia's feature film industry (see box story, page 102) goes back to the earliest days of this century and forms an integral part of Australian cultural history. The Archive is open daily from 9.30 am to 4 pm. Entry is free.

The **Australian National Univer-**

then, Duntroon graduates have served all over the world, always with distinction.

If that heroic tradition was forged in the flames of the Great War, it is worth remembering that the RMC was from the very beginning a forward-looking institution as far as the academic side of its work was concerned. English and Modern Languages were taught there from the very start, and Japanese was added as early as 1917. Cadets could also study Science and Engineering, but the humanities were given parity in every way.

By 1968 the University of New South Wales was to set up an entire Faculty of Military Studies at Duntroon in a move which reflected the academic excellence of the place. That arrangement only terminated in 1986, when the University College was moved to the glittering tri-service Australian Defence Force Academy which has been built just over the hill from Duntroon.

Despite the advent of the Academy, which has usurped some of its academic functions, the RMC retains its unique role. It still provides the military training component for Australia's Army officers, both men and women, whether they are Academy graduates or not. And it continues to act as a regional centre for military excellence, drawing cadets from around the region – New Zealand, Papua New Guinea, Fiji, Singapore, Malaysia and Thailand.

The dream of General Bridges has become a reality.

sity's grounds begin near the Archive and border the lake. The ANU isn't national in the sense that it's necessarily the preeminent Australian university, of course, although some of its students and staff might argue that way. Not many people, though, will dispute their claim that the ANU is the most beautiful university in the country, set in truly glorious grounds. Visitors are welcome to visit the campus, and there are some

public lectures. For the more casual tourist there are delightful waterside walks or bicycle tracks, plus shops, kiosks, a theatre, and restaurants.

In the same direction from the centre (west) but considerably further out on the slopes of Black Mountain are the **National Botanic Gardens**. Over 6000 native plants provide an in-depth picture of many odd and unique Australian examples of flora.

There are exhibitions of how Aboriginal people used native plants for food, and re-creations of natural environments within the grounds. There is also a bookshop, kiosk and information centre. The Gardens are open from 9 am to 5 pm daily. While you are there, it's a good opportunity to take in Canberra's best bird's eye view from **Telecom Tower.** It is a 195 m structure on the top of Black Mountain offering possibly the most panoramic views of the capital from its three galleries (the highest at the 66 m level). It has a revolving restaurant, a snack bar and souvenir shop, and an exhibition area on lower ground floor. It is open from 9 am to 10 pm (tel: 06-248-1911).

And on the same northern shore of the lake, but further west still, is **Yarramundi Visitors' Centre** on Lady Denman Drive. This is actually Stage One of the **National Museum**, and features exhibitions and videos of Australia's history, a working paddle-steamer, and models and plans depicting the Museum's future development. It is a good place to visit with children too, for

Telecom Tower perched on top of
Black Mountain.

the grounds sport a discovery trail and picnic areas. The Centre is open Mondays to Saturdays, from 10 am to 4 pm, and on Sundays from 1 pm to 4 pm, and entry is free.

Finally, one national institution which cannot be overlooked in sport-crazy Australia is the **Australian Institute of Sport**, though it's way out in **Belconnen**. This is where Australia's leading athletes are nurtured through magnificent indoor and outdoor training facilities. It is in many ways a monument to the Australians' passion for physical competition – a passion which reaches the heights almost of religion on special occasions. Public tours of the Institute leave at 2 pm on Wednesdays, Saturdays and public holidays.

Churches and History

Canberra, a young capital in a young country, is understandably not strong on history. But that doesn't mean there is nothing of historical interest at all. For example, the **Free Serbian Orthodox Church of St George** on National Circuit, quite near Capital Hill, is a fascinating replica of an old Serbian village church.

Its hand-painted interior is a miniature masterpiece. The church is open for inspection daily, except Sunday mornings. **All Saints Anglican Church**, open daily, in Cooper Street, **Ainslie**, and a couple of kms from Canberra city centre, has an odd and slightly mournful history. It was originally the railway station of **Rookwood Cemetery** in Sydney, but was transported overland stone by stone and re-erected here as a church.

Quite close to the centre, and before you reach the War Memorial, is **St John's Church and Schoolhouse**. These are Canberra's oldest surviving buildings, built of local limestone, and date from around 1840. They are open Wednesdays from 10 am to noon, and weekends from 2 pm to 4 pm. Giving another glimpse into the past is **Blundell's Farmhouse**, a pioneer farmhouse (now a museum) close to Lake Burley Griffin's north shore, off Constitution Avenue and near the city centre. It was built by Robert Campbell, the owner of Duntroon, as a cottage for his head ploughman, in 1860. It is open daily from 10 am to 4 pm.

Lanyon Homestead is worth a visit but is a fair distance – 30 km south of Canberra. Nevertheless, this historic property where Aboriginal campsites and even a canoe tree remain enjoys the National Trust's highest classification. It features farm buildings part-built by convict labour, landscaped gardens, a park beside the Murrumbidgee River, and even a small gaol – which demonstrates to what extent farmsteads in the early days had to be virtually self-sufficient.

There is a gift shop and a coffee shop. Adjoining Lanyon is the Nolan Gallery which has permanent and changing exhibitions by Australia's most famous artist Sir Sidney Nolan. This is closed on Mondays, but otherwise opens from 10 am to 4 pm daily.

Ethnic Embassies

As the national capital, Canberra attracts the principal overseas missions of foreign countries. These increasingly reflect Australia's deep involvement with the Asia-Pacific region, and several countries have made their embassies into cultural showpieces as well as diplomatic missions. Without leaving Canberra, the visitor can catch vivid glimpses of the Asia-Pacific world of which Australia is a part. Two of the most interesting are the embassies of Australia's nearest neighbours, Papua New Guinea and Indonesia, both in the Yarralumla dis-

trict to the west of Capital Hill. The Papua New Guinea Embassy has an exhibition which dramatically illustrates the lifestyles of that country's tribal peoples, with examples of their colourful costumes, and bizarre idols. It is open Mondays to Fridays from 10.30 am to 12.30 pm and from 2.30 pm to 4.30 pm. At the Indonesian Embassy a special exhibition for visitors depicts the villages and native handicrafts of different ethnic groups within one of the most culturally diverse nations on earth. Open daily from 9 am to 5 pm.

Around and about in Canberra district

Bywong Mining Town is 20 minutes north of Canberra, signposted off the main Federal Highway. It is a gold-mining village of yesteryear recapturing the lifestyle of Australia's original settlements. It sports mine shafts, an open-cut mine, a blacksmith and wheelwright, gold-panning, and ore-crushing batteries and it is open daily from 10 am to 4 pm. There's a warm invitation to take part in most activities, and Bywong is known as an educational centre as well as a tourist sight.

Follow the Barton Highway out towards Yass for about 10 minutes' drive, and near the turn-off on Gold Creek Road are a number of attractions. At Cockington Green is a miniature English village (one-twelfth scale) including castle, thatched houses, an oasthouse and even Stonehenge! There are also (full-sized) sports fields, playgrounds, train rides, and a restaurant. Cockington Green is open daily from 10 am to 4.30 pm. Nearby **Ginninderra Village** has an arts and crafts centre with many stalls of Australian-made souvenirs, clothing and accessories, as well as antiques. It also features weekend entertainment, and has a restaurant. The Village is open daily from 10 am to 5 pm. Close by is the **George Harcourt Inn**, historic **Ginninderra Village Schoolhouse**, and the **Australian Opal and Gemstone Museum**. Adjacent is **Ginninderra Falls and Nature Reserve** where you can see Australia's bush life in its natural state. There are animals, birds, flowers and plants at every turn on the nature trails, and a fine view over the Falls and the spectacular Gorge below. The Reserve is open daily from 10 am to 5 pm.

More wildlife at **Rehwinkel's Animal Park** 24 km north of Canberra off the Federal Highway. Koalas, kangaroos, wombats, black swans, emus and many other Australian birds and animals have made the 50-acre park their home. There is an entrance fee and the park is open daily from 10 am to 5 pm. For those who like a more formal zoo, try **Mugga Lane Zoo** which is in suburban Canberra just south of **Red Hill** and only 10 minutes from Capital Hill by bus or car. With over 100 species of animals and birds. It is open daily from 9 am to 4 pm on weekdays and from 9 am to 5 pm on weekends. Children

under five get in free. Quite a different kind of wildlife is to be found at the **Gundaroo Pub** (tel: 06-295-3677). Free buses take visitors to this typical Aussie country pub where families can enjoy

Fresh country air and landscapes are to be enjoyed on a
motoring route towards Canberra.

traditional barbecues and *damper* –
doughy bread made in an open fire.
Sporty types will prefer **Corin Forest**

Recreation Area, an alpine reserve half-
an-hour from Canberra on Corin Dam
Road. It has an 800-metre alpine/bob-

sled slide (Australia's longest). Skiing and tobogganing are popular from June to September, and there is a licensed cafeteria. The Area is open only on weekends and holidays from 10 am to 5 pm.

Heaven and Earth

Canberra's clear cold skies are ideal for star-gazing, and several world-class astronomical facilities have been built in and around the capital. **Mt Stromlo Observatory**, 16 km west of the city, is the home of National University's Department of Astronomy and features a 188 cm telescope, astronomical displays and a visitors' gallery. Open daily from 9.30 am to 4 pm. **Tidbinbilla Deep Space Tracking Station**, 40 km southwest of Canberra, is one of the western world's three key tracking stations for space exploration. For visitors the Station opens from 9 am to 5 pm daily, free of charge, has mounted displays of model spacecraft, antennae, and space-related photographs, and also puts on video shows. Not far away, is the **Tidbinbilla Nature Reserve**. It covers 5000 hectares of wild country with nature trails criss-crossing it. The Reserve is open from 9 am to 6 pm and sometimes later, with guided evening tours in summer, and there is an information centre.

In Queanbeyan

Canberra, new though it is, already has a "limpet city": Queanbeyan, just over

the border in New South Wales. Queanbeyan has some interesting, if minor, points of interest of its own.

Among them, **Christ Church** (c. 1860) is a fine example of early colonial architecture.

The **District Museum** (1877) is in the former police sergeant's residence and displays interesting relics from the early days, but is only open on weekend afternoons from 2 pm to 4 pm.

The **Millhouse Gallery** (1883) has rare books, antique furniture and arts and crafts and is open from Wednesdays to Sundays from 10 am to 2 pm. Make sure you try to fit these sites in your travel itinerary.

Cooma, a popular ski centre is only an hour and a half by car, outside the capital.

In the Snow Season

A trip from Canberra by road to **Cooma** in the **Snowy Mountains**, one of the main skiing centres, takes about an hour-and-a-half. Here you can photograph the statue of the "Man from Snowy River". Originally this was the title of a verse by Banjo Paterson (see box story, page 100), but was subsequently made into a very successful 1980s Australian film co-starring (as the obligatory Hollywood name) Kirk Douglas.

View some historic buildings before heading through **Berridale** and **Jindabyne** to **Kosciusko National Park** (containing Australia's highest mountain), the aptly named **Perisher Valley**, and **Smiggin Holes**. Then on by railway to **Mt Blue Cow**, **Thredbo Alpine Village** and a chairlift to **Crackenback Range**.

Along the way you'll pass the massive Snowy Mountains hydro-electric scheme where, in the early stages of Australia's massive post-war immigration drive, many thousands of migrants worked out their entitlement to citizenship.

The lifestyle in the northeast quarter of Australia has traditionally been carefree, with the emphasis on having a good time. The one word heard constantly is "fun". Every second car has a bumper sticker reading "Don't worry, be happy!" Maybe this fun-loving attitude springs from the weather, which the state's publicity machine describes as "Beautiful one day, perfect the next". That conveniently overlooks the winter squalls and occasional drenching tropical thunderstorms in summer, but again, who cares? The fact is that Queensland is warmer and sunnier than any other widely settled part of Australia. And you may have noticed that in warm places the people are generally happy and outgoing.

This happy-go-lucky attitude

Fun and carefree lifestyle is the tradition along the northeast state.

Brisbane / Queensland

SUNSHINE PLANTATION

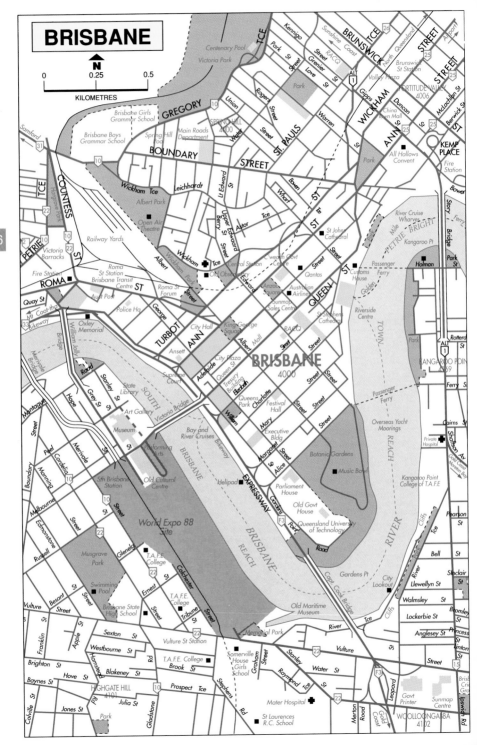

BRISBANE

N

| 0 | 0.25 | 0.5 |

KILOMETRES

Kennigo

BRUNSWICK TCE 26

STREET

Airport

North Queensland

Sunshine Coast

Park St

Greiner St

Love St

Gipps St

RACQ

ALT 1

Valley Plaza

Brunswick St Station

FORTITUDE VALLEY 4006

25

25

Duncan St

McLachlan St

Berwick St

Centenary Pool

Victoria Park

Park

GREGORY

Union St

10

Rogers Street

Warren St

China Town Mall

ANN

25

KEMP PLACE

Fire Station

Brisbane Girls Grammar School

SPRING HILL 4000

Main Roads Department

WICKHAM

St

All Hallows Convent

Brisbane Boys Grammar School

Spring Hill Road

Water St

Street

ST PAULS

Park

Bower

TCE

COUNTESS

BOUNDARY

STREET

ST PAULS

Wharf St

Story Bridge

Samford

Hargrave Park

Wickham Tce

Leichhardt

Lt Edward St

Bowen

ST

St John's Cathedral

River Cruise Wharves

Mile

PETRIE BRIGHT

Kangaroo Pt

Park Rd

TCE

22

Albert Park

Upper Edward

Berry St

Astor

Tce

ST

PETRIE

31

10

Open Air Theatre

Railway Yards

Wickham

Tce

Central Station

C'wealth Govt Centre

Street

ST

Passenger Ferry

Kangaroo Pt

Holman

Ferry

ST

Victoria Barracks

22

Albert

Wickham Park

Old Observatory

Edward

Street

Qantas

Customs House

TOWN

Golden

Fire Station

Roma St Station

Anzac Square

Australian Airlines

QUEEN

Riverside Centre

ROMA

ST

Brisbane Transit Centre

Roma St Forum

Sunmap Sales Centre

St Stephens Cathedral

Park

Rottery St

ALT 1

Quay St

Aust Post

George

King George Square

RACQ

KANGAROO POINT 4169

Mt Coot-tha Bikeway

33

Police Hq

TURBOT

ANN

Albert Mall

Street

Street

Ferry

Cairns

William Jolly Bridge

Oxley Memorial

Ansett

City Hall

BRISBANE 4000

Street

Passenger Ferry

Shafston Av

Private Hospital

Bridge

Adelaide

City Plaza

Queen St

Street

Street

Gold Coast Motorway exit

Merivale Bridge

State Library

Supreme Court

Treasury Building

Eagle

Street

Overseas Yacht Moorings

Stanley St

Grey St

Art Gallery

Victoria Bridge

Queens Park

Charlotte

Festival Hall

Mary

Street

Kangaroo Point College of T.A.F.E.

Hope St

Museum

SOUTH

Performing Arts

William

Executive Bldg

Street

Montague

Peel

Merivale

St

Bay and River Cruises

Bikeway

Margaret St

Botanic Gardens

Music Bowl

Pearson St

Cordelia

BRISBANE

Helipad

St

Alice St

Parliament House

Bell St

Boundary

Manning

Sth Brisbane Station

EXPRESSWAY

Cordelia

Melbourne St

10

Old Cultural Centre

Old Govt House

Sinclair St

Edmonstone St

Street

Queensland University of Technology

River

Llewellyn St

Russell

22

World Expo 88 Site

Glenelg

T.A.F.E. College

Colchester St

Road

Gardens Pt

City Lookout

Walmsley St

Cliffs

Lockerbie St

Bromley St

Musgrave Park

22

Ernest St

T.A.F.E. College

Tribune St

BRISBANE REACH

Capt Cook Bridge

Old Maritime Museum

RIVER

Anglesey St

Princess St

Vulture St

Besant St

Swimming Pool

Brisbane State High School

Sexton St

Vulture St Station

23

River Tce

Vulture St

Stanton St

15

Franklin St

Apple St

Westbourne St

T.A.F.E. College

Brook St

Somerville House Girls School

Graham St

Raymond

Water St

Street

Brisbane

Brighton St

Hove St

Blakeney St

Stephens Rd

22

Vulture

F3

Sunmap Centre

Baynes St

HIGHGATE HILL 4101

10

Prospect Tce

Mater Hospital

Stanley

Tce

Govt Printer

Leopard St

Gold Coast

Coville St

Jones St

Julia St

Gladstone

Park

St Laurences R.C. School

Merton Road

WOOLLOONGABBA 4102

Ipswich Rd

opened the door through which Japanese and other foreign money poured into Queensland in the 1980s. At the time, everybody welcomed the development it brought with it. Only after the horse had bolted did the Government discover that Japan owned much of the stable and had also made an attractive offer for the horse! But then. Australia's "Sunshine State" has always been a place where everybody is welcome.

Queensland's habit of throwing open its doors to all goes back to the early days of free settlement. The state, half tropical and mostly rural, developed a reputation as an easy-going place for people to retire to or holiday in – but where no-one did a great deal, except farm sugarcane. The real fortunes were to be made on the land and in business in the southern capitals, and most go-ahead Australians found the appeal of Queensland rather tepid.

Suddenly in the sixties and seventies they realised that things were changing. The Queensland capital, Brisbane, had always been a pleasant country town with inner suburbs of close-packed, tin-roofed houses built on stilts. Now it was emerging as a small but thriving and cosmopolitan city. It was helped by a steady drift north to the sun, the development of Asian markets on its doorstep, and the rapid growth of mineral industries in Queensland's interior.

By the mid-1980s Brisbane was a city of 1 million people or so, and the fastest-growing metropolis in Australia. Hosting the World Expo '88 put the seal on its civic adulthood.

Development was not confined to Brisbane itself, of course. Many people from all over Australia were choosing to move to the home of the Australian "*dolce vita*" – the Gold Coast, just 60 minutes' drive south of Brisbane. Shrewd developers were transforming mudflats there into the garden estates which now line river and creek frontages. Today in the centre of the Gold Coast glitters the pleasure city of Surfers Paradise – a symbol of the vigour (not to say lust) with which pleasure was pursued in the brash new Queensland of the 1980s.

The population of Queensland – especially of the Brisbane/Gold Coast littoral – has continued to mushroom. There is an endless trickle of families moving north to the sun from Victoria, Tasmania, New South Wales and even South Australia, all of whom have vowed never to shiver through another winter. New Zealanders, who have automatic right of settlement in Australia and whose winters really are chilly, have also joined the queue.

Wages may be considerably higher in Melbourne or Sydney, but again, who cares? It's better up north enjoying Queensland's happy lifestyle. The suburbs of Brisbane now sprawl in every direction, homes have gardens front and back with palms and other trees and shady verandahs. In the newer districts a house is not a home without a swimming pool, and the traditional old stilted Queenslander houses have become sought-after collectors' items.

Brisbane, capital of the Sunshine State.

Brisbane City

It is a city of parks, trees, shrubs and flowers, with the blocks of a towering glass-and-concrete central business district set like gemstones among the greenery. The **Brisbane River** drifts languidly through the centre. Four bridges span it, of which the attractive **Story Bridge** is the best-known and the most central.

The most modern of Brisbane's bridges, the **Gateway Bridge**, is an awesome concrete crescent which hurdles the mouth of the river near the airport and provides a short cut between the Gold Coast in the south and the **Sunshine Coast** in the north. It is privately owned and charges a toll of A$2 per car.

Tidy, wide and of checkerboard orderliness, streets with the names of queens and princesses (Ann, Adelaide,

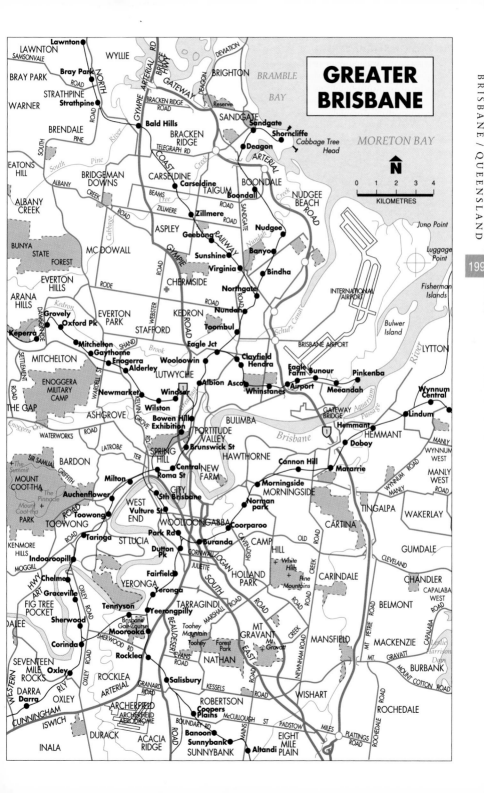

GREATER BRISBANE

LAWNTON
SAMSONVALE
Lawnton
WYLLIE
BRUCE HWY
GYMPIE ARTERIAL RD
DEAGON
GATEWAY
DEVIATION
BRIGHTON
BRAMBLE
BAY
BRAY PARK
Bray Park
ROAD
STRATHPINE
Strathpine
NORTH
BRENDALE
PINE
WARNER
WARNER
BRACKEN RIDGE
ROAD
Bald Hills
BRACKEN RIDGE
TELEGRAPH RD
SANDGATE
Sandgate
Shorncliffe
Reserve
Cabbage Tree
Head
MORETON BAY
EATONS HILL
PINE
River
South
ALBANY
CREEK
BRIDGEMAN DOWNS
CARSELDINE
Deagon
BOONDALE
ARTERIAL
ALBANY CREEK
SOUTH
Creek
Pine
South
Cabbage
BEAMS ROAD
ZILLMERE
RAILWAY
CARSELDINE
Carseldine
TAIGUM
Boondall
SANDGATE
NUDGEE BEACH
ROAD
Creek
BUNYA STATE FOREST
MC DOWALL
ASPLEY
ROAD
ROAD
Zillmere
Geebung
Sunshine
Virginia
Nudgee
Banyo
Bindha
Nundah
ROAD
Juno Point
Luggage Point
GYMPIE
RODE
EVERTON HILLS
CHERMSIDE
WEBSTER
KEDRON
Northgate
ROAD
Nundah
INTERNATIONAL AIRPORT
Fisherman Islands
ARANA HILLS
Grovely
Oxford Pk
EVERTON PARK
STAFFORD
ROAD
Toombul
Bulwer Island
Keperra
DAWSON RDE
KEDRON
Brook
Eagle Jct
Schur's Canal
BRISBANE AIRPORT
LYTTON
Mitchelton
Gaythorne
SHAND
Wooloowin
Clayfield
Hendra
Eagle Farm
Pinkenba
THE GAP
MITCHELTON
Enoggera
Alderley
LUTWYCHE
Albion
Asco
Eunour
Airport
Meeandah
Wynnum Central
ENOGGERA MILITARY CAMP
WARDELL ST
Newmarket
Windsor
Whinstanes
GATEWAY BRIDGE
Aquarium
Passage
River
Lindum
SETTLEMENT ROAD
KEVIN GROVE
Wilston
Bowen Hill
Exhibition
BULIMBA
Hemmant
HEMMANT
WYNNUM WEST
Enoggera Creek
WATERWORKS
ROAD
LATROBE
TER
SPRING HILL
PORTITUDE VALLEY
Brunswick St
Brisbane
Doboy
MANLY
MANLY WEST
ASHGROVE
BARDON
RD
Central
NEW FARM
HAWTHORNE
Cannon Hill
WYNNUM ROAD
MANLY WEST ROAD
SIR SAMUAL
GRIFFITH
The Summit
MOUNT COOT-THA
Milton
Roma St
CITY
Sth Brisbane
MORNINGSIDE
Morningside
Mararrie
TINGALPA
WAKERLAY
Mount Coot-tha PARK
The Pinnacle
Auchenflower
TOOWONG
WEST END
Vulture St
WOOLLOONGABBA
Norman park
CARTINA
KENMORE HILLS
ROAD
Toowong
Taringa
ST LUCIA
Park Rd
Coorparoo
CAMP HILL
OLD
ROAD
GUMDALE
CLEVELAND
Indooroopilly
Dutton Pk
Buranda
CORNWALLOGAN
CAVENDISH
White Hills
Pine Mountains
CARINDALE
CHANDLER
MOGGILL
HWY ART
Chelmer
Graceville
Fairfield
JULIETTE
HOLLAND PARK
CREEK
CAPALABA WEST
BELMONT
ROAD
FIG TREE POCKET
OXLEY ROAD
YERONGA
Yeronga
SOUTH
ROAD
Mt Gravatt
MANSFIELD
MT PETRIE ROAD
CAPALABA
Tennyson
TARRAGINDI
MARSHALL
MT GRAVANT
Leslie Harrison Dam
Sherwood
Yeerongpilly
Brisbane Golf Course
Toohey Mountain
Toohey Forest Park
Gravatt
EAST
NEWNHAM ROAD
MACKENZIE
MT. COTTON ROAD
BURBANK
Corinda
SHERWOOD
Moorooka
BEAUDESER
CREEK
ROCHEDALE ROAD
SEVENTEEN MILE ROCKS
Oxley
Rocklea
NATHAN
EVANS ROAD
MT. GRAVAT
DARRA
Darra
OXLEY
ROCKLEA
WESTERN RLY
OXLEY
Salisbury
KESSELS
ROAD
WISHART
ROCHEDALE
CUNNINGHAM
ISWICH
ARCHERFIELD
ARTERIAL
GRANARD ROAD
ROBERTSON
Coopers Plains
McCULLOUGH ST
PADSTOW
MILES
PLATTINGS ROAD
DURACK
ACACIA RIDGE
ARCHERFIELD AERODROME
BOUNDARY RD
Banoon
Sunnybank
Altandi
MAINS ROAD
EIGHT MILE PLAIN
INALA
SUNNYBANK

N

0   1   2   3   4
KILOMETRES

MORETON BAY

Land Administration Building, Brisbane.

Elizabeth, Charlotte, Mary, Margaret and Alice) all run parallel in a north-east-to-southwest direction. Streets with the names of kings and princes (William, George, Albert and Edward) cut across them at right angles. Even in the centre of the city lovely old buildings have survived – though all too few of them – stucco-fronted and iron-balconied. They make a pleasing counterpoint to the glass-fronted mega-storey office blocks, hotels and government buildings.

The city council's bus and ferry services are absolutely first class. Make inquiries and pick up free timetables downstairs at the **Queen Street Mall** in the bus terminal.

There is also an efficient suburban rail network. Get timetables from the **Transit Centre** (train and interstate bus terminal) at the top of Roma Street to the north of the city centre.

interior of Parliament House, before taking a look at the nearby **Land Administration Building**, also in George Street. This is the former headquarters of the Premier's Department and is reputed to have a haunted corridor on the second floor. Perhaps the ghost of an honest politician? No wonder there hasn't been a sighting since last century!

Old Government House is an exercise in symmetry and style in sandstone. It stands at the same end of George Street at the top of the beautiful **Botanic Gardens**, which are themselves well worth a visit and were cleared by convicts from the bush as the original settlement's vegetable patch. Today the Gardens offer pleasant tree-lined walks in the very heart of the city, bright with flowers and with the blue glitter of the water as a backdrop. Walk up George Street away from the Gardens. The **Treasury Building** on George Street, on the corner with Queen Street, is pure Italian Renaissance and very graceful. Ironically, given its former use, it is currently being considered for use as a casino.

Not far away is **City Hall** (between Ann and Adelaide Streets). This neo-classical Italianate building has an 85 m clocktower fronting **King George Square**. It serves as the main feature of the Brisbane city logo. The clocktower contains an observation level 62 m high, reached by an ornate old lift. The main auditorium of the Hall is a wide expanse unobstructed by any columns, and the seating (for audiences up to 1500) is dismountable, allowing the whole au-

Stately Edwardian and Victorian Treasures

If you appreciate old buildings, you'll greatly admire the superb French Renaissance **Parliament House** at the corner of Alice and George Streets. This is at the Botanic Gardens end of George Street, right in front of the Queensland Institute of Technology, and is a good place to start a Brisbane walkabout. Inquire about inspecting the richly ornamented

The colonnaded Town Hall.

ditorium to be used for exhibitions and other functions. The building also contains an art gallery and small museum. Entrance is free. The **General Post Office**, also in Queen Street, is a sandstone beauty built on the site of the old prison for women convicts.

While you are in the area take a stroll down **Queen Street Mall**. It's not a building, but a few blocks of impressive old shopfronts from the last century and situated right in the heart of the city. Behind each old facade lies a modern shop or department store and hidden beneath the mall is the city's biggest bus terminal. It was a remarkable feat of engineering to scoop this out while all above remained stable. There are several fine arcades in Brisbane and all are full of interesting shops. You will find more beautiful old decor in **Rowes Arcade** between Edward and Adelaide Streets. There are several outstanding examples of church architecture nearby. The **Uniting Church** is in Albert Street, parallel to George, and **St John's Anglican Cathedral** is in Ann Street. But in Elizabeth Street, next to the majestic **St Stephen's Catholic Cathedral**, is a rare jewel – a humble stone chapel now crumbling away that was designed by Augustus Welby Pugin. Pugin was responsible for much of the decorative work on the Houses of Parliament in London.

For some convict history, walk down Elizabeth Street into William Street, which runs parallel to the river. Here you will find the old convict structure called the **Commissariat Stores**, variously used over the years as the Government Storehouse, as Customs House and as a shelter for migrants. Now it is the headquarters of the State's Royal Historical Society. The more notorious of Brisbane's two most famous convict buildings is the **Old Windmill** at Wickham Terrace. Built in 1829, it looks much like any windmill, minus the sails, but has a grim history. Convicts called it the "tower of torture" because they had to shuffle hour after hour on a treadmill to mill the settlement's grain. To find it,

follow Ann Street up to Edward, turn left and follow it along for 300 m: **Wickham Terrace** leads off on your left.

Relax with the River

Brisbane, like all of Australia's state capitals, is essentially a water city and it makes an enjoyable outing on a warm day to take a ride on one of the two *Kookaburra Queen* paddlewheelers. Each makes four daily jaunts for morning tea, lunch, afternoon tea and dinner. Depart from the pier at **Waterfront Place**, at the corner of Creek and Eagle Streets and phone for bookings on (07) 221-1300. Reach this pier by walking through **Queen Street Mall** from George Street, and then continuing along Queen until it crosses Creek. Then turn right towards the water.

In keeping with Brisbane's fun image, another craft – but this time of near aircraft-carrier dimensions – is Brisbane's floating nightclub. Relax among hundreds of palms and other plants on board. It is called **The Island**, and offers music, grog, lots of fun – and an ever changing view of the river (tel: 07-831-5066).

Take in the Arts

The grandiose new **Cultural Centre** stands just across **Victoria Bridge** on the south bank of the **Brisbane River**. Its main venue is the 2000-seat **Lyric**

Painting up in Warana.

Theatre where ballet, opera, musicals and other big cast presentations are staged. The concert hall holds almost 2000, while the **Cremorne Theatre** seats 300 for performances of special appeal. Also within the Centre are the **State Library and Art Gallery**. Exhibits are drawn from the state's extensive collection, or from visiting exhibitions. The Gallery is open daily from 10 am to 5 pm and entrance is free.

For details of performances and exhibitions ask at the City Hall front desk for the detailed "What's On" leaflet, or call the Centre direct on (07) 840-7229. There are guided tours of the Centre's various attractions, too, and the whole complex is on such a grand scale that such a tour isn't a bad idea. The Cul-

tural Centre also houses the **Queensland Museum** with thematic displays of Queensland's human, natural and technological history. This opens daily from 9 am to 5 pm, and entrance is, once again, free.

Brisbane's **Chinatown** consists of a few blocks imaginatively rebuilt in Chinese style with all the evocative smells, sounds and good food of the East. It is just a few minutes northeast of the city centre in **Fortitude Valley** and a taxi ride should be about A$3.50.

An **Arts and Crafts Market** is staged every Sunday morning at the **Riverdale Centre**, 123 Eagle Street, between the city and Fortitude Valley, and close to the ferry pier. Among the junk there are lots of interesting things to see and buy

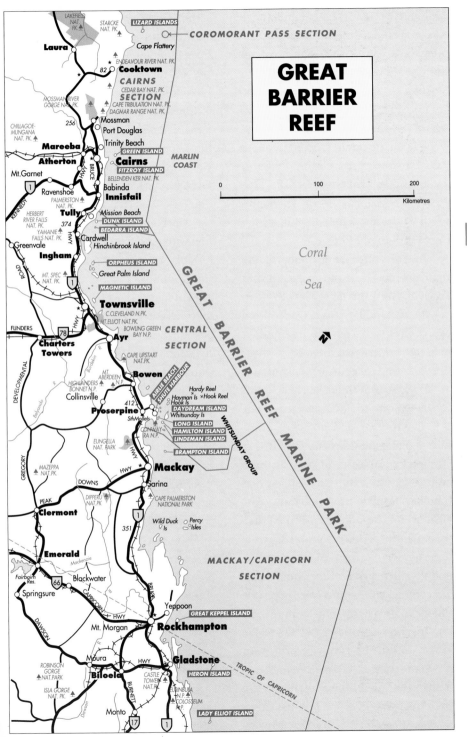

LAKEFIELD NAT. PK.

STARCKE NAT. PK.

LIZARD ISLANDS

COROMORANT PASS SECTION

Cape Flattery

Laura

ENDEAVOUR RIVER NAT. PK.

82   Cooktown

CAIRNS
SECTION

CEDAR BAY NAT. PK.
CAPE TRIBULATION NAT. PK.
DAGMAR RANGE NAT. PK.

MOSSMAN RIVER GORGE NAT. PK.

256   Mossman

Port Douglas

CHILLAGOE-MUNGANA NAT. PK.

Trinity Beach

GREEN ISLAND

MARLIN
COAST

Mareeba

Atherton

Cairns

FITZROY ISLAND

Mt. Garnet

BELLENDEN KER NAT. PK.

Ravenshoe

PALMERSTON NAT. PK.

Babinda

Innisfail

HERBERT RIVER FALLS NAT. PK.

Tully

374

Mission Beach

DUNK ISLAND

YAMANIE FALLS NAT. PK.

Cardwell

BEDARRA ISLAND

Greenvale

Hinchinbrook Island

Ingham

ORPHEUS ISLAND

MT. SPEC NAT. PK.

Great Palm Island

MAGNETIC ISLAND

FLINDERS

Townsville

C. CLEVELAND N. PK.

MT. ELLIOT NAT. PK.

Coral

Sea

GREAT BARRIER REEF MARINE PARK

78   Charters
Towers

Ayr

CENTRAL
SECTION

BOWLING GREEN BAY N.P.

DEVELOPMENTAL

CAPE UPSTART NAT. PK.

MT. ABERDEEN N.P.

HIGHLANDERS BONNET N.P.

Bowen

AIRLIE BEACH
SHUTE HARBOUR

Hardy Reel

Collinsville

412

Hayman Is   × Hook Reel
Hook Is

DAYDREAM ISLAND

Proserpine

Whitsunday Is

Sth Mollels

LONG ISLAND

HAMILTON ISLAND

EUNGELLA NAT. PARK

CONWAY RA N.P.

LINDEMAN ISLAND

BRAMPTON ISLAND

WHITSUNDAY GROUP

MAZEPPA NAT. PK.

DOWNS

Mackay

Sarina

PEAK

DIPPERU NAT. PK.

CAPE PALMERSTON NATIONAL PARK

Clermont

351

Wild Duck
Is

Percy
Isles

Emerald

MACKAY/CAPRICORN

SECTION

Fairbairn Res.

66   Blackwater

Springsure

CAPRICORN

Yeppoon

GREAT KEPPEL ISLAND

HWY

Mt. Morgan

Rockhampton

Moura

HWY

Gladstone

Biloela

CASTLE TOWER NAT. PK.

HERON ISLAND

TROPIC OF CAPRICORN

ROBINSON GORGE NAT. PARK

EURIMBULA N.P.

ISLA GORGE NAT. PK.

COLOSSEUM

Monto

17

LADY ELLIOT ISLAND

GREAT
BARRIER
REEF

while buskers provide the entertainment. A second outdoor market adjoins it and afterwards you can take an escalator upstairs for a snack. Budget travellers looking for cheap novels and knick-knacks can try the Sunday morning **flea market** at the **Rocklea Market**, Sherwood Road, **Rocklea**. It opens at about 7.30 am and starts closing down at 11.30 am, so don't leave it too late, especially since it's several kilometres south on the Ipswich Road. But, it is on the suburban rail line.

And if you're in Brisbane at the right time, don't miss out on the **Warana Festival**. For seven days every September the city indulges in a Queensland **Mardi Gras** with a parade, free outdoor entertainment, open-air food festival, fireworks and (of course) plenty of fun.

Early street Village is in McIlwraith Avenue, Norman Park, on the eastern side of the river and about a seven-minute cab ride from the city. It is a remarkable tableaux of colonial Brisbane. It boasts a collection of heritage buildings ranging from slab huts to an elegant homestead, all furnished and decorated in period style and set in a large garden. You can make a day of it and stop there to have lunch and to buy a few things at the souvenir shop. The Village is open daily from 9 am to 4.30 pm. For enquiries phone (07) 398-6866.

A genuine historic home is New**stead House**, a grand homestead built in 1846 on the banks of the river at **Breakfast Creek**, a few minutes drive northeast out of the city towards the airport, where visitors are welcome to view the house and its furnishings. It is open Mondays to Thursdays, 11 am to 3 pm and on Sundays from 2 pm to 5 pm. Breakfast Creek itself is one of the most famous tourist spots in and around Brisbane and now has a number of attractions. Just over the road from Newstead House is the **Boardwalk Complex**: in fact a tunnel beneath the road connects it to Newstead House.

The Boardwalk is a mod-old confection with an amusing clocktower, fashionable restaurants, tea and coffee shops, antiques, books and free parking. Budgeteers, get fish and chips and take a seat downstairs to watch the passing river traffic, including Venetian-style gondolas. On the other side of the water is one of the most photographed pubs in Australia – the famous **Breakfast Creek Hotel**. One glance at its beautiful lines and you, too, will reach for your camera. Followers of the harness races gather here on Saturday and Wednesday evenings for a beer and giant sizzling steak before heading next door to **Albion Park** for "the trots".

Mt Coot-Tha Gardens is only 6 km west of the city, and well worth a visit. It affords a fine view over Brisbane and within the grounds you can also see rainforest, lagoons, ponds and tropical plants all under a large dome. It also has a magnificent Japanese garden, a planetarium, cafeteria and souvenir shop. It is open daily from 9 am to 5 pm, though the planetarium is closed on Mondays and Tuesdays and does not

Waiting to be fleeced at a woolshed in Samford.

admit children under the age of six.

New Farm is an historic and charming near-city parkland suburb with many old colonial-style homes. It's on the north bank of the Brisbane River and a couple of kilometres from the city. Get a copy of the pamphlet "Heritage Trail New Farm" before catching a ferry from the pontoon at the foot of Edward Street in the city to New Farm Park, and then spend a couple of hours in pleasant tranquillity.

In spring the park is a stunning vision of purple as its many jacaranda trees burst into bloom. One of Brisbane's best-known venues is **Lone Pine Sanctuary** at Jesmond Road, Fig Tree Pocket, upstream of the city and best reached by cruiser. It features sheep, kangaroos and koalas (including one which rides on a dog's back).

Lone Pine goes in for the hands-on approach when it comes to animals, which makes it an ideal place to take children. But it is also does important work in animal breeding. Now Japanese-owned, it supplies koalas to many Japanese zoos. It is open daily from 9 am to 5 pm. It is a good idea to take a "koala cruise" from **Golden Mile Wharf**, departing 1 pm daily, and combine river sightseeing with koala cuddling. Call (07) 229-7055 for details.

You will find some of the same tactile approach to native and adopted Australian animals at the **Australian Woolshed**, 148 Stamford Road, Ferny Hills, just 20 minutes from the centre.

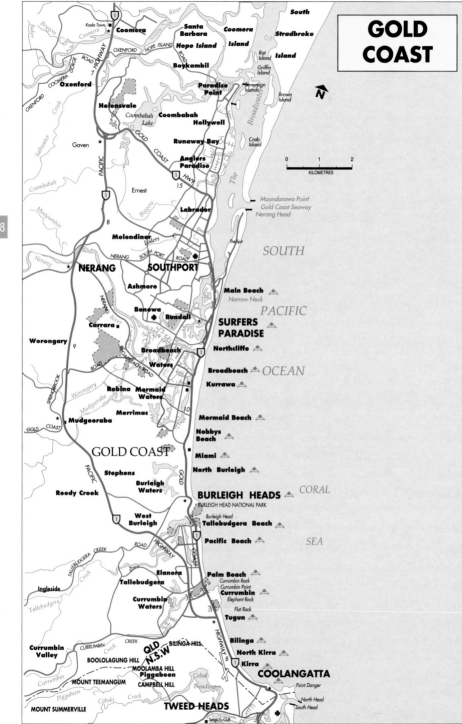

GOLD COAST

N

0   1   2
KILOMETRES

Baker

Brygon

Coomera River

River

South

Koala Town

Coomera

OXENFORD

Santa
Barbara

Coomera
Island

South
Stradbroke
Island

Hope Island

Hope Island

Boykambil

Rat
Island

Griffin
Island

Oxenford

Coomera Creek

HIGHWAY

ROAD

Sultwater

Helensvale

Paradise
Point

Sovereign
Islands

Brown
Island

The Broadwater

Coombabah
Lake

Coombabah

Gaven

PACIFIC

GOLD

Runaway Bay

Crab
Island

Coombabah

COAST

Hollywell

Ernest

HWY

Anglers
Paradise

The Spit

Moolendinar

Biggera

Waters

15

Labrador

Moondarawa Point
Gold Coast Seaway
Nerang Head

Moeyumbin

Nerang

8

NERANG

Ladders

SOUTH

PORT

The Spit

SOUTH

Nerang

NERANG

Nerang River

Ashmore

SOUTHPORT

ROAD

PACIFIC

Main Beach

Benowa

Bundall

Narrow Neck

Carrara

Worongary

9

Broadbeach
Waters

BROADBEACH ROAD

SURFERS
PARADISE

OCEAN

Northcliffe

Worongary

Robina

Mermaid
Waters

Broadbeach

Kurrawa

Mudgeeraba

Merrimac

10

Mermaid Beach

Mudgeeraba

GOLD

Nobbys
Beach

SPRINGBROOK

COAST

Miami

ROAD

Stephens

North Burleigh

GOLD COAST

Reedy Creek

Burleigh
Waters

GOLD

BURLEIGH HEADS

CORAL

BURLEIGH HEAD NATIONAL PARK

PACIFIC

West
Burleigh

Burleigh Head

Tallebudgera Beach

HIGHWAY

ROAD

Pacific Beach

SEA

TALLEBUDGERA

CREEK

Elanora

COAST

Palm Beach

Ingleside

Tallebudgera

Currumbin Rock
Currumbin Point

Tallebudgery

Creek

Currumbin
Waters

Currumbin

Elephant Rock

Flat Rock

Tugun

HIGHWAY

Currumbin
Valley

CURRUMBIN

CREEK

Creek

BILINGA HILL

QLD
N.S.W

Bilinga

BOOLOLAGUNG HILL

MOOLAMBA HILL

Piggabeen

North Kirra

GOLD

Kirra

MOUNT TEEMANGUM

Currumbin

CAMPBELL HILL

Cobaki

COOLANGATTA

Point Danger

Piggabeen

Cobaki
Broadwater

North Head

MOUNT SUMMERVILLE

Cobaki

Creek

TWEED HEADS

South Head

Seagull's Club

Skyscraper skyline.

Here you can watch sheep-shearing and sheepdogs at work (a sight not to be missed if it's your first time), and hand-feed 'roos or cuddle koalas. You can also have some true-blue Oz tucker there and briefly experience bush life. For inquiries phone (07) 351-5366.

Sporting Brisbane

Where leisure and fun occupy people's minds most of the time, as they do in Australia, there is bound to be a lot of interest in sport of all kinds.

In Queensland, with its miles of unspoiled beaches and warm waters, that means any sport connected with the sea. Since the weather is warm to hot most of the time, non-participatory out-door spectator sports are popular too, particularly rugby in winter and cricket in summer. Horse-racing, trotting and greyhounds are also very big in Queens-land.

At the weekends, horse-racing takes place not only in Brisbane and on the Gold Coast, but in all the main cities opposite the Barrier Reef and in many inland centres, too. So does toad-racing, incidentally, but you'll probably have to see that before you believe it.

Likewise there is a strong following for harness racing throughout the coastal areas of the state. You may be certain that at least a couple of fixtures are being staged somewhere every day except Sundays.

Beach days and holidays on the gleaming sands.

Try the Gold Coast

Surfers Paradise is the central city of the **Gold Coast**, an hour's drive to the south of Brisbane. The Gold Coast is a sophisticated holiday resort area spread along 42 km of beach and bursting at the seams with international-quality facilities – hotels, restaurants, elegant shops, arcades and more. Stunning white surf beaches run invitingly mile after mile down south to where New South Wales begins. Combers dash on to the

Lazing about under the sun.

sand, rolling in from the far side of the Pacific under an azure sky. Set well back from the water's edge are so many high-rise hotels and apartment blocks that the skyline fleetingly resembles Hong Kong. Most stores have bilingual signs in English and Japanese, just in case you were wondering who among Queensland's visitors has the most money to spend.

There is nothing historic to view: whatever there once was has all been torn down and redeveloped. The names of the suburbs indicate the nature of the place – Isle of Capri, Sorrento, Rio Vista, Miami Keys, Mermaid Waters, Paradise Waters and so on. Cheap? Well, there are those who think the whole place is pretty tacky, but people who choose to live there find homes anything but cheap. Not that the kind of people who want to live in **Surfers** are likely to worry much about that.

Endless modern mansions sprawl on the banks of the **Nerang**, and along the many canals running off it, each with its own mini-beach. Take a cruise to see how the other half lives. Typical fares are: adults, A\$16, children, A\$10 and that includes soft drinks.

Besides sightseeing, there's much to enjoy, but first a warning. The Australia-wide recession began to bite in 1990/91 and since the Gold Coast is where people tend to splash their money around, the place has attracted criminal elements. Take care with cameras and handbags, treat smooth-talking

Seeing the Gold Coast
from the air.

strangers with caution and don't flash your cash. People walking alone after midnight are putting themselves at risk.

But on the brighter side there is so much to see and enjoy here, and most of it within easy reach. **Seaworld**, on **The Spit**, puts on a great show with dolphins, trained seals, and aquabatics. Take a look round by monorail.

Fisherman's Wharf, next to Seaworld, offers entertainment, with a tavern, cocktail bar, children's playground, shopping village, and restaurants. And also on The Spit is the **Marina Mirage**. You can walk around the marina quays to see the array of sleek launches, yachts and other craft. For more shopping and entertainment try **Paradise Centre**, right in the heart of

the city with scores of souvenir shops. Take the escalator up to **Grundy's** entertainment centre and international food court. But beware – children will spend a fortune here if you let them.

Moving a little out of town, you can get a (windswept) bird's eye view of the whole glorious scene from the open cockpit of a *Tiger Moth* bi-plane from **Carrara Airport**, at the **International Raceway** 4 km inland of the Surfers. Take your camera for some truly dramatic shots – but don't let go of it! Coming down to earth again, it's worth exploring **Pacific Fair** at **Broadbeach** just to the south of Surfers. This is one of the largest shopping resorts in the Southern Hemisphere and there are shopping complexes here selling everything from antiques to everyday sundries. It is also a fun place for children, with restaurants too, if you want to make a day trip out of it.

Jupiter's Casino, also at Broadbeach, offers more than you might think in the way of family entertainment. Besides the plethora of gambling games, including the *dinkum* Oz game of two-up, there are international shows, nightclubs, top restaurants, a café and an old-time pub. To encourage a bit of free spending Jupiter's theme is "You only live once". A monorail links the casino with the up-market **Oasis Shopping Centre** on the other side of the road.

For gentler spirits, and especially for animal and bird lovers, **Currumbin Bird Sanctuary** is a must. It is 12 km to the south of Surfers on the Gold Coast

Marina homes at Sanctuary Cove on the Coomera River, north of Surfers Paradise.

Highway and on the way to **Coolangatta Airport**. Visitors here can feed gorgeous lorikeets and cockatoos, as well as many other birds and native animals, and pose with them for photos. Or, if it's time for a little relaxation after the hectic pace of pleasure in Surfers, simply take it easy and commune with nature in a tranquil setting.

There are several beauty spots and tourist attractions up the length of **Currumbin Creek**, which stretches several kilometres inland through some fine countryside. Try **Olsen's Bird Garden** in **Currumbin Valley** for more feathered friends.

About 10 km north of Surfers Paradise on the Pacific Highway around **Coomera** and **Oxenford** (about 50 km south of Brisbane) are several other attractions.

Sanctuary Cove on the **Coomera River** is an extravagant tourist development including a top-class hotel and international resort, shops, restaurants, golf course and marina. It oozes wealth and symbolises the opulence of the tourist property boom in the 1980s, and you might find it worth a visit from that point of view alone.

Dreamworld near Coomera is a Disney-style theme park with a strong Australian flavour. It had, at the last count, 27 fun rides, and the obligatory koalas and kangaroos, along with a full range of shops, and restaurants. Dreamworld is open daily from 10 am to 5 pm.

Close by at **Koala Town**, (yes, our furry friends once again make an appearance) are lots of other rustic delights to see here, including sheep-shearing, cow-milking, the feeding of baby animals, and horse-shoe throwing. There's a re-enactment of a bushranger holding up a horse-drawn coach, and an Aussie outback performance.

There are kangaroos, dingoes, peacocks and snakes to see, and boat rides on the adjoining Coomera River. Crocodile feeding is a big attraction, but don't let that put you off the boat trips.

Koala Town is open Wednesdays to Sundays

Evening entertainment at Broad Beach.

from 10 am to 5 pm. For the more active, **Wet 'n Wild**, a little further south, offers a giant waterslide, a toboggan drop, and a wave pool, and is also open daily from 10 am to 5 pm.

Go North, Young Man

You'll find it hard to wrench yourself away from the man-made allure of the Gold Coast and Brisbane but there's much more to enjoy up north. By road, head past the **Glasshouse Mountains** (or stop off to explore them) and drive up beyond the **Sunshine Coast**, a gentler version of the Gold Coast. At **Noosa Heads** blocks of high-rises and a few trendy shops and restaurants conceal the beach. From here head for the Great Barrier Reef resorts starting with **Gladstone** and moving north through several attractive stop-over points including **Rockhampton**, **Mackay**, **Townsville** and **Cairns**. Before you get there, though, you will pass close by one of Queensland's offshore wonders – and not, for a change, built on or around the **Barrier Reef**. This is **Fraser Island**, a great hummock of sand standing 240 m

Heron Island.

proud of the sea and over 100 km long, just a couple of hundred kilometres north of Brisbane. Heavily forested and with some unparallelled camping and walking facilities beside the freshest lakes you'll see anywhere, Fraser is ideal for non-five-star accommodation. But you can't go without a four-wheel-drive (unless you hoof it) and you need a permit to camp there, which is best obtained in advance from the tourist bureau in Brisbane.

Most visitors to coastal Queensland will be drawn principally to the Reef, and with good reason. But it's worth noting that on the way north there are many other attractions, of which Fraser Island is just one. There are numerous state forests and national parks along the **Great Dividing Range** and its northward extensions, and all of these are well provided with campsites and walking trails. With the glory of the beaches and the Reef so close at hand, it's possible to overlook the inland beauties of Queensland, and that can be a pity.

Life along the reef

Gladstone is 540 km north of Brisbane and is the closest major land centre to the Reef. Offshore is **Heron Island**, a captivating coral cay not only surrounded by a wide variety of marine life, but with its own population of tropical birds and turtles.

Explore the Reef by boat from

The Great Barrier Reef

One of the wonders of the world, the Great Barrier Reef is actually a conglomeration of 2900 reefs and some 900 islands, many of them cays or coral islands.

It stretches for more than 2000 km along the Queensland coast, starting about 75 km north of Bundaberg and stretching beyond the northernmost point of Australia, Cape York. It is the largest marine park in the world, and can be regarded as the largest living organism on earth.

For the Reef is a living entity made up of colonies of coral which interact with lime-producing algae. It contains 300 types of coral, most of which contribute to building the Reef and several of which are named for their appearance – brain, mushroom, staghorn, plate and slipper corals. When it dies it is covered by algae whose limestone content not only preserves the coral skeleton, but provides a base on which fresh coral may form and grow. Thus the Reef is growing all the time, albeit very slowly, and has the richest biological diversity of any reef system in the world.

About 1500 different species of fish and other sea creatures, many of exotic colours and bizarre appearance, inhabit the Great Barrier Reef. From a glass-bottomed boat you will see a kaleidoscope of living colour and in any one sighting you will see at least some of this breathtaking array of marine life. The Reef's inhabitants include, to name a very few, butterfly fish, parrot fish, sweetlips, monocle bream, barracuda, coral trout, Spanish mackerel, sea snakes, rabbit fish, eels, epaulette and leopard sharks, seahorses, manta rays, squid, sea slugs, beautiful anemones, starfish, trumpet fish, cuttlefish, octopus, shrimps, crabs and much, much, more.

Of course, snorkellers and scuba-divers can see far more of the ocean life as they get close to the reefs and their myriad dwellers, but they also run a few risks. Apart from the obvious danger of sharks, the Reef is home to some toxic and highly dangerous creatures so you are well advised to make your first underwater forays with the help of someone who knows the ropes. Creatures that should sound a danger signal if

Snorkelling on the reefs.

you get too close include stonefish, blue-ringed octopus, Crown of Thorns starfish, some cone shells such as the textile cone, moray eels, sea snakes, pufferfish, porcupine fish and toadfish.

The warm waters of the Reef are the breeding grounds for humpback, minke and killer whales. They are also home to a large number of turtles and dugong, also known as sea cows or manatees.

Deep-Sea Perils

Put on your snorkelling mask and fins and swim into another world.

Today, the Reef faces two perils. Originally the main one was man. If every visitor were to snap off a piece of coral for a souvenir the accessible parts of the Reef would slowly disappear and the whole ecological cycle be thrown out of balance. But men can be controlled, and have been since the Reef opened up to tourism in the 1950s and 1960s.

The second danger is the Crown of Thorns starfish, which feeds on hard and soft corals, gorgonians (sea whips), sea urchins, clams and algae. These starfish, which are covered with thousands of poisonous spines that cause a severe reaction in humans, attach themselves to a section of coral and kill it within four to six hours.

Starfish infestations were first recorded in 1962 and now almost a third of the reef is affected by them. Their natural enemy is the triton shell, but these are found only in comparatively small numbers on the reef as against the Crown of Thorns, the female of which produces 20 million eggs yearly.

However, there is dispute as to just how permanently the Reef will be damaged by the Crown of Thorns starfish, and some suggestion that the infestation is only a cyclical phenomenon. If so, the Reef has recovered before, and will probably recover again. Certainly, coral reefs do seem to have extraordinary powers of recovery and repair. The entire Great Barrier Reef has grown in only the last few thousand years. More immediate dangers may spring from man's activities on the coast. Sugar plantations now reach right down to the shoreline, previously covered by rainforest. The run-off

from fertilisers and pollution from towns and resorts are probably not doing the coral any good. Coral needs exceptionally clean water in which to thrive.

But we have, thankfully, entered a more caring age. Australians care passionately about the Reef, in rather the same way that they care about Kakadu, as a symbol of all that is best and most beautiful in their country. Tampering with the Reef in any way – particularly the possibility of exploring for oil anywhere near it – is a very hot political potato indeed.

There are now two key centres of Reef research, both in Townsville. These are James Cook University, and the Australian Institute of Marine Science, both of which have active programmes to monitor reef life and the populations of marine flora and fauna. Besides which, the parks authorities keep a very firm grip of who is allowed to do what, and local people and tourist operators take their concerns very seriously indeed.

Such concern increases among the public as more people gain access to the Reef and see its wonders for themselves. In that sense, increased tourism is actually of benefit to the Reef. It's an example, if you like, of democracy in action, and a refutation of the old elitist idea that only specialists could really understand such complex ecosystems and only they could be entrusted with their protection.

With this kind of commitment from the Australian people, the Great Barrier Reef seems to face a bright future.

Exploring the azure.

Gladstone, and in town enjoy super-fresh seafood. **Rockhampton** lies 639 km north of Brisbane. Motor on a few miles to **Rosslyn Bay Harbour** then take a ferry out to **Great Keppel Island** for some sea, sun, sailing, swimming, snorkelling and sports which include tennis, squash, horse riding, water-ski-ing, parasailing, golf and volleyball. There is a nightclub and disco too. Nearby **Yeppoon** is one of several fast growing coastal resorts. If you're weary-ing of sun and sea rest up in "**Rocky**" for a while: it has a languid lifestyle and some delightful old buildings – the **Customs House** is a must.

Mackay, at 973 km north of Bris-bane and in the tropics proper, is an attractive port city. Already the sugar

Romantic setting of Airlie Beach.

Life on the reef island.

of these islands sport their own laid-back resorts, of varying levels of luxury, where tomorrow is even more enjoyable than today. **Hamilton** also has an animal reserve and dolphin pool.

Moving yet further up the coast, **Townsville** (1369 km north of Brisbane) has a cosmopolitan lifestyle, with five-star hotels, a casino, sophisticated resorts, an international airport, and a walk-through aquarium. It is also just 40 minutes by ferry to **Magnetic Island**, with 20 tropical bays and some 4000 hectares of national park. It's a mecca for walkers and lovers of wildlife, which abounds. In the same vein, mas-

capital of Queensland, it now enjoys still more prosperity thanks to tourism. There are a number of resorts in and around Mackay, and it is the base for cruises to the offshore **Whitsundays** and **Brampton Island**.

Airlie Beach and **Shute Harbour** are coastal towns 160 km north of Mackay, incidentally served by a fair-sized airport. These are probably the most popular jumping-off points for the Reef island resorts, with plenty of cruises from these adjoining ports to **South Molle, Hamilton, Lindeman** and other islands in the Whitsundays group. You can fly out to several of them too, either by helicopter or fixed-wing plane. All

Rowing around the reefs.

Cairns, a world class big-game fishing centre.

sive **Hinchinbrook Island** is not far north.

Totally unspoiled, it is the world's largest offshore national park. Townsville has an international airport with direct connections to New Zealand and other flights to the Pacific and the United States.

It is also an important rail junction for inland Queensland. The city is an important departure point for many reef islands. It's paradise, but it helps if you're well bankrolled.

Cairns (1718 km north of Brisbane) is the true boom city of northern Queensland. Though some of the gloss has come off its get-rich-quick atmosphere following the Australian recession and the crash of many of the country's cor-

porate glitterati, tourism is still king in Cairns thanks to its proximity to the Reef and to its international airport. It is the natural point of entry to Australia for visitors from the Pacific Rim, particularly Japan, and it drops them neatly in the middle of all the action. There are five-star hotels, luxury resorts, encircling rainforest, magnificent game-fishing – everything except skiing, and all at the visitor's fingertips. This is relaxation tropical-style. War buffs should note the **House on the Hill** whence *Z-Force* commando raids on Japanese-held territory were directed during World War II. Now it's a motel.

Cairns is almost entirely ringed by rainforest, and for anyone who may be temporarily "reefed-out" the city offers

Taking in the sun.

the best opportunity to explore a little further inland. The forests here have been regenerating naturally and virtually undisturbed for over 100 million years: they are massive, majestic and incredibly beautiful.

Take a four-wheel-drive tour through some of the parks – you can get one for half-a-day if you don't want to be away from the hotel bar for too long.

The **Atherton Tablelands** is a 150-km stretch of tropical country inland of Cairns, and worth a separate trip to see its volcanic lakes, its forests and its birdlife. The forests continue north up the ridge of mountainous country to form a backdrop to **Port Douglas** and the former gold-mining town of **Cooktown**, named in honour of Captain James Cook whose ship was holed on the reef.

Port Douglas, until ten years ago

Out fishing for marlin off Cairns.

hardly more than a fishing village, now has one of the ritziest international resorts on its very doorstep in the form of the **Mirage Port Douglas**.

But if glamorous resorts are not your scene, this is the part of North Queensland where the true enthusiast will find the wild and wonderful **Mossman Gorge**, and 36 km further still the township of **Daintree**.

From here on it's four-wheel-drive only, at least for the moment, a jumping-off point for the **Daintree Rainforest**, and the only half-explored **Cape York** region. It's symbolic that here is where an international consortium plans to build a base for exploration even further afield: the **Cape York Spaceport**.

Getting there

Most visitors fly to the Barrier Reef resorts, either to Cairns or Townsville, on a package deal that includes accommodation in either place, cruises to the reef and stop-overs in resorts on the islands. Here are some examples of the costs of one-way airfares:

Melbourne to Cairns, A$358 and to Townsville, A$332; Sydney to Cairns, A$299 and to Townsville, A$269; Brisbane to Cairns, A$241; and to Townsville A$206. For return air fares, double these amounts – but don't forget to shop around. Airfares in Australia are increasingly competitive. Hotel rates in the region range from about A$30 to

Beach Culture

Beaches are something that Australia has plenty of – 36,000 km of them, to be precise.

That's a longer coastline than any other country on earth, and is approximately the circumference of the planet. Added to the fact that most of the island continent's coastline remains more or less unspoiled. Add to that Australia's climate is agreeable almost everywhere, and in most places downright hot.

Put all of this together, and it is no surprise that the "beach culture" is a key part of the Australian way of life.

For generations, sun, sand and surf have been inseparable from the Australian ethos. That started out as a matter of necessity. All of Australia's state capital cities, and many other towns, are port settlements, and the economic life of the country from the earliest times revolved around the sea.

The growth of beach-based leisure went hand-in-hand with economic growth. But Australia's beaches, while matchless in their beauty, can be treacherous too. There are rips, dangerous tides, and unwelcome fellow-swimmers like stinging jellyfish, octopuses, and even sharks. In response to the dangers of the sea, local groups of aquatic fanatics formed surf lifesaving clubs all around the country.

The skill and occasional heroism of Australia's lifesavers is unquestioned. They still save scores of lives every year, and the sight of their twin flags – marking the safe and supervised zone for swimmers – is a welcome sign of security on any beach.

But surf lifesaving has also become the focus of a whole range of recreational activities. Surf carnivals are a regular part of the beach calendar right across Australia.

Surfboats manned by superfit oarsmen battle it out through crashing blue water. Young men – mostly amateurs – pit themselves in gruelling athletic contests in and out of the water for the honour of winning the coveted "Iron Man" title for their district.

These kinds of beachside activities have come to symbolise much that is distinctive in the

Sea shells and sea gulls on the seashore.

Australian character – a love of the outdoors and of fierce physical competition, a certain unashamed hedonism, an addiction to the sun. It's no wonder that one of Australia's best-known artists on the international stage is Ken Done, who built his reputation with his carefree and childlike beach scenes. No wonder too that among Australia's most profitable manufactured exports (particularly to Japan) is high-quality beachwear.

There have been changes over the years. Within the last decade Australians have finally come to accept a connection between their love of the sun and their extraordinarily high incidence of skin-cancer.

The beaches today are a little less crowded by people with beautiful bodies, slowly cooking themselves to death.

Meanwhile other forms of beach-based culture have experienced a boom as Australians have become wealthier and more adventurous. This is especially true in Queensland, which boasts some of the very finest beaches and a climate which varies from subtropical to tropical.

Luxurious beach resorts have sprung up along the coast and on the string of islands which run the 2300-km length of the fabulous Great Barrier Reef.

For those who prefer to rough it (comparatively) four-wheel-driving has caught on in a big way. It is now possible to drive for scores of kilometres along Queensland's beaches, with camping often permitted just a few yards from the breaking surf.

Fraser Island to the north of Brisbane offers the last word in fourwheeled beach leisure. The largest sand island in the world, its sandy tracks can only be negotiated by four-wheel-drive vehicles – and in the season it is crowded with them.

Largely because of its beaches, Queensland in fact leads the way in Australia's tourism boom. Fully 60 percent of in-bound tourists to Australia name Queensland as their primary destination.

Virtually all of them plan to spend some time in, on, under, or just beside the sea.

Beach culture has become big business.

about A\$164 a night for a shared double room. There are good train and road coach services up the coast from Sydney and even further south, and these can be quite an adventure and reasonably priced. But it is such a very long way that you need a good deal of time.

There are various other rail trips through inland Queensland too, for the real enthusiast, and the tourist bureau will be able to advise you about those.

Tourist Information Centres can be found at the following addresses:

Brisbane:
196 Adelaide Street
Tel: 07-221-6111,
Fax: 07-221-5320 (or go to the information kiosk, Queen Street Mall).

Sydney:
75 Castlereagh Street
Tel: 02-232-1788
Fax: 02-231-5153

Melbourne:
257 Collins Street
Tel: 03-654-3866,
Fax: 02-650-1847

Adelaide:
10 Grenfell Street
Tel: 08-212-2399,
Fax 08-211-8841

Perth:
55 St George Terrace
Tel: 09-325-1600
Fax: 09-221 3092

Adelaide, capital of South Australia, is a delightful city, a leafy, friendly place of open-air cafes and fine old buildings. It has been dubbed the "City of Churches" and that gives the visitor a glimpse of its essential character: quiet, conservative and dignified.

In fact the Adelaide of today has moved a long way from that stereotype, but it has managed to retain much of its original peaceful charm.

Even today it is not a city which moves at breakneck speed. Its streets must be walked in leisurely fashion if you are to appreciate it. As if its Victorian designers wanted to encourage you to do just that, Adelaide is built on a simple grid pattern around five squares, making it easy to find your way about. Transport is especially good, even if you choose not to walk. There is a good bus service, a cen-

Adelaide's superb town planning reflected the vision of William Light, South Australia's first Surveyor,

tral train station, one tramline, and even a futuristic O-Bahn rapid transit busway right through the city. In fact it's the longest O-Bahn in the world at 12 km, running from suburban **Tea Tree Plaza Shopping Centre** in the north to Paradise Interchange on the far side of Adelaide.

Adelaide was the vision of Colonel William Light, South Australia's first Surveyor-General in the 1830s.

Opinionated he may have been, but he was also a superb town planner. Through his foresight and determination Light made Adelaide the cultured pearl that it is today. He was in bitter conflict with the first Governor, Captain John Hindmarsh, who wanted a utilitarian capital that would also serve as a port.

Hindmarsh's scheming, besides frustrating Light at every turn, caused a lengthy delay to the development of agricultural settlements on the rich pasturelands that are the citiy's hinterland.

The land went unsurveyed and unsettled while the two bickered – and more than 1000 starving would-be farmers subsisted on emergency food supplies from New South Wales.

After two years, Hindmarsh was dismissed, but he left with a smile on his face, having made a fortune from land speculation. Light, meanwhile, had resigned in disgust and he died in poverty soon afterwards.

However the new governor, Colonel George Gawler, instated Light's plans

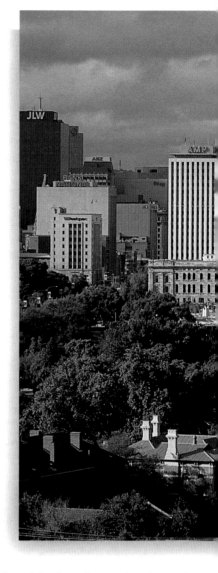

for Adelaide and immediately set about encouraging agricultural development. Adelaide is eternally grateful to its planner, and thus today, **Light's Vision** is a real place, a lookout on the top of **Montiefiore Hill**. Here, a kilometre's walk from the city centre, Light's statue gazes out over an unparallelled view of his city and its environs.

Built on a simple grid of five squares, the city of churches is leafy and delightful.

On Foot in Adelaide

Adelaide's **SA Government Travel Centre** is the place to start discovering the city. It is at 18 King William Street in the city centre (tel: 08-212-1644; fax: 08-

212-4251) and provides a wide choice of pamphlets and brochures. Alternatively, before you head for South Australia you can get all the information you need from the Centre's branch offices in Sydney at 143 King Street (tel:02-232-8388; fax: 02-232-8680) or in Melbourne at 25

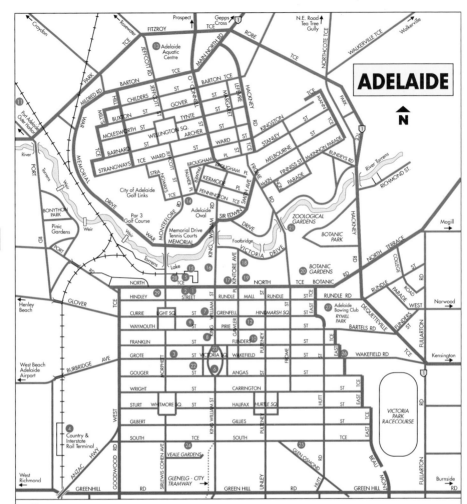

ADELAIDE

↑ N

Key

- ① Australian Airline Office
- ② Ansett Airline Office
- ③ Central Bus Terminal
- ④ Interstate Railway Terminal
- ⑤ Adelaide Metropolitan Railway Station
- ⑥ Glenelg tram Terminal
- ⑦ Metropolitan Bus Infomation Office
- ⑧ General Post Office
- ⑨ Australian Passport Office
- ⑩ YMCA
- ⑪ YMCA
- ⑫ Royal Automobile Association Of S.A.
- ⑬ Adelaide Aquatic Centre
- ⑭ Light's Vision, MonterFiore Hill
- ⑮ Adelaide Casino

- ⑯ Adelaide Festival Centre
- ⑰ National Soldiers War Memorial
- ⑱ Migration and Settlement Museum
- ⑲ Mortlock Liabrary
- ⑳ Botanical Gardens
- ㉑ Zoological Gardens
- ㉒ Adelaide Central Market
- ㉓ Victoria Square Fountain
- ㉔ Veale Rose Gardens
- ㉕ Himeji Japanese Gardens
- ㉖ Australian Formula 1 Grand Prix Circuit
- ㉗ Rymill Park
- ㉘ Adelaide Convention Centre
- ㉙ Living Arts Centre

The Parliament House, a gracious old building of marble on granite, which took some 56 years to complete!

Elizabeth Street (tel:03-614-6522; fax: 03-614-6967). The toll-free number is 008-88-2092 from anywhere in Australia outside Adelaide. The Centre will help you arrange any of the scores of tours on offer in and around Adelaide.

The Travel Centre, within easy reach of **Adelaide Railway Station**, makes a convenient point to start an exploratory walk along North Terrace, the finest of Adelaide's boulevards. As a first move, come out of the Centre, turn left and cross King William Street, then cross to the north side of North Terrace. Here you will find a cluster of Adelaide's sights, all within a stone's throw, and grouped close to the station.

South Australia's fine **Parliament House**, is a gracious building with ten

Corinthian columns. It's built of Kapunda marble on granite foundations. It seems that things didn't move too fast in Adelaide's early civic history: the building was started in 1883 and not finished until 1939! Look for the stone lion which is part of a royal coat of arms and which originally decorated the Houses of Parliament in London. Parliament House is open to the public when the members are sitting, with viewings from 2 pm.

A visit there isn't complete, however, without calling in on **Old Parliament House** next door. This was built in 1855 as South Australia's original Legislative Council Chamber, and is now a museum of political history with displays and audio-visual programs. It's

Among its evening entertainment, a formal-style casino.

the perfect place to orientate yourself on South Australia's history – and it also has a courtyard restaurant. While on the subject of history, you can hardly miss the **South African War Memorial** on the corner of North Terrace and King William Road (King William Street becomes King William Road north of that junction). The Boer War of 1899-1902 was the first major overseas conflict in which Australians served and this bronze monument commemorates the fallen. The War has given rise, incidentally, to one of Australia's most successful films of the past few years – *Breaker Morant*.

This cluster of buildings on the north side of North Terrace is not wholly given over to civic pride and history, however. Roulette wheels spin merrily at the city's

Casino, equidistant from Parliament House and the city railway station. In fact, Adelaide's casino used to *be* the railway station. It's worth visiting, not necessarily for a flutter, but simply to observe this remarkable metamorphosis. Of course, if you do have a touch of the gambling bug, the casino has 98 gaming tables which might help cure it. Virtually next door is **Adelaide Convention Centre**, which was the first of its kind in Australia, and hosts sporting events and exhibitions as well as conventions for up to 3500 people.

Strike west now along North Terrace for about 1 km until it ends at its junction with West Terrace. It is worth just making this walk to take in the sweep of Adelaide's finest boulevard with

Everyone loves a parade.

its stately buildings on your left, and acres of greenery on your right. Adelaide is surrounded by great swathes of parkland on all four sides. You could be forgiven for thinking the good Colonel Light had joggers in mind when he laid the city out. Flat and delightfully green, Adelaide is a fitness freak's paradise.

Having made the walk, you'll find yourself outside the fine 1884 Newmarket Hotel, on the southern side of the Terrace. The hotel incidentally features a magnificent free-standing open stairway. Opposite and in the parklands to the northwest of the end of North Terrace don't miss **Adelaide Gaol** complete with hanging tower. Now almost 150 years old, the gaol is a splendid piece of 19th-century architecture and

was in use up until 1988. Return to North Terrace, and retrace your steps along the south side of the Terrace taking time to call in at the **Living Arts Centre** at the junction with Morphett Street, which is the home of Adelaide's biennial Festival Fringe and occupies the site of old factories. On the opposite corner is the state's oldest Anglican church, the **Holy Trinity**. The tower houses the original 1836 clock shipped out from London.

Turn right here off North Terrace into Morphett Street, then left into **Hindley Street**, itself a magnificent thoroughfare and home to many of Adelaide's finest restaurants and liveliest nightspots. Walk eastwards to King William Street (a couple of hundred metres) and turn right into it. On the corner of Hindley and King William you will find **Edmund Wright House**, named after the architect who built it in 1876 for the Bishop of South Australia.

Now the office of Births, Deaths and Marriages, it features some splendid decoration, especially the ceiling of the entrance foyer, and there is a musical performance staged here every Wednesday lunchtime. Walk on south down King William, past the 1867 **General Post Office**, with its clock reckoned to be the Australia's most accurate GPO clock.

This brings you into **Victoria Square**, incidentally the terminus for the quaint 1929 tramway which will take you down to the beach at **Glenelg** in about 30 minutes.

On the south of Victoria Square is the 1869 **Supreme Court**, built of local sandstone. Rounding the square and walking north again up the other side you can't miss the **Cathedral Church of St Francis Xavier**, built in stages between 1858 and 1926 and the centre of Adelaide's Catholic life. It holds five masses daily.

Walking north a few metres back into King William Street , pay a visit to

Geometrics in the Square.

the **Telecommunications Museum** on the corner of the Square.

Nearby is the **Old Treasury**, on the corner of Flinders and King William Streets. Bits of this building date right back to 1839 – about as far as you can go in South Australia. The Old Treasury houses a unique collection of drafting and surveying equipment, and is dedicated to the exploration and settlement of South Australia. Then stroll on a few metres up King William Street to see another expression of civic pride, the **Town Hall**. It's reminiscent of civic buildings in Genoa and Florence, and was designed in 1859 largely by Edmund Wright, who was not only an architect but was also mayor of Adelaide. Much of the soul of the city is to be found on display here in the **Queen Adelaide Room** and the **Colonel William Light Room**. These rooms contain, respectively, memorabilia of the Queen after whom the city is named and the Surveyor-General to whom it owes its uncompromising design.

Shops, Culture & Car Racing

Walking on as far as Grenfell Street, you find yourself in the heart of Adelaide's **shopping district**. It is a distinct area, bounded by Grenfell in the south, North Terrace in the north and King William and Pulteney Streets to the west and east respectively.

Rundle Mall forms its central pedestrian artery, running from King William Street to Pulteney, and there are a dozen or more arcades and complexes clustered here, catering to every imaginable shopping taste.

If you're not too loaded down with purchases by then, and still have some energy left, stroll east along Grenfell for about half-a-kilometre to the **Tandanya Aboriginal Cultural Institute**. This is the first major Aboriginal cultural centre of its kind and scale in Australia, and has a performing arts gallery, arts and crafts workshops and other facilities. It is owned and managed by Aboriginal people. Incongruously enough, this living testimony to an ancient culture is right on the edge of the distinctly 20th-

century motor racing circuit of the annual **Adelaide Grand Prix**, which twists through a number of streets here on the edge of the city proper. For those interested in other sorts of racing, they will find that the horse-racing course at **Victoria Park** is also only about a kilometre from Tandanya, just off Wakefield Road. You can find that by following the zigzag of **East Terrace** southwards and turning left onto **Wakefield**.

To continue our original walking circuit, however, go northwards up East Terrace on leaving Tandanya and after maybe 200 m this will lead you back into North Terrace. If it's that time of day, this is a good point for a rest, for at 288 North Terrace is **Ayers House**, the state headquarters of the National Trust which also houses two fine restaurants.

The house took nearly 30 years to build, starting in 1846, and was the home of Sir Henry Ayers, seven times premier of South Australia, who also gave his name to Ayers Rock (now Uluru). It's open from 10 am to 4 pm Tuesdays to Fridays and in the afternoons on weekends.

Bounding the Terrace on the far side of the road (that is, the northern side) is the **Botanic Gardens** founded in 1855, adjacent to the grounds of the University of Adelaide.

The Gardens boast the largest **conservatory** in the Southern Hemisphere, with 4000 plants and even a miniature rainforest. There is a small entry fee for the conservatory. If Adelaide's parklands are the emeralds in the city's crown,

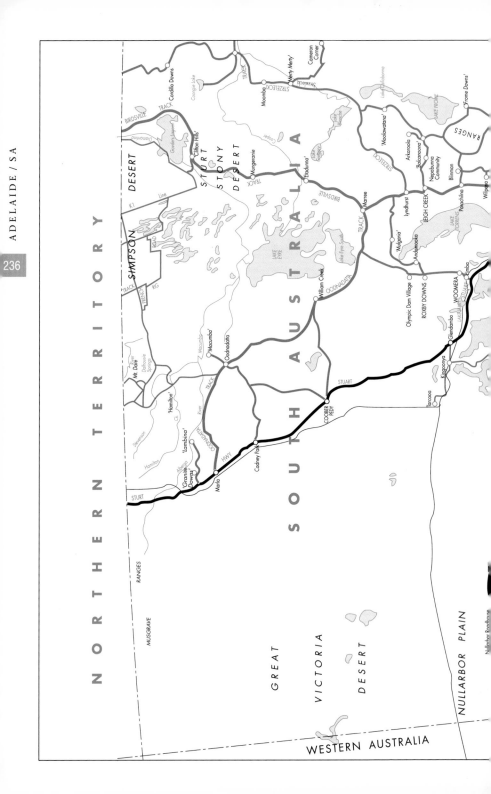

NORTHERN TERRITORY

SOUTH AUSTRALIA

SIMPSON DESERT

STURT STONY DESERT

STURT STONY DESERT

GREAT VICTORIA DESERT

NULLARBOR PLAIN

WESTERN AUSTRALIA

RANGES

MUSGRAVE RANGES

Cameron Corner

'Merty Merty'

Moomba

STRZELECKI

Strzelecki

Lake Blanche

Lake Frome

FROME RANGES

'Frome Downs'

Cordillo Downs

Goongie Lake

BIRDSVILLE TRACK

Diamantina

Goyders Lagoon

'Clifton Hills'

Mungeranie

Cooper

'Moolawatana'

Arkaroola

'Balcanoona'

Nepabunna Community

Blinman

Parachilna

STRZELECKI

Line

K1

Etadunna'

BIRDSVILLE TRACK

Marree

LEIGH CREEK

Lyndhurst

'Mulgaria'

Andamooka

LAKE TORRENS

TRACK

Lake Eyre

Lake Eyre South

William Creek

OODNADATTA

RAIG

RIG

TRENCH TRACK

Mt. Dare

Dalhousie Springs

Hamilton

River

Stevenson

Hamilton Cr.

'Macumba'

Macumba

Oodnadatta

RIVER

OODNADATTA TRACK

OODNADATTA

'Lambina'

'Granite Downs'

Alberga

Marla

STURT

Cadney Park

HWY

STUART

COOBER PEDY

Olympic Dam Village

ROXBY DOWNS

WOOMERA

Glendambo

Kingoonya

Tarcoola

Nullarbor Roadhouse

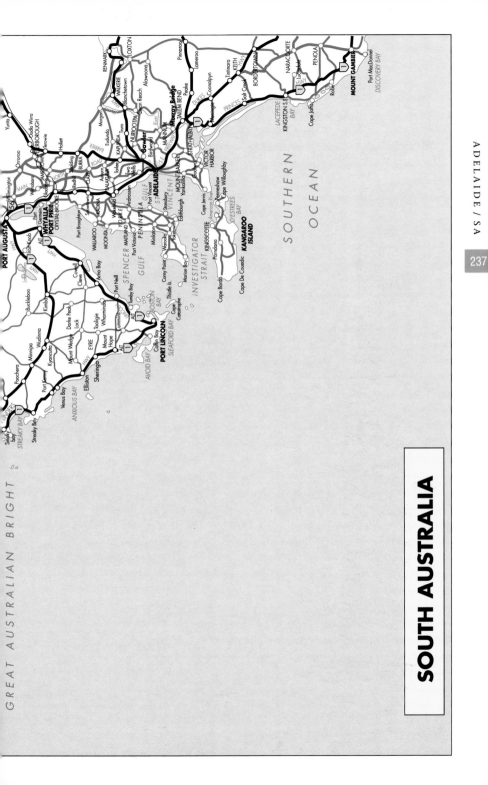

SOUTH AUSTRALIA

GREAT AUSTRALIAN BRIGHT

STREAKY BAY
Smoky Bay
Streaky Bay
Poochera
Venus Bay
Minnipa
Wudinna
Kyancutta
Port Kenny
Mount Wedge
Darke Peak
Lock
Toolligie
Mount Hope
Sheringa
Elliston
ANXIOUS BAY
EYRE
Cummins
AII
HWY
Wharminda
Tumby Bay
AII
Coffin Bay
PORT LINCOLN
AVOID BAY
SEAFORD BAY
Cape Catastrophe
BOSTON BAY
Cape Wanna
Thistle Is.
Corny Point
Marion Bay
Warooka
INVESTIGATOR STRAIT
Pondana
KINGSCOTE
KANGAROO ISLAND
Cape Borda
Cape De Couedic
Cape Gantheaume
D'ESTREES BAY
Penneshaw
Cape Willoughby
American River
Edithburgh
Minlaton
Port Victoria
MAITLAND
YORKE
Port Broughton
WALLAROO
MOONTA
Ardrossan
Yorketown
Stansbury
MOUNT BARKER
Cape Jervis
Normanville
VICTOR HARBOR
Goolwa
Delamere
STRATHALBYN
FLEEUR
MANNUM
Meningie
PRINCES
Coonalpyn
Tintinara
KEITH
BORDERTOWN
Port MacDonnell
DISCOVERY BAY
MOUNT GAMBIER
PENOLA
Robe
Cape Jaffa
KINGSTON S.E.
LACEPEDE BAY
NARACOORTE
Lucindale
Padthaway
Salt Creek
Kingston
Yunta
Oodla Wirra
Orroroo
PETERBOROUGH
Terowie
Hallett
BURRA
MAIN
Wirrabara
Melrose
Wilmington
NORTH
561
Port Germein
Port Pirie
WHYALLA
PORT PIRIE
Iron Knob
Iron Baron
MAIN
HWY
PORT AUGUSTA
LINCOLN HWY
Kimba
Buckleboo
Cleve
Cowell
Arno Bay
Port Neill
CRYSTAL BROOK
Gladstone
Reding
Auburn
Clare
STATE
Balaklava
Snowtown
Kadina
Maitland
MID NORTH
Blyth
Owen
Two Wells
Tarlee
Kapunda
Freeling
Gawler
Birdwood
Nuriootpa
TANUNDA
Truro
Eudunda
Morgan
Swan Reach
MURRAY BRIDGE
TAILEM BEND
DUKES
Pinnaroo
Lameroo
Alawoona
Peake
Blanchetown
WAIKERIE
WALKERIE
Berri
BARMERA
RENMARK
LOXTON
SPENCER GULF
GULF ST VINCENT
PENINSULA
YORKE PENINSULA
ADELAIDE
Gawler
Two Wells
Port Vincent

SOUTHERN OCEAN

Ayers House, once home to Sir Henry Ayers, former premier of South Australia, whose name is given to the famous rock.

then the Gardens constitute the jewel of them all, with spectacular views, heritage buildings, and a fine licensed restaurant. They are open daily "sunrise to sunset" with free guided tours at 10.30 am on every Tuesday and Friday (except Good Friday).

Museum Mania

Rejoin North Terrace and follow it westwards. Along its northern side, museum maniacs will find what they've been looking for. There is a **Museum of Clas-**

sical Archaeology in the **Mitchell Building**, within the grounds of Adelaide University between North Terrace and Frome Road. Also within the University (in the **Union Building**) is the **Union Gallery** with shows of contemporary art, jewellery and ceramics. Cross Frome Road and continue towards the city centre along North Terrace. Within a few hundred metres you will find the **South Australian Museum**, the **Art Gallery of South Australia**, the fine concert venue **Elder Hall**, and just off the Terrace, the **South Australian Police Museum**. This is in the old barracks of the mounted police, built in 1851 (open weekday afternoons only). If you want a break from all of this, cross over North Terrace to view the second oldest church in the city, **Scots Church**, at number 237. It has some fine stained glass, and its original organ from the 1850s.

Back on the northern side of the road, the corner of Kintore Avenue and North Terrace is guarded by the **National Soldiers' War Memorial** sculpture, commemorating the fallen of WW I. On this corner is another clutch of buildings for culture vultures. There is the **Royal South Australian Society of Arts** with permanent and special interest fine arts exhibitions. Nearby is the white marble **State Library**, with the fine old **Mortlock Library** with some fascinating exhibits of books, writing materials and memorabilia of old Adelaide (but closed Wednesdays and Sundays). Turn right up Kintore for a "must

see" museum – the **Migration Museum** at number 82, in the restored remnants of **Adelaide's Destitute Asylum**. It tells the story of the people who came to found this distant colony. It's open from l0 am to 5 pm during the week but on weekends in the afternoon only.

Stroll back down to North Terrace, turn right and walk a few metres to the junction with King William Road. You are now immediately opposite your starting point at the Travel Centre. On this corner you will find the grand 1838 **Government House**, the earliest surviving regency building in Adelaide, which offers tours of the splendid gardens. Next to it are the **Prince Henry Gardens**, with plaques set in the footpath to commemorate key contributors to South Australian progress.

Opposite this tranquil garden scene is the modern **Festival Centre** on King William Street which seats up to 4000 during the city's Festival of Arts held in March of every even-numbered year. This is Adelaide's big event, and has led to the state's soubriquet "the Festival State" (you'll see that on car number plates). No visit to Adelaide is complete without a stroll around the Festival Centre, even if it isn't festival month. There are theatres, concert halls and open-air performing areas – often in use – as well as cafés and bistros overlooking the river.

North Adelaide

Determined walkers from the city can

St Peter's Cathedral, housing the heaviest and finest bells in the southern hemisphere.

continue north up King William Road from the Festival Centre and through **Elder Park** (there are 20-minute boat-trips up the Torrens to the **Adelaide Zoo** from here on the *Popeye Launch*). This route will take you across the Torrens, past Light's Vision on Montiefiore Hill

to the left, and past **Adelaide Oval** – probably the prettiest cricket ground and sporting venue in the country. This brings you to the doors of **St Peter's Cathedral.** A grand church, it took seven years to build in the 1870s, and today boasts two soaring spires and the heavi-

Outside the Maritime Museum, one of the numerous
museums to be found in this city.

must is the South Australian **Maritime Museum** in Lipson Street. Here a small but splendidly evocative exhibition transports you into the cramped berth of a migrant windjammer heaving its way from England to the new world Down Under. Try to imagine undergoing months of danger and hardship, only to be faced on arrival with the task of settling this dry and unforgiving land, so very different from home. The Museum displays one of the best collections of maritime artifacts in Australia, including historic vessels moored at the wharf, an 1869 lighthouse and several restored buildings (it's closed on Thurs-

est and finest bells in the Southern Hemisphere. The largest weighs seven tons.

Golfers will find three fine courses in North Adelaide, and there is a major tennis court complex on the north bank of the Torrens off War Memorial Drive. Out the other side of North Adelaide on Jeffcott Road is the **Adelaide Aquatic Centre**, with a variety of leisure pools as well as standard facilities for the serious swimmer and diver (tel: 08-344-4411). There's good shopping in North Adelaide too, with the old world charm of Melbourne Street a special attraction.

You'll need to drive for 25 minutes out to the northwest to visit **Port Adelaide**, but it's worth it. One

Naval exhibits inside the Maritime Museum.

There are 7 distinct wine-growing areas within in a few hours' drive of Adelaide.

days and Fridays, though, except during school holidays).

Indeed **Port Adelaide** itself and the whole port area reeks of history. There are some wonderful old Victorian buildings, antique shops with nautical knick knacks, wooden quays and fascinating old ships – and some fine restaurants, too. You can tour the old port by horsedrawn carriage, or cruise the blue waters on the 1919 ketch *Falie* or on the *Captain Proud* luxury paddle cruiser. There is also an aviation museum, a railway museum with 26 locos and two operating steam trains, a glassworks, a fresh fish market, an art gallery and the 1855 Port Dock Brewery Hotel on Todd Street – still very much in the business of selling beer.

Best reached by tram, the seaside suburb of **Glenelg** – try spelling it backwards – has a special attraction in the form of its **Old Gum Tree**. At Glenelg in 1836 the proclamation establishing the new settlement of South Australia was read in the shade of a tree which, although long-dead, is still standing. Nearby are two cannons from *HMS Buffalo*, the ship that brought the proclamation party to the site. There is a re-enactment every year on 28 December. *HMS Buffalo* herself has been lovingly rebuilt to the original admiralty plans at a cost of A$1.5 million. She is moored beside **Adelphi Terrace**, and houses a splendid collection of curios, logbooks and photographs. Nearby is an aquarium and a good restaurant.

Glenelg is a pretty seaside suburb with a fine beach, picnic areas and barbecues, and is particularly popular with the children. There is also **Shell Land**, at the corner of Mary and Melbourne Streets, with an international collection of shells on show and shell jewellery for sale.

Hard Times on Kangaroo Island

Offshore in St Vincents Bay is **Kangaroo Island**. You can reach it by ferry from Port Adelaide or from Cape Jervis down the Main South Road from Adelaide city, or fly to one of three airfields on the island. Don't be fooled by the map into thinking it's a small place. It just looks that way because South Australia is so huge. In fact Kangaroo Island is well over 150 km long. But it is a wonderful place to visit if you have the time, especially if you are interested in history.

The story of the island reveals that South Australian life was not always God-fearing. Sealers, shipwrecked sailors, mutineers, escaped convicts and other rogues long occupied Kangaroo Island. Seals, once counted in millions

especially in the migratory season, were quickly wiped out with brutality. That put paid to the sealers' livelihood, but Kangaroo Island then became a settlement of cut-throats who lived for piracy and violent crime. Many lived with Aboriginal women they enslaved after murdering the menfolk. Take pity on honest seafarers who, shipwrecked on this rocky coast, swam ashore only to be confronted by these heartless brigands.

A hint of Kangaroo Island's colourful past is given by some of the place names still in use – Seal Bay, Devil's Kitchen, Pelican Lagoon and American River. Today it makes for an excellent (and thankfully more peaceful) stay with lots to see – seals, sea lions, fairy penguins and of course kangaroos. Visitors can explore caves, go on camel-back safaris, fish from the rocks, or simply collect seashells from the shore. The stout-hearted can even spend an eerie night in an old lighthouse keeper's cottage.

The Wine Country

Within a few hours' drive of Adelaide there are seven distinct wine-growing regions: Barossa Valley, Clare Valley, Riverland, Adelaide Hills and Plains,

Little Germany in the Barossa Valley north of Adelaide,
especially at Schuetzenfest.

Murraylands, McLaren Vale and the Wine Coast and Coonawarra and the South-East. An eighth area, Eyre Peninsula, is several hundred kilometres further to the west. It would be impossible to visit all of these on anything but a major tour, but it is worth glancing here at some of the charming winegrowing areas within reach of Adelaide.

Perhaps the **Barossa Valley** wineries are no better than hundreds in the other regions, but the quaintness and colour of the Barossa, a fascinating little bit of Germany set in verdant valleys only 50

Rolling landscape of the Murray River valley.

ern tip of the Valley, complete with singing birds, a barrel piano, and even an 1840s musical church. Move on to **Tanunda** in the heart of the Valley where the **Kev Rohrlach Museum** is worth a visit: it houses everything from battle-axes to speedcars. The Barossa Valley is a must for everyone who has time. But perhaps you should spare a little time for some of the other winelands too.

The next obvious stop is the **Clare Valley**. **Kapunda**, some 20 km north of

km north of Adelaide, give it that extra touch. If you're driving, first take the road through **Gawler** and on the outskirts look hard, very hard, for a small sign almost hiding the way to the Barossa Valley. Your perseverance will be well rewarded. Soon you will be wondering whether this isn't really part of the Rhine. The towns and villages with coffee shops, bakeries and pastry shops – many with German signs – will make you feel like breaking into the *Drinking Song from The Student Prince*. And there is some drinking to be done, unless you are driving of course.

In the Australian tradition, you can sample wines at dozens of vineyards and wineries throughout the region, and buy only if you feel like it. Apart from drinking in the atmosphere and the wine, you should also try a splendid German-style meal. After that, by way of a change, head for the **Mechanical Music Museum** at **Lyndoch** at the south-

Hahndorf – a German enclave.

Visits to the wine country often give the opportunity to sip wine in the tasting rooms.

Gawler, was once a thriving copper-mining town which still retains some interesting streets and a large statue of a Cornish miner. If it's the history of the region which really catches your fancy, then drive an extra 60 km from Kapunda to **Mintaro**. There are a number of slate, stone and timber buildings here which are over 130 years old (old indeed for this part of Australia) and have been declared historic treasures.

On the other side of Adelaide, to the southeast, is **Hahndorf** in Adelaide's hinterland among the Southern Vales wine district. To get there from the state capital take the South Eastern Freeway for about 25 km to Mt Barker then turn northwest for 5 km on a local road. Here in Hahndorf you will find traditional German sausages and cuckoo clocks, arts and crafts, and a wonderful collection of Hans Heysen's Australian paintings at the local art gallery. Then head back on to the same road for 5 km to **Bridgewater** to inspect the old flour mill and restored water wheel.

Depending on how much time you have, it can be a worthwhile trip indeed to visit the Murraylands and Strathalbyn. At **Strathalbyn**, an hour's drive south from Adelaide via Reynella, you can admire the colonial buildings that served as backdrop for the film *Picnic at Hanging Rock*, a haunting and beautifully filmed masterpiece of 1970s Australian cinema. Then cut southeast another 30 km to the state's original port of **Goolwa**, where the Murray River paddle wheelers and other vessels from upriver once discharged their cargoes of wool and grain. Drive around the **Fleurieu Peninsula** on the way back to Adelaide – the circuit from Goolwa is only about 100 km – and stop off to fish or bathe. The beaches are wonderful, there are spectacular landforms, and old mine-workings to explore at Talisker.

The **Heysen Walking Trail** starts from Cape Jervis, and stretches for hundreds of kilometres to the northern Flinders, but you don't have to walk that far to enjoy the beauties of the area. Then find your way back via **Hallett Cove**, just on the southern fringe

The Rotunda provides a pleasant stop for tired feet.

of Adelaide, and there, ponder the tracks left by glaciers that slowly inched their way into the sea 270 million years ago. The trip, though lengthy, offers frequent rest-stops at the wineries which dot the countryside. It's always a good idea to buy your wine at source. Wine tasting is an integral part of a tour of any of the South Australia winelands – and if you buy direct from the winery you know exactly what you are getting. Besides, you won't find them cheaper anywhere in Australia.

Most vineyards and wineries will sell by the bottle, and virtually all of them are set up to have wine freighted to your home, anywhere in the world. These practical considerations aside, nothing quite beats the atmosphere of sipping wine in a sun-flooded tasting room, overlooking the vineyards where the grape was grown. Buying a bottle or two is the best possible way of recapturing the experience long after you have come home.

Wine Festivals

Most of the wine regions have an an-

MFP – Adelaide: But What is it?

Adelaide has just won a glittering prize: the city has been selected as the site of the new Multi-Function Polis (MFP).

The proposed Australian-Japanese "city of the future" (known as the MFP) was up for grabs. Adelaide won it against stiff competition from Australia's supposedly more aggressive state capitals – including a strong challenge from Sydney. Admittedly the South Australian capital was second choice: Brisbane was offered the MFP first, but the Queensland Government couldn't or wouldn't bite the bullet when it came to resuming land for the massive project. Adelaide showed it was prepared to do whatever was necessary, so the MFP came south.

For Adelaide, it was a bit like being chosen as site for the next Olympics. Press releases went out, South Australian politicians crowed over their victory, a body called MFP-Adelaide was set up and glossy brochures issued.

The only fly in the ointment is that nobody quite seems to know what the MFP *is*. This is how MFP-Adelaide's brochure describes it:

"A unique form of urban development which brings together advanced technology and brainpower to help shape the world's future in an environment designed for living, working, and relaxing."

This doesn't help. Other literature isn't any more precise. It uses phrases like "strategic thinking", linking "technology" and "culture", and baldly declares that, whatever it is, the MFP is going to contribute "to the growth of the Pacific Rim and the greater world economy."

It's unkind to mock. At the very least the planners – and they include some very big names in Australia and Japan – have been prepared to boldly go where others fear to tread. And they are quite specific about the logistics behind the development. Pie in the sky it is not.

MFP-Adelaide will be built on 3500 hectares of land, a 20-minute drive northwest of Adelaide's central business district, and just 15 minutes from the airport. It will be developed over 15 or 20 years as a mosaic of "villages" separated by parks, lakes and forests, and eventually housing 100,000 people. A World University will be set up there. Several transnational technology companies (not just Japanese ones) have expressed a desire to be part of the project.

The MFP, so the planners say, will have a separate identity but will be integrated into the life of Adelaide – the population of which it will boost by over 10 percent. The "future-oriented industry groups" which will form its core have already been designated. For the record they are: education, information and telecommunications, health, leisure and entertainment, environment, construction and design, and advanced transport services.

Perhaps it is as it should be that no two people seem to be able to agree as to what form

nual "bash" where the bonhomie is infectious and participants eat, drink and make merry in the near-certain knowledge that tomorrow they'll regret it. With Germanic gusto the Barossa Valley stages no less than four annual festivals and another every second year, but other wine regions celebrate in style too.

Here is a sample of what is on offer on the festival calendar.

January – *Oom Pah Festival* gets the year under way in the Barossa Valley.

March – *The Essenfest*, a food festival, and the *Best of Barossa Banquet*, are both staged in the Barossa Valley.

March/April – The Barossa's biennial *Vintage Festival* is held in the week beginning on Easter Monday on uneven-numbered years.

May – The *Adelaide Cup* long weekend is always a cause for celebration in the state capital, and the *Gourmet Weekend*

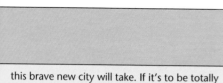

this brave new city will take. If it's to be totally new, after all, it should be hard to describe in terms of any existing city.

And it is worth pointing out that Adelaide, despite its reputation for conservatism and even for sleepiness, has shown in recent years an unexpected commitment to innovation and technology. It isn't all wineries and wheatfields nowadays.

Adelaide is, for example, the heart of some of Australia's most advanced defence and aerospace industries – and that is very advanced. Much of this grew out of the location at Woomera in South Australia after World War II of the Anglo-Australian rocket testing range. That attracted a range of international high-tech companies to the area and saw the Australian Government's Defence Science and Technology Organisation headquartered in the area. More recently, Adelaide was chosen as the site to build six brand-new Swedish-designed submarines for the Royal Australian Navy – a contract worth over US$3.5 billion.

Adelaide is experienced in handling big projects with a high-technology base. In the hands of its South Australian hosts, the MFP could just turn into something very special for Australia. If you want something to show your grandchildren, take a trip out to the wasteland and mangrove swamp where it's going to be built and take a few photos.

is held in the Clare Valley.

August – They are at it again in the Barossa Valley, with the *Classic Gourmet Weekend.*

September – If you haven't had enough by now, try the *Food and Wine Affair* at Stirling, in the Adelaide Hills about 25 km southeast of Adelaide.

October – The aptly named *Southern*

Indulgence Festival and the *Bushing Festival*, both at McLaren Vale and the Wine Coast.

October/November – Riverland's *Wine Festival* is a biennial event held in uneven years.

The Pioneers of South Australia

Many visitors content themselves with a wine tour of some kind, and it's certainly a pleasant way to see the richer country within reach of Adelaide. But, if time is available, the state has a great deal more to offer. Wine, although long an important industry, has only recently achieved its multimillion dollar status. The original settlers broke the land for wheat, or fenced it for sheep, or even fossicked in it for gems. Most of their activities were involved with obtaining or moving or selling these commodities, and the relics they left bear witness to their struggle to succeed in a hostile land. Let's take a tour around South Australia and stop off at some of the sights those pioneers have left.

The historic port of **Robe**, about 260 km south of Adelaide on the Princes Highway, has streets made especially wide to enable large horse-drawn wagons to turn with ease.

Some of the buildings, declared national treasures, are worth a visit, particularly the original police station and courthouse, the customs house and

Young helper out in opal country, which begins 600 km north of Adelaide.

telegraph station. It was here that the noted Australian poet Adam Lindsay Gordon, recuperating in one of the fine hotels following a bad fall from a horse, met and married the publican's niece. You can still lift a glass at the pub, the **Caledonian Inn**.

Chinese gold-diggers disembarked in Robe after their long voyage from Canton and immediately started the long overland trek to the Victorian gold-fields at Ballarat. Some, however, used their shovels to make an early fortune by digging wells along the route so they could sell water to their parched countrymen. Talking of water, move on towards **Beachport** some 50 km south of Robe.

Here, biblically named the **Pool of Siloam**, is a lake six times more salty than the sea. When you reach **Mt Gambier**, 80 km further south, you can sample the extraordinarily fresh water drawn from the **Blue Lake** in the crater of a 5000-year-old volcano. The lake supplies the town's water, too. Incidentally, halfway between Beachport and Mt Gambier, at **Millicent**, there is an extraordinary exhibit in the museum – a bicycle built for 35. It's not much to do with colonial history, but it's undeniably something you don't see every day!

Explore the Murray Country

Head due east out of Adelaide for about 150 km on the Sturt Highway, named after the man who first navigated the mighty Murray. Soon after crossing the great river you come to **Barmera**: nude bathing is allowed at **Pelican Point Beach**, if you're into that sort of thing, and nearby **Lake Bonney** was where Sir Donald Campbell made his water speed record attempt in 1964. However, in this small town it doesn't feel like much has happened since. Another 50 km takes you to pretty **Renmark**, with some old wineries, river cruises on the *MV Barrangul*, **Hardings Folklore Gallery**, and just a little further north some really fine views over the river from **Head-**ings **Cliff Lookout**.

For a shorter trip to the great river, come out of Adelaide and head due east for **Murray Bridge**, about 75 km down the Dukes Highway. This is a water-skiers haven, but there is also a **Butterfly House**, the **Murray River Fish Aquarium** and a **Puzzle Park** – which isn't just for kids.

About 25 km north of Murray Bridge on the Murray River at **Mannum**, the 1890s paddle steamer, *Marion* is anchored as a floating museum that tells the saga of the paddle wheelers on the inland waterways.

South Australia's opal country begins about 600 km north of Adelaide. The main opal fields are at **Andamooka**, about 60 km out from the former rocket testing range of **Woomera**, and at **Coober Pedy**, almost 300 km further north.

At Andamooka you will be flabbergasted to find a home made entirely of beer bottles (empty, of course). The heat is so intense in these regions – it can reach as much as 45°C – that whole populations live underground. Coober Pedy's shops, motels, church and even the museum are all deep in the relatively cool earth. If you're an opal fancier, toss a spade and a *kepi*, or cap, in the boot and head out for the *Opal Festival* in October.

One important tip when buying opals or any other stones, produce your passport to establish that you are a *bona fide* traveller and you will be spared the sales tax.

Perth / WA

253

The rugged coastline of Western Australia is rich in history. Portuguese and Dutch ships touched land here as early as the 16th century. When, as late as 1829, the British founded a city on the banks of a river they were to call the Swan, it was a river that the Dutch navigator Wilhelm de Vlamingh had first explored in 1697. That city was Perth, and today it is perhaps the most pleasant of Australia's state capitals.

Re-enactment of the quaint and old, at the Town Hall in Fremantle, Perth's port.

Much of Western Australia's wealth comes from its goldfields in and around Coolgardie and Kalgoorlie, but agriculture is a mainstay of its prosperity, with wheat and sheep farms concentrated in the southern part of the state.

In the north there are large mineral deposits, particularly of iron ore, around such places as Mt Tom Price.

Western Australia is the largest of

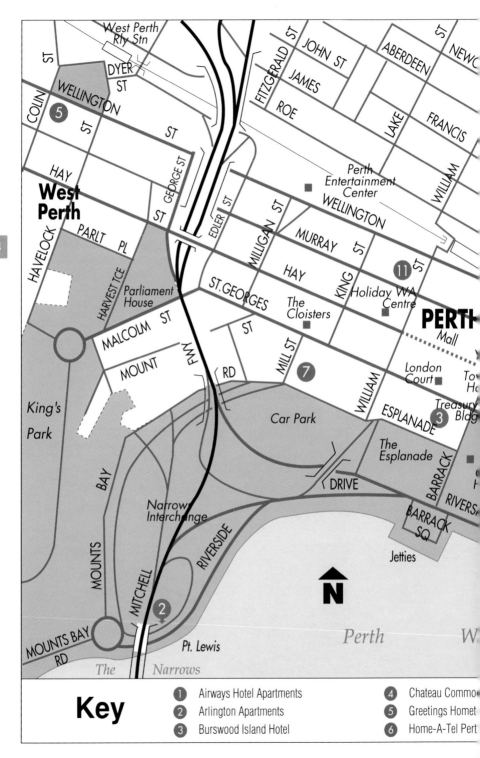

West Perth Rly Stn

ST

DYER ST

WELLINGTON

COLIN ST

5

ST

GEORGE ST

ST

HAY

West Perth

PARLT PL

HAVELOCK

HARVEST TCE

Parliament House

MALCOLM ST

MOUNT

FWY

King's Park

BAY

RD

MOUNTS

MITCHELL

RIVERSIDE

Narrows Interchange

2

MOUNTS BAY RD

The Narrows

Pt. Lewis

FITZGERALD ST

JOHN ST

JAMES

ROE

ABERDEEN

NEWC

ST

LAKE

FRANCIS

NEWG

WILLIAM

Perth Entertainment Center

WELLINGTON

EDLER ST

MILLIGAN ST

MURRAY ST

HAY

ST. GEORGES

The Cloisters

ST

MILL ST

7

Holiday Inn

KING ST

WA Centre

11

ST

PERTI

Mall

London Court

To H

WILLIAM

ESPLANADE

3

Treasury Bldg

The Esplanade

DRIVE

BARRACK

RIVERSI

BARRACK SQ

Car Park

Jetties

N

Perth W

Key

1. Airways Hotel Apartments
2. Arlington Apartments
3. Burswood Island Hotel

4. Chateau Commo
5. Greetings Homet
6. Home-A-Tel Pert

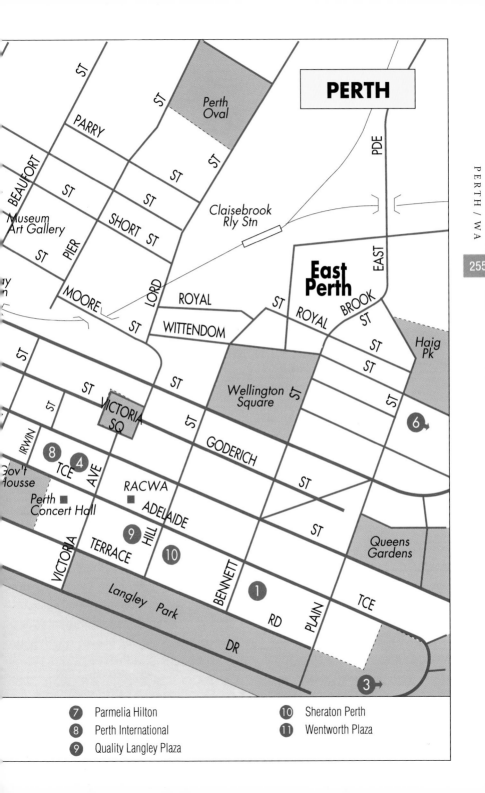

PERTH

255

Perth Oval

PDE

ST

PARRY

ST

ST

BEAUFORT

ST

ST

SHORT ST

Claisebrook Rly Stn

EAST

East Perth

Museum Art Gallery

PIER

ST

LORD

MOORE

ST

WITTENDOM

ROYAL

ST

ROYAL

BROOK

ST

Haig Pk

ST

ST

ST

ST

Wellington Square

ST

ST

6

VICTORIA SQ

ST

ST

GODERICH

ST

ST

IRWIN

ST

8

4

ST

AVE

RACWA

ADELAIDE

ST

ST

Queens Gardens

Gov't Housse

Perth Concert Hall

VICTORIA

TERRACE

9

HILL

10

BENNETT

1

TCE

Langley Park

RD

PLAIN

3

DR

7	Parmelia Hilton	10	Sheraton Perth
8	Perth International	11	Wentworth Plaza
9	Quality Langley Plaza		

Perth's pretty and proud of it.

Australia's six states, occupying almost half the continent. Its capital, on the coast of the Indian Ocean, in some ways stands apart from Australia's other major cities.

Perth is closer to Bali, Jakarta and Singapore than to Melbourne or Sydney. This helps make Perthites a little isolationist in their attitudes to the rest of the country, which they group together under the name "the Eastern States".

In fact, last-century Western Australia wanted to secede from the Commonwealth and go it alone.

Some residents still wish it had, believing they are treated as the "poor country cousin" of the more populous and wealthier states.

Proud And Pretty

Perth is a pretty city, and proud of it. It is clean, thanks to that same civic pride, and it is green, full of parks, gardens and tree-lined suburban streets. The air rolling in from the Indian Ocean or whipping up from the Swan River is fresh and cool, except during stifling high summer days in January and February where occasional daytime temperatures rise well above 40°C. It is also a friendly place where most locals go out of their way to help visitors enjoy their stay.

Although Perth has a small, almost rectangular city centre contained between the Swan River and the central railway station making it easy to find your way about, it is still worth collecting some tourist brochures from the **WA Tourist Centre**, 772 Hay Street (tel: 09-322-2999; fax: 481-0190, or call toll-free on 008-993-333 from anywhere in the country). The Centre is open from 8.30 am to 5.30 pm Mondays to Fridays, from 8.30 am to 4.45 pm on Saturdays and from 9 am to noon on Sundays. There are branch offices in other cities: in Sydney, at 92 Pitt Street, (tel: 02-233-4400); in Melbourne, at 35 Elizabeth Street, (tel: 03-614-6833); in Brisbane, at 243 Edward Street, (tel: 07-229-5794); and in Adelaide, at the corner of Grenfell and King William Streets, (tel: 08-212-1344). In any of these offices you will get all the help you need. You will learn there are five free **City Clipper** sightseeing buses which circle the inner city area and also take in the immediate suburbs, including the interesting ethnic dining area at **Northbridge**.

City Centre Walking

Start off by striking right across the city centre from the Tourist Centre. This involves emerging on Wellington Street, then leaving the railway station behind you to walk through **Forrest Chase**s **Shopping Precinct** until you hit **Murray Street Mall**, parallel to Murray on the far side of the Chase. Cross Murray Street, and then move from north to south (that is, towards the river). You will be heading for St Georges Terrace, and on

Walk right into ye olde tudor England (c. 1937!)

the way you will have to cross Hay Street Mall, parallel to Murray Street. This will take you through all of Perth's best shopping, and it will be surprising if you can manage to avoid making detours and doublebacks through the arcades and malls which crowd the area. Probably the best known of these is **London Court**, a charming arcade which appears to be a little bit of olde tudor England, but was actually built in 1937. It runs between St George Terrace and Hay Street in the centre of Perth, and is a marvellously imaginative open-air arcade of interesting little shops. But there are at least another score of shopping streets and malls and arcades crammed into this small square of Perth – Gledden, Piccadilly, Trinity, City and Wesley Arcades,

Perth is green, full of parks, gardens and tree-lined suburbs.

to name just a handful. While in the area it is worth making a detour along Hay Street for a couple of hundred metres westwards. Just past the junction with King Street is **His Majesty's Theatre** on the left. This wonderful theatre, built last century in traditional style, has recently been authentically restored. It is Perth's main venue for theatre, opera and ballet.

This is the heart of old Perth, and most of the city's historic buildings are within a short distance of here. Stroll down **The Cloisters** towards St Georges Terrace. The Cloisters and nearby **St George's Cathedral** were built in 1858. Turn left into the Terrace a little way and along on the righthand side of the street is **Government House** in its fine formal gardens. Completed in 1864, this official residence of the State Governor has Gothic arches and turrets a little reminiscent of the Tower of London. This is one of several interesting old buildings in St George Terrace, others including the **Deanery** built in the 1850s opposite Government House and one of the oldest houses still standing today. Another is the **Old Perth Boys School** at number 139 St Georges Terrace, which was Perth's first Government school and opened in 1854. It looks like a church, but in fact was always a school. Today it has been restored by the National Trust, and it serves as a gift shop, heritage centre and information bureau.

Set in the grounds of **Stirling Gardens** and almost adjoining Government House is the majestic **Supreme Court** building of 1897, and not far from here – also in St Georges Terrace – is the **Concert Hall.** Orchestral recitals, folk music and concerts are held at this venue. Walking through the Government House and **Supreme Court Gardens** brings you out on the Swan River frontage of the city, near **Barrack Street Jetty.** On the way through the Supreme Court Gardens you will pass the **Perth Music Shell**, the venue for outdoor summer concerts. Also in the Gardens is the **Francis Burt Law Museum**, which has a fascinating display of objects related to the history of law and lawmaking. It embodies the **Old Court House** of 1829.

A variety of ferries and cruises leave from Barrack Street jetty, but a popular one is the ferry ride to South Perth. On landing at the Mends Street jetty a five-minute walk takes you up to the **Zoological Gardens** in Labouchere Road.

Its garden setting is ideal for a wide variety of Australian and foreign animals, reptiles and birds. Or take a bus to the Zoo from the city centre. It is open daily from 10 am to 5 pm.

On returning to the Barrack Street jetty, turn right and follow the waterfront parkland along the **Swan River**, perhaps taking time to stroll in **Langley Park**, right on the water. Crossing the Park is Victoria Avenue, and you should walk back up into the city along the length of this thoroughfare until it ends in Victoria Square, with **St Marys Cathedral** set in the centre amid its own gardens. Off the eastern side of the square is Goderich Street, and just a few metres down this is **Perth Mint**, originally established in 1899 and open on weekdays and Saturday mornings. Retrace your steps into Victoria Square, cross it and on the far side Murray Street emerges, and leads back right into the shopping district south of the railway station, where you started out from.

Go right through it on Murray and out the other side. This time, turn right into William Street and cross the railway line. Just north of the line is Perth's magnificent **Western Australian Museum** complex.

The museum has a variety of exhibits from old cars and meteorites to wildlife displays, and is open from Monday to Thursday from 10.30 am to 4 pm and on Friday to Sunday from 1 pm to 5 pm. Among its many fascinating displays is the **Old Gaol**, a brilliant example of colonial architecture which has been painstakingly restored to give a glimpse into the less happy days of Perth's history.

The art gallery in Perth's impressive **Cultural Centre**, near the railway station in James Street and almost next door to the museum, has a well-tailored collection of Australian, European and Aboriginal art. The centre, which also has a good gift shop, is open daily from 10 am to 5 pm. Not strictly cultural, but fascinating nevertheless, is **Small World** in **Parliament Place**.

A miniature world of cars, trains, houses and lots of other little things to be enjoyed by all children under the age of 80! It is open from Sunday to Friday from 10 am to 5 pm and on Saturday from 2 pm to 5 pm. Follow James Street westwards until it is possible to cross back over the railway line again, and finish your walk at Perth's imposing **Entertainment Centre**. This large auditorium in Wellington Street hosts major productions like rock concerts, musical spectaculars and big-time basketball matches.

Perth's Arboreal Gem

The 400-hectare spread of mainly natural bushland which is today **Kings Park** is set on a hillside only a few minutes by road from the city centre. An energetic walker could manage it with no problems, following St Georges Terrace to the western end, then turning left towards the greenery. The views of the city and the hinterland from the Park are breathtaking. To the east, framed by the blue waters of the Swan River, are the tall buildings of the city of Perth while below, the gentle arc of the **Narrows Bridge** gracefully links the two sides of the river and provides a frontispiece for the full spread of orange-roofed suburbs that stretch almost as far as the eye can see.

Isolation from the rest of the wealthier states has not prevented Perth's development over the last decade.

Kings Park was declared inviolate by the city fathers of the previous century as an example of the type of land settled by the first pioneers from as early as 1829. This scrubland, dotted with trees, sets Perth apart from Australia's other major centres. The soil, fertilized only by fallen leaves and a not too generous rainfall, plays host to some 5 million visitors a year who thread their way along the pathways in this treasure house of wildflowers, including the magnificent red and green kangaroo paw, wild orchids, banksia trees and blackboys. A scene of such beauty, your natural inclination may be to pick a flower or two, but don't! First, it could be seen as desecration of a wonderful living memorial to yesteryear. Second, there is a hefty fine. Apart from the profusion of wildflowers, there is a garden of rare and endangered species, a botanic garden, and glasshouses bursting with colour. The park, which is open from 9 am to 7 pm has a restaurant, snack bar, information centre, picnic lawns and children's playgrounds. There are also barbecue areas.

The best time to visit Kings Park is in late September or early October, when summer's early warmth produces a vivid explosion of colour from the wildflowers and other indigenous plants. At this time Kings Park also hosts the *West Australia Wildflower Festival*.

Besides being dedicated to those Australians who gave their lives in war, the memorial within the Park commemorates the courage of the early settlers who faced not only the hazards of a strange and wild land, but the initial hostility of its earliest occupants too.

Keen-eyed visitors looking across at the Narrows Bridge from Kings Park may spot the sails of the **Old Mill** at the far end of the bridge, in the grand old suburb of South Perth. Built in 1835, it was Perth's original flour mill and today, faithfully restored, contains many fascinating relics of the pioneering days. An unusual monument for Australia, where windmills look curiously out of place, it is well worth a closer look.

State Emblem

You should see at close hand the state's emblem, the **black swan**, thought to be mythical creatures until the early explorers found they were very much alive and well.

Take a cab or a bus either to **Lake Monger** or **Hyde Park**, in the inner-city suburbs of **Leederville** and North Perth respectively.

At Lake Monger the swans take titbits of bread and cake from your hand, but take care, they might snap at you while you're snapping photos of them. If you're lucky you may see a stately mum convoying her clutch of newly hatched cygnets across the water.

Interestingly, cygnets are all white

The statue of Captain Fremantle.

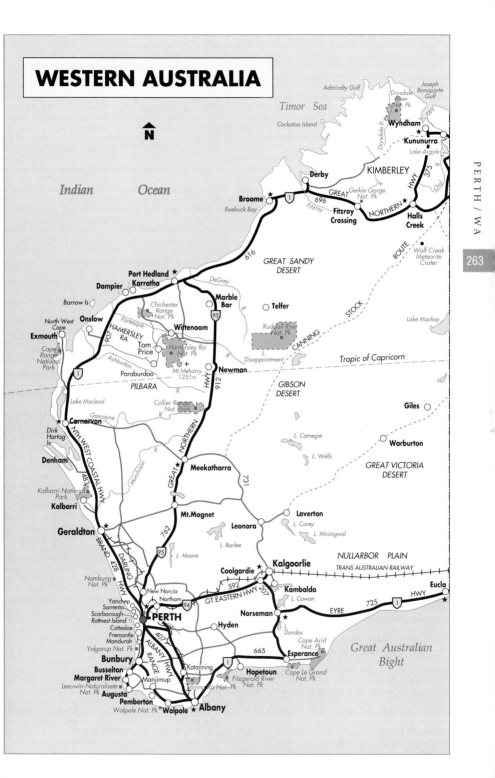

WESTERN AUSTRALIA

N

Indian   Ocean

Timor Sea

Admiralty Gulf

Joseph Bonaparte Gulf

Cockatoo Island

Drysdale River Nat. Pk

★ **Wyndham**

○ **Kununurra**

Lake Argyle

Drysdale R.

KIMBERLEY

Derby ●

GREAT *Geikie Gorge Nat. Pk*

Broome ★

Roebuck Bay

Fitzroy

Fitzroy Crossing

NORTHERN ★

Halls Creek

696

Wolf Creek Meteorite Crater

375

Ord

R

HWY

ROUTE

STOCK

616

GREAT SANDY DESERT

DeGrey

Port Hedland ★

Dampier

Karratha

Marble Bar ●

95

Telfer ○

Lake Mackay

Chichester Range Nat. Pk

North West Cape

Onslow ●

HAMERSLEY RA

Wittenoom ●

Fortescue

Ruddall River Nat. Pk

CANNING

Exmouth

Cape Range National Park

Tom Price

Hamersley Ra Nat. Park

Ashburton

Paraburdoo ●

+ *Mt.Meharry 1251m*

Newman ●

L. Disappointment

Tropic of Capricorn

907

R

HWY

912

PILBARA

Collier Range Nat. Park

R

Gascoyne

★ **Carnarvon**

GIBSON DESERT

Barrow Is ○

Lake Macleod

Dirk Hartog Is

Denham

483

Murchison

NTH WEST COASTAL HWY

NORTHERN

GREAT

★ **Meekatharra**

731

L. Camegie

L. Wells

Giles ○

Warburton ○

GREAT VICTORIA DESERT

Kalbarri National Park

Kalbarri

762

Mt.Magnet ●

95

Leonora ○

L. Barlee

Laverton ○

L. Carey

L. Miningwal

★ **Geraldton**

BRAND

DARLING

428

HWY

L. Moore

NULLARBOR   PLAIN

Coolgardie ★

Kalgoorlie ●

TRANS AUSTRALIAN RAILWAY

Nambung Nat. Pk

592

Kambalda ●

L. Cowan

Eucla ○

New Norcia

Northam

207

HWY

★

Yanchep

Sorrento

Scarborough

Rottnest Island

94

GT. EASTERN HWY

Norseman ●

L. Dundas

EYRE

725

HWY

1

PERTH

Cottesloe

Fremantle

Mandurah

Hyden ●

Cape Arid Nat. Pk

Great Australian Bight

Yalgorup Nat. Pk

ALBANY HWY

407

Cape Le Grand Nat. Pk

665

Esperance ●

Bunbury

Busselton

Margaret River

Manjimup

RANGE

Katanning

1

Hopetoun ●

Fitzgerald River Nat. Pk

Leeuwin-Naturaliste Nat. Park

Augusta

Pemberton

Stirling Ra Nat. Pk

Walpole Nat. Pk ★ **Walpole** ★ **Albany**

fluff and become jet black only as they mature. Hyde Park is worth a visit in its own right. There are many other species of wildfowl on its ornamental lake, and the trees of the park are especially beautiful in autumn.

PERTH / WA

Entertainment

It is estimated that Perth's population of 1.1 million or so have over 15000 restaurants to choose from. The variety is naturally bewildering, but it is especially worth looking out for fine Japanese cuisine, for which the local seafood is a key ingredient.

The Japanese have long been associated with the Western Australian coast because of the old pearl fisheries, and their culture appears to have taken root more firmly here than elsewhere in Australia.

Perth does of course have all the usual big city attractions associated with a wealthy lifestyle and international standing, but one deserves special mention.

The **Burswood Island Casino** is a short distance out of the city, off Great Eastern Highway in Victoria Park. The casino offers 24-hour action on its 110 gaming tables.

You can retire to one of the many restaurants and bars once you weary of the tables. It is closed on Christmas Day, Anzac Day and Good Friday. Even then there is plenty of action, for the resort complex includes a five-star hotel and a top-class golf course along with numerous other attractions.

Fremantle, Perth's Port

This quaint old city with a fishing village atmosphere is just 19 km down the Swan River from the capital and has scarcely changed in 150 years. Get there by car, bus, or – best – by train. But after arrival, it is best enjoyed on foot. As host to the 1986 America's Cup, Fremantle sprang temporarily into frenzied activity, but has subsequently quietly settled back into its olde world atmosphere. It wasn't always so.

Between 1942 and 1944 Fremantle was a base for British and American submarines operating in the Indian Ocean against the Japanese. Troopship convoys also anchored off Fremantle in the early days of the war to allow soldiers from New Zealand and "the Eastern States" a last leave on Australian soil before going into action in Greece, Syria and the Western Desert.

A replica of the ship Captain James Cook used to explore much of Australia's eastern coastline, the *Endeavour*, is on show at the **Fishing Boat Harbour**, facing the **Esplanade** and near the Museum. It provides a sobering insight into how small the vessels were that the great seafarers of yore used. The *Endeavour* is open daily from 10 am to 4 pm. Moving into our own century, the yacht that won for Australia the America's Cup, the *Australia II*, is on show at the

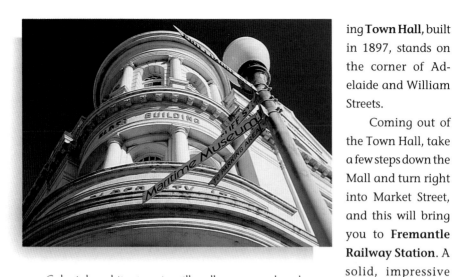

Colonial architecture is still well-preserved and appreciated by Perthites and visitors.

ing **Town Hall**, built in 1897, stands on the corner of Adelaide and William Streets.

Coming out of the Town Hall, take a few steps down the Mall and turn right into Market Street, and this will bring you to **Fremantle Railway Station**. A solid, impressive structure completed in 1907, it faces Phillimore Street and backs onto the waters of **Fremantle Harbour**. Cross back through the town centre to emerge on Marine Terrace, which runs along the ocean frontage of Fremantle. Here at number 16 you will find **Fremantle Gaol**, an even more solid building, built, ironically, by convicts between 1850 and

Sails of the Century exhibit in B Shed, Victoria Quay. Another famous yacht on view here is solo yachtsman Jon Sanders' *Parry Endeavour*. Viewing time is between 10 am and 4 pm daily.

Famous Old Buildings

The **Round House** was built at the west end of High Street in 1831 as a gaol, and is now the state's oldest building. Again, almost next door to the Museum, it offers excellent views of Fremantle from its lookout and is open daily from 10 am to 5 pm.

Moving inland a few metres up **High Street Mall**, the charm-

A famous old, the Round House in Fremantle.

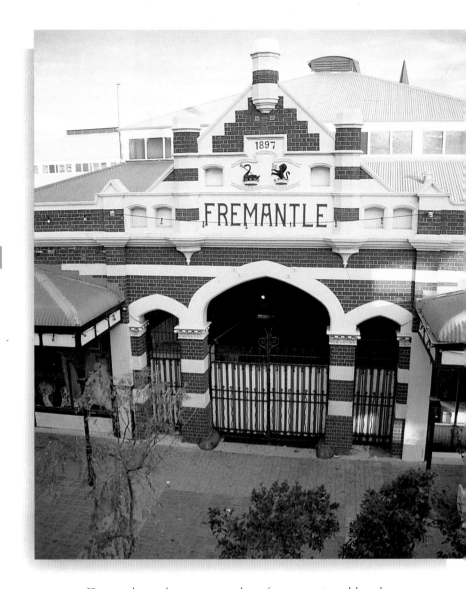

Fremantle market, a great place for souvenirs, old and new.

1858. For visiting hours, consult the chief warder as it is still in use for its original purpose.

Fremantle Market is a likely place to snap up an unusual souvenir or antique. A great variety of stalls offer an even greater variety of treasures, old and new.

On the corner of South Terrace and Henderson Street a few metres back from the sea, it is open from 9 am to 9 pm on Fridays. Saturdays' opening hours are from 9 am to 5 pm and Sundays' are from 11 am to 5 pm.

Rottnest, a holiday isle, a hop away from Perth.

Fresh Seafood Treats

On the **Fremantle Esplanade** and close to the **Maritime Museum**, **Fishing Boat Harbour** is where to eat fresh seafood cooked while you wait. At weekends you can also tap your feet to the sound of jazz bands. Another option is to get fish and chips wrapped in newsprint and enjoy the fresh air in the nearby park.

Just back from the water is the **Port Authority** building in Cliff Street: visit the observation tower there for an overview of the harbour and its workings. There are tours every hour from Monday to Friday starting at 9.30 am. Live freshwater and saltwater crocs from West Australia's Kimberley region can also be seen in Fremantle, though thankfully not in the wild. The saltwater ones are the man-eaters, while the freshwater species is supposed to be human-friendly, but who is going to put it to the test?

Fremantle Crocodile Park is situated a little further out of the centre in Mews Road, and it is open daily from 10 am to 5 pm. It boasts the **Hard Croc Cafe** for anyone who finds that watching man-eaters gives them an appetite.

And a Little Out of Perth...

A tour with a difference is a 19-km trip by sea from Perth to **Rottnest Island** to see the quokkas, rodent-like mammals which the Dutch navigators of 350 years ago mistook for rats. Of course Rottnest has much more to offer – beaches, seafood and a very relaxing holiday atmosphere. Landlubbers can catch a plane there and back.

Back on the mainland **Gallop House** is a gracious colonial home in **Birdwood Parade**, in the suburb of **Nedlands** near the **University of Western Australia** and below **Kings Park**. The University is well worth a visit in its own right, incidentally, with splendid grounds and outdoor auditorium venues for the annual *Festival of Perth*.

Gallop House is beautifully refurnished in 1870s style by the National Trust. But remember, it is only open on Sunday afternoons. Call the Trust for more information (09-386-4363).

There is a winding waterfront walk from Nedlands to **Claremont**, and this will take you to **Claremont House**. It is a wonderful place to picnic beside the river. Then wander through this former school, built around 1860.

Situated in Victoria Avenue, Claremont, it is open on Wednesdays, Saturdays and Sundays from 2 pm to 5 pm. If the sight of all this wealth is giving you a thirst, arrange a visit to the **Swan Brewery**, at 25 Baile Road, Canning Vale.

Here at the home of Western Australia's famous beer, you can watch how Swan Lager and Emu Bitter are made, then enjoy a "cold one" on the house. Advance bookings must be made by calling (09) 350-0222.

Millionaires Aplenty

Perth seems to foster an entrepreneurial spirit that has spawned its own **Millionaires' Row**. You'll find it by heading south from Perth towards Fremantle. Turn off Stirling Highway at Crawley, just past the University of West Australia, and find your way to Jutland Parade and Victoria Avenue, Dalkeith, then move on to Peppermint Grove. It is hard to know which to drink in first – the palatial homes of the multi-millionaires or the beautiful bays of the Swan River, its blue waters lapping the hulls of sleek racing yachts and cabin cruisers. On the basis of recent corporate history, the beauties of the Swan River would seem to be more reliable!

Sport and Fun in the Sun

Perth is noted for its sporting activities, especially cricket in summer and Australian Rules football in winter. The near-city coastline is dotted with more than 30 splendid surfing beaches, two of the most notable being **Scarborough** and **Cottesloe**. Some advice for swimmers: don't swim outside the patrolled area marked by flags – there are some strong currents along this coast. If you are caught in a rip current or need help, hold up one arm vertically to signal to the lifesavers. Always swim with the group rather than go far on your own, and never swim after dark.

For racegoers there is Saturday and holiday **racing** at **Ascot** in the summer and **Belmont Park** in the winter. Harness racing fans will enjoy Friday night trotting races at Gloucester Park in East Perth.

Fixtures are also periodically staged at **Richmond Raceway** in East Fremantle. Form guides and full details appear in the sports pages of the daily papers. Speedcars and motorcycles send up showers of gravel and clouds of exhaust smoke as they roar round the showground speedway track at Claremont on Friday nights during spring and summer.

At **Cables Water Park**, Troode Street, Spearwood (just south of Fremantle) cable tow-ropes whiz waterskiers abound for the ultimate thrill on water. There is instant tuition available, and gear for beginners.

Visit the Wine Country

Take a pleasant day tour northeast from Perth through the historic towns of **Guildford** and **Midland Junction**, both well worth an inspection stop, to the lush **Swan Valley** on the upper reaches of the river. This is wine-and-food country with a list of delights for the weekend tripper. In Dale Road, **Middle Swan**, is one of Australia's most renowned vineyards and winery – **Houghton's** – where the cellars and their samples will bid you welcome. At Guildford try to see the historic **Rose and Crown Hotel** with its remarkable mini-museum and coach-horse stables. There's fine food and drink here, too. Other day tours can be taken to interesting pioneer farming centres such as **York, Toodyay** and **Northam**, all less than 100 km east of Perth. All three have historic buildings and imposing farm homesteads, while the road to Northam also takes you past El **Blanco Caballo** with performing white horses.

Underwater Encounters

A pleasant drive due north of about 50 km from Perth on Wanneroo Road leads to **Yanchep**, where the national park has fascinating crystal caves as well as koalas, emus, kangaroos and black swans.

En route drop in on the **Gumnut Factory** and **Pioneer Town** in Prindiville Drive, Wanneroo, to see glimpses of old Australia as well as many hand-crafted souvenirs. It is open daily from 9 am to 5 pm. After Wanneroo on the way back, turn off right to the **Underwater World** at **Sorrento Beach**, where you can walk through undersea glass tunnels and meet face-to-face some of the 5000 marine creatures which live there.

Follow the coast road back, past such spectacular ocean swimming beaches as **Cottesloe**, where Prince Charles swims when he comes to Perth. This route in turn takes you over the Swan River and into Fremantle. Even more rewarding while heading north may be a visit to **New Norcia**, 140 km

Monkey Mia, 911 km north of Perth has attracted worldwide interest for its dolphin community.

inland up the Great Northern Highway. This remarkable mission was established in 1846 by Italian Benedictine monks to help the Aboriginals. The monks simply arrived, and wandered off into the bush to find their "lost sheep". The monastery is still run by the Benedictine Order and is very Italian in style, as is the abbey, while the museum contains works by Raphael, Titian and other old masters.

The whole settlement is an extraordinary tribute to the dedication of its iron-willed founders. It is still an orphanage with over 200 children calling it home.

New Norcia has a fine old hotel, walking tracks, and is surrounded by small country settlements and areas of great natural beauty.

Pearls, Dolphins – and Bombs

If you really hit the northern trail, it's unlikely you will want to miss **Monkey Mia.** Here the dolphins come right inshore to welcome you and can be patted as if they were family pets (though it's as well to use some caution). The phenomenon has attracted interest worldwide as probably the only example of wild dolphins "adopting" an entire human community. The dolphins are even known to drive schools of fish inshore for local anglers to catch. But it's a long way to go. Monkey Mia is 911 km north

Not exactly prepared for heavy traffic, the Shark Bay terminal.

of Perth on the coast in **Shark Bay**, just south of Carnarvon. Still, a trip there, if something of a major undertaking, can be combined with a tour of interesting coastal towns where the Portuguese and Dutch landed hundreds of years ago – long before the British. In the museum at **Geraldton**, for example, there are old cannons, coins, pottery and other relics of these often involuntary visits. Even further north is **Broome**. The story of Broome could have been written by Somer-

set Maugham. Once it was the pearling capital of the world, where Japanese, Koepangers and Malays dived for shell from hundreds of pearling luggers. But when Mr Mikimoto developed cultured pearls and Broome became a near-ghost town.

During WW II Broome was thought to be one of the safest places for flying-boats from the then Dutch East Indies to land planeloads of civilian refugees, but Japanese bombers caught some just as they alighted in **Roebuck Bay**.

More than 70 women and children lie buried in the cemetery. Ironically, not far away are the remains of Japanese pearl divers who died of the bends.

At low tide the remains of the flying boats can still be seen in the bay. Today Broome is enjoying a new lease of life thanks to an English peer, Lord Mac-Alpine, who has bought up much of the town and transformed it into a booming tourist resort.

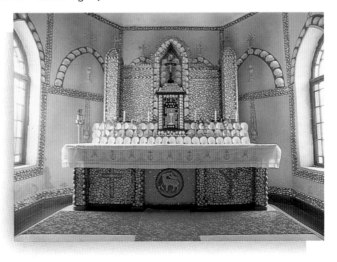

The altar at the Beagle Bay Mission, Broome.

Bad Luck for the *Batavia*

On a June morning more than 360 years ago the Dutch East India Company ship *Batavia* struck a low-lying reef and sank to the bottom. Of her 316 passengers and crew only 124 were to survive the catastrophe and the mutiny and murder which followed it.

Today, it is hard to imagine the scope of such a disaster. For these Dutch seafarers were about as far from help and from home as it was possible to be. They were in among the Abrolhos Islands off what is now Geraldton in Western Australia. Captain Cook was not to "discover" the eastern coast of Australia for another one-and-a-half centuries. And the vast and apparently empty western shore of Terra Incognita was not settled by Europeans until well into the 19th century. Yet the Dutch sailed these dangerous waters in some strength during the 17th and 18th century. They were there in sufficient numbers, indeed, to lose other great ships along this coast: the *Vergulde Draeck* in 1656, the *Zuytdorp* in 1712 and the *Zeewijk* in 1727.

There were other ships wrecked along this treacherous shore, including the British *Tryal* (1622), and well into modern times the Abrolhos group has continued to claim victims. A Greek oil tanker narrowly escaped her doom there as recently as July 1991. But it is the old pre-settlement wrecks which are of special interest to the archaeologists and researchers of the Western Australian Maritime Museum in Fremantle. Painstaking research in Dutch archives

during the 1950s and 1960s and years of searching the seabed pinpointed the location of these wrecks. Archaeologists and conservation specialists have been working on them ever since.

The *Batavia* has yielded most secrets so far. Marine archaeologists have recovered more than 30 tonnes of her original timbers – about one-sixth of the ship's hull. After years of treatment and restoration the stern of the *Batavia* is being assembled in the Museum to form a unique and fascinating exhibit. It is the first project of its kind anywhere in the world involving a 17th-century Dutch ship.

There is a wealth of other shipwreck material on display: coins, cannon, navigation equipment, fittings and personal effects from the Dutch wrecks and from other foundered vessels. All this is backed up by a comprehensive video and published material. Taken together, it is the only collection in Australia to tell the story of European contact with the island continent in the 150 years before Captain Cook. For Australians and visitors alike it is a unique spyhole into a more remote past.

Find the Museum at the corner of Cliff Street and Marine Terrace in Fremantle, just outside Perth. But don't get confused. The Western Australian Museum now has four separate properties in Fremantle alone, each with its own particular slant on history.

They are all worth a visit. But for a special experience, don't miss the *Batavia*.

And Going South...

Heading in the opposite direction take the coast road through Fremantle down to **Rockingham**, 40 km south of Perth. **Rockingham Museum** is on the corner of Kent Street and Flinders Lane, and houses a mini-submarine used by Australian "Z" Force special agents to sabotage shipping in Japanese-held wartime ports. The museum has other memorabilia from the district as well, and is open from 1 pm to 4.30 pm daily, except Mondays. Or, for a less warlike Rockingham adventure, take the ferry to **Penguin Island** to see the fairy penguins from March to December. Other birdlife is also spectacular and don't forget your swimming gear.

On the way back, call in at **Adventure World**, **Bibra Lake**, not far south of Fremantle. This offers rides, native animals, waterways and various other

The pensive Pinnacles, near Mt Augustus, the largest rock in the world.

activities especially aimed at entertaining the kids. It's open from mid-November to late April from 10 am to 5 pm.

For inquiries call them on (09) 417-9666. It's possible to cut inland from here down Forrest Road for 20 km or so, which will bring you out on the South-western Highway at **Armadale**.

This picturesque hillside township is a pleasure to visit in its own right, and features attractions such as **Pioneer World** and a quaint **Elizabethan Village**. The **Cohunu Wildlife Sanctuary** is off the main road near **Gosnells** on the way back.

Rocks Around the Clock

Anyone who has the time to extend their southward exploration should not miss the unique rock formations just out of the wheat-farming town of **Hyden**, 350 km south east of Perth.

Wave Rock, 50 m high, appears to be a gigantic wave frozen by time and is estimated to be two-and-a-half million years old. In the same district there are other unusual rock formations known descriptively as the **Hippo's Yawn** and **The Humps**.

Town Hall of Kalgoorlie, in the gold mining district.

POST AND TELEGRAPH OFFICE

You should also make the extra trip along to **Bates' Cave**, erstwhile hiding place of an Aboriginal cannibal and murderer called "Mulka the Terrible", whose victims purportedly included his mother. There are other natural formations 200 km north of Perth in the **Nambung National Park**.

The Pinnacles, limestone pillars up to six metres high, are the fossilised remains of an ancient forest. And further still **Mt Augustus**, twice as large as Ayers Rock (Uluru) and the biggest rock in the world, is 1200 km north of Perth.

Gold Fever

West Australia's goldfields were once fabulous producers. The **"Golden Mile"** of Kalgoorlie-Boulder just oozes mining history. If you make this 595-km trip east from Perth there is a lot that is of interest.

Tours can be arranged to several adjacent mining ghost towns. Gold was first discovered in **Coolgardie** in 1892. Within five years it had a population of 25,000 in and around the town, 26 hotels, three breweries, seven newspapers and two stock exchanges. There's not much to show for all of this in Coolgardie today, though its history makes it a fascinating place to visit.

Kalgoorlie is an exception, and still thriving, helped by the fact that today it is an important stop-over on the **Indian Pacific Railroad** that links this vast continent from west to east.

277

The Northern Territory looks as if somebody once laid a set-square on a map of Australia, drew two vertical lines up to the northern coast and a horizontal one across the centre, then surveyed the three strokes and said, "that takes care of all that remote land – we'll call it the Northern Territory".

The Territory's south-north axis stretches roughly 1670 km from the northern border of South Australia to the shores of the Timor and Arafura Seas. It separates Queensland from Western Australia

Except for famous places of touristic pilgrimage, nothing can prepare you for the starkness of the desert.

by more than 1000 km from east to west. It is big, it is almost empty, and it is remote. Cattle have always been its main industry and some cattle stations are larger than entire European countries. Round-ups are often carried out by helicopter. The two main cities are Alice Springs in the south, and the port of Darwin in the north,

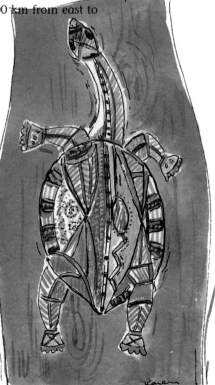

The beauty of Ayers Rock changes by the hour.

connected by 1500 km of the Stuart Highway, known locally as "the Track". In terms of human settlements, there's not much else bigger than a farmstead, and the entire population of the Territory would fit into Melbourne Cricket Ground and leave it 25 percent empty.

Before beginning your trip, pick up some pamphlets from the Northern Territory Tourist Bureau's offices. There are branches in Sydney (tel: 02-262-3744), Melbourne (tel: 03-670-5007), Brisbane (tel: 07-229-5799), Adelaide (tel: 08-212-1133) and in Perth (tel: 09-322-4255).

fishermen from the East Indies, long before the white man knew it existed. As it grew in this century it attracted adventurers, islanders from the Torres Strait, Japanese pearl-divers, Chinese traders, Papuans, Filipinos and others who liked the easygoing lifestyle and a drink or two to combat the heat. Add to this cocktail Aboriginal hunters and their womenfolk, and some British Empire-builders, and you've got Darwin.

In 1839 the natural harbour here was named Port Darwin by Captain J. Wickham of *HMS Beagle* in honour of one of the ship's earlier passengers, the naturalist and exponent of the Theory of Evolution, Charles Darwin. It was not until 1869 that Surveyor General George Goyder finally fixed the site for the Territory's principal town – called Palmerston then. The Federal Government took control of the Territory from South Australia in 1911, and changed the name of the port to Darwin.

Darwin is not like any of the other Australian state capitals. Since the Northern Territory is still administered largely from Canberra, it is doubtful whether you can really call Darwin a "capital" at all. Even aside from the question of its status, Darwin is different. It is home to about half the population of the Territory, but that still makes it only about one-twelfth the size of Perth, and one-fortieth the size of Sydney. Its small size, and the heat, and the extraordinary cultural diversity of its people – and maybe their fondness for the odd cooling beer too – all give Dar-

Darwin: Not So Much a City, More a Melting Pot

The 80,000 inhabitants of Darwin comprise a racial bouillabaisse of Greeks, British, Indonesians, Chinese, Italians, Japanese and Aboriginals, among others. For centuries it was a landfall for

Darwin, one of the few main cities of the Territories.

win an informal "manana" atmosphere.

But if the town is a happy-go-lucky place where friendliness is infectious, there is a serious side to its history too. In WW II Darwinians endured more than 60 Japanese bombing raids. At least 300 people died and sunken ships still ring the harbour. Then on Christmas Eve in 1974 a natural tragedy struck. Cyclone Tracy, the most powerful cyclone recorded in Australian history, smashed through the port delivering hammerblows that killed more than 100 people. Only 400 of the town's 11,000 buildings were left intact and nearly 6000 homes were destroyed.

Characteristically, Darwin rolled up its sleeves and built a modern town on the devastated site of the old one. A few

of the original buildings remain, tough old stone structures that have survived many a "big blow". They include the humble **Brown's Mart** that was built in 1885 by a former mayor. It has had several careers. Once it did sterling service as a brothel and, immediately after that, became the police headquarters.

Other noteworthy buildings include the **Old Victoria Hotel** of 1891 in The Mall. This is where you will probably start any Darwin walkabout because this is also where the **Tourist Bureau** is situated. The Old Victoria is of more than architectural interest. Its lunches in the palm garden are legendary, which makes it a good place to finish your walk too. The Mall is set about 100 m back from the **Esplanade**, which runs

Darwin's Mindil Beach markets where a variety of peoples of Papuan, Philippino, Japanese, Chinese, Aboriginal and Australian stock gather.

behind the city's two principal wharves. It's not hard to find: the town centre is only about a kilometre long and rather less across. You might stroll down to the Esplanade, and have a look at **Government House**, a few metres to your right as you face the ocean.

Retracing your steps, take a walk in Cavenagh Street, where the old **Chinatown** used to be before Cyclone Tracy blew away nearly all of it. Just a couple of old stone buildings are left, but the Chinese have always been a potent force in Darwin and still own great chunks of the town. Take the time to seek out the **Northern Territory Museum of Arts and Sciences**, which has a heavy emphasis on Aboriginal and island cultures. While on the subject of museums, look in also at the **Telegraph Museum** at Lyons Cottage.

In this vast country where communications has been so vital, the story of the Overland Telegraph across the width of the hostile land is an epic in itself. Darwin was once the first Australian link in the telegraph line from Java, thus connecting the continent with the rest of the world and spanning in minutes the gulf of distance which had taken weeks to cross before. You should also see **Christ Church Cathedral**, where Cyclone Tracy left only the porch and the altar, made of a large log. And another must is **St Mary's War Memorial Cathedral** which has a pearlshell altar, an Aboriginal Madonna and Child, and a gold-inlaid cross.

*Indonesian satay at the
market stalls.*

For a real experience of Darwin's cosmopolitan character, walk out to **Mindil Beach** when the sun goes down. Here, a couple of kilometres north of the town centre, the stalls of the night market offer delicacies from a bewildering range of cuisines and souvenirs from a plethora of cultures. It's only walking distance from here to Darwin's **Beach Casino,** which demands a hefty stake and attracts some big Asian money. If you're visiting the area in daylight, take a car or a cab the remaining two or three kilometres to **East Point Reserve**. The **War Museum** is here, with quite a collection of authentic military debris, all the more vividly evocative because of Darwin's closeness to the action in the desperate days of WW II. This route will

take you past another grim reminder of bygone years, **Fannie Bay Gaol**, built in 1883 and now a museum, complete with hangman's noose. Close by is **Fannie Bay Racecourse**, where local meets take place every Saturday. The big event is the Darwin Cup in August.

Venturing out of Darwin: Do's and Don'ts

The Northern Territory is about the size of Western Europe, and hardly anybody lives here. There are only three towns of any note: Darwin, Katherine and Alice Springs, and though none of these could be described as a metropolis, almost every Territorian lives in or around one of them. It follows that a great deal of the Territory is still very rugged country indeed, very remote, and potentially very dangerous. That is naturally one of its great attractions, but there is no point in taking unnecessary risks when visiting the great unknown. Commonsense will avoid most problems, but there are some special safety hints which even Australian visitors – being mostly city dwellers – sometimes overlook.

Swimmers, beware! Between October and May NEVER take a dip in the sea. The sea wasps (also called box jellyfish) can be deadly dangerous. You should be aware of the ocean's sharks too, though generally they are an over-rated threat. Not so over-rated, however, are the dangers from crocodiles. They are not at all uncommon in the

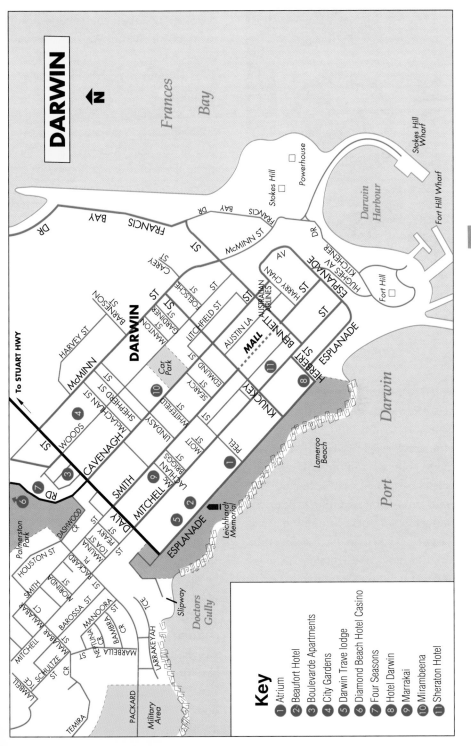

DARWIN

N

Frances Bay

To STUART HWY

DARWIN

Stokes Hill Wharf

Powerhouse

Stokes Hill

Darwin Harbour

Fort Hill Wharf

Fort Hill

FRANCIS BAY DR

BAY DR

McMINN ST

CAREY ST

FORELCHE ST

GARDINER ST

MANTON ST

BARNESON ST

HARVEY ST

ST

ST

ST

LITCHFIELD ST

AUSTIN LA

HUGHES AV

HARRY CHAN AV

KITCHENER DR

ESPLANADE

AUSTRALIAN AIRLINES

McMINN

McLACHLAN ST

SHEPHERD ST

WOODS

CAVENAGH

SMITH

MITCHELL

DALY

EDMUND ST

WHITEFIELD ST

SEARCY ST

LINDSAY

McLACHLAN ST

BRIGGS

MOTT ST

PEEL

KNUCKEY

BENNETT ST

HERBERT ST

ESPLANADE

MALL

Car Park

RD

ST

DASHWOOD CR

HOUSTON ST

SMITH

MORINDA ST

MAUNA LOA ST

PEART ST

PACKARD ST

MITCHELL

MALABAR CT

SCHULTZE CR

BAROSSA ST

NEPTUNA CR

MANOORA ST

BAMBRA CR

MARBELLA

LARRAKEYAH TCE

PACKARD

TEMIRA

Military Area

Palmerston Park

Doctors Gully

Slipway

Leichhardt Memorial

ESPLANADE

Lameroo Beach

Port Darwin

① ② ③ ④ ⑤ ⑥ ⑦ ⑧ ⑨ ⑩ ⑪

Key

① Atrium
② Beaufort Hotel
③ Boulevarde Apartments
④ City Gardens
⑤ Darwin Trave lodge
⑥ Diamond Beach Hotel Casino
⑦ Four Seasons
⑧ Hotel Darwin
⑨ Marrakai
⑩ Mirambeena
⑪ Sheraton Hotel

*Never smile at a crocodile,
especially while swimming!*

waters of the Top End (the coastal fringe of the Territory). They can reach several metres in length, and have taken a number of people in recent years. It's fair to point out that in most cases the people concerned were behaving with what looks, with hindsight, to be astonishing foolhardiness. Swimming across estuaries known to be the favourite haunt of dangerous crocs, for instance, or wading out into estuarine waters to fish, while casting offal bait in all directions. People do seem to have trouble believing that so hideous a threat can really exist outside of horror films. But, as the saying goes, you better believe it! There are plenty of crocs in the quieter waterways on the outskirts of Darwin itself. Watch for the crocodile warning

signs, always take them seriously, and if in doubt – ask a local. And yes, they can move on land, too. Faster than a horse, some say, and they can be big enough to eat one too.

Also, if you stray from the road or established tracks there is the danger of getting lost. Don't take risks. Don't go it alone. If you are driving, take extra cans of petrol and water. In some places it's 200 km to the next fuel station. Also take water, spare tyres, tubes, water, puncture-repair outfit, pump, fan-belt, water, coil, condenser, radiator hose, distributor points and most importantly, lots and lots of water. Tell people where you are going, and when you expect to arrive (and, please, don't forget to tell them when you do arrive). The police will not think you are a wimp for doing this, but they may be less than sympathetic if they have to spend three days in the desert looking for you because they didn't know where you were headed. Of course, you may be past caring by then. If anything does go wrong, the cardinal rule is – stay with the vehicle. Sit in the shade, wear a hat, and wait. In virtually every case when the Outback claims someone's life through thirst, it has been because they wandered off "to try to get help". Don't do it!

The roads here are mainly unfenced, and the stock often more than half wild. A high speed collision with a wandering bull camel can be an unpleasant experience for all parties concerned, so watch how you go. For other reasons, try to avoid hurting any native wildlife. Some

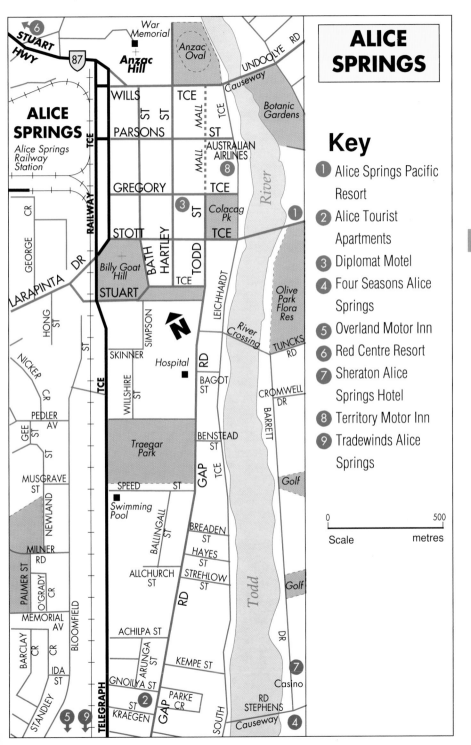

ALICE SPRINGS

Key

1. Alice Springs Pacific Resort
2. Alice Tourist Apartments
3. Diplomat Motel
4. Four Seasons Alice Springs
5. Overland Motor Inn
6. Red Centre Resort
7. Sheraton Alice Springs Hotel
8. Territory Motor Inn
9. Tradewinds Alice Springs

Scale 0 — 500 metres

of these tend to gather around road kills, so be especially careful if you see a dead animal on the road. All native animals and birds are protected. Even crocodiles are protected – which means that they can kill you, but you can't kill them.

One other very important point is the need to respect Aboriginal culture. About 25 percent of the total population of the Northern Territory is Aboriginal or Islander, and between them they own about half of the land area. The vast area of **Arnhem Land**, on the eastern side of **Kakadu**, is home to many Aboriginal and Islander people living as closely as possible to their traditional lifestyle. Written permission is required to enter Aboriginal-owned land, apart from when you are travelling on a public road, and requests must be made well in advance. Not having a permit can result in a A$1000 fine. The cattle, sheep and other livestock are the property of the land-owners. Leave it that way.

Kakadu National Park

While remembering all of these words of caution, you don't want to stifle your sense of adventure entirely. The Northern Territory has some of the world's most dramatic natural sights to offer, and probably the best treat of all is **Kakadu National Park**. You can reach it by driving east out of Darwin. After about 40 km the Stuart Highway branches south and the Arnhem Highway almost due east. Follow the Arnhem Highway for another 100 km or so, and you arrive at Australia's most dramatic and most famous national park.

Here is wild beauty such as you may never see again in our shrinking world. Far bigger than several small nations, its 130300 hectares cover six different topographical regions. They include the floodplains of the **Alligator** and **Wild Man Rivers**, mangrove-covered tidal flats in **Van Diemen's Gulf**, and woodlands, forests and wetlands where the natural order of the reptile and bird worlds has remained unchanged for millennia. Astonishingly, no native species of animals have been lost from Kakadu, though half the native marsupials and rodents have disappeared from some other parts of Australia. Invasion by exotic animals and plants have been kept to a minimum.

Two waterfalls, **Jim Jim** and **Twin Falls**, send cascades crashing more than 100 m into clear rock pools in the far southern part of Kakadu while at **Obiri** and **Nourlangie Rocks** there are galleries of Aboriginal rock paintings thousands of years old. One wildlife tour into the Park (and there are many, to choose from) features crocodiles which leap at the armour-plated glass that separates them from you, just in case you needed convincing about their ferocity. Deadly saltwater crocodiles can be seen basking in the mudflats or trawling the water if you take a cruise on the **South Alligator River**.

While on the subject of crocs, Kakadu's leading hotel is the **Four Seasons**

Kakadu National Park in the Northern Territories.

Crocodile Hotel at **Jabiru**. If you're on a helicopter flight, have your camera ready as you approach – the hotel is built in the shape of a crocodile. A favourite dish here is barramundi, the succulent fish of the region's rivers. There are plenty of less exclusive accommodation, motels and campsites, and literally scores of companies organise tours for varying lengths of time, and of varying degrees of hardship, through this nearly untouched wilderness. It is significant that the owners of Kakadu are the Aboriginal people, whose under-

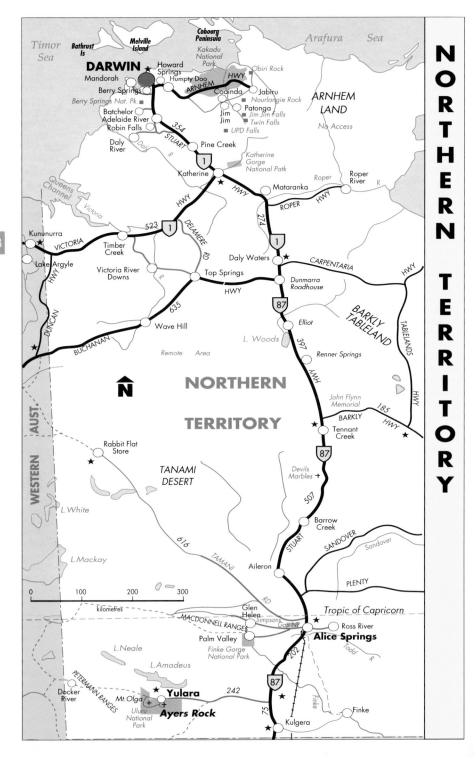

Timor
Sea

Bathrust
Is

Melville
Island

Cobourg
Peninsula

Arafura   Sea

DARWIN
Mandorah
Berry Springs
Berry Springs Nat. Pk.

Howard
Springs
Humpty Doo

Kakadu
National
Park

Obiri Rock

HWY
ARNHEM

Coainda
Jabiru
Nourlangie Rock
Patonga
Jim Jim Falls
Twin Falls
UPD Falls

ARNHEM
LAND

No Access

Batchelor
Adelaide River
Robin Falls
Daly
River

354

STUART

Jim
Jim

Pine Creek

Daly R.

Katherine

1

HWY

HWY

Katherine
Gorge
National Patk

Mataranka

Roper

Roper
River

R

Queens
Channel

523

1

DELAMERE RD

HWY

Kununurra

Lake Argyle

VICTORIA

Timber
Creek

Victoria River
Downs

R

Top Springs

Daly Waters

1

274

ROPER

HWY

CARPENTARIA

HWY

BARKLY
TABLELAND

TABLELANDS

HWY

Dunmarra
Roadhouse

HWY

635

HWY

Wave Hill

DUNCAN

BUCHANAN

Remote   Area

N

NORTHERN

TERRITORY

Rabbit Flat
Store

*TANAMI
DESERT*

87

Elliot

397

HWY

L. Woods

Renner Springs

John Flynn
Memorial

185

BARKLY   HWY

Tennant
Creek

87

WESTERN   AUST.

L. White

616

TAMANI

L.Mackay

Devils
Marbles +

507

Barrow
Creek

STUART

SANDOVER

Sandover

0   100   200   300
kilometres

L.Neale

L.Amadeus

MACDONNELL RANGES

Palm Valley

Finke Gorge
National Park

Glen
Helen

Simpsons
Gap NP

Aileron

RD

PLENTY

Tropic of Capricorn

Ross River

Alice Springs

202

Todd

R

PETERMANN RANGES

Docker
River

Mt.Olga +

Uluru
National Park

★ **Yulara**

Ayers Rock

242

87

57

Finke

★ Kulgera

Finke

Original primitive aboriginal art found on an abandoned rock formations.

standing and love of the land is so profound. They have leased it to the Commonwealth of Australia for use as a national park.

Heading South on "the Track"

It's about 350 km from Darwin to Katherine, the Territory's third largest town (it is home to 8000 people). The route is due south through tall and deceptively monotonous eucalyptus forest down the Stuart Highway. The road became a vital link in the Allies' supply chain as WW II progressed and there are a number of abandoned airstrips to be visited *en route* by aviation buffs. Sattler,

Strauss, Livingstone and Hughes Airstrips are all within a few miles of Noonamah, and not far off the road. There are other traces of the War, too.

Manton Dam, 25 km before Bachelor, was built as part of the pre-War build-up to supply Darwin with water, and the pipeline can still be seen running beside the road. Darwin now gets most of its water from the much bigger Darwin River Dam. And about 120 km from Darwin is the most poignant reminder of all, the **Adelaide River War Cemetery**. Among the 786 WW II graves here are those of nine people killed by the first Japanese bombs to hit the Post Office in Darwin in 1942.

On then for another 110 km to **Pine Creek**, watching out for snakes crossing

Leisure on the outback.

the road (don't get out to be friendly). Workers on the Overland Telegraph at this remote place found traces of gold here in 1872, and for a while there was a miniature goldrush, mostly by Chinese workers. Not many fortunes were made, but as recently as 1985 a company established an open cut goldmine here. It is possible to reach Jabiru by road from here, incidentally, allowing a circular trip to or from Kakadu.

Ninety km further south on the Stuart Highway is Katherine, at the edge of the southern more arid lands. First stop has to be the spectacular **Katherine Gorge**, now called **Nitmiluk** by its Aboriginal owners (again it has been leased back to the Commonwealth). The river cuts through 13 gorges and the lined

faces of their ancient rock walls bear mute testimony to the water's scouring passage over millions of years. Take a boat trip to capture it all on film from close quarters. Yes, there are crocodiles in the water, but they're the freshwater variety which live predominantly on fish, so you can swim in safety. Check with a local if you're still a little wary.

Many different walking trails begin from the visitors' centre, so take your pick – anything from an hour to five days. **Edith Falls** is another spot in **Nitmiluk National Park** where the water is unbearably inviting. Here a large clear waterhole, amid towering rock walls, is fringed with greenery. But just because it is safe to swim here, don't assume the same applies at **Katherine**

Low-Level Nature Park. While this is a favourite haunt of the local folk for picnics and swimming, they are ultra careful during and after the wet-season flooding because the saltwater crocs do penetrate this far inland.

Adventurous types can gleefully hire a canoe and do their own thing up and down the gorges, but again, not in the **Big Wet**, when floods turn the sedate watercourse into a mad torrent. You could go on a fishing tour to try and catch a barramundi, the region's most tasty fish. Bait and lines are supplied. You can inspect uranium mines or turn your hand to bird and wildlife spotting at the **Red Lily Lagoon**, where you can also photograph the stately jabiru, a beautiful wading bird. Try learning a bit about life-saving trees, watch an Aboriginal spear-throwing demonstration, and see how they kindle a flame with fire-sticks.

Katherine has come a long way since Jeannie Gunn visited it in 1902 before writing **We of the Never Never**. Then it had a telegraph station, a pub and a police station, plus a population of six. In the 1880s it was intended to be the junction of an extended Pine Creek railway to meet the line coming north out of South Australia, but the northern section was abandoned (although you can still see stretches of it along the Stuart Highway). The southern section did reach Katherine, but not until 1926. Today, however, Katherine is modestly prosperous, thanks mostly to the tourist trade, but also to the RAAF's F/A-18 base at **Tindal** nearby. Agriculture is still important, and despite the apparent dryness of the land opening up to the south, the largest dairy farm in Australia is to be found in the region, and is included in some tours.

There's no Town like Alice

Head southwards now into that drier country if you really feel rugged. It's a long way, about 1200 km from Katherine to Alice Springs on the Stuart Highway, with not a whole lot in-between except Tennant Creek. Most intelligent people fly there. However, there are some points of interest if you are at ground level. About 27 km out of Katherine, the limestone basin has been worn into some weird shapes, and hollowed into caves. These are the **Cutta Cutta Caves.** Don't be alarmed if you hear odd noises from above, it's just the bats. Not ordinary bats, but the rare orange horseshoe bat and the endangered ghost bat. Don't dally too long if you're en route to Tennant Creek: it's 714 km away.

Next stop is **Mataranka**, and you'll be familiar with the country around here if you've seen the film *"We of the Never-Never"*. Take a moment to have a look at the graves of the real characters who took part in that pioneering drama. There's a **thermal pool** here with a constant temperature of 34°C as the centrepiece of a small nature park. Swimming is permitted, but no skinny dipping. Then it's back on to the highway for your next diversion. **Tennant Creek** features some old gold mines and diggings, an **Old Telegraph Station**, and all the usual services.

Take a look at the **Burnt Shirt Mine**, perhaps, and at the town itself. You are now just over 500 km from "the Alice" as they all call it up here. On the way down you will pass the **Devil's Marbles**. This extraordinary collection of large boulders, balancing one on top of the other and grouped in piles across a wide valley, have mystical significance for the Aboriginal people, and it's easy to see why.

The southern part of the Territory was long known as the "Dead Heart" of Australia, but the tourist authorities are manfully striving to change that name to the "Red Heart" or the "Red Centre". The only city of the Centre, **Alice Springs**, is where the bull's-eye would be, if Australia were a dart-board. It was the English author Neville Shute's book **A Town Like Alice**, and the subsequent film, that initially drew international attention to the place.

Today, far from being the dusty, one-horse, pioneer town of Shute's story, it is a recognized tourist centre. The Alice sits astride an area of timeless, sun-baked desert where Aboriginal tribal people are only a few generations from the Stone Age, and where the rust red of the land contrasts vividly with the blue of the sky. The land may be primitive, but the town is not. It is home to 25,000 people and boasts modern hotels and motels, a casino, swimming pools, sports

facilities and city shopping. But there is history to see too. Old stone buildings dating back to 1872 are a legacy of the settlement's original role as a relay station on the **Overland Telegraph** line, when it was known as Stuart. The name was changed in 1933 when the telegraph station was closed.

Largely responsible for this work

Devil's Marbles on the way to see Alice.

was Charles Heavitree Todd, who supervised the stretching of the single "singing wire" of the telegraph atop 36000 poles northwards across 2000 km of unexplored country. It took just two years and was completed in 1872 – only ten years after Stuart had become the first white man to cross the continent from south to north. Todd is remembered in a number of placenames.

The Alice is named after his wife; the Todd River on which the town stands obviously owes its name to him. And the Todd River runs (when it runs) through

The Tragedy of Burke and Wills

In the history of exploration, failures often make better stories than well planned successes.

That must be why everyone knows about Scott of the Antarctic while few remember Amundsen. The Australia of the last century, so harsh a land and so vast, could hardly be without its own story of heroic and failed endeavour. In 1860 Robert O'Hara Burke and John Wills provided it.

As with so many debacles of discovery, this one sprang from a race. The young settlements of Australia were at this time distinct colonies, each one a separate economic entity. They vied with one another to open up new areas for settlement and new trade routes, and funded a series of expeditions by such men as Eyre, Leichhardt, Stuart and Sturt.

The lavishly funded Burke and Wills expedition was Victoria's attempt to win the honour of crossing the arid interior of Australia and reaching the Gulf of Carpentaria before rival South Australia could manage it.

The Irishman Burke (who led the expedition) and the Englishman Wills were an ill-assorted pair. Though Wills was a competent astronomer and meteorologist, Burke was – of all things – a police inspector. Neither knew anything of exploration. Burke was quite ignorant of the sciences, which in itself made him an odd choice, since the expedition was mounted by the Royal Society of Victoria. Of his courage there can be little doubt, but his motives are another matter. He was madly in love with a Melbourne actress, and perhaps he hoped to impress the lady.

Burke and Wills started out from Melbourne with 12 companions, 21 tons of baggage and 25 camels on 20 August 1860. They left most of the party at Menindie on the River Darling, where they established a base camp. Then they pushed north with about half the complement to Coopers Creek in central Australia.

The idea was that they should wait here until the bulk of the expedition could come up. But Burke was impatient. Taking Wills and two other companions, Gray and King, he struck out to walk the 1250 km north to the sea – a feat never achieved by any white man.

Astonishingly, they made it, and reached the Gulf in two months. This was longer than they had hoped, but did not constitute a disastrous delay. In their absence, they knew, the rest of the expedition would have come up from Menindie to Coopers Creek, and there would be food and shelter waiting for them. They turned about and plodded back

The return trip did not go so smoothly. Gray could not stand the pace and died of fatigue. Their supplies ran dangerously low. But they kept up the same punishing pace, and finally reached Coopers Creek, weak and exhausted.

Here, instead of a heroes' welcome, food and rest, they found the camp abandoned. They had missed the relief party – by just seven hours. The drama now took on the aspect of a classical tragedy. The three survivors were spent, and had only two exhausted camels left. Though the relief party was probably less than 20 km away, the trio had not the strength to overtake it. They rested for two days before setting out in a last desperate bid for their lives. They aimed not to overtake the rest of the expedition, which would recede from them more and more quickly, but to reach a remote police post at Mount Hopeless, 250 km away.

They were not up to it. After another two months, Burke and Wills died of hunger, exhaustion and despair in June 1861. Only John King survived, rescued by the Aboriginals whom Burke had despised.

Heavitree Gap near here, a place of pools and waterholes where you will see a vivid profusion of birdlife. Just north of the town you can visit the original **Telegraph Station**, and even the waterhole optimistically dubbed "**The Springs**".

Tough And Rugged

The Territory has always been a land of

Bronco-busters at Alice Springs.

tough Aboriginal survivors and rugged immigrant individualists. Yet it owes its greatest debt to the kindly missionary, the Rev John Flynn, founder of the Inland Mission that gave a better life, education and medical care to thousands of native people especially in the harsh period between the wars. Father Flynn also founded one of the institutions of outback life, the Flying Doctor Service. It was at the **Hermannsburg** **Mission**, 130 km west of Alice Springs, that the Aboriginal landscape artist Albert Namatjira perfected his art, becoming the most famous man in Central Australia in the 1950s, but dying soon after achieving fame. He is buried in Alice Springs. If you are visiting the Mission, take time to call in at the **Finke** **Gorge National Park** just to the south. Places like Hermannsburg and the Alice itself were supplied for many years by

Bare-back cattle rides are not faint experience.

camels, often in camel trains sixty beasts long driven by **Afghan** drivers. These became largely redundant after the arrival of the railroad from **Oodnadatta** in South Australia in 1928 and many were turned loose. They roam the Territory in enormous numbers today, numerous enough for the authorities to put up road warning signs (see page 318). However, out of gratitude for their work, the new railway was christened **"The Ghan"** some say because the train took over the job of the camels and their Afghan drivers, others because they helped build the railroad.

Today Alice Springs is restoring the original Ghan Railway in the largest community project ever undertaken by the town. It's well worth a visit.

Side trips with a Difference

It is common for visitors to Alice Springs to believe that now they are here, sights like **Uluru (Ayers Rock)** are just a hop, skip and a jump out of town. The Rock is actually 470 km to the southwest, which makes it rather more than a pleasure drive.

Fortunately, regular coach and air services link the Alice with Uluru. Many tourists believe their visit to Australia would be incomplete without a visit here to drink in the spiritual legacy of Uluru, the colour-changing monolith with a Dreamtime of its own.

Native lore lays down that Uluru was created by the Earth Mother and her devotees millennia ago. Now they sleep in the mountain, stirring only, but never appearing, at times when the Aboriginals perform the rituals handed down from tribal elders.

The Loonba bird guards the rock, they say, and shrills a warning if danger approaches. Legend has it that one such cry many ages ago angered Wanambi, the snake more than 100 metres long which once dwelt coiled around the uppermost parts of the Rock. In his rage Wanambi reared up and flung himself into the skies halting the rains, causing droughts, and inflicting other punishment on the Aboriginals.

Those visitors of less vivid faith concentrate on filming its spectacular changes of colour – burning red at sunrise as the starry sky itself changes to cobalt blue, rust red to earth brown as the setting sun draws a cloak over this eighth wonder of the world. They also inspect its caves and wall paintings, walk around the base or climb to the top 400 m above the plain to get a spectacular view of the surrounding desert (careful: a good few people have died doing this).

An admission fee is now charged to Uluru which has been returned to the Aboriginal people as a cultural heritage site. It was leased back to the Commonwealth by the Pitjantjatjara people as a national park which also embraces the bizarre **Kata Tjuta Domes**, formerly known as **The Olgas**.

Just 32 km from Uluru this collection of 36 curious rocky humps in the desert are almost certainly the remains of what was once a monolith many times the size of Uluru, which has been worn down by time, wind and erosion to the present shapes. Somebody definitely lacking the soul of a poet once likened them to "giant red potatoes on a kitchen draining board".

Many visitors are pleasantly surprised to find that Kata Tjuta is at least as fascinating as Uluru. Try taking a light plane flight from Uluru to see them from the air. If you are staying in the area you will probably find yourself at the **Yulara** tourist oasis with its hotels, motels and campsites.

This development has mushroomed only half an hour's drive from the Rock, but – rather surprisingly – it is tastefully designed, blending with the landscape. As part of the development, shabby 1960s motels which cluttered the base of Uluru have now been swept away, so that the natural environment has actually been improved by a tourist development. Is this a first? There is a range of accommodation and facilities at Yulara, including even lockable tents for budget travellers.

Beehive Of Tours

The Alice is like a beehive of tour operators. They use limousines, coaches, minibuses, four-wheel-drive vehicles, light planes and even balloons to show visitors all manner of sights in such places as the **Artlunga Historical Reserve**,

Rainbow Valley, the **Simpson Desert** or the **MacDonnell Ranges**. From here you get breathtaking views of **Standley Chasm** and **Ormiston Gorge**.

The **Hermannsburg Aboriginal Settlement** and the **Finke River** watercourse, which is thought to be the oldest in the world, can also form part of your itinerary. Depending on your choice of tour, you can watch native elders creating attractive Aboriginal dot paintings depicting scenes from the Dreamtime, learn to throw a boomerang, or go hunting for lizards and eat damper (roughly-made bush bread) washed down with billy tea at a desert campsite.

This is also where you can satisfy your curiosity about Aboriginal customs and beliefs, and even get a glimpse of a *corroboree* site where sacred dances are performed. Then wash off some of the sweat and dust in a rock pool or find out about the **Royal Flying Doctor Service** – so vital where distances are measured in hundreds or even thousands of kilometres. If you are fascinated by this vast landscape there are extraordinary rock formations and meteor craters that make impressive photographs and camel rides are a novel, if jerky experience.

The camel is making a definite comeback as a beast of tourist burden, carrying people on safaris for days or weeks into the wilderness. Or cap the day's strangeness with a night under the stars, secure in the knowledge that the possibility of rain is very remote. Here is prehistoric Australia in all its primitive grandeur.

Getting to the Northern Territory

The fastest way is by jetliner either to Alice Springs or Darwin. Some approximate single fares to Alice Springs are A$230 from Adelaide, and A$285 from Melbourne. To Darwin the fares are about A$350 from Adelaide and A$406 from Melbourne. From Sydney, it costs around A$300 to fly to the Alice and A$400 to Darwin. Return fares are nor-

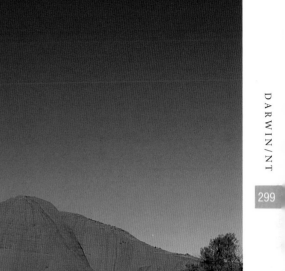

*After Katherine and Alice (Gorge and Spring), meet big Olga,
shaped in bizarre-looking domes.*

mally double, but shop around for discounts. Since deregulation in 1990 domestic airlines have been slashing fares in all directions, and besides, many tour operators offer attractive package deals.

The national coach lines operate services on these very long routes. The fare from Adelaide to Alice Springs is about A$124, and from Adelaide to Darwin about A$238; from Melbourne the figures are A$165 and A$265; and from Sydney, A$206 and A$275. For those with time on their side there is a direct rail service from Adelaide to Alice Springs via the modern version of the Ghan. The air-conditioned train takes 24 hours for the 1559 km journey, much of which is across the desert landscape. It currently costs A$270 for a sleeper in first class; economy seats are cheaper. Cars and caravans can be carried on the train for an extra fee.

Tasmania is the most English of the Australian states in appearance, atmosphere and weather. "Tassie" is the heart-shaped island south of Victoria and is Australia's smallest state. In fact it's about the same size as Ireland, which may not seem so very small after all. Because Tasmania draws heavily on nature for its charm – rugged mountains, temperate rainforests, glacial lakes, rivers, streams and beaches – it follows that outdoor activities rank high here. Fishing, sailing, rafting, canoeing, caving, bushwalking and cycling all add up to a very special way of life. Dozens of holiday packages of different durations and budgets are constructed around these activities alone. Due to the island's compactness, only 190 miles (300 km) from top to bottom and 180 miles (280 km) wide, no area of natural beauty which is on any kind of a road is more than

"Tassie", most resembling England in climate and terrain.

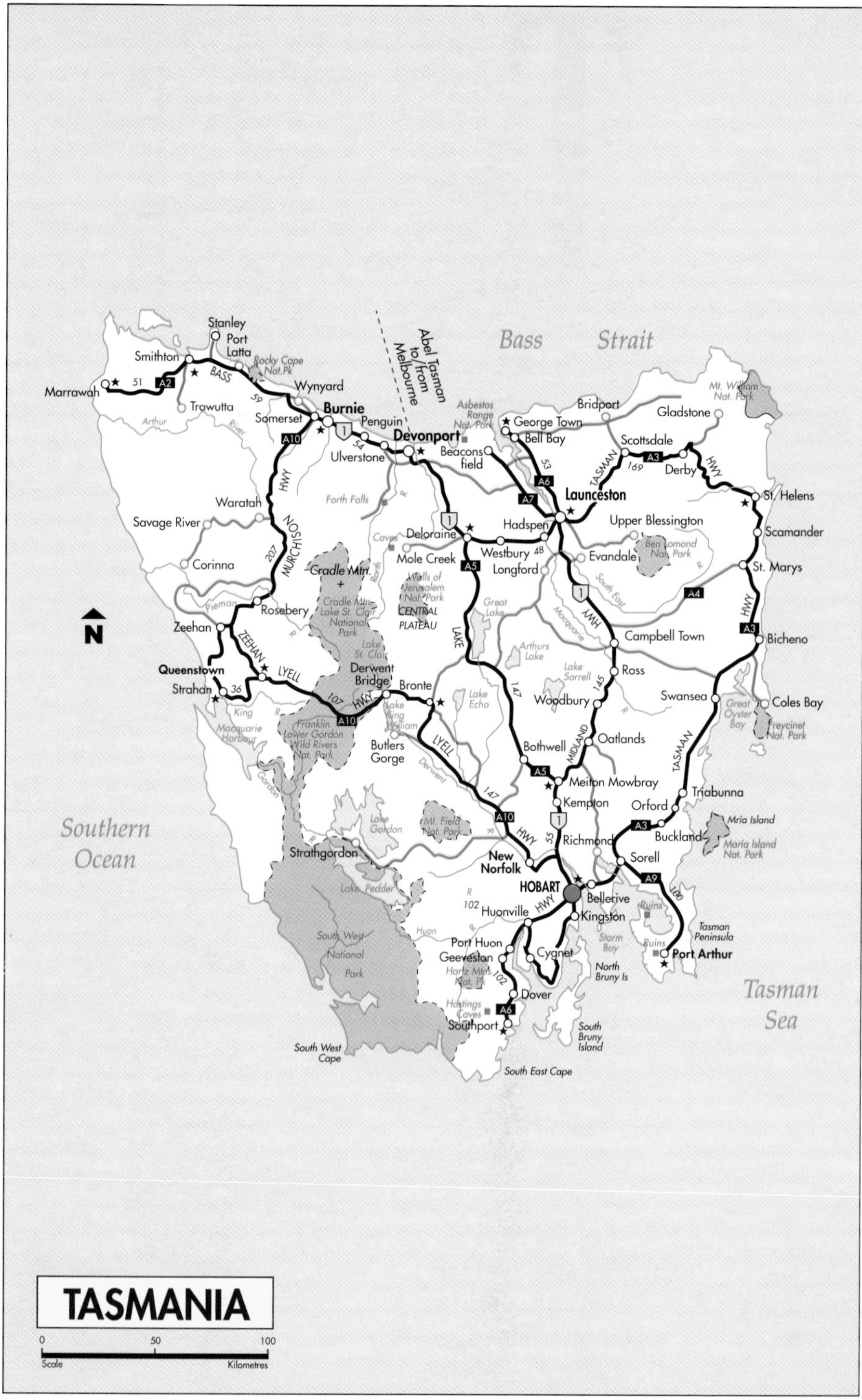

Bass Strait

Marrawah ★ 51 A2
Smithton
Stanley
Port Latta
Rocky Cape Nat. Pk.
Trowutta
Wynyard
Somerset
Penguin
Burnie
Devonport
Ulverstone
Beaconsfield
Abel Tasman to/from Melbourne
Asbestos Range Nat. Park
George Town
Bell Bay
Bridport
Gladstone
Mt. William Nat. Park
Scottsdale
Derby
St. Helens
Scamander
St. Marys
Bicheno
Coles Bay
Freycinet Nat. Park
Great Oyster Bay
Swansea
Triabunna
Maria Island
Maria Island Nat. Park
Launceston
Hadspen
Upper Blessington
Ben Lomond Nat. Park
Evandale
Longford
Westbury 48
Deloraine
Mole Creek
Walls of Jerusalem Nat. Park
Cradle Mtn.
Lake St. Clair National Park
Cradle Mtn-Lake St. Clair National Park
CENTRAL PLATEAU
Great Lake
Lake Echo
Arthurs Lake
Lake Sorell
Campbell Town
Ross
Woodbury
Oatlands
Bothwell
Melton Mowbray
Kempton
Orford
Richmond
Sorell
Buckland
Waratah
Savage River
Corinna
Rosebery
Zeehan
Queenstown
Strahan
King Macquarie Harbour
Franklin Lower Gordon Wild Rivers Nat. Park
Derwent Bridge
Bronte
Butlers Gorge
Strathgordon
Lake Gordon
Lake Pedder
South West National Park
Mt. Field Nat. Pk.
New Norfolk
Huonville
Port Huon
Geeveston
Hartz Mtn. Nat. Pk.
Hastings Caves
Southport
Dover
Cygnet
North Bruny Is
South Bruny Island
South East Cape
South West Cape
HOBART
Bellerive
Kingston
Storm Bay
Port Arthur
Tasman Peninsula
Tasman Sea
Southern Ocean

N

TASMANIA

0   50   100
Scale   Kilometres

half a day's drive away from anywhere else – although on some occasions you may need a four-wheel-drive vehicle to get there. The sight of people togged up with ropes, picks and backpacks for yet another outdoor adventure is as common here as it is in Switzerland.

"Tassie" really is a prime destination for nature-lovers and many visit its shores regularly from the mainland and return singing its praises. New Zealanders often fly directly from Auckland and Christchurch to tour Tasmania and compare its cold ruggedness with that of their own land.

Increasingly, on the back of Australia's tourist boom, visitors come from much farther afield too. They find Tasmania generally cooler, more peaceful, and less... well, brash... than most of the rest of Australia.

Hotels in Tasmania

Tasmania is fully geared for tourism with heated rooms in all accommodation and heated indoor swimming pools in the luxury hotels. Before booking your hotel, check whether it has a heated pool. You will certainly appreciate it on a nippy day.

On the other hand, you may wish to experience history first-hand by staying in one of the colonial cottages. These single and double-storey guesthouses, some built by convicts, are a delightful mix of old furniture and decor and modern fixtures. You can even stay in the old gaolhouse at **Bicheno** on the east coast.

But this is only one of several score picturesque places to stay. To get details on colonial cottages and other accommodation make enquiries at the **Tasmanian Travel Centre** at 80 Elizabeth Street, Hobart (tel: 008-300-211). Tasmania casts a wide net to attract tourists and has branch offices in Sydney at 149 King Street (tel: 02-233-2500); in Melbourne at 256 Collins Street (tel: 03-653-7999); in Brisbane at 217 Queen Street (tel: 07-221-2744); in Adelaide at 32 King William Street (tel: 08-211-7411); in Perth at 100 William Street (tel: 09-321-2633); and in Canberra at 5 Canberra Savings Centre, City Walk, (tel: 062-47-0888).

Government House holds stately in Hobart.

Hobart: the Quiet Capital

It is a sobering thought that the next landmass south of Tasmania is Antarctica. That's why the island's capital, Hobart, is the headquarters for Australia's scientific and exploratory expeditions to the South Pole. The last Austral-
ian port of call for these intrepid people is the southern settlement of Kingston. Hobart is also the headquarters for the nation's principal marine research program conducted by experts of the Commonwealth Scientific and Industrial Research Organisation (CSIRO) in the fields of fishing and oceanography.

For true-blue city dwellers there are

in the 30 years following the first settlement. Happily the chill hand of redevelopment and modernisation has not yet grasped Hobart and it looks much the same today as it did at the turn of the century with many of its lovely old buildings still intact.

City Walking

Let's start from the Tourist Bureau in Elizabeth Street. Turn right down Elizabeth Street towards the harbour. From the water's edge on **Franklin Wharf** you should be able to see **Parliament House** a couple of hundred metres over to your right. This grand old building, dating from 1840, is one of numerous public buildings constructed by convicts, and it began life as the Customs House. The erstwhile bonded stones in the basement still bear the broad arrows that signify prison labour. Having surrendered its original premises to Parliament, the customs service pampered itself with a new highly ornamented and very photogenic structure nearby. This "new" **Customs House** dates from 1902, and stands almost beside the original building. Make a detour at this point up Murray Street, which runs down one side of **Parliament Square**.

About 200 m up Murray you will discover **St David's Cathedral**. Among its treasures are five solid silver altar vessels presented by King George III in 1803. Another claim to fame is that one of Tasmania's bishops, Bishop Montgo-

some places even in Hobart where the pulse of city life is felt, though it's scarcely more than a quiet throb. This capital is a cosy sort of place, perfectly located on the banks of the Derwent River beneath the shelter of nearby Mt Wellington, on the southeast coast of the island and facing – perhaps symbolically – away from the mainland. It is an intensely historic city, founded in 1804 and with several fine buildings erected, especially

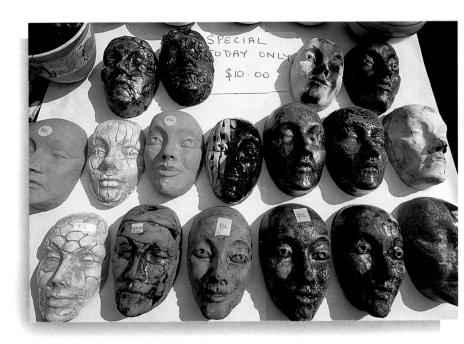

Tasmanian craft are often made of wood, leather and clay.

mery, was father of the wartime Field Marshal Montgomery of El Alamein fame. Now walk back down to Parliament Square.

Running along behind Parliament Square is **Salamanca Place**. Lovely old sandstone warehouses line the docks here. Perhaps because of Tasmania's next-to-nature lifestyle many of its inhabitants are skilful craft workers who sell their creations of wood, leather and clay every Saturday in the **Salamanca Market**. This is a must for all visitors.

Crossing Salamanca Place – which is a street, rather than a place – walk down Gladstone Street to the **National Trust Office** at the junction with Harrington Street, where a second information bureau is located. On the far side of

Harrington Street you will see **Anglesea Barracks**. Guarded by an 18th-century cannon, this establishment incorporates buildings dating back to 1814 (the year before Waterloo). It is open from Monday to Friday but for exterior inspection only – the Army still uses it. Entry is free.

Turning into Harrington, heading towards the port and bearing left into **Castray Esplanade** after a few metres walk, you will find the **Van Diemens Land Folk Museum** on your left. When you emerge from the museum (for you wouldn't think of passing it unvisited!) continue down Harrington and then branch right into Secheron Street after about 300 m. That will bring you to the famous **Battery Point** area of Hobart.

This fascinatingly former mariners'

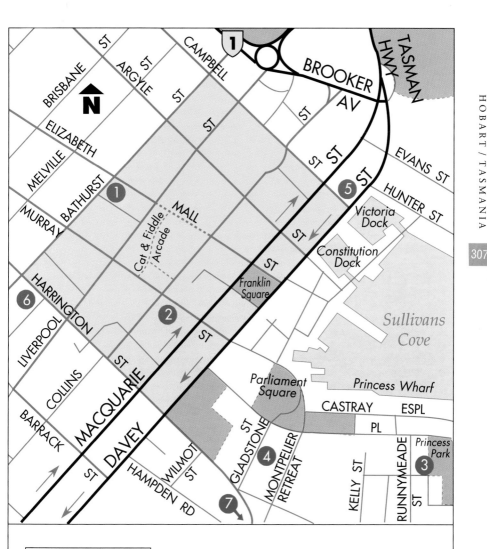

HOBART

Key

1 Hobart Midcity Motor Inn

2 Innkeepers Hadleys Orient Hotel

3 Innkeepers Lenna of Hobart

4 Salamanca Apartments

5 Sheraton Hobart Hotel

6 Westside Hotel

7 Wrest Pt Casino Hotel

Shopping at Salamanca Market, amidst stalls and sandstone warehouses.

manca Market again, with **Kellys Steps** just behind.

Walk on, following the water's edge past Parliament House again and emerge on **Brooke Street Pier**. A wide variety of tourist river cruises and ferries leave from here. Inquire at the Travel Centre about half and full-day river cruises and coach tours to beauty spots and other locations.

Follow Franklin Wharf round to **Constitution Dock**, which is the focal point of the water-

village has tiny cottages on hilly streets and an occasional grand mansion thrown in for contrast. It has remained unchanged for more than a century. The **Maritime Museum** on Battery Point has a fine collection of maritime items, including models, covering the sailing ship and steamship eras, as well as maps and other memorabilia dating back to Abel Tasman's discovery of the island in 1642. The entry fee for adults is A\$2, and children get in free.

Rejoining the Esplanade, follow it round until it takes you past the **Postal and Telegraphic Museum**, and Sala-

front, teeming with fishing boats and pleasure craft. You can buy fresh fish straight off the boats and have it cooked for you on the spot.

Constitution Dock is even livelier in December and January, when it plays host to the massed yachts of the Sydney/Hobart and Melbourne/Hobart racing fleets. Those are events not to be missed if you are in Hobart at the right time.

Just behind the dock, in Argyle Street, is the **Tasmanian Museum and Art Gallery**. This houses relics and depictions of the harsh times faced by the early settlers of Van Diemens Land, later

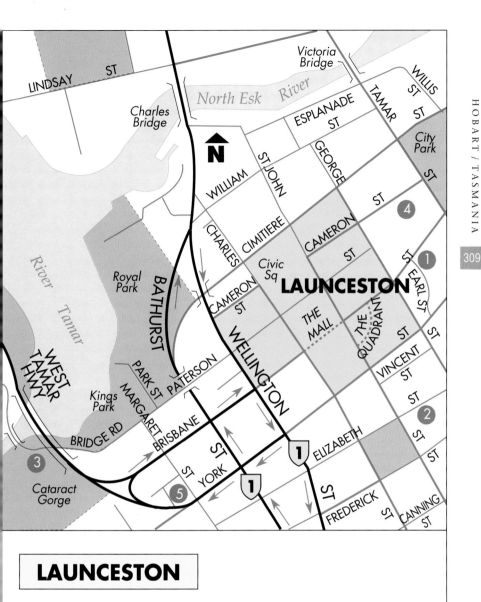

LAUNCESTON

Key

 1 Great Northern Hotel

2 Innkeepers Colonial Motor Inn

3 Innkeepers Penny Royal

4 Launceston International Hotel

5 The Old Bakery

re-named Tasmania. It is open daily from 10 am to 5 pm and entry is free. Across the road is the **Town Hall** (1864). Hobart's civic dignitaries ensured that they carried out their deliberations in a fittingly handsome stone building which is well worth inspecting.

Walk up Argyle Street away from the water as far as Collins Street, and turn right into it. A little way along Collins you will be able to see the charming **Theatre Royal**, Australia's oldest. It has been painstakingly restored and is certainly worth a visit even if nothing is showing.

It was a great favourite of Vivien Leigh and Laurence Olivier on their post-war Australian tours. Of course, Hobart is not all history. You will certainly feel a change of pace in the **Wrest Point Casino** in **Sandy Bay**, just to the south of the city centre.

The casino comes complete with cabaret, and a fine revolving restaurant on top of a 64 m tower, which gives incomparable views of the city and harbour. And if that proves too much excitement, relax for a while in the **Botanical Gardens**, within the huge green expanse of the **Queens Domain**, to the north of the city centre.

Two of the prime attractions of the Botanical Gardens are the **Conservatory** and the **Japanese Garden**, but also make a point of inspecting **Arthurs Wall** to see how tropical plants were grown in these temperate climates in the old days. The Gardens are open daily from 8 am to 4.45 pm. Entry is free.

On the Outskirts

Mt Wellington, which looms over the city of Hobart, is a 25-minute drive west up the Huon Highway, branching off right after about 5 km from the city. It takes you to lookouts that give dazzling views of the city and the sea, and there are some attractive walks around the summit for the enthusiast.

Also in the outskirts of Hobart on

Hobart has developed gracefully since Abel Tasman's founding of the island in 1642. Mt Wellington presides over Hobart.

the way out to Mt Wellington is the **Cascade Brewery** – the country's oldest brewery and second oldest company. Inspections are welcome. Tasmania is noted for its chocolate factories and a visit to the **Cadbury-Schweppes** complex at Claremont is a must, particularly for chocaholics! Buy your tickets from the Travel Centre, adults A$7, children A$3.50 and then take the ferry trip north up the Derwent River from Ho-

bart. Of course you get a sample or two, but remember it is only open for visits in the morning from Monday to Friday. Try also the **Tasmanian Transport Museum**, on the road north at **Glenorchy**. This is also where you will find the **Derwent Entertainment Centre**, which is where most of Hobart's large-scale musical, exhibition and sporting action takes place. Crossing the **Bowen Bridge** near here you will arrive at **Risdon**

Walking the Wilderness

A huge area of Tasmania's national parkland is now listed as a World Heritage Area, judged by UNESCO to be among the planet's great natural treasures and worthy of preservation for all time. No one who goes there could disagree.

The adjoining parks total almost 1.4 million hectares – more than a fifth of Tasmania's total area. They comprise one of the last large temperate wilderness areas on earth, a kaleidoscope of soaring alps, white water and numberless lakes and tarns.

Much of this terrain has never even been explored, but it is protected by its own remoteness, not by any exclusivity conferred by its World Heritage listing. World Heritage status in fact encourages sympathetic and sensitively-managed use of wilderness areas, with the object of helping people understand them better. There can be no better way to establish a rapport with the wilderness than to walk through it, and no one who walks Tasmania's wilderness emerges without a sense of privilege.

One of the world's most spectacular walking trails has to be the **Overland Track** from **Cradle Mountain** in the north 60 km to the shores of **Lake St Clair**. A number of adventure tour operations take groups along the Overland Track, generally over a period of five to ten days, depending on the enthusiasm and fitness of the walkers and the places of interest visited on the way. **Cradle Huts** of Launceston is one of the best known (Tel: 003-312 006) and runs the only private accommodation along the length of the walk in the shape of well-appointed huts.

Other operators, like Craclair of Devonport (Tel: 004-243 971), guide their walkers from one spectacular campsite to the next.

The walk takes visitors across alpine plateaux, beside highland lakes and tarns and through forests of pine and myrtle, all between 800 m and 1200 m above sea-level where the air is clearer than anyone but a mountaineer is likely to have experienced before. Other walks in or around the northern half of the World Heritage Area lead around Cradle Mountain or to the jagged **Walls of Jerusalem**, or further south to the summit of **Frenchmans Cap** through forests of 2000-year-old Huon pine.

It is not necessary to be commando-fit for this sort of thing. The organised walks are all accompanied by well-trained guides, and several of the excursions allow two days or so at a base camp, so that stiff muscles can relax and sore feet recover. All of these trips can be geared to cater for people with only a few days to spare,

Rustling ferns, cascading waters and the
buzz of insect life…aah!

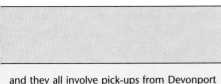

and they all involve pick-ups from Devonport (where the trans-Tasman ferries come in) or from Launceston, linked by air with the rest of Australia. With proper timing, someone in Melbourne is only three or four hours away from the start of a walk they are likely never to forget.

The **Southwest National Park** abuts the Cradle Mountain-Lake St Clair, and there is dramatic walking to be had in this even more rugged territory. Best-known are the **South Coast Track** and the **South West Track**, which starts from **Scotts Peak Dam** and is accessible from Hobart.

It is possible to tackle these tracks and others in the Heritage Area without a guide, but that is an undertaking only for the very experienced. This land is terrific to look at, and terrible to get lost in, and it does not easily forgive people who treat it with disrespect.Now two variations on the wilderness theme, for those who love the water.

Travelling by water can be the only way to get to see some of these remote areas, particularly in the aptly named Franklin-Gordon Wild Rivers National Park, the third of the major parks to make up the Heritage Area.

Companies like Peregrine (their head office is in Melbourne on 03-663-8611) will take you whitewater rafting down the torrential Franklin River if you have as little as five days to spare, or as long as a couple of weeks. They pick up from Hobart. At the other extreme, troutfishing in Tasmania has been elevated by devotees almost to the status of a religion.

Brown trout and some rainbow trout were introduced to Tasmania's rivers in the 1860s and today they have developed into populations of the wildest, wiliest and most highly-prized sporting fish in the world.

As always, the attraction of fishing is as much to do with what you see as what you catch. There can't be a much more pleasant way of spending an evening than beside one of Tasmania's 3000 lakes, with the promise of a mountain lodge and a blazing fire to come. Catching a fish would be almost a nuisance.

Pick up details on troutfishing in Tasmania from any of the Tasmanian Travel Centres across the island state or in any Australian state capital.

Cove, now an historic site, but once the location of the first European settlement in Tasmania (1803). Coming back into town on Brooke Avenue, stop off at **Runnymede** historic homesite.

Hell in the South

Morbid curiosity makes the notorious penal settlement here at **Port Arthur** the island's most-visited area, a couple of hours drive out of Hobart on the Tasman Peninsula to the east of the capital. The shell of the main convict-built prison block still stands gauntly guarding its grisly secrets. This was the most dreaded of Australia's prisons between 1830 and 1877. Port Arthur was chosen to house the most hardened criminals because it was thought escape-proof. In the stormy seas around the prison lay such swirling mantraps as the Mighty Blowhole and the Devil's Kitchen.

The only way in and out was along Eaglehawk Neck and here savage hounds were tethered, baying for blood. Convicts, harnessed to ropes, were even used to pull a carriage containing passengers and supplies.There's a lot to see in and around this grim place, where A$9 million has been spent on restoration work for the benefit of modern-day visitors. There is a replica of the old convict-operated sawmill, and a convict outstation where you can spend the night in much more comfort than did the poor wretches of 150 years ago. The museum has a number of gruesome exhibits, and there is the shell of the old prison church and the forbidding model prison where prisoners in solitary confinement had to remain completely silent as a punishment. Transgressors, of course, suffered even more cruel treatment. There is even a ferry trip to the **Isle of Dead** where 1769 convicts and 180 freemen lie buried. About 11000 convicts actually survived the horrors of the penal settlement to gain their freedom, though it's hard to see how. A drive of about 100 km south of Hobart takes you through the **Huon Valley** and some of the island's prettiest orchard country. Tasmania has been nicknamed "The Apple Isle".

The same route will take you close to the spectacular **Hartz Mountains National Park**, and finally to the **Hastings Caves**. There's a thermal pool you can bathe in and you can have a look at the limestone caves daily from 11.15 am to 1.15 pm and 2.15 pm to 3.15 pm. Entrance to the cave costs A$4 for adults and A$2 for children, the pool costs adults A$1 and children A$0.50.

Second City

Tasmania's second city, **Launceston**, a few hours' drive north from Hobart, has a quaint village atmosphere. **Yorktown Square** is a graceful colonial shopping area you'll want to film.

The Old Umbrella Shop is a delightful gift shop dating from the 1860s.

Cataract Gorge only just outside the city centre beside the **Tamar River** is a must, especially if it has been raining heavily and there is a formidable overspill. You can see it at close quarters from the chairlift. This exciting experience costs A$3 for adults and A$2 for children. At the other extreme of entertainment, Launceston also boasts a **casino** at the **Federal Country Club**. Launceston has a number of notable old buildings. Take a look at **Macquarie House** on Charles Street in the centre, and the nearby **Batman Fawkner Inn** on Cameron Street, which still takes guests.

The **Queen Victoria Art Gallery and Museum** on Paterson Street, abutting **Royal Park** beside the **North Esk River**, houses the best contemporary craft collection in Tasmania, and a fine collection of early colonial paintings – besides one of only three planetaria in Australia. It also displays a complete joss house, which was used by Chinese tin miners in northeast Tasmania in the last century.

Villages and Resorts near Launceston

Grindlewald is a quaint Swiss-style village resort in the Launceston district with self-contained chalets, two restaurants (which are closed on Sundays), tennis courts, a golf course and **The Mouse House** for children. Situated in the village of **Hadspen**, about 7 km west of Launceston on the Bass Highway, is **Entally House**. This beautifully furnished colonial home is the end result of a rags-to-riches story. Its original owner, Thomas Reibey, was the son of a woman who, aged 13 years, was transported from England for stealing a horse. She married an officer who resigned his commission to become a shipowner and merchant and one of the colony's earliest, wealthy settlers. Reibey's own son became premier of Tasmania. Entally is open daily from 10 am to 12.30 pm and 1 pm to 5 pm. The entrance fee for adults is A$4, for children it is A$1.50.

Not too far away is **Devonport**, in the centre of the north coast. It is a pretty port in its own right, and there are some interesting Aboriginal rock carvings to be seen at the nearby **Mersey Bluff**. The passenger and vehicle ferry, the Abel Tasman, that links Tasmania to Melbourne, sails to and from Devonport, taking 14.5 hours each way. **Burnie** is a 40-minute drive west along the coast. Moving back south, on the main A1 road about 40 minutes out of Devonport you'll come to the pretty town of **Deloraine**. It is worth stopping off here, if you're on your way down to Launceston, and taking a look at **King Solomon's Cave** and **Marakoopa Cave**.

Outlying Islands

The Tasmanian coastline is dotted with smaller islands, many of them uninhabited, but several others offering tour-

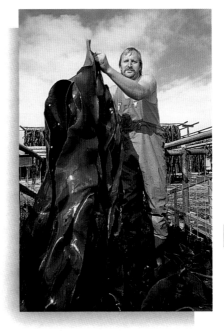

Working at giant bull kelp on King Island, northwest of Tasmania.

ist attractions in their own right. Consider a trip to the **Furneaux Group** and in particular **Flinders Island**, off the northeast tip of Tasmania, where mutton-birds, other birds and fish abound to the delight of nature lovers. **King Island**, to the northwest of Tasmania, offers scuba diving, fishing and rugged sightseeing, as well as a well-known cheese and dairying industry. **Diamond Island**, off Bicheno on the east coast, is home to a colony of fairy penguins and can be visited on foot at low tide.

Maria Island, 60 km further down the coast, is now a national park. It has the remains of the original probationary station for convicts from Port Arthur, as well as traces of Tasmania's first wine and tanning industries.

So you've seen the *Crocodile Dundee* movies, you're young in body and/or mind, and want to do it tough, huh? Well, step on up: Australia's going to suit you right down to the ground. What follows is a list of some of the many adventurous pursuits you can enjoy in this rugged, challenging country. To take up the challenge, consult a tourist bureau for details of tour operators, or phone The Australian Experience toll free line on 008-331-373 (fax: 03-650 - 5570).

Adventure Travel

317

There's no lack of adventure pursuits, bumps or humps, in the Australian outdoors.

Across the Country

Bushwalking and Trekking: Here's a way to experience the REAL Australia, humping your *bluey* (carrying your *swag* – that is, anything you need – on your shoulders) as you follow in the footsteps of the Aborigines on walkabout. A wide variety of trekking adventures are available in all states, and of course you'll have experienced trail guides to show you Nature's (and the Aborigines') secrets. You'll meet all sorts of true-blue Australians (including some of the insectivorous type you'll wish you hadn't), and if it's a clear night your "hotel" in the Great Outback won't be a five-star, but a five-million-star one. The dingoes won't disturb your sleep – they don't bark – but don't count on a quiet night. Other things will snap, crack, rustle and screech until dawn. What sort of things? It's better not to look; just pull the blanket over your head and ask the guide in the morning. If you survive the first night, you'll probably be alright for the rest of the trip. Don't forget the mosquito repellent, though. There isn't much you can do about the flies, the ants and the rest of the biteys that come with the territory. Grubs in the sand, sand in the grub!

Camel trekking: This is real Outback stuff. Camels were brought to Australia in the early days because of their ability to plod long distances for several days without water. They were used by Indian camel-drivers to take food and water to diggers in remote areas, such as the goldfields of Western Australia. They also lumbered trustingly into many unknown regions, carrying supplies for the men who explored the Great Outback. When railway lines and roads eliminated the need for these "ships of the desert", as they were called, their owners turned them loose and they thrived in their adopted home on the edges of the desert. But before you decide to fling a leg across one, be warned that they're the jerky, one-hump model (the steadier, two-hump variety is up

Xinxiang way in China). South Australia offers six-night camel treks around **Kangaroo Island** or the **Flinders Ranges**, while those of sterner stuff might prefer an adventurous, if bumpy, 14-day picnic of sorts exploring the **Finke River Gorge** of Central Australia which starts from Alice Springs. There are also one-week safaris to less rugged locations starting from the Alice.

Hit The Trail!

Trail Riding: Have you read Banjo Paterson's stirring verses in **Clancy of the Overflow** or **The Man from Snowy River**? If so, your heart may have raced a little faster as you pictured yourself there sitting sweatily in the saddle with the doughty drover who was the hero of these sagas of Australian bush life. (If you haven't heard of Paterson, try to get one of his books. They portray truly the tough life in the "bush" before Australia struck it rich). Nowadays the droving is done from the seat of a roaring motorcycle or a four-wheel-drive vehicle and, in the more remote stations, by helicopter.

Today's trail-riding adventures will transport you back to the cattle-droving days that Paterson portrayed so evocatively. The loneliness of the high country; the grandeur of the Snowy Mountains; the excitement of cutting through mountain trails, your sure-legged horse dodging rabbit-holes, and you ducking beneath low branches, following the forgotten bullock trails of the pioneers, one horse to carry you, one for your *swag* and other gear; living off the land and sleeping under the stars – here is high adventure for the would-be horseman.

No matter what else you do, watching the sheepdogs in action is a must. The intelligence of these marvellous dogs simply has to be seen to be believed as they whip around the outside of a flock of sheep to drive them from one paddock to another. You will be almost open-mouthed with amazement as you watch a single dog's uncanny skills as she forces 50 or more sheep to do her bidding. It's a memory of the Australian bushland that you will treasure. New South Wales, Queensland, Victoria and Western Australia all offer trail rides. In Western Australia, the trail goes deep into the **Cockburn Ranges** along the early stock routes; this one's tough going and NOT for first-timers.

Better not to look, sometimes! Queensland offers great rapids.

Water Sporting

Whitewater Rafting: Australia's surging rivers can offer a real challenge to the most experienced whitewater rafters. If whirling past rocks and snags doesn't get your adrenalin going, some operators spice up things with cliff-face abseiling, and sometimes a pickup by helicopter. Make sure the price includes helmets, safety equipment, camping gear, wetsuits, boots, accommodation and meals (and someone to cook 'em).

Tasmania offers 125 km of wild river rafting over 11, 12 or 14 days down the **Franklin River**, or 5 days down the **Lower Franklin**. One trip includes some seaplane excitement, and all start from Hobart. In New South Wales, it's down the **Shoalhaven River** through rugged gorges that are as adventurous as those

Canoeing, sculling, kayaking for those who prefer calmer waters.

in the Franklin River. Start from **Nowra** for an 11-day trip, or from **Goulburn** for a 5-day trip, and end with a helicopter pick-up from the river.

A 4- or 5-day trip, which begins by bus from **Coffs Harbour**, takes you down the less challenging **Nymboida River** and through the Drop, Hidden Elbow and Chute.

In Victoria, the route is from Buchan down the Snowy River for a 5- or 6-day excursion, and a 5-day trip goes from Stratford through the Amphitheatre and Final Fling of the Mitchell River.

In Queensland, an 11-day trip leaves from Cairns, then a helicopter drops you next to the torrent of the Herbert River with its many waterfalls and rapids (and abseiling is thrown in

for further adventure). Also originating from Cairns is a shorter and less ferocious trip down the North Johnstone and/or Tully Rivers.

Canoeing and Kayaking: Most states offer canoeing and kayaking excursions which are a little more sedate, and far safer, than running the rapids. Encounter nature in her serenity and commune with life in the creeks and rivers. Don't forget your sleeping bag!

Diving: Where else but Queensland's Great Barrier Reef for a diving holiday par excellence exploring this watery wonderland? Experienced scuba divers can live aboard a dive boat anchored atop the reef and drink in its beauty, while novices can head for the **Whitsunday Islands** or **Port Douglas**

Biking possibilities range from cattle country to snowy mountains.

to begin courses with expert underwater tutors, culminating in a proficiency certificate. However, if you're an experienced diver looking for something really out of the way, why not try an Indian Ocean diving tour 250 km out from **Broome**, where you will dive from a converted trawler which doubles as home for 9 days.

Snow to Sky

Cross-country Skiing: Trips are confined to snow season in Victoria, between late June and September. You'll brush up on your skiing, learn basic snow-camping techniques, and after two days of roughing it you'll get a few

nights' warm sleep in Bogong Jack Lodge. These excursions start from **Mt Beauty**.

Mountain Bike Touring: Victoria offers some of the best bike tours through cattle and gold-strike country. One, starting from **Wangaratta**, is a 7-day trip that will tone up every muscle in your body. The price includes bikes, helmets, camping gear – and somebody who knows the way! Queensland offers a 7-day cycling tour of the **Atherton Tablelands** which starts from Cairns, while in Tasmania you can try a 9-day flip around the **Eastern Highlands**. Go for it!

Motorcycle Touring: Ah, so there is a way for softies to do all those interesting bike tours without all the sweat and leg cramps – on a powerful motor-

Hot-air ballooning, though not a regular sport for most, can be arranged through a good travel agent.

cycle. These tours are similar to the cycle tours, but of shorter duration.

Hot-Air Ballooning: Most states have balloon flights, generally tied in with land tours and other attractions. By tradition, balloon flights usually end with the intrepid participants sharing a bottle of champagne – once they're back on solid ground…Cheers!

Four-Wheel-Drive Safaris: From the relative comfort (give or take a few million bumps) of your van, cut across country and really experience the Great Outback. But absolutely DO NOT stray from your party – this is a land where inexperienced people still get lost, sometimes forever. Camp under the stars, or spend the night at Outback lodges or in cattle-station homesteads. These tours are offered by every state, but are a speciality in Western Australia, Queensland and the Northern Territory.

Whatever or wherever it is, bring along your swag bag and pack your drink, for adventure travel means miles out.

Sightseeing with a Difference

Aboriginal Cultural Encounter: If you wish to experience a culture almost as old as the land itself and see sacred sites, view cave paintings, learn about Dreamtime, listen to the lulling tones of the *didgeridoo*, and hear tales of ancient folklore, join an Aboriginal tour from Alice Springs. Aboriginal guides will instruct you in hunting "bush tucker" including lizards and plants, and also point out medicinal shrubs. You will return with a new appreciation of human survival in the harshest part of Australia.

Outback Mailman Tour: Here is some seat-of-your-pants fun. Make ar-rangements with the tourist bureau in Alice Springs to hop aboard the postie's plane and fly with him as he delivers mail to Outback cattle stations and Aboriginal communities. This tour leaves from Alice Springs at 7 am Thursdays, Fridays and Saturdays. It's about 7 hours of sightseeing with a difference, with about 14 happy meetings with Outback folk. Be prepared for a few bumpy landings! Take your camera and food with you.

Queensland Sailing-Ship Adventures: All sorts of square riggers sail from Airlie Beach, Shute Harbour, Cairns, Townsville and Hamilton Island for voyages of between 6 and 8 days around the Great Barrier Reef. Star of the show is the *Bounty*, a full-scale replica of Captain Bligh's infamous vessel.

Making it up Uluru, sacred rock of the Aborigines, is a sport on its own.

Four-wheel Drives: Australian Dream Machines

Australia is one of the world's premier markets for four-wheel-drive vehicles.

Nissan sells about 700 Patrols every month when business is good, and Range Rover about 1400 in a reasonable year. More than 200000 people have bought Toyota Landcruisers since their Australian debut way back in 1959. And bear in mind that these are the expensive marques. Suzuki, Subaru, Lada, Mitsubishi and Daihatsu, among others, all sell rough country vehicles like hot cakes.

In 1990, over 66000 four-wheel drives were registered in Australia. That's about half the total sales of light commercial vehicles and not far short of 20 percent of the combined total for all new passenger and light commercial vehicle sales across the entire country.

You might think that's unsurprising. Australia after all is a rough rugged country of dirt tracks and deserts, and Australian drivers are all hairy-chested Crocodile Dundee types, right? Wrong. In fact the four-wheel-drive phenomenon says something very particular about Australians and the way they like to be seen by the world. "At least 70 percent of the people who buy the more expensive four-wheel drives never take them off-road," says a spokesman for JRA, which distributes Range Rovers in Australia.

Chris Mullett, an adventurer journalist who runs a four-wheel-drive school at Moss Vale south of Sydney (Tel: 048-691-235) conducts courses for hundreds of drivers every year and leads dozens more on remote adventure safaris. He reckons that his typical client is between 35 and 45, married with two children, and earning at least A$40000 a year.

"There is a better-than-even chance that the limit of such a client's safari experience is negotiating the gravel track to the golf club. His expensive vehicle has probably never even had low-range gears engaged."

And more surprises! Nissan says that up to 25 percent of its Patrol sales are directly to women, and many more sales are actively influenced by women. JRA says that though men usually buy Range Rovers, women use the vehicles up to 40 percent of the time. The upmarket four-wheel drives are advertised in adventure magazines – but are more actively promoted in the business press and even in women's journals. Says Chris Mullett:

"Hardly any of the people who buy four-wheel drives will actually drive round Australia. But all of them want to."

The four-wheel drive in Australia, then, is largely the stuff that dreams are made on. By and large they are bought by city folk who yearn for a wide open country which few of them will ever traverse. "Pitt Street cowboys" – they are scornfully dubbed by those Australians who really do work the land. But this odd situation has something to offer the visitor to Australia. For the very possession of these vehicles, bought for reasons of status or romance, is tempting ever larger numbers of urban Australians to use them. Not to drive across Outback torrents on a bridge of crocodiles, necessarily, but to discover the wonders of Australia's wilderness

Above deck, this beauty is all sailing ship with 8000 glorious square feet of wind-stretched, creaking canvas, while down below there are modern airconditioned cabins.

Sea Pleasures

Whale Watching: Between late July to September, from cliffs overlooking South Australia's Great Australian Bight, you can observe the behaviour of the endearing **Southern Right Whales** who move close inland to mate and rear calves.

Other sea creatures enjoying the ocean include dolphins, sea lions, fur seals and osprey. There are also many caves to explore in this area. Jumping-

within a reasonable distance of the cities. Services, tours, hire companies and training schools have sprung up to meet that need.

Virtually every holiday town has some local operator offering four-wheel-drive trips. Even in as little as half-a-day you can be driven through some spectacular scenery by someone who knows his or her way around. Several companies now offer extensive four-wheel-drive bus tours of Australia's wildernesses, lasting up to a month. Many people who take them, even if they have previously groaned at the idea of an organised tour, find these very special experiences are the quickest way to see the country and meet people.

Range Rovers and Patrols, the 4-wheel drive art of staying on course in the outback.

You can hire a four-wheel drive easily and not too expensively for trips of your own, and they can be rented complete with safety equipment and camping gear. The National Parks and Wildlife Service and the various state forestry commissions will advise you of four-wheel-drive routes and will make sure you are clear about the do and don'ts. About 12000 Australians belong to four-wheel-drive clubs today. You could do worse than make first contact with one of these (the tourist people or the parks service will know a number to call). These clubs frequently organise trips on which passengers may be invited, they know the country well, and they cringe at the idea of being considered "bush-bashers". Most of them are committed environmentalists, and very often they are family people who just want to see a little bit more of their own country.

So Australians are turning their four-wheel-drive dreams into reality. It's a great opportunity to tag along for the ride.

off point for these excursions is Ceduna. You may even be asked to take part in a spot of scientific whale research. The adventure holidays detailed above are just a grab-bag of what's on offer. Australians love their country and there are endless opportunities for them to share it with you.

If there is something you have always wanted to do, Australia's probably the place to do it! Enquire about your special interest at a tourist bureau. They will steer you in the direction of some rugged outdoor type who will arrange a croc-shooting trip, a wild buffalo hunt from a helicopter, an emu shoot, a face-to-face encounter with a Great White shark, barramundi-fishing in the lakes of Arnhem Land or anything else you care to dream up.

Consult an encyclopaedia of sports and, almost certainly, you'll find that every single sport listed there is played somewhere in Australia. A combination of the country's wonderful climate and the competitive nature of the average Australian has produced both a nation that is obsessed with sport and a hall of fame featuring world champions in almost every field of sporting endeavour. Sometimes, it seems that if Australians aren't playing sport, then they're either watching it or talking about it!

Watch it or do it. Australians have a great obsession with a sporting event, at a personal or national level.

Generally speaking, business shutters in Australia come down at 5 pm on Fridays, and from then until 9 am the following Monday, the waking hours of Australians are devoted to having a good time. There are playing fields, sports grounds and swimming pool complexes in every city and country town. You'll see balls being kicked, hit, struck, thrown, tossed or flung. There'll be throngs of people swimming, surfing, diving or riding the waves, while others will be snorkelling beneath the water, or sailing, paddling or racing on its surface in all types of craft. And still more will be fishing from boats, jetties, rocks or the shore.

In the countryside, you'll find peo-

Sports & Recreation

Australia's coasts go on forever and its sea sports
are equally endless. Brisbane.

ple hiking, hunting, climbing, fishing, picnicking, studying, filming and taking photos. And of course the sky will have its share of parasailers, balloonists, parachutists and pilots all enjoying the great blue yonder. No element of earth goes unused when Australians set out to enjoy themselves. For specific details of whatever sport you're interested in, ask at the local tourist bureau, check the sports section of your newspaper, or look in the Yellow Pages of the telephone directory under "Clubs".

Joining In Yourself

If the pursuits listed below aren't your style, choose from any number of rec-reational pursuits – squash, horse-riding, ten-pin bowling, lawn bowls, water skiing, grass skiing, indoor cricket, ballooning, canoeing, caving, croquet, ice and roller skating and rock climbing. Sporting clubs often have reciprocal agreements with overseas clubs and will extend temporary membership rights to visitors upon proof of membership.

Boating and Sailing: Australians love boating – and when you see the sparkling waters of the rivers, lakes and oceans, so will you. Charter a boat and sail or cruise through the Whitsundays, off the Great Barrier Reef, or join the many sailcraft on Melbourne's Port Phillip Bay, Hobart's Derwent River, the Sydney Harbour or Perth's Swan River.

Camping: Hire a four-wheel-drive

vehicle and experience first-hand the secrets of the Australian bush. Check with the local tourist bureau for information on camping regulations and the location of camping grounds. It's wise to camp only in these designated sites, as the bush can be unpredictable.

Cycling: There are cycling tracks through parks, around waterways and in rural areas. Hire a bike and cycle around the Swan River in Perth, the south bank of Melbourne's Yarra River or the Botanic Gardens in Brisbane, or try the Coronation Drive Bikeway from Brisbane along the river bank to St Lucia. For cross-country cycle tours, see Adventure Travel (page 321).

Diving and Snorkelling: On the east coast, explore the world-famous Great Barrier Reef; dive in the beautiful waters of New South Wales at Port Hacking, Broken Bay or Sydney Harbour's North Head; or discover the many shipwrecks in Melbourne's Port Phillip Bay. In the west, there's the Rowley Shoals, 14 hours by boat from Broome; the Ningaloo coral reefs off Exmouth; and Rottnest Island, just off Fremantle, with its reefs, caves and shipwrecks. The Port Noarlunga Reef near Adelaide is also a popular diving spot. Other diving expeditions are described in Adventure Travel (page 320).

Fishing: You can take on the big fish all along the east and northwest coasts of Australia. The most famous area for gamefishing is Cairns (Queensland), where you can hunt marlin, mackerel, tuna, barracuda and sailfish

from September to November. Try Bermagui (New South Wales) from late November to June for marlin, tuna and sharks, or Exmouth (Western Australia) for mackerel and many other gamefish.

In the Northern Territory, fish with the locals by day or night, especially around Bathurst Island and Darwin, for the barramundi (June to November), as well as jacks, tarpon and mackerel.

Rainbow and brown trout can be found in the Tasmanian lakes, the rivers of the Australian Alps (Victoria and New South Wales), the Onkaparinga River on the outskirts of Adelaide, and in the southwest of Western Australia, at Pemberton. You'll find fishing grounds for a wide range of species all over Australia. Tourist bureaus can provide maps and local tips, and be sure to find out about fishing licences, bag limits and seasons for protected species.

Golf: There are over 1200 public and private golf courses in Australia. In some, the rough can be very rough indeed and quite unlike anything you've ever seen before! Golf clubs can be hired, but bring your own shoes. Some tour operators offer special golf holidays that provide access to the famous courses of Australia.

Hiking: Hiking, or bushwalking as it is usually called, gives you the chance to experience at close hand Australia's delightful animals, birds and wildflowers. There are walking trails through the many National Parks which are found from coast to coast, covering all types of terrain and climatic zones.

Windsurfing on the Barrier Reef.

Organised tours can be arranged through bushwalking clubs, or check Adventure Travel (page 317) for some more adventurous ideas.

Hunting and Shooting: Consult tourist bureaus about game seasons, firearms laws and the special hunting and shooting tours that are available in the north of Australia. Remember that all native animals are protected, and stock, which is the property of the landowners, cannot be hunted.

Snow Skiing: Enjoy Australia's snow season, from late June to Septem-

Tasmanian snowfields are at Mt Field (1 hour from Hobart) and Ben Lomond (1 hour from Launceston). Cross-country skiers should refer to Adventure Travel (page 321).

Swimming and Surfing: Australia's beautiful and expansive beaches are world renowned. Surfers will want to head for Sydney's surf beaches – Manly, Harbord, Whale Beach and Palm Beach – the Gold Coast of Queensland or the rugged beaches in the southwest of Western Australia near Margaret River and Augusta. Swimmers will find the choices endless. Perth is famous for coastal beaches such as City, Cottesloe, Floreat, Scarborough and North Beaches, as well as its nude beach, Swanbourne. Sydney's harbourside beaches at Balmoral and Nielsen Park are very popular, but sadly its ocean beaches have become badly polluted in recent years.

A few words of warning about swimming in Australia: the oceans can be treacherous, so always swim between the flags, and if the shark siren sounds – get out quick! In northern Australia, avoid swimming in the ocean between October and May, when the stinging box jellyfish are prevalent. And finally, when in the north, pay serious attention to signs warning about the presence of crocodiles. They're not joking!

Tennis: Public and private tennis courts can be found all across Australia. Many hotels and most resorts have their own courts, or you can call the nearest tennis club if you'd like to challenge a local. You can hire racquets, but don't

ber, in the mountainous regions of the southeastern states. In New South Wales, the place to go is Kosciusko National Park, including the resorts of Thredbo, Perisher-Smiggins, Guthega, Mt Blue Cow and Mt Selwyn. Victoria's High Country snow resorts are Mt Buller (only 3 hours' drive from Melbourne), Falls Creek, Mt Hotham and Mt Buffalo. The

People-watching, sport for the eyes.

forget your tennis shoes.

Just Watching

If spectator sports are more your style, you won't be disappointed either. And if you can't be there in the flesh, chances are your favourite sport will be shown on television. All you need is the time to watch it! Australian television networks show live telecasts of cricket, Australian Rules football, horse racing, basketball, tennis, golf, soccer, surfing, wrestling, boxing and car racing, while highlights of rugby, greyhound racing, hockey, table tennis, athletics, swimming, yachting and many other sports are shown on regular sporting programmes.

And now a few words about the Big Three spectator sports in Australia.

Cricket: Without doubt, cricket is god in summer. Test series (played over 3 to 6 matches) and 1-day matches keep interest at fever pitch as the home side pits itself against teams from England, New Zealand, the West Indies, India, Pakistan and Sri Lanka. Crowds of 30000 to 90000 people invade the grounds at Sydney, Melbourne, Adelaide, Perth and Brisbane, while millions more stay glued to their TV sets. At any time, you are likely to be accosted by a total stranger and asked, out of the blue, "Oooja thinkll win, mate?" (Who do you think will win, mate?). Is there a man alive brave enough to reply that he neither knows nor cares? No! A response such as "We're juskiddin to 'em, doncharekkon?" (We're just kidding to them, don't you reckon?) will satisfy your questioner, and you will have passed one of Australia's biggest tests with flying colours.

Aussie Rules Football: In the states where it is played, Australian Rules football – or Aussie Rules – dominates television programming, social life and conversation throughout winter. The game originated in Victoria during the 1850s gold rush, when gold-seekers amused themselves between excursions into the fields by playing a rough game based on Gaelic football. It was not until 1866 that the rules of the game were drawn up and made official. The people of Victoria are absolutely fanatical about Aussie Rules, living and breathing it for six months of the year. In other states,

Surfers Paradise.

the people are merely crazy about it. The game has always been one to inspire rivalry, and this escalated several years ago when Queensland and Western Australia (followed by South Australia in 1991) joined the prestigious Victorian Football League to form a national league, the Australian Football League (AFL). The complacency of Victorian teams and fans alike was shattered by the good performances put in by the other states, and it seemed at one stage in 1991 that the unthinkable might happen – that a Melbourne team might lose the Grand Final crown! However, their supremacy, though dented, was spared. The AFL Grand Final is considered one of the most exciting sporting events in the country, and fans travel to Melbourne from all over the country to experience its special blend of the agony of defeat and the ecstasy of victory.

Horse Racing: In every state, on every day and most nights except on Sundays, racing of some sort is taking place. On Saturdays, there is a staggering programme of racing (galloping with jockey) in the daytime and harness racing (pacers with reinsmen) at night. Not only do gamblers bet on events taking place in their home city and in other parts of their state, they can also bet on interstate races. In Queensland, for example, gamblers – or punters as they're called – can have a fling during the daytime on the horse-races in Brisbane, on the Gold Coast and at Caloundra (all in their home state), plus the full card of races in Sydney, Melbourne and Adelaide – and the last four races on the

The Aussies love a bet. Melbourne.

Phar Lap and the Melbourne Cup

Australians are keen racegoers, and it seems entirely appropriate that one of their national heroes has four legs. The great chestnut racehorse Phar Lap has been dead for 60 years, yet his name is still a household word to Australian children who have never even seen a horserace. A feature film about him has appeared in the last few years. His untimely death is still hotly debated in pubs across the land. After his death in California, the great horse's hide was stuffed and is now on display in the **Museum of Victoria** in Melbourne. His enormous heart – at some 6 kg twice the size of an average horse's heart – went to the **Institute of Anatomy** in Canberra. And his skeleton was shipped to the land of his birth, New Zealand, where it remains today. So great was his hold on the imagination that Phar Lap, mounted for display in his glass case in Melbourne, still draws crowds, especially in early November – the time of that greatest of all Australian horseraces, the Melbourne Cup.

The Melbourne Cup is an institution in itself. Launched in 1861, when just 7000 people attended, the two-miler put Australia on the international racing map. It has been dubbed the greatest all-age handicap in the world. By the early 1920s, nearly 120000 spectators were attending the event. Nowadays the racetrack attendance is huge but irrelevant. Television has taken the Melbourne Cup into every home and pub and club across the country. It is attended by royalty. It falls on the first Tuesday of November and is marked in Victoria by an official public holiday, and across the rest of Australia by an unofficial one. Only barmen and restaurant owners do any work on Melbourne Cup Day.

The great Phar Lap was born in New Zealand in 1927, and was bought as a yearling for the knock-down price of 160 guineas by Australian trainer Harry Telford. The big ungainly horse was so unpromising that the owner for whom he was bought at first refused to pay for his training. He was launched onto a racing career in Sydney, but for his first nine races showed every sign of justifying his critics' doubts. Though he had one minor win, he was unplaced in the other eight races.

In September 1929, something extraordinary happened. He came second in the Chelmsford Stakes in Sydney. Then he won his next three races over a two-week period. Only a month before, the big red horse had been a 25-to-one outsider even in fairly minor races. Now he was a hot tip for the forthcoming Melbourne Cup. He was rapidly sent to Melbourne, where he won again in one of the warm-up races. Phar Lap started the 1929 Melbourne Cup as favourite. Indeed, Phar Lap started as favourite in three successive Melbourne Cups – the only horse ever to do so. But such are the vagaries of racing that he only won on one occasion, in 1930. He came third in the 1929 Cup, when he had not reached his full potential, and was unplaced in the 1931 event, when he was probably sick.

The Melbourne crowds adopted Phar Lap as their own and he was based in the Victorian capital from then on. He recorded one other third in a race early the next year, then on 1st March 1930 struck the mother lode of winning form. He had nine successive wins, then a second place. Then 14 more wins, and another second. Then eight more wins. So firm a favourite was he that bookmakers sometimes refused to take bets on him. These were the Depression years in Australia, and people badly needed a winner. But the purses for big races in Australia were getting smaller, and Phar Lap's owners took a fateful decision: to ship the horse to the United States to race for some of the big money on offer there. Phar Lap raced only once overseas, at the Agua Caliente Handicap in Mexico on 20 March 1932. Characteristically, he won it hands down. Sixteen days later he was dead, poisoned on a California farm. Some said, and still say, that he was deliberately killed. Certainly he had enemies. He had been shot at on one occasion in Australia. But it seems much more likely the death was a tragic accident. Nothing could replace Phar Lap in the hearts of Australians. But his startling record endures. Phar Lap started 51 times for 37 wins, 3 seconds and 2 thirds. His total stake winnings were £66,738, an enormous sum in those days. That made him one of the top-earning horses of all time, and represented a fantastic return on Telford's 160 guineas. His racing career lasted less than three short years.

other side of the continent, in Perth.

The racing clubs concerned cooperate by programming their events to allow a 5-minute gap between each race. And a special television network called Sky Channel darts from racetrack to racetrack to show viewers all over Australia all 48 or so races in one hectic afternoon. The procedure is repeated at night, with harness racing and/or greyhound meetings screened from three or four different tracks.

Punters can place their bets at the racetrack or at the Totalisator Agency Board (TAB) shops, which are equipped with electronic bet-taking machines connected to the various courses. The turnover from these TAB agencies, makes gambling Australia's fourth biggest industry. Racing is not confined to the capital cities. Australia abounds with many hundreds of racecourses, harness racing tracks and dog racing tracks. The pride of many an otherwise undistinguished country town is its racetrack.

Australia's most important race is the Melbourne Cup a handicap run over 3200 m at Flemington Racecourse in Melbourne on the first Tuesday of November. The country's premier racetrack is named after Robert Fleming, who operated a nearby abattoir that supplied the meat for steaks and pies sold to early racegoers. The stake money offered for the major races regularly tops A$1 million, while races worth A$500000 are almost common place. One champion racehorse, "Better Loosen Up", has amassed stakewinnings of A$5

million, while a few dozen other runners are "equine millionaires", having topped the A$1 million mark.

January

Perth	Perth Cup
Melbourne	Australian Open Tennis Tournament

February

Melbourne	Australian Masters Golf Tournament

April

Melbourne	Stawell Gift Easter Foot Running Carnival
Darwin	City to Surf Fun Run

July

Darwin	Darwin to Ambon (Indonesia) Yacht Race

July–August

Darwin	Darwin Cup Carnival

August

Sydney	City to Surf Fun Run

September

Melbourne	AFL Grand Final

October

Adelaide	Australian Formula One Grand Prix
Bathurst	Bathurst 1000
NSW	(production car race)

November

Sydney	NSW Golf Open
Melbourne	Melbourne Cup

December

Sydney	Sydney to Hobart
Hobart	Yacht Race

Ready, steady, go.

Aussie Food

Australia is the land of plenty, and nowhere is this more evident than in its cuisine. Local cuisine is based on the use of the country's wonderful selection of fresh ingredients – world-renowned beef and lamb; seafood from the expansive coastline and many waterways; rich dairy products; and a wide variety of fruit and vegetables found in the many climatic zones Australia occupies.

Cheese, wine, bread, fruit..... the good life where food is concerned.

Whatever style of cooking you enjoy, you will find it in Australia. This variety is a direct result of the immigration programme. Until the late 1940s, the menu in an Australian restaurant was dull, stodgy and unimaginative. Then along came the immigrants who soon set about providing themselves with the sort of fare they once enjoyed at home. The Italians set the pace and soon other nationalities followed suit. Staid Austral-

*Coastal and riverine harvest complement
Australia's other produce.*

ians accustomed to a lifetime of roast beef and Yorkshire pudding at first shunned the new cuisine and the wine it was washed down with, but soon their taste-buds became more adventurous and they began to experiment enthusiastically. Ethnic cafés became the "in" places for a whole new generation, and imaginative cuisine had come to stay in Australia. Choose from African, Chinese, French, Greek, Indian, Indonesian, Italian, Japanese, Korean, Lebanese, Malaysian, Spanish, Thai, Vietnamese and many others. Each capital city has its inner-city ethnic enclaves – Italian or Greek for example – where you can enjoy cosmopolitan cuisine at very affordable prices.

The range of eating establishments is just as wide. In all major cities, there are first-class restaurants, family-style bistros, cafes and tea-rooms, pubs and wine bars that serve counter meals, fast-food outlets, and inexpensive food markets. Eating in one of Australia's many top quality restaurants is a worthwhile experience, but it won't be cheap. Dinner is likely to be a long drawn-out affair, taking the better part of an evening, but if time is precious inform the waiter. Some mid-range restaurants offer fixed-price set meals or buffets, but most are *á la carte*. If you don't want to dole out too many dollars, try the department stores or chain stores where restaurants and cafés offer a square meal for A$6 or so.

Unfortunately, the choice of food

and restaurants outside the city areas is less diverse. Although resorts and major tourist centres are well served, small country towns may only offer the hotel dining room, the local pub, a few snack bars and possibly a Chinese restaurant.

City Menus

The following is a quick round-up of specialties offered in the capital cities:

Adelaide: Try Hindley Street for a wide variety of different restaurants, and don't forget to wash your meal down with one of the excellent wines from the Barossa Valley.

Brisbane: Brisbane's specialties include Moreton Bay bugs (small, squat crustaceans similar to lobsters), reef fish, the huge Queensland mud crabs, beef, and tropical fruit such as the unique strawberry mango. The inner-city suburbs of Milton (look for the mini Eiffel Tower), Paddington and New Farm offer some top-notch restaurants, while Fortitude Valley is the location of a very upmarket Chinatown with a wide variety of Asian restaurants.

Canberra: Canberra has more restaurants per head of population than any other Australian city, so the choices are endless.

Darwin: Top End specialties are barramundi (local freshwater fish best served grilled), prawns, squid and barbecued buffalo steak. Dress codes for dining out are very relaxed in Darwin, as they are for everything else.

Hobart: The cooler climate in Tasmania produces a delightfully different menu. While in Hobart, try scallops, crayfish, tuna, abalone, mutton birds, venison, quail, rainbow and brown trout from mountain lakes, Tasmanian salmon, strawberries and raspberries (December to April), apple pie with rich King Island cream, a wide variety of excellent cheeses, liqueur honey and local apple cider.

Melbourne: Melbourne is Australia's culinary capital, with over 2000 restaurants. Bay scallops, oysters, mussels, fish, dairy foods and cheese are among the specialties on offer. There is a boundless supply of top-class restaurants, while for hearty ethnic meals head for the suburb of St Kilda, heart of the city's nightlife. Try Lygon Street, Carlton, for Italian food served alfresco; Little Bourke Street for Chinese; Lonsdale and Siva Streets, Richmond, for Greek; or Sydney Road, Brunswick, for Turkish.

Perth: Perth is famous for its seafood, especially rock lobster, WA dhufish and snapper, marron (local freshwater crayfish), crabs and prawns. Sample some for yourself at one of the many seafood restaurants located on the river. The city's nightlife centre is Northbridge, where you'll find an abundance of ethnic restaurants, pubs and street cafés.

Sydney: Sydney is a close rival of Melbourne for the title of culinary capital. Try rock oysters, lobster, crabs and prawns at a harbourside seafood restaurant such as the justly famous Doyle's; or go ethnic at Leichhardt or

Australia remains one of the most self-sufficient in dairy and agricultural produce.

Darlinghurst (Italian), Cleveland Street, Surry Hills (Lebanese) or Liverpool Street (Spanish). There are lots of trendy coffee shops in the pretty terraced suburbs of Glebe and Paddington, while the historic Rocks area offers an interesting variety of traditional pubs and taverns.

Restaurant Codes

It's always wise to make a restaurant reservation, especially on Fridays to Sundays, and always ask whether the restaurant is licensed (sells alcohol) or BYO (bring your own wine or beer). If you need help in choosing a restaurant, consult one of the guide books available from tourist bureaus, check the Yellow Pages of the telephone directory or ask a local.

Restaurant hours vary widely depending on the style of establishment and from state to state. Watch the time: generally, orders are taken until 9 or 10 pm for dinner, but can sometimes stop as early as 2 pm for lunch. Also, if staying in a hotel, check the breakfast hours or you'll step out of the lift still rubbing your eyes and find breakfast ended at 9.30 am or even earlier. Still, you won't starve: fast-food outlets, pizzerias, ethnic restaurants, coffee shops and snack bars all have very flexible hours, and most major hotels have 24-hour coffee shops. Many of the finest restaurants in the country serve – at great expense – dishes with unusual

Bush Tucker

When the great 19th-century Australian explorers Burke and Wills perished of malnutrition in the red centre of the continent, they died surrounded by food.

Their Western prejudices prevented them from learning how to survive on bush foods of the kind that the Aboriginals nearby thrived upon. Their less famous companion John King did in fact live through the ordeal, but only because the Aboriginals force-fed him after he became too weak to resist.

Certainly to the Western observer the Australian bush – and especially the arid zones – can look pretty bare of nourishment. The truth is that bush food is not scarce. But it isn't necessarily very palatable either. Witchetty grubs are probably the most famous item of bush tucker. The grubs are the maggots of a large moth and live in tree trunks and roots. Some bush gourmets like them tossed in hot ash, but they can be fried, or – for those with strong stomachs – eaten raw. It's best to pull out the intestines first, though. They tend to be full of half-digested wood.

Rather tastier are honey-ants. These ants hold large droplets of honey in their swollen abdomens, which is every bit as sweet as bees' honey. The grubs of all kinds of ants can be found by smashing open old tree stumps, and are extremely nutritious and quite edible if toasted on a hot stone. Separate ant grubs from dirt by tossing them in water. The grubs float. They will keep you alive, but you need a lot of them to make a meal. The Aboriginals also used to eat march flies, which at least makes a change from having them eat you.

Snakes have a delicate flavour not unlike chicken, and even the venomous ones are quite safe to eat. They are not always safe to kill, however, and since Australia has its fair share of poisonous snakes it may be as well to avoid them. Lizards are a better bet, and the big goanna – which can get to 4 or 5 feet long – has plenty of meat on his bones.

Virtually all mammals and birds are edible, as elsewhere. Some are said to be quite delicious, particularly flying fox.

Vast numbers of Australian plants are edible and nutritious too. A recent scholarly survey summarised several hundred of these into some 240 pages. But the Australian bush is not a cornucopia of luscious fruit. There are coconut palms in the tropical north, and mangoes, figs, a slender native banana, and a form of "bush lemon". But in general, as one survival expert puts it, most Australian native fruits are still at the "crab-apple" stage of evolutionary development, at least as far as non-Aboriginal tastes are concerned.

The red fruit of the Walking Stick Palm is a useful food, though, and was responsible in one famous case for keeping plane crash survivors alive. There are also yams and tubers, but these should be boiled first, since some are poisonous raw. The prickly pear cactus can be eaten when the spines have been singed off, and has the advantage that it is easily recognised. Various waterplants and even slimy green freshwater algae can be (and have been) lifesavers. The study of bush food is in vogue today in Australia. Army Major Les Hiddens, who has devoted his military career to studying survival foods, has become a media star with several series' of very popular TV programmes behind him. A few avant-garde delicatessens and restaurants even offer examples of the least repellent bush tucker for sale in the cities.

Most knowledge of native foods, though, still resides with Australia's Aboriginal population. While white Australians have been traditionally conservative about food, it seems many of them may now be prepared to learn from the original inhabitants.

Australian Wine

Today Australian wines sell all over the world and make up a multimillion-dollar export industry for the nation.

Yet even now few people would automatically associate the land of kangaroos and koalas with fine vintages and a great gourmet tradition. Perhaps that's something to do with the image that Australians have built up for themselves. They have traditionally seen themselves as unpretentious and egalitarian folk. Their traditional drink is beer – the honest workingman's beverage. Wine, or so the myth used to go, is associated with elegance and elitism.

This is quite unfair. In fact the history of wine in Australia goes back to the very beginning of European settlement. Captain Arthur Phillip, who led the First Fleet of settlers and convicts to Botany Bay in 1788, brought vine cuttings with him. The Mediterranean climate and good soil of New South Wales had already been noted as ideal for viticulture.

Those first cuttings, planted where Sydney's Botanic Gardens now stand, did not thrive. But soon the cause of wine was taken up by the Macarthurs, the great family of pastoralists who founded the merino wool industry in the colony. By the early 1800s, the Macarthurs had extensive vineyards at their family seat at Camden Park just outside Sydney. From there thousands of cuttings were sent to help found the South Australian wine-growing industry.

This proved to be a good move. So good, indeed, that South Australia is now known as "the wine state" and produces over 60 percent of Australia's wine. Plenty is still grown in New South Wales, though, and a little still comes from the Camden Park area. In Victoria there were also promising beginnings. The first Governor of the state, Charles La Trobe, had a Swiss wife. They encouraged Swiss vignerons to settle in Victoria, and for many years it was the premier state for wine production.

Despite these promising beginnings, Australia's potential for producing good quality wine for the table was not fully realised until after WW II. An influx of European migrants and a growing level of contact with the rest of the world helped change the Australian attitude towards wine.

Even dedicated beer drinkers began to consider wine as an option with the advent of the Australian-invented wine cask, a "box" of wine usually holding four litres. While the wine cask may have sent a shudder down the spines of purists, it permitted wine to compete head-to-head with beer in terms of price.

It also incidentally helped dispel the elitist myth surrounding wine-drinking. During the 1970s and 1980s the industry boomed, and today Australian wines of all kinds win international awards at shows around the world. Casks still sell well, but many Australians now have very well-educated palates indeed, and it would be a rare social occasion at which beer was the only drink on offer.

A fascinating by-product of the Australian wine boom has been the growth of an associated tourist industry.

Several of the major wine-growing areas are close to major cities. The Hunter Valley and even the Mudgee Vineyards are within striking distance of Sydney, for example, and the Barossa and Clare Valleys are not far from Adelaide. These regions and others like them are dotted with vineyards and wineries. All of them welcome casual visitors who call in to taste a little wine, and to buy a bottle or two, or occasionally even a case.

Guest houses have sprung up on and around some of these wine-growing properties. It is possible to take a hot-air balloon flight over the vineyards and come back to a champagne breakfast. Or to visit half-a-dozen vineyards in a horsedrawn carriage and stop for a picnic lunch overlooking a *billabong*.

Many wineries are small family concerns, and a weekend visiting them can be a delightful and intimate experience – and incidentally a good way to learn about wine. Many Australian vignerons are directly descended from German or French settlers of the last century, and are happy to talk about their craft. Indeed, some areas still strongly reflect their European origins, which can make visiting them an even more charming experience.

Australians have taken a well-established industry, and have enriched it with something of their very own.

local or native ingredients such as witchetty grubs (see Bush Tucker, page 345), kangaroo, camel, crocodile and buffalo. However, you won't find a style of cooking that is distinctively Australian, or anything that could be called a national dish. There are a few local "specialties", though:

Damper (coarse unleavened bread cooked over a campfire) and *billy tea* (brewed in an open tin can called a billy, with a eucalyptus leaf thrown into the brew) – both remnants of Australia's pioneering days. The *pavlova*, a meringue creation filled with cream and fruit that is purported to have been named after the Russian ballerina Anna Pavlova. *Meat pie and tomato sauce*, a variation of which is the *Adelaide Floater*, a meat pie in a soup filled with mushy peas and topped with tomato sauce. *Vegemite*, a thick, black vegetable extract used as a sandwich spread and much loved by Aussie children and adults alike. The *lamington*, a sponge cake iced with chocolate and coconut and usually split in half and filled with fresh cream. The *Great Aussie Barbecue*, a national pastime on weekends, in which steak, chops and sausages are sizzled on outdoor hotplates and eaten with the traditional accompaniments of bread, salads and the inevitable bush flies! And to accompany all this wonderful food? Try a local wine or one of Australia's famous lagers. Australian beer is fairly strong and is drunk icy cold. Each state produces its own brews and of course each will tell you its brew

Great Aussie past time.

is best. The main brands are Foster's (Victoria), Castlemaine XXXX (Queensland), Swan (Western Australia) and Cooper's Sparkling Ale (South Australia). There is also a growing number of boutique brewers, such as the Matilda Bay Brewing Company which offers such deliciously named varieties as Redback Lager, Dogbolter and Brass Monkey Stout. Beer can be bought in large bottles, cans ("tinnies"), stubbies (small bottles) or on tap.

Australian wines enjoy an international reputation especially the excellent cabernet sauvignons and chardonnays. *Vin ordinaire* is sold cheaply in flagons and casks and is of a fairly good quality. When you order "house wine" by the glass or carafe in a restaurant, this is what you'll get!.

At first sight, Australia is a destination in itself.

The populous southeastern seaboard cities, where most Australians live and where most visitors initially touch down, seem a very long way from anywhere else. Having made the effort to get there, travellers may feel that there is enough to see within Australia without worrying about other overseas destinations. In that respect it is a little like the United States – it's not really on the way anywhere else.

To some extent this is an illusion, and unless the visitor is aware of the options there is a chance of missing out on some fascinating sidetrips.

In ceremonial paint a tribesman in Papua New Guinea prepares for the annual Sing Sing.

Beyond Australia

New Zealand

New Zealand is the obvious example, frequently and mistakenly missed by visitors because they assume it must be similar to Australia and not really worth the extra trip. Some Australians will perpetrate this myth. Aus-

Taking in the Franz Josef glacier in New Zealand.

tralians and New Zealanders are friendly rivals, and Aussies are reluctant to admit their trans-Tasman neighbours might have anything that Australia lacks.

It certainly pays to remember that these are two quite separate and inde-

pendent nations, despite the superficial similarity of flag and accent. Visitors will be reminded firmly about this point if they fail to acknowledge it.

Having said that, the two countries share a great deal in terms of cultural heritage, pioneer spirit, easy-going atti-

has a tiny population of 3 million plus, and an economy which has been to hell and back in the last few years, though optimists say it is now recovering.

Apart from all this, New Zealand is in fact quite different from Australia, and indeed the North and South Islands are quite different from each other. Most visitors will fetch up in the North Island at Auckland first, New Zealand's biggest city but not the capital (that's Wellington). There are those New Zealanders who hate Auckland as sprawling, noisy and industrial: but these are comparative terms. Most big city visitors from abroad will find it has the expected metropolitan appurtenances – including some excellent restaurants in Queen Street and Quay Street – but is rather quiet and slow-moving. They might also find it pretty expensive. New Zealand has low income tax, but a high consumption tax, which is fine if you live there, and not so fine if you don't. Watch out especially for the cost of hiring a car. Unless you do it as part of a package, it can be outrageous.

All these points, good and bad, apply to New Zealand as a whole. There is an endearingly old-fashioned sense to the place. Farmstay holidays in particular – and there are scores of these to choose from – benefit from this rather homely charm. Try staying in an old pub in the main street of a small country town to get the authentic flavour of New Zealand. You'll find the accommodation quaintly outmoded, and the people warm and welcoming and with a wry,

tudes and friendliness to tourists. They are also growing closer economically. The recent Closer Economic Relations Treaty between them forms a two-nation South Pacific Trading Bloc, and citizens of one country have automatic right of residence in the other. Australia is, however, easily the dominant partner in this relationship. New Zealand

laid-back humour. As a society, it is somehow less brash than Australia.

New Zealand, like Australia, is becoming a more multicultural society. But in a sense it always was one. Its own indigenous people, the Maoris, retain a vibrant culture which makes itself felt assertively.

Part of the TV news is broadcast in Maori, the language is routinely taught in schools, and Maori issues are hot political potatoes. The vigour of Maori culture – their dances, stories and military prowess permeate New Zealand life – gives the country special interest. Yet in country areas the New Zealanders of European stock can seem more British than the British.

As for places to visit on the North Island, try a trip up the dramatic **90 Mile Beach** (actually a mere 90 km in length) which sweeps up to **Cape Reinga**. The Cape is at the northernmost tip of New Zealand, where the swirling currents of the Tasman Sea and the Pacific boil in a gigantic maelstrom. It is from here that the spirits of the dead Maori begin their long journey home to their ancestral land of Hawaiki, whence their forefathers voyaged to find this land they call Aotearoa ("the Land of the Long White Cloud") about 1000 years ago.

Stay a couple of nights at **Russell** on the **Bay of Islands**, north of Auckland on the east coast. This sleepy hamlet was – incredibly – once known as the hell-hole of the Pacific, full of drunken whaling-men and grogshops (90 of them). It was also the site of symbolic signings of treaties with the Maoris and subsequent fighting over them, and was briefly even the capital. Today, it's hard to believe its past status. Take the "milk run" out on a catamaran around the chain of islands in the bay, each island with its own story.

Moving south down the coast you should see on the Coromandel Peninsula the remains of the vast forests of *kauri* – native conifers which live for thousands of years and which the white man took for spars and masts. And no-one on the North Island misses **Rotorua**, a few hours south of Auckland. Here for centuries the Maori people lived in uneasy symbiosis with volcanic activity – mud pools, hot geysers and constant clouds of sulphurous fumes. The present tourist town stinks of it, but the residents claim they don't notice the smell, and many of them heat their houses with geothermal energy. Volcanic activity is widespread across the North Island, and has caused more than one major catastrophe since the coming of the white man.

It is a reminder of just how new and raw this country is, which in part explains the steeper more jagged topography of New Zealand when compared to Australia.

A visit to **Wellington** is a must, the windy city is one of the prettiest capitals in the world. It is on the southern tip of the North Island. From here a ferry trip across the Cook Strait will take you to the South Island.

Get away from it all on a beach in Fiji.

New Zealand's South Island is a strange and sometimes forbidding land of soaring alps, creeping glaciers and bottomless fjords. Like the North Island, it is studded with lakes, many of breathtaking loveliness.

The South Island remained largely unexplored by the European until the later years of the last century, and today it represents perhaps the last truly untouched wilderness in Australasia. It is best known for its winter sports, with some of the world's finest skiing and climbing.

Its troutfishing and walking are also unrivalled, and the coastline, with deep tranquil sounds and long empty beaches, offers spectacular scenery and matchless fishing. It is even possible to take a train across the mountains for one of the most dramatic rides of your life.

Get to New Zealand by Qantas or Air New Zealand or a range of other international airlines direct from any of the east coast Australian cities. It takes about three hours, or about the same as flying from Sydney to Perth.

There are several flights in both directions daily. Auckland and Wellington on the North Island, and Christchurch on the South Island, are all served by international flights. The best way, if you have time, is probably to take a trans-Tasman package deal. At least until the recent price wars among deregulated Australian domestic airlines it was actually cheaper to fly to New

Savour the Balinese culture, not too many hours away.

Zealand from Sydney or Melbourne than to some other Australian destinations, and trans-Tasman routes are still extremely competitive.

Bali

For a different kind of experience altogether, try **Bali**. Modern mass air travel has put this idyllic tropical Indonesian island just six hours away for Australian holidaymakers from the southeastern cities – 150000 of them go there every year. That has its downside. The southern resort towns of **Sanur** and **Kuta Beach** (renowned for its surf) are virtually Australian tourist colonies. You may well find the streets packed with large-

bellied lobster-coloured men in singlets on their way to one of the dozens of "genuine Aussie pubs" which have sprung up to cater for them, complete with Australian beer.

It's not true to say the Balinese have remained untouched by this invasion. There's plenty of pressure from the locals for tourists to buy everything from fake watches to on-the-spot massages. But on the other hand it is astonishing to what extent the Balinese people have retained their identity, their serenity and their essential good humour. Just a very little way out of the main tourist areas will put you more closely in touch with one of the world's gentlest and most colourful cultures.

Take a trip to **Ubud** in the centre of

the island, an artists' colony which still retains its charm, though increasingly "touristy" itself. Or carry on up to the far north coast (the island takes about two hours to drive across) for sheer hedonism and stay at one of the black-sanded beach resorts near the old capital of **Singaraja**.

A more down-to-earth experience can be had by taking a half-hour flight, or a longer boat-trip, to the neighbouring island of **Lombok**, or even to the smaller islands beyond that wander anywhere off the beaten track and you can rediscover much of the richness of Balinese dance, dress and ritual which so enchanted the Europeans who first visited it.

It is astonishingly cheap to reach Bali from virtually any of the Australian international airports. On a package deal, the canny traveller can often go and stay there for a week or two for less than it would cost to stay in Australia for the same period of time. The Australian dollar is strong against the Indonesian rupiah. Living in Bali can be cheap indeed, even if you decide to do the adventurous thing and find your own accommodation – easily the best way to enjoy the island.

South Pacific Islands

Several Pacific island destinations are within easy reach of Australia's east coast, and tourism is rapidly developing into the major dollar-earner for them.

In response, a wide range of hotel accommodation has sprung up on virtually every Pacific island. Airlines operating from Australia offer a bewildering variety of tours, sometimes combining several destinations. Even weekend package deals are now available to several Pacific destinations.

It needs to be said, though, that in general they offer fairly standard fare for the casual visitor – fine beaches, snorkelling, sailing, varied cuisine and more-or-less luxury accommodation. There's nothing wrong with that, of course, but it would be difficult and expensive to travel to most of these destinations independently, and difficult to find much to do there even if you did.

Most Australians seem to regard Pacific island holidays as get-away-from-it-all vacations, and all of them cater for that taste rather than for the more adventurous type who wants to mix it with the locals.

New Caledonia

New Caledonia was France's penal colony in the South Pacific. Nowadays visitors are generally much more eager to get in than to escape, though there have been some violent clashes in the cause of independence in recent years. It remains a French possession, and the Frenchness of the capital Noumea and of the whole archipelago is part of its special charm.

South Pacific sunset. Vanuatu.

French is the official language, though English is widely spoken, and French cuisine dominates the cafes and restaurants. There is a wide range of hotel and budget accommodation.

New Caledonia is near-tropical in climate, with fabulous weather year-round to enjoy watersports. Yacht charter groups do a particularly lively trade. They offer craft with or without skippers and provisioning, and hire them to novices or old salts, for trips across the tranquil lagoon or across the 70 km of blue Pacific to the Isle of Pines. New Caledonia is one of the largest islands in the Pacific, and is about 3 hours out of Sydney by Qantas, UTA or Air Caledonia.

An hour or so further east by jet from Noumea, or about 3 hours direct from Brisbane or Sydney by Air Vanuatu, lie the 83 islands that make up the nation of **Vanuatu**.

Vanuatu offers luxury accommodation, fabulous sunsets, great seafood and general hedonism. But its particular fame is its scuba diving. It is possible to get full international certification in a couple of weeks if you are there for that long.

Not much further out, and still within easy reach of Australia, is another tropical jewel, **Fiji**, where the South Pacific science of catamaran-building was taken to heights which approached European shipbuilding before the colonial powers eclipsed it. Even now Fiji retains more of a sense of independent history than some of the other island nations, while offering the same kinds of leisure attractions.

The determined traveller can use Australia and/or New Zealand as a base for a whole range of more distant Pacific island explorations beyond these few. **Tonga**, **Samoa**, **Tahiti**, and the idyllic **Cook Islands** are all served by jet flights from eastern Australian cities.

Papua New Guinea

Those who prefer adventure and hard work to lounging in the sun, and can't get their fill of it in Australia, might find it in **Papua New Guinea** just to the north. A visit there would be a special thrill for history buffs, who can trek across the rugged Kokoda Track which crosses this wild and remote land from north to south.

Japanese and Australian troops fought to death over this fiendishly hostile terrain in World War II and a company called New Guinea Expeditions in Sydney is among a number of adventure travel operators which cater for enthusiasts who want to experience the Track for themselves.

Naturally there are less strenuous vacations to be had in Papua New Guinea, though currently the capital of Port Moresby has a dreadful reputation for violent crime. For the rugged adventurer, the inland fastnesses of PNG would be hard to beat, but for the pleasure-seeking holidaymaker it is probably best

avoided. Two gentler but still unusual island experiences lie off Australia's east coast, closer at hand for visitors to Sydney and Brisbane.

Lord Howe Island is 700 km northeast of Sydney and the same distance southeast of Brisbane, a tiny piece of New South Wales set in the Pacific, but so different from the mainland that visiting it is like travelling to a distant country. It is just 11 km long and 2 km wide, and consists almost entirely of two mountains guarding a crystal lagoon. Visiting it is a very special experience. Only 300 people live there permanently, and only 400 visitors are allowed at any one time.

There are no 5-star hotels, and the largest resort will take only 85 guests, so the emphasis is on informality and clean comfort rather than luxury. It's a wonderful place for diving, bushwalking, birdwatching and reef-viewing. There's not a fancy nightclub to be seen.

Norfolk Island is 1600 km out from the Australian coast, and is served directly from several Australian cities, often by flights which link it to Lord Howe for visitors who want to see both. Norfolk Island was settled by a group of the mutineers from *HMS Bounty* and their Polynesian womenfolk early in the 19th century, and today blends European and Polynesian cultures in a fascinating cocktail. Even now it preserves a level of independence from Australia, granted by Queen Victoria, and as a result of that act of reconciliation it is today a tax-free shopper's paradise.

TRAVEL TIPS

ACCOMMODATION

The big cities have a full range of accommodation options for the visitor, from plush five-star hotels to economy hotels and hostels, motels (you don't have to be driving a car to get a room), backpacker lodges and boarding houses. For longer stays, there are holiday flats and furnished units in the main resort areas. On arrival at a domestic airport, railway or bus station, look for the tourist information kiosk and check what's available in your price range. If you are arriving from overseas, it is advisable to make a firm booking in advance, even if it's only for one night.

Package tours are a good option once you begin city-to-city sightseeing, as you are always assured of a clean, comfortable room at your next destination. These can be arranged through domestic airlines, bus lines and state railways.

Outside the cities, towns offer mainly hotel and motel rooms, or perhaps a caravan park. Bookings are essential during peak periods such as school holidays.

AIR TRAVEL

A price war among the three established domestic operators, Ansett, Australian and East-West has resulted in pace-setting bargains, forcing operators to slash prices. Now, all sorts of bargain packages are on offer, so shop around. There are also a variety of concession fares for students and senior citizens. If arriving in Australia on the national carrier, Qantas, remember it also has cut-rate flights between capitals.

Important country towns are linked by air to their respective capitals, and it is hoped deregulation will also cause a reduction in fares on these feeder routes. Because of the immense distances in Australia, it is usually necessary to fly between major centres and also to some of the remote outback regions, unless time is on your side.

AIRPORT TRANSFERS

Airports in all Australian capitals are generally quite a long way from the city. Unless you arrive in the middle of the night, there usually will be a bus service operating from the airport to the city, even on Sundays and holidays. Check details about these buses at the tourist information kiosk, and also ask about approximate taxi fares.

Sydney has a marvellously efficient public transport system. The Airport Express bus service runs from the international to the domestic airport, then into the city, stopping in the main tourist areas such as the Central Railway Station and Chinatown. It terminates at Circular Quay, arriving just in time for you to catch a hydrofoil across the harbour to Manly, if that is your destination. The bus drivers are very helpful, your map, and perhaps a question or two to a passerby, will get you to your accommodation.

Adelaide's regular bus service between the airport and the city stops near the main hotels, and the drivers will gladly give you helpful advice.

Melbourne's Tullamarine Airport is a long way out, but a mini-bus service operates between the airport and Spencer Street Railway Station in the city. From there, it is a quick taxi ride to your hotel.

Brisbane has a magnificent domestic airport, but its international airport is shabby. There is an efficient bus service into the city. However, if you have a party of four, then a taxi ride there will be faster and more comfortable.

Perth and **Hobart** have regular airport–city bus services. Take the cheaper bus or the faster taxi, whichever suits your needs. There is no bus service from **Canberra** airport.

AREA CODES

Area codes for phoning interstate and overseas are listed in the front of the White Pages of the telephone directory.

For local calls, dial only the local number. For other calls within Australia, dial the area code (listed for the capital cities as follows) + local number

To call overseas, dial 0011 + country code (given first in the following list of some major cities) + area code if applicable (listed second) + local number

ARRIVAL PROCEDURES

On arrival in Australia, you will hand over your passport, immigration card and quarantine and wildlife declaration. The purpose of the quarantine and wildlife declaration is to prevent disease being brought into Australia via produce or animal products.

Do not treat this declaration lightly. After passing through Immigration, proceed to the carousel to collect your luggage, and you will probably need a A$1 coin for a trolley. You must then choose the standard green (nothing to declare) or red (something to declare) channels to pass through Customs. There are severe penalties for trying to cheat Customs.

At last you're through the doors and into Australia. Look around carefully before pushing your trolley out of the building. Find the information desk, enquire about transport and take copies of pamphlets that may be of help, particularly a map and the booklet entitled "This Week in Sydney" (or whatever city you've just arrived in). If you don't have a hotel booking, study the large coloured board giving details, including location and price, of hotel and other accommodation. There is a free phone attached.

Unless you arrive very late, there will almost certainly be a money changer available. You'll get the same rate here as in the banks in the city. *Hot tip*: In the departure lounge of the airport you're departing from, buy a small amount of money of the country you're flying to – in this case, Australia. Then you'll be assured of having some of the country's currency in your pocket.

BANKING HOURS

Banks in Australia keep more liberal hours than do those in some countries, though generally their doors stay firmly bolted on Saturdays, Sundays and holidays. Times vary a little from state to state, but on weekdays expect banks to open at 9 or 9.30 am and to close at 3.30 or 4 pm On late night shopping days, branches in some suburban shopping complexes may stay open until 5 or 6

pm, while on Friday evenings the city branches of major banks keep similar hours. In the cities, some banks open a branch for a few hours on weekends (check with the local tourist bureau). City branches usually have *Bureaux de Change* with experienced staff, while suburban branches may not.

BARGAINS

Hot tip: Pick up a copy of any sort of backpackers' guide or information from the local tourist bureau and study it for money-saving ideas. The "flip-flop brigade" passes on to its fellows all manner of tips on good, cheap restaurants, bars and night spots, and clean, cheap accommodation.

BUSINESS HOURS

In general, business hours are from 9 am to 5.30 pm on Mondays to Fridays and from 9 am to noon on Saturdays, but many an office may start winding down by about 4.30 pm on a weekday and 11 am on Saturday mornings.
Weekly Holiday: Sunday.
Government:
Monday-Friday: 0900-1700 hrs.
Saturday: closed
Banks:
Monday-Thursday: 1000-1500 hrs
Friday: 1000-1700 hrs
Saturday: closed
Commerce & Industry:
Monday-Friday: 0900-1700 hrs.
Saturday: 0900-1200 hrs.

CAMPING

Camping grounds and caravan parks are found all over Australia, many situated in picturesque settings near beaches, lakes and rivers, near popular tourist attractions or within National Parks. Guides providing information on location, facilities and price can be obtained from tourist bureaus.

Generally, facilities include electricity, water supply and ablutions blocks. On-site vans with full facilities (linen, crockery, appliances, etc) can be hired fairly cheaply at most caravan parks.

CAR RENTAL

Car rental kiosks are situated in airports and railway stations, as well as in many city, suburban and country town locations. Prices vary enormously, so shop around if you have the time (numbers are listed in the Yellow Pages of the telephone directory under "Car And/Or Minibus Rental").

You will need to produce your valid local driver's licence or an international driver's permit. The day rate quoted usually includes third party insurance and unlimited free km within the metropolitan area.

CLIMATE

The climate varies from dry tropical in the Northern Territory (Darwin) into sub-tropical in Queensland (Brisbane) and New South Wales (Sydney) to Mediterranean in South Australia (Adelaide) & Western Australia (Perth).

CLOTHING

What clothing to take, and how much of it, depends on where you're going, at what time of the year, and whether you'll be attending any formal functions. If your visit is purely for pleasure, stick to clothes that can be used by day and by night.

If you are coming from the northern hemisphere, remember that Australia is "Down Under" where the seasons are at the opposite time of the year to what you are accustomed to. Winter starts in June, spring in September, summer in November and autumn in April, although the seasonal periods can be a bit elastic depending on which part of the country you are visiting.

Generally, medium weight clothing with a topcoat is suitable for the winter months. Light weight clothing is suitable for the summer. Light weight clothing is suitable year round in the Northern Territory. Formal evening attire is not needed.

Melbourne is Australia's most proper city when it comes to dressing for dinner. Sydney is casual chic; Adelaide and Perth make a half-hearted effort at sophistication; Hobart dresses up because of the cold; Brisbane is ultra casual; while in Darwin a gentleman absolutely must wear a T-shirt and flip-flops before entering a dining-room!

Hot tip: If you're going to Melbourne, Canberra, or especially Tasmania in winter, take lots of very warm clothing, plus an umbrella. You'll need them.

COACH TRAVEL

Coach travel, though time-consuming, is an economical way of seeing Australia. Operators such as Deluxe Coachlines, Bus Australia, Greyhound and Ansett Pioneer offer special passes that can add up to big savings if you're planning on criss-crossing the country. Coaches are generally comfortable and well appointed, with air-conditioning, toilets, adjustable seats and head-rests, and some have sound and video systems.

Here's grab-bag of interesting trips:
• *Sydney – Brisbane* via the coastal Pacific Highway (you don't see much of the sea) takes between 15 and 27 hours, depending on stops. An alternative route is via the inland New England Highway through rolling farmland with mountain views (17.5 to 27 hours).
• *Sydney – Melbourne* via Parramatta, Yass, Gundagai and Albury takes 13 hours, while the route via Canberra takes 13.5 hours.
• *Brisbane – Melbourne* via Goondiwindi, Dubbo and Deniliquin, inland from Sydney, has 26 stops and takes 24.5 hours.
• *Adelaide – Brisbane* going north-east across the country through Mildura, Coonabarabran and Goondiwindi, far inland from Melbourne and Sydney, takes 27 hours.
• *Brisbane - Townsville* northwards along the coast beside the Great Barrier Reef takes 19.5 hours.
• *Brisbane – Cairns* continues past Townsville to one of the fastest growing resort towns off the Barrier Reef, taking 24 hours.

Longer trips to more exotic destinations include Cairns–Alice Springs via Townsville, inland from Charters Towers to the giant mining town of Mt Isa, and south through Three Ways and Tennant Creek, a trip lasting 31 hours. From Alice Springs, you're just a comparably short hop from Ayers Rock, now called Uluru.

The Townsville–Darwin trip follows the same route to Three Ways, then travels north through Katherine, a journey of 37.5 hours.

CONSULS, EMBASSIES AND TRADE MISSIONS

Consuls are located in various state capitals and are listed under "Consuls" in the White Pages of the telephone directory. Embassies and trade missions are based in Canberra.

Brisbane:

Australia: 127 Creek St.;	229-3222
Belgium: 12 Brookes St.;	854-1920
Denmark: 127 Creek St.	271-2233
Finland: 123 Eagle St.	831-1911
Germany, W.: 26 Wharf St.	221-7819
Great Britain: 193 North Quay	221-4933
Italy: 158 Moray St.	358-4344

Japan: 68 Queen St.	831-1438
Mexico: 40 Queen St.	229-3577
Netherlands: 260 Queen St.	831-1779
New Zealand: 288 Edward St.	221-9933
Norway: 633 Wickham St.	854-1855
Philippines: 131 Elizabeth St.	221-1477
Sweden: 30-36 Herschell St.	221-9977
USA: 383 Wickham Ter.	839-8955

CREDIT CARDS

Internationally recognised credit cards such as American Express, Diners Club and Visa are accepted in most hotels, retail outlets, restaurants and petrol stations. If a restaurant does not display the customary credit card stickers at the entrance, check with the waiter before ordering.

CUSTOMS AND QUARANTINE

Australia is meticulous in controlling its quarantine regulations, which have been successful in keeping out various human, animal and crop diseases prevalent in other countries. Should a passenger accidentally bring in an affected item, an enormous amount of damage could be done to human health and rural production. The first person aboard any plane arriving from overseas is a Quarantine Service Inspector, who thoroughly sprays the passenger compartment before passengers disembark.

Prohibited items include food products, including fresh, frozen and canned meats, salami, dairy products and eggs; and any articles, including souvenirs, made from animal products. Also coming under close scrutiny, if not outright embargo, are plants, seeds, fruit, vegetables or wood and any articles made from plant products.

You cannot bring in products made from the skins, feathers, bones or any other part of a protected species of wildlife. This covers clothing, accessories, handbags, shoes, trophies, ornaments and souvenirs made from such protected species as turtles, alligators, crocodiles, tigers, leopards and other members of the cat family, elephants (especially ivory products), rhinoceros, whales and zebras. A certificate from an overseas retailer stating that the animal concerned was bred in captivity and legally farmed for its skin is of no use. The only documentation accepted by Australia is an export permit from the relevant wildlife authority in the country where you made the purchase. Otherwise, all such items are confiscated and subsequently destroyed.

Illegal drugs are strictly prohibited, and penalties for drug-related offences are severe. Most weapons and firearms are prohibited. Those that are not, require an Australian customs permit which must be issued before arrival, and you must inform your carrier that you wish to travel with a weapon.

The importation of cordless telephones and citizen band radios is prohibited unless they are approved by the Australian Department of Transport and Communications (GPO Box 594, Canberra ACT 2601; fax: (06) 274 8169).

Travellers over 18 years of age may bring in one litre of alcohol of any sort; 250 cigarettes or 250 grammes of tobacco products; and other dutiable articles worth not more than A$400 (A$200 for travellers under 18 years). All travellers are allowed, duty-free, personal clothing and footwear excluding items of fur and other animal skins; and a reasonable supply of personal hygiene and grooming items, but not perfume concentrate or expensive jewellery. Far more generous allowances are made for the goods of migrants and Australians returning from residence overseas (for details, contact the Collector of Customs, GPO Box 8, Sydney NSW 2001; fax: (02) 226 5997).

There are also regulations applying to your departure from Australia. Australian wildlife may not be exported. With koalas, frill-necked lizards and many other unique and protected species attracting so much attention overseas, strict precautions are taken to prevent their illegal export – and penalties for smugglers are severe. It is also illegal to export (without licence) items regarded as being part of the national heritage. Examples include works of art; historic books, documents, maps, stamps, coins and furniture; Aboriginal artefacts; objects associated with the country's social, military and sporting history, and its scientific and technological development; mineral specimens, ancient fossils and archaeological finds; and important items associated with Australia's film, television and photographic industries (for details, contact the Cultural Heritage Unit, Department of Arts, Sport, the Environment, Tourism and the Territories, GPO Box 787, Canberra ACT 2601; fax: (06) 274 1123/1324).

LOCAL CUSTOMS

A suit is necessary in Sydney and Melbourne. In Brisbane, local businessmen may wear a shirt, tie and shorts, however, visiting businessmen should wear a lightweight suit on their initial interview.

Prior appointments are necessary for all business and Government visits. Business handshaking is customary at the beginning and end of business meetings. Before any business discussions begin you will be expected to indulge in light conversation about Australian sights, cultural events and sports. Presentations should be detailed and complete. Do not conceal problem areas. Australian businessmen appreciate honesty and a sense of humour, efficient and hardworking. Business contracts will be well-defined and firm. A great deal of business is transacted over drinks. A businessman who volunteers a drink check out of turn would be considered rude. The established custom of buying a drink in turn is to buy when it is your "shout" ("Who is in the Chair?") If invited to a businessman's house, it is appropriate to bring flowers or alchohol. It is advisable to be punctual or early but never late.

DANGEROUS SPECIES

While Australians are generally friendly folk, there are some inhabitants that are not. Visitors travelling from city to city face no risk of encountering any of these nasties, but those who wish to go to the beach or take part in adventure holidays should read on.

Do not plunge into either ocean or river without checking whether the area is prone to sharks, crocodiles, box jellyfish, the blue-ringed octopus or sea snakes.

Nine Australians have been killed by **sharks** in the past 10 years, while a number of surfboard riders have been attacked and injured. Sharks are mainly found in the sea, but they also enter estuaries and rivers. However, the number of shark attacks compared to the many people who swim is extremely small.

Five people have been taken by **crocodiles** in the past 10 years. The saltwater crocodile is a predator that attacks man without provocation. In water, it glides up to its prey with only two eyes and its nostrils showing. On land, it appears from nowhere and with great speed clamps its jaws onto the victim.

The **box jellyfish** kills at least one swimmer every year. It is found in an arc running from the top of Western Australia across the coast of the Northern Territory and down the Queensland coast as far south as Mackay. The jellyfish are most prevalent in summer, from November to March, and are more likely to appear when conditions are invitingly calm. Looking like a blob of gluey white jelly shaped like a bell and sometimes as big as a bucket, the creature pulses silently through the water trailing up to 16 tentacles as long as 3 metres. The faintest touch of a tentacle can be fatal. Highly virulent poison is injected into the victim's skin, while a sticky substance ejected simultaneously ensures that the tentacle clings to the flesh. An antivenene must be administered immediately. The victim feels indescribable pain and can die within minutes of either heart failure or inability to draw breath. The affected skin looks slashed and raw. Vinegar must be applied to remove the tentacles, or they should be picked off with tweezers. Mouth-to-mouth resuscitation should be given while the antivenene is rushed to the scene.

The **blue-ringed octopus** is no frightening denizen of the deep, but a pretty creature about the size of a man's hand at full span. It is washed into rock pools along every part of the coast. Children who go adventuring amid seaside rocks often come upon one and pick it up out of curiosity. The bite is painless, but within one and a half hours the victim could suffer fatal breathing failure. When disturbed, the creature mottles itself with a series of electric-blue rings, or spots appear all over its body. This is nature's warning!

Australian waters are home to no fewer than 30 species of **sea snake**, and their venom is reputed to be more potent than a cobra's. Happily, they are shy creatures and only bite if disturbed.

Go hiking in the countryside only in the company of an experienced bushman, and, when in dense bush, try to follow exactly in his actual footsteps. He knows what unwelcome surprises may be lying in wait. Australia has 14 dangerous **land snakes**: the Death Adder, Spotted Brown, Western Brown, Spotted-headed Snake, Eastern Brown, Copperhead, Tiger, Taipan, Fierce, King Brown or Mulga, Collett's Snake, Spotted or Blue-bellied Black Snake, Red-bellied Black Snake and the Rough-scaled Snake. The most poisonous of these is the Fierce Snake, which secretes enough poison to kill a quarter of a million mice, but is less than 2 metres long. Next comes its yellowy-brown cousin, the Taipan, which bites its prey again and again. The Tiger Snake raises itself cobra-style, and hisses before striking several times with great speed. Victims must be given immediate aid – a pressure bandage above and below the bite, covering all of the affected limb, followed by antivenene. The bandage prevents the poison from spreading while medical help is sought. The limb must be kept still for the same reason.

There are a list of "do-nots" to remember while enjoying the Australian bush:

• Do not put your hand into rabbit burrows or hollows in dead trees on the ground.

• Do not reach up into the hollow formed by the branches of a tree to see if it contains a bird's nest, as some snakes hide there.

• Do not kick dry leaves and twigs; this is one of the habitats of the Death Adder. They also burrow into dry sand or gravel.

• Do not lift aside a dead branch, or put your hand into a crevice in the rocks.

• Do not go tramping through thick grass in wet, swampy areas, the territory of Tiger Snakes, Copperheads and Red-bellied Black Snakes. If you leave a cleared path, look down before taking each step; a snake may be basking in a pool of sunlight. Remember that they're beautifully camouflaged and hard to see.

Australia also has some of the world's nastiest **spiders**. The Funnel-Web spider is the most dangerous, and is known to have killed 14 people in the past 60 years. It lives in suburbia in parts of New South Wales, Victoria, Tasmania and Queensland, hiding in garden sheds, beneath houses, or in dark corners. In mountainous bushland, it is found in trees. This spider is reddish-brown to black and its nest is like a sausage skin of silk, rather than a funnel. The male is the smaller but deadlier sex. Treatment is the same as for snakebite: apply a pressure bandage, keep the limb immobile and inject antivenene as soon as possible.

The Red-back spider's markings, a thick red stripe or blob in the middle of its fat black body, serves as warning. This spider is known to have killed a dozen people. Oddly, its poison is slow-acting and the victim can get to a doctor for an injection of antivenene. Unlike the Funnel-Web, the female is the aggressor. Although no bigger than one joint of a finger, the fearless Red-back attacks lizards, mice and even Funnel-Webs, particularly at night.

Another species found in suburbia is the Trap-door Spider, which makes its nest in a hole in the ground and then covers it with a trap-door of earth or bark. The pain of its bite is felt immediately, and the victim should seek medical attention as soon as possible. If the spider has been killed, it should be taken with the victim when aid is sought, so that the correct antivenene can be administered. If not, a description should be given.

A trip into the Australian bush is nothing like a jaunt into the English countryside. Most city-dwelling Australians wouldn't venture there without an expert to lead them. The bush is home to a number of other "nasties" such as the scrub tick, fiddleback spider and scorpion, while other sea-going dangers include the stinging Portuguese Man-O-War and bluebottle, and the deadly stonefish, butterfly cod and red rock cod with their needle-sharp poisonous spines. So take care if you intend to venture on the wild side.

DEPARTURE TAX

On leaving Australia, travellers over 12 years of age pay a A$20 departure tax. An exemption stamp is required for children under 12. Departure tax stamps can be purchased at airports or post offices in Australia and should be affixed to the traveller's airline ticket.

DISABLED TRAVELLERS

Few countries in the world are better equipped to handle the needs of disabled travellers than Australia. As disabled Australians are regular travellers, the country's international and domestic airports, along with railway stations, bus terminals and other transport services, are well-equipped to cater for their needs. Also, thanks to the helpfulness of most Australians, somebody will quickly come to the assistance of a disabled person when required.

DOCUMENTS

It is a good idea to photocopy in duplicate your travellers' cheques, credit cards, bank drafts and any other essential documents you will be taking with you, including the vital pages of your passport and your visa for Australia.

Place one set in a stout envelope and tape it to the inside of your suitcase. Leave the second set with somebody at home who is prepared to take a collect call in an emergency. If a problem arises, you will have a flying start in arranging replacement documents. Also give your contact at home a copy of your itinerary and, if taking an extended holiday, keep in touch by phone occasionally to let your contact know where you are. Remember to keep a running tally of travellers' cheques as you use them, as you will need to know the numbers of the remaining cheques in the event of theft or loss.

A passport and visa are required to enter Australia. It is advisable to consult with Australia's Embassy or Consulate in your country as there are a few exceptions. All travellers must fill out a passenger card in English which is to be presented when arriving and departing. Travellers who will be continuing the journey without leaving the aircraft do not require a passenger card. An international certificate of vaccination for cholera is required if arriving from an infected area. An international certificate of vaccination for yellow fever is required if arriving from an infected area within 6 days. It is advisable to have a vaccination for typhoid.

Entry is prohibited to holders of Taiwan passports and members of South African sports teams. Entry is also prohibited to racially selected sports teams unless they have special permission from an Australian government representative.

Consider making a will before departure.

DRIVING

Visitors may drive in Australia for three months on a valid licence issued in their own country. For longer stays, an international driver's permit is required. The licence or permit must be carried while the visitor is driving. International driving permits are preferred but are not legally required.

Seat belts are compulsory.

ELECTRICITY

The electricity supply in Australia is 240 volts, 50 cycles, alternating current, and three-pin power sockets are used.

EMERGENCIES

Phone 000 for ambulance, police or fire brigade. Look on the first page of the telephone directory White Pages for emergency numbers such as those for hospitals, treatment for poisoning or marine stings, or the lifeline crisis service.

FESTIVALS (MAJOR)

January
New South Wales
Sydney's arts festival, the Festival of Sydney, presents an extensive programme of cultural performances as well as an array of more light-hearted entertainment. Undoubtedly, one of the festival highlights is the free concerts in the park, when thousands of music lovers picnic under the stars listening to internationally acclaimed performers.

In the town of Tamworth, Australia's premier country music festival draws artists and diehard fans from all over the country.

February
Western Australia
The Festival of Perth is held over three weeks in late February and March, presenting a stimulating programme of arts from all over the world, as well as the best Australia has to offer.

March
Australian Capital Territory
The Canberra Festival presents a ten-day calendar of arts and other events to celebrate the city's birthday. Among the most popular events are the birdman rally, balloon gathering, and the grand finale concert.

South Australia
Australia's premier cultural event, the Adelaide Festival of Arts, is staged throughout March in even-numbered years. A spectacular fireworks display opens the Festival, turning Adelaide into a city of non-stop entertainment for three weeks.

Victoria
Melbourne lets its hair down for Australia's most famous carnival, the Moomba Festival. Moomba is an Aboriginal word meaning "Let's get together and have fun" – and fun is the theme of this ten-day festival. The entertainment climaxes in an extravagant city parade presided over by the King of Moomba, a different local personality each year. In the country town of Ballarat, the annual Begonia Festival is a must for flower-lovers.

Easter Events
New South Wales
The Royal Sydney Show, an immense rural exhibition, encapsulates the heart of the New South Wales countryside and delights adults and children alike.

South Australia
The Barossa Valley Vintage Wine Festival is a celebration of wine-making – and wine-drinking. It's held in odd-numbered years, commencing Easter Monday and continuing until the weekend.

May
Northern Territory
Alice Springs hold its Bangtail Muster, a festival featuring sporting events and street parades.

August
Western Australia

In the North West, the historic pearling town of Broome, now a major tourist resort, hosts the Festival of the Pearl, featuring a gala ball and mardi gras.

September
Queensland
Brisbane's Warana Spring Festival celebrates springtime with a feast of cultural and fun events culminating in a grand city parade.

Flower-lovers should head to Toowoomba, an hour and a half's drive inland from Brisbane, where the September Carnival of Flowers is held.

Victoria
Melbourne hosts the International Festival of the Arts, a programme of music and theatre featuring top Australian and overseas performers.

October
New South Wales
On the northern coast of New South Wales, Grafton celebrates the Jacaranda Festival with its streets a riot of violet-blue blooms from the Jacaranda trees.

Northern Territory
There's lots of fun to be had at Alice Springs at the Henley-on-Todd "Regatta", in which neither the eccentric sailors nor the boats get wet, as it's staged in a dry river-bed.

November
New South Wales
Celebrate the year's cherry harvest with the locals of the country town of Young, where it's Cherry Festival time.

Western Australia
Perth's port city of Fremantle stages Fremantle Week, with a different theme each year. This vibrant city's many artists and artisans, along with traders and community groups, present a week of parades, performances and exhibitions celebrating some aspect of life in Fremantle.

HEALTH MATTERS
Drinking water is safe everywhere. Do not bathe at unguarded beaches (sharks are abundant) and do not attempt to explore the interior by yourself. Pharmaceuticals and toiletries are reasonable priced.

Emergency medical assistance will be rendered in Brisbane at Royal Brisbane Hospital (Tel: 253-8111), in Melbourne at the Royal Melbourne (Tel: 347-7111), St.Vincent's (Tel: 41-0221), Prince Henry's (Tel:62-0261) or Queen Victoria Hospital (Tel: 665-5206). In Perth, Royal Perth Hospital (Tel: 325-0101). In Sydney, Sydney Hospital (Tel: 230-0111) or Hospital Emergency (Tel: 339-0477).

Medical services are excellent in Australia, but fees are high. Visitors are not covered for medical insurance under the government Medicare Scheme, so seriously consider taking out hospital and medical insurance for your trip. Usually, for little extra cost you can also get coverage for loss of money or baggage, forced change of itinerary or being stranded by missing a pre-paid flight.

If you have a special medical condition that requires an unusual prescription, bring a sufficient supply with you, as well as a doctor's certificate and prescription or letter explaining why you are carrying so much of a particular medicine.

To prevent sore eyes, remove your contact lenses when flying. And don't assume you'll be able to get your particular contact lens solution in Australia; take a supply with you.

Unpleasant as it is to contemplate, there is a chance that you may develop diarrhoea on your travels, although the water in Australia is quite safe to drink from the tap, and health standards are very high. Before departure, get a preventative pill or mixture from your doctor or chemist. Much of the fun of travelling is exploring, and the best exploring is done on foot. Be sure your shoes are comfortable.

AIDS has taken root in Australia, though not as severely as in some countries. If you engage in sexual intercourse, take the necessary precautions.

INTERPRETATION SERVICE
If you need something interpreted urgently, a 24-hour Telephone Interpreter Service is available. The number is listed in the Emergency section of the telephone directory White Pages.

LOCAL LAWS
Australians are generally law-abiding and the country runs on a self-disciplinary code known to all by the slogan "Do The Right Thing". The police, like everybody else, are easygoing and helpful. They turn a blind eye to most trivial misdemeanours – but this amiability ends abruptly with anything seriously illegal.

Drugs are absolutely and positively a no-no! All entry points are staffed with people (and sniffer dogs) highly skilled in drug detection. Do not try to bring any type of narcotic into Australia, for yourself or anyone else. Australian attitudes to drugs hardened several years ago when two nationals were executed in Malaysia for drug offences, and community anger reached boiling point after a nation-wide drugs-related spree of house-breakings and muggings.

Do not drink and drive. Just three glasses of beer could put you over the legal limit, and the fact that you are a visitor will not excuse you. Random breath-testing for alcohol is a fact of life on the roads in Australia. Police in marked or unmarked cars may order you at any time to pull off the road and to submit to a breath sample. If over the limit, you will be taken down to the lock-up until you can arrange bail. Subsequently, you will be fined over A$1,000 and barred from driving for the rest of your holiday.

Parking signs in some cities can be a little confusing. One roadside sign in green might read: "Parking, pay meter fees, 9 am – 6 pm", while just around the corner another sign in green indicates: "Parking, pay meter fees, 10 am – 4 pm". At the first, you'll probably get a rare bonus of free parking after 6 pm At the second, you could get a ticket, or even be towed away, if you park between 4 pm and 6 pm, because below the green sign there could be a red one stating "No parking 4 pm – 6 pm". Always look for the red sign which overrides information on a green sign.

Road traffic in Australia travels on the **left side of the road**, British style. The use of **seatbelts** is compulsory.

LUGGAGE

Hot tip: It can be folly to draw attention to yourself with ostentatious and expensive luggage wherever you travel, and that includes Australia. The only person you might be impressing is the very last one whose attention you wish to attract.

MONEY MATTERS

Australian currency is decimal, the dollar (100 cents equal one dollar) being the basic unit. Notes come in $100, $50, $20, $10 and $5 denominations, while coins come in $2, $1, 50c, 20c, 10c and 5c denominations. Two cent and 1c coins are being phased out, although there are still some in circulation.

You may bring into Australia up to A$5,000 worth of Australian or foreign currency. If you have more than this amount, you must inform Customs on arrival and file a report. On leaving the country, there is a A$5,000 limit on Australian or foreign currency being taken out. You must file a report with Customs if over the limit with foreign currency, although your woes will be lightened if you have the written approval of the Reserve Bank of Australia.

When cashing travellers' cheques, there is no variation in rates from bank to bank. You will be asked to produce your passport to verify your identity. At all international airports, there is a *Bureau de Change*, which uses the same rates as the banks in the city. These are open for longer hours than banks during weekdays, and provide a money-changing service at weekends and on holidays. But note that such service is NOT round-the-clock. *Hot tip*: Try to avoid changing money at your hotel as their rates are usually lower than the banks'.

NEWSPAPERS AND MAGAZINES

Australia has a very vigorous press. The morning newspapers, mostly broadsheets, tend to concentrate on politics and financial matters and, while generally conservative, are by no means stodgy. Afternoon papers, mostly tabloids, run glaring headlines about crime and scandal (preferably political) leavened with girlie pictures and other froth and bubble. Morning and weekend papers carry the majority of classified advertising. Saturday and Sunday morning papers are usually thick and heavy, and some have weekly magazines as well. Newspapers that cost 50 cents on a weekday go up in price to between 90 cents and a dollar for the fatter weekend editions.

News-stands carry hundreds of glossy magazines on an endless list of subjects. Overseas newspapers and magazines are generally found on sale only in the large newsagencies in the centre of each capital city, or at the airport bookshop. Often, these publications are out of date and prices are high. Ethnic newspapers are printed in a variety of languages such as Chinese, Vietnamese, Japanese, Italian, Greek and Polish. Generally, these are sold in those districts where certain ethnic groups are concentrated.

PHOTOGRAPHY AND FILM

A wide choice of film – colour slides and negatives – is available from outlets like camera shops, pharmacies, department stores and supermarkets. Many also have fast-developing facilities for running off postcard-size prints from negatives in a few hours, while slides must be sent away for processing, which takes a couple of working days. Shop around if you're buying several rolls; sometimes pharmacies under-cut even the supermarkets. If you need running repairs to your camera, use a reputable camera shop, which will try to rush your repair through once you explain you're an international visitor.

POSTAL SERVICES

Post is delivered once a day and only on weekdays. Post offices are closed on Saturdays, Sundays and public holidays. Domestic postal charges are very high, and overseas parcel post is ruinously expensive, even if you choose sea mail instead of air mail. Check the White Pages of the telephone directory for the location of your nearest post office. Incidentally, everybody calls the post office the "Cheepeeeohhh", or GPO for General Post Office.

PUBLIC HOLIDAYS

National public holidays in Australia are New Year's Day, Australia Day (the closest Monday to 26 January), Good Friday, Easter Monday, Anzac Day (25 April), Christmas Day and Boxing Day. Other public holidays vary from state to state and year to year. Tourist bureaus will be able to provide you with a calendar of public and school holidays current for your year of travel.
Principal National Holidays:
1 Jan
26 Jan
13 April* - 16 April*
25 April
12 June
25 Dec
26 Dec
* Christian holiday – varies each year.

RADIO AND TELEVISION

The Australian Broadcasting Corporation (ABC) operates Australia's government-funded, non-commercial network of radio stations and one television station (Channel 2). Each state also has a variety of commercial stations supported by advertising revenue, most of which belong to the national Seven, Nine or Ten networks.

National commercial television networks offer late-night news with a difference. On Channel 7, the news is served up as humorous tidbits during a one-hour variety show hosted by comedian Steve Vizard. Alternatively, a monologue

report with offbeat comments is offered on Channel 9 by the highly opinionated Clive Robertson, known as "Robbo", about whom American comedienne Whoopi Goldberg declared "I could drink his bath-water"!

ABC's Channel 2 telecasts consistently good programmes, including news, current affairs, drama, comedy and documentaries.

International visitors interested in what's been happening in the world should watch the excellent nightly newscast at 6.30 pm on SBS, the ethnic channel. Like the ABC, SBS offers intelligent and entertaining viewing, with no commercials. Its fare also includes steamy continental dramas, with original soundtrack and English sub-titles.

AM and FM radio stations offer a very wide choice of listening – classical music, opera, rock, pop, heavy metal, sport and talkback radio. Melbourne even has a full-time Italian-English station. For informative, entertaining radio, the ABC is strongly recommended. Most capitals have an ethnic station offering half-hour programmes in Czech, German, Spanish or Italian, interspersed with music. There are a plethora of talk shows on Australian radio. Sit almost anybody before a microphone and off they'll go with unbending views on everything from rooting out corruption to not rooting out trees, from what's wrong with the country to what's wrong with the sex cycle of the vanishing echidna.

The ABC presents a gem from 8 to 10 am on Sunday – "Australian All Over", hosted by a whimsical bushwhacker called "Macca" (Ian MacNamara). Here's a programme that will give you an insight into the character of the true-blue Aussie bushie. You'll hear poems, bird songs, ditties, folklore, tales of floods and droughts, cheerio calls, community announcements, and callers from the South Pole to truckies out back of beyond. It is a marvellous programme, so try to catch it one Sunday.

RAIL TRAVEL

There are fast, comfortable train services linking the five capital cities on the continent. The Trans-Australia service (the "Indian Pacific") that links Perth with the eastern states travels a vast distance, so you need a lot of time to spare – 65 hours, in fact! However, the following trips are relatively comfortable:

• Sydney–Melbourne: 12.5 hours
• Sydney–Brisbane: 14 hours

- Melbourne–Adelaide: 12 hours
- Brisbane–Mackay: 18 hours
- Brisbane–Townsville: 25 hours
- Brisbane–Cairns: 31 hours.

There are special rail passes and discount fares available for overseas visitors, such as Caper Fares (for advance-purchase tickets), the Austrail Pass (for unlimited travel within a chosen period of time) and the Kangaroo Road 'n' Rail Pass (for unlimited travel on government rail services and Greyhound coaches). Check with your travel agent for details.

RELIGION

While Christianity is the predominant faith in Australia, all forms of religion and worship flourish without hindrance. Visitors should make enquiries at the tourist bureau in whichever city they are visiting. Addresses, telephone numbers and directions will gladly be given.

RIVER CRUISES

In the mid-19th century, paddle-wheelers and a variety of other craft began plying the inland river systems of New South Wales, Victoria and South Australia, mainly along the 2,600 km of the Murray River. Echuca, where the Campaspe River meets the Murray, became Victoria's second biggest port, after Melbourne. Its wharves were a remarkable complex of different level landings to accommodate a wide variety of vessels. There were steam-driven wool-presses nearby to bale the wool that was to be transported to Port Eliot, on the Great Australian Bight in South Australia, and then on to Britain. Echuca's waters, bustling with traffic, saw all sorts of feuds and nautical skulduggery.

Paddle-wheelers still churn gently down the Murray waters, but they are beautiful reproduction craft such as the *Murray River* and *Proud Mary*, both floating hotels offering six-day cruises. At Echuca look for the old brothel in the main street overlooking the wharf. In the upstairs room of a prominent waterfront building, a seated waxwork harpy surveys the scene, looking to serve the whims of the passing trade.

Ports in all states operate seagoing services such as ferries and catamarans to resorts and tourist attractions either on outlying islands or up-river. The best example is Sydney Harbour, where passenger-laden craft constantly criss-cross the waters. Also particularly busy are craft operating from ports along the north coast of Queensland to the many hundreds of island resorts.

ROAD TRAVEL

Doing at least part of your trip by road is highly recommended if you have the time. The scenery is breathtaking and you will pass through bush-ranger country, goldfields and historic towns; spot kangaroos by the road; pass many varieties of magnificently coloured birds; and see flocks of sheep as large as your field of vision and endless fields of sunflowers. If you follow the occasional road-side tourist signs – they are brown and white – to scenic drives, look-outs and other vantage points, you'll really have the chance to drink in the beauty of this rugged land.

Don't just drive through the country towns, where you'll discover friendly folk, and charming buildings crafted in styles you thought had gone for ever. If the weather's kind, buy sandwiches and have a picnic in the park, or follow the signs to a tourist information office and pick up a map and some details of the district's history and attractions. Set off on a sightseeing trip and you may find you like the place so much that you might like to spend the night.

You're sure to find a Chinese restaurant in the bigger towns, or if you'd prefer a tender T-bone with two eggs, grilled tomatoes and chips, try a counter lunch or dinner in a country pub – but check the meal hours, which are usually strictly set. Your tourist brochures will recommend other places to eat. At Returned Soldiers' League clubs, a simple signature and address will give you guest membership and entry to a restaurant of good standard.

There are clean, cheap motels dotted along the major highways, as well as some very luxurious ones. The larger towns offer hotel accommodation, but you may have to share the bathroom. When choosing a motel, consider its distance from the main road, as trucks thundering past at night could disturb your sleep. Drive up and ask not only the price but what extra facilities are provided, such as a restaurant or a pool. Some have all sorts of attractions – for example, the Thunderbird Motel, just out of Tamworth on the way to Sydney, has a vintage car museum and a small zoo. Some of the motel chains offer inducements to keep your patronage from town to town, and a reservation service so you can be sure of a room at your next stop. Motel rooms are usually equipped with tea-making facilities and television, and sometimes in-house video. Breakfast, ordered in advance, is generally served through a hatch in your room at whatever time you wish. All motels display "Vacancy" or "No Vacancy" signs, and the best rooms in the best motels are allocated on a first-come, first-served basis. An increasingly popular way of touring by road, especially with a groups of half a dozen or so friends, is to hire an 11-seater van. Road-weary children can have a snooze stretched out on one of the back seats and adults can share the driving and the hire charges. You may also consider hiring a campervan and, like the hermit crab, carry your home with you wherever you travel!

Road travel is recommended for the eastern part of the country, but think twice before attempting to cross the Nullarbor between the Perth in the west and Adelaide in the east. It is 2,725 km through the desert, and is not most people's idea of a holiday drive. The possibility of breakdowns or floods adds an element of danger.

Choose from the following **Sydney to Melbourne** routes:
• Along the Hume Highway, via Goulburn, the home of the Big Merino; historic Gundagai, where the "dog sits on the tuckerbox"; and Albury on the New South Wales–Victoria border (877 km). The Hume Highway is also known as the Crystal Highway because fast-moving vehicles throw up stones which sometimes shatter the windscreens of other vehicles, thus the roadsides is littered with "crystal".
• Down the Olympic Way, via Bathurst, Young and Wagga Wagga to Albury and south through Victoria (963 km).
• Through the national capital, Canberra, chilly Cooma in the Snowy Mountains and Sale (1,038 km).
• Down the coastal route through Nowra, Bega and Sale (1058 km). A visit to Canberra, south from Goulburn on Highway 23, is definitely recommended. If the children want to see the dog and tuckerbox statue at Gundagai, make a small detour from Canberra through Yass to Gundagai, then continue south to Melbourne.

The following routes from **Melbourne to Adelaide** are recommended:
• Due west along the Western and Dukes Highways through Ballarat, which is well worth a stop-over, Ararat and Bordertown (724 km). If you like Ballarat, you should also make a detour north to Bendigo, another old goldmining centre. From Bendigo, proceed to Castlemaine, then west to Ararat and on to the Western Highway.

• Along the semi-coastal Princes Highway west through historic Warrnambool and Mt Gambier (910 km).

Routes from **Sydney to Brisbane** include:
• Along the Pacific Highway, which sometimes hugs the coastline and is dotted with towns and resorts such as Taree, Coffs Harbour, Port Macquarie (the small detour is well worth it), Grafton (a mass of gorgeous violet jacarandas trees in spring), Coolangatta and the fabulous Gold Coast (1,002 km). Another worthwhile detour is to Woolgoolga, 25 km north of Coffs Harbour, where the predominantly Sikh population, which owns most of the district's banana plantations, has built a large, traditional Sikh temple with life-size elephant statues.
• Up the New England Highway, through magnificent pastoral and mountain scenery and a succession of delightful towns such as Scone (pronounced Scohne), Armidale and Glen Innes, then over the border through Warwick and up to Brisbane (1,017 km).
• Combine the previous two routes for the best of both worlds. Enjoy the charm and beauty of the New England Highway to Glen Innes, then head west to Grafton for 159 km to join the Pacific Highway. From here it's 300 km north to the Gold Coast.

North from Brisbane is a tropical paradise. The first leg is a good day's drive of 639 km to Rockhampton through Gympie, Maryborough and Childers, all very interesting places offering enjoyable breaks in the drive. A detour of 50 km from Childers takes you to Bundaberg, famous for its rum. From Rockhampton, it's 334 km to Mackay, 396 km to Townsville and 349 km to Cairns, a total distance of 1,718 km. It's a long haul, and before setting out from Brisbane you should make sure tropical storms aren't expected so you don't encounter flooded roads. Accommodation ranging from simple and inexpensive to five-star quality is available in towns all along the route.

If you wish to drive in one direction only, to save time and repetition, it is relatively inexpensive to put your car on the train for the return journey

SEA TRAVEL
Liners no longer ply the coastal routes from capital to capital, but the handsome ferry *Abel Tasman* operates between Melbourne and Devonport, on the north coast of Tasmania,

taking vehicles as well as passengers. It is an overnight trip, with the ferry sailing from Melbourne every second day.

A faster alternative to the traditional ferry is the super sleek trimaran, *Seacat*, which carries more than 300 passengers and about 100 cars on a four and a half hour high-speed trip once a day in either direction. The 35-knot-plus trimaran operates from Port Welshpool, about an hour's drive south-east of Melbourne, to George Town, on Tasmania's north coast. This is 40 minutes closer by road to the capital, Hobart, than is Devonport, the arrival point of the *Abel Tasman*. The *Seacat*'s sails at 8.30 am from George Town, arriving at Port Welshpool at 1 pm, then departs from Port Welshpool at 2 pm, completing its round journey at 6.30 pm.

SHOPPING

Although Australia is not famous as a shopping destination, nonetheless a staggering array of unique products for visitors to buy. It must be said that prices are generally high, but so too is the quality of goods offered. For serious shoppers, some capital cities such as Melbourne, Sydney and Adelaide offer shopping tours (check with the local tourist bureau), and a publication entitled *Your Shopping Guide to Australia* is available from the Australian Tourist Commission.

Aboriginal Art and Crafts

Aboriginal paintings and handicrafts can be bought in retail outlets in the major cities as well as from their sources in the more remote regions of Australia. There is a wide selection to choose from – paintings, bark paintings, boomerangs, weapons, carvings, basketware, fish nets and hooks, didgeridoos, hand-painted fabrics, and pottery. Aboriginal art has an international reputation and has become very popular in recent years, so don't expect it to be cheap.

Bush Clothing

Oilskin cattlemen's coats (Drizabones) and cattlemen's hats (Akubras) have become very fashionable articles of clothing and are available in most cities. Members of the British Royal Family have been photographed wearing Drizabone coats, and of course Paul Hogan made the Akubra famous in his *Crocodile Dundee* films.

Fashions

You can find fashions by top local designers such as Trent Nathan, Prue Acton, Stuart Membery,

Jenny Kee and Adele Palmer in the sumptuous department stores and designer boutiques throughout Australia. Quality leisurewear, pure wool suits, leather clothing, and tropical and desert design fashions are good buys.

Handicrafts

Australia's many handicraft stores sell a multitude of quality gift and decorative items – for example, pottery (Bendigo pottery is a particular favourite with visitors); items made from local timber such as jarrah and blackboy (Western Australia), and Huon pine, myrtle and blackwood (Tasmania); clocks set in polished mallee root; dried wildflowers and floral art; woolcrafts; and sculpture. There are very vigorous arts communities in rural and outback Australia, and it's well worth looking into the arts and crafts outlets that abound in almost every country town.

Jewellery

Exquisite jewellery is fashioned from Australia's rich supply of precious stones – sparkling white, champagne, cognac and the extremely rare pink Argyle diamonds from the North Kimberley region of Western Australia; pearls farmed from the waters off Broome; sapphires and other precious stones from Queensland; and of course the brilliant opals (see below) for which Australia is famous. These are set in locally produced gold and silver, and unique pieces are also made from Western Australian iron-ore.

Leather Goods

Designer leather clothing and other leather goods are very popular. In recent years, ventures into emu farming in the North West of Australia have resulted in the production of excellent quality emu leather products.

Opals

An ancient poet described opals in the following terms:

In the opal you shall see the living fire of the ruby, the glorious purple of the amethyst, the sea-green of the emerald, a blue more brilliant than the sapphire, all together in an incredible pattern of light.

These shimmering stones are widely mined in South Australia, New South Wales and Western Queensland. The main types are "white" or "milky" opals from Coober Pedy (South Australia), the coveted "black" opals from Lightning Ridge (New South Wales), and "boulder" opals from Quilpie (Queensland). The "boulder" is generally conceded to be the most attractive because of its brilliant colour and bright pattern.

The Coober Pedy fields are the largest in Australia; in fact, most of the world's precious opal is mined there. The name "Coober Pedy" is a very descriptive Aboriginal term for the method of mining used – it translates as "white men in a hole". When buying opals, look for colour, brilliance, pattern and clarity, and always buy from a reputable dealer. Examine your choice under a magnifying glass to make sure it is a solid stone rather than several chips, and to check for blemishes. A broad splotchy pattern is valued more highly than a dotty pattern.

You may have heard somewhere that opals bring bad luck to their wearers. Not so. This was a sly rumour started by diamond dealers when sales of opals began to affect the diamond trade. In fact, opals bring their owners very good luck – really top grade stones (prices range from A$30 to A$450,000) have increased in value by up to 25 percent a year over the past decade.

Sheepskin Products

Rugs, car-seat covers and footwear made from sheepskin are excellent value.

Souvenirs

If buying souvenirs like cuddly toy koalas or kangaroo-skin products, look at the trademark before handing over your cash as often these are mass-produced in another country – and it could be embarrassing to give a friend an Australian gift only to find out that it was made in Hong Kong, China, Taiwan or Korea. You will find hundreds of souvenir items – T-shirts, tea-towels, placemats, calendars and almost anything else you can think of – printed with the distinctive designs of Ken Done, who cleverly combines bright colours with simple, almost childlike forms.

Wine

Australian wines are of excellent quality and value and provide Australia with a flourishing export industry (see page 346). Major wine centres include the Hunter Valley in New South Wales; the Rutherglen district in Victoria; the Barossa and Clare Valleys, the Coonawarra region and McLaren Vale in South Australia; and the Swan Valley and Margaret River regions of Western Australia. Sample as much as you like while you're in Australia, but if you're planning to take some home with you, check the duty-free

allowance of the country of your destination.

Woollen Products

Australia is famous for the quality of its wool. Designer fashions in pure wool, hand-knitted woollen sweaters etc are excellent buys.

Shopping Bargains

Bargains are hard to come by in Australia, but here are a few tips for dedicated bargain-hunters:
• All major centres have markets, usually open all weekend, selling a wide variety of cheap goods such as clothing, arts and crafts, jewellery, health foods and dried flowers.
• Shopping tours offered in Sydney and Melbourne take in a few factory outlets as well as the designer boutiques.
• You will be amazed at how inexpensive coffee-table books are in Australia. Every city has cut-rate bookstores (such as **Bookworld**) with a plethora of top-quality books on matters Australian and general interest topics. But be warned: the high-quality art paper used in such books adds to their weight, so be selective or your luggage could tip the scales!
• Keep an eye open for end-of-season sales in department stores and designer boutiques, when prices are often slashed dramatically to clear the way for the new season's stock.

Duty-free Shopping

Travellers can avoid paying Australia's 14 percent sales tax by shopping at the many duty-free stores located at airports as well as in city and suburban locations. Similarly, when buying jewellery at general retail outlets, produce your passport to establish that you are a *bona fide* traveller and your purchases will be duty-free.

Shopping Hours

Shops are open generally from 8.30 or 9 am to 5 or 5.30 pm on Mondays to Fridays, with late-night shopping to 9 pm on at least one day per week (usually Thursdays and/or Fridays). On Saturdays, hours vary considerably from state to state, but shops are open for at least half a day. Markets and some tourist-oriented shops are open on Sundays. Specific hours for the capital cities are as follows:

Adelaide
9 am – 5.30 pm Monday – Thursday; 9 am – 9 pm Friday; 9 am – noon Saturday

Brisbane
8.15 am – 5.30 pm Monday – Thursday; 8.15 am – 9 pm Friday; 8.15 am – 4 pm Saturday; 10 am – 4 pm Sunday (major city complexes only)

Canberra
9 am – 5 pm Monday – Thursday; 9 am – 9 pm Friday; 9 am – noon Saturday

Darwin
9 am – 5.30 pm Monday, Tuesday, Wednesday, Friday; 9 am – 9 pm Thursday; 9 am – 1 pm Saturday

Hobart
9 am – 6 pm Monday – Thursday; 9 am – 9 pm Friday; 9 am – noon Saturday

Melbourne
9 am – 5 pm Monday – Wednesday; 9 am – 9 pm Thursday, Friday; 9 am – 5 pm Saturday

Perth
8.30 am – 5.30 pm Monday, Tuesday, Wednesday, Friday; 8.30 am – 9 pm Thursday; 8.30 am – 5 pm Saturday

Sydney
8.30 am – 5.30 pm Monday, Tuesday, Wednesday, Friday; 8.30 am – 9 pm Thursday; 8.30 am – 4 pm Saturday; 10 am – 4 pm Sunday (many, but not all, stores)

TAXIS

Taxi ranks can be found everywhere, or you can phone for a taxi for a small additional charge (numbers are listed in the Yellow Pages of the telephone directory).

Nothing works faster and with more efficiency than the meter of a cab. As you open the door, before you even open your mouth to give the destination, the digital display on the meter will have begun its silent yet remorseless journey into your pocket. Taxis are recommended strictly for shorter trips.

TELECOMMUNICATIONS

Telephone calls can be made from the numerous telephone boxes located in cities, suburbs and country towns. There is a public telephone section open at all times at every post office. Red phones are only for local calls (30 cents; 10c and 20c coins accepted), while other calls may be made from green, gold or blue phones (10c, 20c,

50c and $1 coins accepted). A blinking light on the phone warns you when to insert more coins. It may be bothersome to use a public call box, but it's much cheaper than going through the hotel switchboard. Check the telephone directory or with the long-distance operator for details of costs. Credit card phones, which accept all major international credit cards, are located at airports, many hotels and in other city locations.

TIME ZONES

Being such a vast land mass, Australia operates on three different times, and to add to the complexity some states adopt day-light saving (putting the clock forward one hour) in summer.

New South Wales (Sydney), Victoria (Melbourne), Queensland (Brisbane) and Tasmania (Hobart) are 10 hours ahead of Greenwich mean time (GMT). South Australia (Adelaide), being slightly west of these states, is nine and a half hours ahead of GMT, while Western Australia (Perth), which is very much farther west, is eight hours ahead of GMT.

TIPPING

Tipping is not generally widespread in Australia. A service charge is not added to restaurant bills, but it is customary at better class restaurants to leave a tip (not more than 10 percent) for exemplary service. Australians in the service industry such as hairdressers, airport porters and taxi drivers do not usually expect a tip, the one exception being hotel porters.

The tip scale is as follows; Taxis: none. Porters: A$1 per piece of luggage. Hotels, Restaurants & Nightspots: 10%. Chambermaids: A$1 per week. Barbers & Beauticians: 10 per cent. Doorman, Ushers, Attendants & Small Services: 50 cents.

VISAS

To enter Australia, you will need a valid passport and a current visa, with the exception of holders of New Zealand passports, who do not need a visa. Visas may be obtained free from the Australian High Commission, Embassy or Consulate in your country.

WEIGHTS AND MEASURES

The metric system is used for all weights and measures. For those accustomed to the imperial system, tape measures, rulers, scales etc. are usually marked in both metric and imperial units.

DIRECTORY

ACCOMMODATION

The following is a broad selection from the many types of accommodation available in the capital cities of Australia. It has not been possible to publish a comprehensive list, which would require an entire book itself, and it should be noted that the publishers do not consider those establishments omitted due to the limitations of space to be unworthy of recommendation.

Adelaide
Five-Star
Hilton International
233 Victoria Square
Adelaide 5000
Tel: 217 0711

Hyatt Regency
North Terrace
Adelaide 5000
Tel: 231 1234

Terrace Adelaide
150 North Terrace
Adelaide 5000
Tel: 217 7552

Luxury
Adelaide Meridien
Melbourne Street
North Adelaide 5006
Tel: 267 3033

Adelaide Parkroyal
226 South Terrace
Adelaide 5000
Tel: 223 4355

Hindley
65 Hindley Street
Adelaide 5000
Tel: 31 5552

Moderate
Adelaide Travelodge
208 South Terrace
Adelaide 5000
Tel: 223 2744

Grosvenor Hotel
125 North Terrace
Adelaide 5000
Tel: 231 2961

Hotel Adelaide
62 Brougham Place
North Adelaide 5006
Tel: 267 3444

Budget
Central Backpackers
139 Franklin Street
Adelaide 5000
Tel: 231 9355

City Central Motel
23 Hindley Street
Adelaide 5000
Tel: 231 4049

Newmarket Hotel

1 North Terrace
Adelaide 5000
Tel: 211 8533

Brisbane
Five-Star
Hilton International
190 Elizabeth Street
Brisbane 4000
Tel: 231 3131

Powerhouse
Cnr Hunt Street and Kingsford
Smith Drive
Hamilton 4007
Tel: 862 1800

Sheraton Brisbane
249 Turbot Street
Brisbane 4000
Tel: 835 3535

Luxury
Abbey Hotel
160 Roma Street
Brisbane 4000
Tel: 236 1444

Gazebo Hotel
345 Wickham Terrace
Brisbane 4000
Tel: 831 6177

Mayfair Crest
Cnr Ann and Roma Streets
Brisbane 4000
Tel: 229 9111

Moderate
Albert Park Motor Inn
551 Wickham Terrace
Brisbane 4000
Tel: 831 3111

Brisbane Parkroyal
Cnr Alice and Albert Streets
Brisbane 4000
Tel: 221 3411

Tower Hill Motor Inn
239 Wickham Terrace
Brisbane 4000
832 1421

Budget
Dorchester
484 Upper Edward Street
Brisbane 4000
Tel: 831 2967

Marrs Town House
391 Wickham Street
Brisbane 4000
Tel: 831 5388

Soho Motel
333 Wickham Terrace
Brisbane 4000
831 7722

Canberra
Five-Star
Hyatt Hotel
Commonwealth Avenue
Yarralumla 2600
Tel: 270 1234

The Pavilion
Cnr National Circuit and Canberra Avenue
Forrest 2603
Tel: 295 3144

Luxury
Country Comfort Inn
102 Northbourne Avenue
Braddon 2601
Tel: 249 1411

Lakeside International
London Circuit
Canberra City 2601

Tel: 247 6244

Olims Canberra Hotel
Cnr Limestone and Ainslie Avenues
Canberra 2608
Tel: 248 5511

Moderate
Acacia Motor Lodge
65 Ainslie Avenue
Canberra City 2601
Tel: 249 6955

Diplomat International Hotel
Cnr Canberra Avenue and Hely Street
Griffith 2603
Tel: 295 2277

Telopea Park Motel
16 New South Wales Crescent
Forrest 2603
Tel: 295 3722

Budget
Downtown Speros Motel
82 Northbourne Avenue
Canberra City 2601
Tel: 249 1388

Macquarie
18 National Circuit
Barton 2600
Tel: 273 2325

University House
Balmain Crescent
Acton 2601
Tel: 249 5211

Darwin
Five-Star
Beaufort International Hotel
The Esplanade
Darwin 0800
Tel: 82 9911

Sheraton Darwin
32 Mitchell Street
Darwin 0800
Tel: 82 0000

Luxury

Darwin Travelodge
122 The Esplanade
Darwin 0800
Tel: 81 5388

Diamond Beach Hotel Casino
Gilruth Avenue
Mindil Beach 0801
Tel: 46 2666

Moderate
Atrium Hotel
Cnr Peel Street and The Esplanade
Darwin 0800
Tel: 41 0755

Mirambeena Tourist Resort
64 Cavenagh Street
Darwin 0800
Tel: 46 0111

Top End Frontier Hotel/Motel
Cnr Daly and Mitchell Streets
Darwin 0800
Tel: 81 6511

Budget
Cherry Blossom
108 The Esplanade
Darwin 0800
Tel: 81 6734

Darwin Motor Inn
97 Mitchell Street
Darwin 0800
Tel: 81 3901

Tiwi Lodge Motel
53 Cavenagh Street
Darwin 0800
Tel: 81 6471

Hobart
Five-Star
Sheraton Hobart
1 Davey Street
Hobart 7000
Tel: 35 4535

Wrest Point Hotel Casino
410 Sandy Bay Road
Hobart 7005
Tel: 25 0112

Luxury
Hadley's Orient Hotel
34 Murray Street
Hobart 7000
Tel: 23 4355

Innkeepers Lenna of Hobart
20 Runnymede Street
Battery Point 7004
Tel: 23 2911

Westside Hotel
156 Bathurst Street
Hobart 7000
Tel: 34 6255

Moderate
Hatchers Hobart Motor Inn
Fountain Roundabout
Hobart 7000
Tel: 34 2911

Innkeepers St Ives
67 St Georges Terrace
Battery Point 7004
Tel: 30 1801

Wrest Point Motor Inn
410 Sandy Bay Road
Hobart 7005
Tel: 250 0112

Budget
Astor Private Hotel
157 Macquarie Street
Hobart 7000
Tel: 34 6384

Cromwell Cottage
6 Cromwell Street
Battery Point 7004
Tel: 23 6734

Marquis of Hastings Hotel/Motel
209 Brisbane Street
Hobart 7000
Tel: 34 3541

Melbourne
Five-Star
Hyatt on Collins
123 Collins Street
Melbourne 3000
Tel: 657 1234

Menzies at Rialto
495 Collins Street
Melbourne 3000
Tel: 620 9111

Rockman's Regency
Cnr Exhibition and Lonsdale Streets
Melbourne 3000
Tel: 662 3900

Luxury
Elizabeth Tower
792 Elizabeth Street
Melbourne 3000
Tel: 347 9211

Old Melbourne Hotel
5-17 Flemington Road
North Melbourne 3051
Tel: 329 9344

Savoy Park Plaza Hotel
630 Little Collins Street
Melbourne 3000
Tel: 622 8888

Moderate
Chateau Melbourne Hotel
131 Lonsdale Street
Melbourne 3000
Tel: 663 3161

Flagstaff City Motor Inn
45 Dudley Street
Melbourne 3000
Tel: 329 5788

Magnolia Court
101 Powlett Street
East Melbourne 3002
Tel: 419 4222

Budget
Backpackers City Inn and Carlton Hotel
197 Bourke Street
Melbourne 3000
Tel: 650 4379

Kingsgate Hotel
131 King Street
Melbourne 3000
Tel: 629 3049

North Motalodge
113 Flemington Road
North Melbourne 3051
Tel: 329 7433

Perth
Five-Star
Burswood Resort
Great Eastern Highway
Victoria Park 6100
Tel: 362 7777

Hyatt Regency
99 Adelaide Terrace
Perth 6000
Tel: 225 1234

Observation City Resort Hotel
The Esplanade
Scarborough 6019
Tel: 234 1000

Luxury
Fremantle Esplanade Hotel
46 Marine Terrace
Fremantle 6160
Tel: 30 4000

Perth Parkroyal
54 Terrace Road
Perth 6000
Tel: 325 3811

Vines Resort
Verdelho Dive
Ellen Brook 6055
Tel: 96 1711

Moderate
Chateau Commodore
417 Hay Street
Perth 6000
Tel: 325 0461

Kings Ambassador
517-519 Hay Street
Perth 6000
Tel: 325 6555

Quality Princes Hotel
334 Murray Street

Perth 6000
Tel: 322 2844

Budget
Inn Town Hotel
Cnr Pier and Murray Streets
Perth 6000
Tel: 325 2133

Murray Lodge
718 Murray Street
West Perth 6005
Tel: 321 7441

Pacific Motel
Cnr Stirling and Harold Streets
Mt Lawley 6050
Tel: 328 5599

Sydney
Five-Star
Hilton International Sydney
259 Pitt Street
Sydney 2000
Tel: 266 0610

Regent of Sydney
199 George Street
Sydney 2000
Tel: 238 0000

Sebel Town House
23 Elizabeth Bay Road
Elizabeth Bay 2011
Tel: 358 3244

Luxury
Hyde Park Plaza
38 College Street
Sydney 2010
Tel: 331 6933

Old Sydney Parkroyal
55 George Street
The Rocks 2000
Tel: 252 0524

Waratah Inn
220 Goulburn Street
Sydney 2000
Tel: 281 4666

Moderate
Bayside Hotel

85 New South Head Road
Rushcutters Bay 2027
Tel: 327 8511

North Sydney Travelodge
17 Blue Street
North Sydney 2060
Tel: 955 0499

Park Regis Motel
Cnr Castlereagh and Park Streets
Sydney 2000
Tel: 267 6511

Budget
Backpackers Headquarters
79 Bayswater Road
Sydney 2011
Tel: 331 2520

Criterion Hotel
Cnr Pitt and Park Streets
Sydney 2000
Tel: 264 3093

Roslyn Gardens Motor Inn
4 Roslyn Gardens
Kings Cross 2011
Tel: 358 1944

AIRLINES — DOMESTIC
Adelaide
Ansett Airlines
205 Greenhill Road
Adelaide 5000
Tel: 233 3322

Australian Airlines
144 North Terrace
Adelaide 5000
Tel: 217 3333

Brisbane
Ansett Airlines
733 Ann Street
Fortitude Valley 4000
Tel: 854 2828

Australian Airlines
247 Adelaide Street
Brisbane 4000
Tel: 223 3333

East-West Airlines

195 Adelaide Street
Brisbane 4000
Tel: 854 2296

Canberra
Ansett Airlines
Jolimont Centre
Northbourne Avenue
Canberra City 2600
Tel: 13 1300

Australian Airlines
Jolimont Centre
Northbourne Avenue
Canberra City 2600
Tel: 13 1313

Darwin
Ansett Airlines
46 Smith Street
Darwin 0800
Tel: 80 3333

Australian Airlines
16 Bennett Street
Darwin 0800
Tel: 82 3311

Hobart
Ansett Airlines
178 Liverpool Street
Hobart 7000
Tel: 38 0800

Australian Airlines
4 Liverpool Street
Hobart 7000
Tel: 38 3511

East-West Airlines
126 Collins Street
Hobart 7000
Tel: 11 2411

Melbourne
Ansett Airlines
465 Swanston Street
Melbourne 3000
Tel: 668 2222

Australian Airlines
50 Franklin Street
Melbourne 3000
Tel: 665 3333

East-West Airlines
215 Swanston Street
Melbourne 3000
Tel: 668 2033

Perth
Ansett Airlines
26 St Georges Terrace
Perth 6000
Tel: 323 1111

Australian Airlines
55 St Georges Terrace
Perth 6000
Tel: 323 3333

Sydney
Ansett Airlines
Cnr Oxford and Riley Streets
Sydney 2000
Tel: 268 1111

Australian Airlines
Cnr Hunter and Philip Streets
Sydney 2000
Tel: 693 3333

East-West Airlines
54 Carrington Street
Sydney 2000
Tel: 268 1166

**AIRLINES – MAJOR
INTERNATIONAL**
Adelaide
Air New Zealand
Tel: 212 6525
British Airways
Tel: 238 2138
Cathay Pacific
Tel: (008) 212 1655 (toll free)
Continental
Tel: 212 6155
Garuda
Tel: 22 1317
Japan Airlines
Tel: 212 2555
Malaysian Airline System
Tel: 231 1671
Qantas
Tel: 237 8541
Singapore Airlines
Tel: 238 2700
UTA French Airlines

Tel: 232 1466
United Airlines
Tel: 231 1821

Brisbane
Air New Zealand
Tel: 299 3044
British Airways
Tel: 229 3166
Cathay Pacific
Tel: 229 9344
Continental
Tel: 832 3666
Japan Airlines
Tel: 229 9916
Malaysian Airline System
Tel: 229 9888
Qantas
Tel: 833 3747
Singapore Airlines
Tel: 221 6300
UTA French Airlines
Tel: 221 5655
United Airlines
Tel: 221 7477

Canberra
British Airways
Tel: (008) 11 3722 (toll free)
Continental
Tel: (008) 42 2266(toll free)
Garuda
Tel: (008) 22 1317 (toll free)
Malaysian Airline System
Tel: (008) 26 9998 (toll free)
Qantas
Tel: 275 5411
Singapore Airlines
Tel: 247 4122
United Airlines
Tel: 248 9184

Darwin
Garuda
Tel: 816 422
Qantas
Tel: 464 666
Singapore Airlines
Tel: 411 785
Royal Brunei Airlines
Tel: 410 966

Hobart
Air New Zealand

Tel: 136 107
British Airways
Tel: 347 433
Cathay Pacific
Tel: 380 800
Continental
Tel: 222 122
Pan Am
Tel: 676 307
Qantas
Tel: 345 700
United Airlines
Tel: 222 611

Melbourne
Air New Zealand
Tel: 654 3311
British Airways
Tel: 602 3500
Cathay Pacific
Tel: 602 2088
Continental
Tel: 602 5377
Garuda
Tel: 654 2522
Japan Airlines
Tel: 654 2733
Malaysian Airline System
Tel: 654 3255
Qantas
Tel: 602 6026
Singapore Airlines
Tel: 605 2555
UTA French Airlines
Tel: 62 2982
United Airlines
Tel: 602 2544

Perth
Air New Zealand
Tel: 325 1099
British Airways
Tel: 322 5011
Cathay Pacific
Tel: 322 1377
Continental
Tel: 481 1688
Garuda
Tel: 481 0963
Japan Airlines
Tel: 322 0333
Malaysian Airline System
Tel: 325 4499

Qantas
Tel: 322 0222
Singapore Airlines
Tel: 322 2422
UTA French Airlines
Tel: 325 6922
United Airlines
Tel: 321 2719

Sydney
Air New Zealand
Tel: 223 4666
British Airways
Tel: 232 1777
Cathay Pacific
Tel: 231 5122
Continental
Tel: 249 0222
Garuda
Tel: 262 2011
Japan Airlines
Tel: 262 2011
Malaysian Airline System
Tel: 232 3377
Qantas
Tel: 957 0111
Singapore Airlines
Tel: 236 0111
UTA French Airlines
Tel: 247 1821
United Airlines
Tel: 237 8611

ANIMAL PARKS
Australian Capital Territory
Rehwinkel's Animal Park
Mack's Reef Road
Bungendore 2621

New South Wales
Australian Wildlife Park
Wallgrove Road
Eastern Creek 2766

Featherdale Wildlife Park
217-229 Kildare Road
Doonside 2767

Koala Park
84 Castle Hill Road
West Pennant Hills 2120

Waratah Park Wildlife Reserve
Namba Road

Duffys Forest 2084

Northern Territory
Yarrawonga Wildlife Park
Palmerston 0830

Queensland
Bunya Park Wildlife Sanctuary
Bunya Park Drive
Eatons Hill 4037

Lone Pine Koala Sanctuary
Jesmond Road
Fig Tree Pocket
Brisbane 4069

South Australia
Cleland Conservation Park
Summit Road
via Greenhill Road
Summertown 5141

Tasmania
Bonorong Park Wildlife Centre
Briggs Road
Brighton 7403

Tasmanian Devil Park
Arthur Highway
Taranna 7180

Tasmanian Wildlife Park
Mole Creek Road
Mole Creek 7304

Victoria
Healesville Sanctuary
Badger Creek Road
Healesville 3777

Western Australia
Cohunu Wildlife Park
Mills Road
Kelmscott 6111

CREDIT CARD EMERGENCY NUMBERS (toll free)

GENERAL POST OFFICES

TOURIST BUREAUS
Adelaide
South Australian Government Travel Centre

18 King William Street
Adelaide 5000
Tel: 212 1644

Northern Territory Government Tourist Bureau
9 Hindley Street
Adelaide 5000
Tel: 212 1133

Queensland Government Travel Centre
10 Grenfell Street
Adelaide 5000
Tel: 212 2399

Tourism Tasmania
32 King William Street
Adelaide 5000
Tel: 211 7411

Travel Centre of New South Wales
7th Floor, Australian Airlines Building, 144 North Terrace
Adelaide 5000
Tel: 231 3167

Victorian Tourism Commission Travel Centre
16 Grenfell Street
Adelaide 5000
Tel: 231 4129

Western Australian Tourist Centre
T&G Building
Cnr King William and Grenfell Streets
Adelaide 5000
Tel: 212 1344

Brisbane
Queensland Government Travel Centre
196 Adelaide Street
Brisbane 4000
Tel: 833 5255

Northern Territory Government Tourist Bureau
48 Queen Street
Brisbane 4000
Tel: 229 5799

Tourism Tasmania
217 Queen Street
Brisbane 4000
Tel: 221 2744

Travel Centre of New South Wales
Cnr Queen and Edward Streets
Brisbane 4000
Tel: 229 8833

Victorian Tourism Commission Travel Centre
221 Queen Street
Brisbane 4000
Tel: 221 4300

Western Australian Tourist Centre
243 Edward Street
Brisbane 4000
Tel: 229 5794

Canberra
ACT Tourism Commission
65-67 Northbourne Avenue
Canberra City 2600
Tel: 245 6464

Tourism Tasmania
5 Canberra Savings Centre
City Walk
Canberra 2600
Tel: 47 0888

Darwin
Northern Territory Government Tourist Bureau
31 Smith Street Mall
Darwin 0800
Tel: 81 6611

Hobart
Tourism Tasmania
80 Elizabeth Street
Hobart 7000
Tel: 30 0211

Northern Territory Government Tourist Bureau
93 Liverpool Street
Hobart 7000
Tel: 34 4199

Victorian Tourism Commission Travel Centre
Trafalgar Centre
126 Collins Street
Hobart 7000
Tel: 31 0499

Melbourne
Victorian Tourism Commission Travel Centre
230 Collins Street
Melbourne 3000
Tel: 619 9444

ACT Tourism Commission
102 Elizabeth Street
Melbourne 3000
Tel: 654 5088

Northern Territory Government Tourist Bureau
415 Bourke Street
Melbourne 3000
Tel: 670 5007

Queensland Government Travel Centre
257 Collins Street
Melbourne 3000
Tel: 654 3866

South Australian Government Travel Centre
25 Elizabeth Street
Melbourne 3000
Tel: 614 6522

Tourism Tasmania
256 Collins Street
Melbourne 3000
Tel:653 7999

Travel Centre of New South Wales
388 Bourke Street
Melbourne 3000
Tel: 670 7461

Western Australian Tourist Centre
35 Elizabeth Street
Melbourne 3000
Tel: 614 6833

Perth
Western Australian Tourist Centre
Cnr Wellington Street and Forrest Place
Perth 6000
Tel: 483 1111

ACT Tourism Commission
77 St Georges Terrace
Perth 6000
Tel: 25 1533

Northern Territory Government Tourist Bureau
62 St Georges Terrace
Perth 6000
Tel: 322 4255

Queensland Government Travel Centre
55 St Georges Terrace
Perth 6000
Tel: 325 1600

South Australian Government Travel Centre
Wesley Centre
93 William Street
Perth 6000
Tel: 481 1268

Tourism Tasmania
100 William Street
Perth 6000
Tel: 321 2633

Victorian Tourism Commission Travel Centre
56 William Street
Perth 6000
Tel: 481 1484

Sydney
Travel Centre of New South Wales
19 Castlereagh Street
Sydney 2000
Tel: 231 4444

ACT Tourism Commission
14 Martin Place
Sydney 2000
Tel: 233 3666

**Northern Territory Government
  Tourist Bureau**
345-347 George Street
Sydney 2000
Tel: 262 3744

**Queensland Government Travel
  Centre**
75 Castlereagh Street
Sydney 2000
Tel: 232 1788

**South Australian Government
  Travel Centre**
143 King Street
Sydney 2000
Tel: 232 8388

Tourism Tasmania
149 King Street
Sydney 2000
Tel: 233 2500

**Victorian Tourism Commission
  Travel Centre**
430 George Street
Sydney 2000
Tel: 299 2288

**Western Australian Tourist Cen-
tre**
92 Pitt Street
Sydney 2000
Tel: 233 4400

**EMBASSIES & HIGH COMMIS-
SIONS IN CANBERRA**

Argentina
58 Mugga Way,
Red Hill
Tel: 95 1570

Austria
107 Endeavour Street,
Red Hill
Tel: 951 533

Bangladesh
11 Molineaux Place,
Farrer
Tel: 861 200

Belgium

19 Arkana Street,
Yarralumla
Tel: 732 501

Brazil
10 Forster Crescent
Yarralumla
Tel: 731 202 / 732 373

Britain
Commonwealth Avenue,
Yarralumla
Tel: 706 666

Burma
85 Mugga Way,
Red Hill
Tel: 950 045

Canada
Commonwealth Avenue,
Yarralumla
Tel: 733 844

Chile
10 Culgoa Court,
O'Malley
Tel: 862 430

China
247 Federal Highway,
Watson
Tel: 412 446

Cyprus
37 Endeavour Street,
Red Hill
Tel: 952 120

Denmark
15 Hunter Street,
Yarralumla
Tel: 732 195

Egypt, Arab Republic of
125 Monaro Crescent,
Red Hill
Tel: 950 394

Fiji
9 Beagle Street
Red Hill
Tel: 959 148

Finland
10 Darwin Avenue,
Yarralumla
Tel: 733 800

France
6 Perth Avenue,
Yarralumla
Tel: 705 111

Germany, Federal Republic
119 Empire Circuit,
Yarralumla
Tel: 733 177

Greece
Stonehaven Crescent,
Yarralumla
Tel: 733 177

Holy See
2 Vancouver Avenue,
Red Hill
(Office & residence of the
Apostolic Pro-nuncio)
Tel: 953 876

Hungary
79 Hopetoun Circuit,
Yarralumla
Tel: 823 226

India
3 Moonal Place,
Yarralumla
Tel: 733 999

Indonesia
8 Darwin Avenue,
Yarralumla
Tel: 733 222 / 958 911

Iran
14 Torres Street,
Red Hill
Tel: 952 544

Iraq
48 Culgoa Circuit,
O'Malley
Tel: 861 333

Ireland
Arkana Street,

Yarralumla
Tel: 733 022

Israel
6 Turrana Street,
Yarralumla
Tel: 731 309

Italy
12 Grey Street,
Deakin
Tel: 733 333

Japan
112-114 Empire Circuit
Yarralumla
Tel: 733 244

Jordan
20 Roebuck Street,
Red Hill
Tel: 959 951

Kenya
33 Ainslie Avenue,
Canberra City
Tel: 474 688

Korea, Republic of
113 Empire Circuit,
Yarralumla
Tel: 733 044

Lebanon
27 Endeavour Street,
Red Hill
Tel: 957 378

Malaysia
7 Perth Avenue,
Yarralumla
Tel: 731 543

Malta
261 La Perouse Street,
Red Hill
Tel: 950 273

Mauritius
43 Hampton Circuit,
Yarralumla
Tel: 811 203

Mexico

14 Perth Avenue,
Yarralumla
Tel: 733 963

Netherlands, The
120 Empire Circuit,
Yarralumla
Tel: 733 111

New Zealand
Commonwealth Avenue
Yarralumla
Tel: 733 611

Nigeria
7 Terrigal Circuit,
O'Malley
Tel: 861-322

Norway
3 Zeehan Street,
Red Hill
Tel: 956 000 / 7333 444

Pakistan
59 Franklin Street,
Forrest
Tel: 950 021

Papua New guinea
Forster Crescent,
Yarralumla
Tel: 733 322

Peru
111 Monaro Crescent,
Red Hill
Tel: 951 016

Philippines
1 Moonah Place, Yarralumla
Tel: 732 535

Poland
7 Turrana Street, Yarralumla
Tel: 731 208

Portugal
8 Astrolabe Street, Red Hill
Tel: 959 992

Singapore
Forster Crescent, Yarralumla
Tel: 733 944

South Africa
Corner State Circle and Rhodes
Place, Yarralumla
Tel: 732 424

Spain
15 Arkana Street, Yarralumla
Tel: 953 872 / 733 555

Sri Lanka
35 Empire Circuit, Forrest
Tel: 953 521

Sweden
Turrana Street, Yarralumla
Tel: 733 033

Switzerland
7 Melbourne Avenue, Forrest
Tel:733 977

Thailand
111 Empire Circuit Yarralumla
Tel: 731 149

Turkey
60 Mugga Way, Red Hill
Tel: 950 227

USSR
78 Canberra Avenue, Griffith
Tel: 959 033

USA
Moonah Place, Yarralumla
Tel: 705 000

Uruguay
Adelaide House, Phillip
Tel: 824 418

Vietnam
6 Timbara Crescent, O'Malley
Tel: 866 059

Yugoslavia
11 Nuyts Street, Red Hill
Tel: 951 458

Zambia
33 Ainslie Avenue
Canberra City
Tel: 472 088

PHOTO CREDITS

Australian High Commission : front endpaper, 3, 14/15, 22, 32, 96/97, 99, 102, 152, 168/169, 185, 192/193
Australian Tourist Commission : 62, 166, 172, 174/175, 183, 188, 190/191, 194, 280
Antiques of the Orient : 11, 12, 17, 18/19
Paul Forster : 68, 124
Jill Gocher : 60, 79, 292/293, 295, 296
Hotel Conrad & Jupiters Casino : 198, 214
Bob King : viii (bottom), viii/ix (top), ix (top), ix (bottom), xv (bottom), 33, 64, 67, 71, 72, 73, 77, 78, 80, 81, 84 (top), 85, 117, 119, 125, 127, 129, 130, 211, 213, 250, 290, 323, 327, 334, 335
Ashwin Mehta : 5, 38, 51, 70 90 (bottom), 112, 136/137, 148, 151, 156, 221, 312
Northern Territory Tourist Division : 281, 282, 284
Alistair McNaughton : 262, 266, 270, 271 (top), 274/275
Pro(file)/Sonia Berto : 157
Pro(file)/Robert Dellapiana : 25, 28, 42/43, 155, 234, 247, 298/299, 315
Pro(file)/Suzanne & Nick Geary : cover
Pro(file)/Dominic Sansoni : 104/105, 138
Pro(file)/Paul Steele : xv (top Left), xvii, 2, 31, 35, 47, 48/49, 58, 216, 218/219, 222, 224, 276, 287, 316, 328
Radin Mohd Noh : 57, 76, 178
Retna Pictures/Chris Beall : 113, 217 (top left), 217 (top right), 278/279, 289
Barry Silkstone : back endpaper, xi (top), xi (middle), xiii (top), xiii (bottom left), xiii (bottom right), xiv (top), xiv (bottom), 59 (bottom)
Geoffrey Somers : xi (bottom), xii (top), 6/7, 131, 146, 147, 204, 207, 209, 210, 212, 215, 217 (bottom), 220 (top), 220 (bottom), 223, 300, 322, 330, 332/333, 342
Morten Strange : 65 (left), 65 (right)
Tourism Office South Australia : 226, 231, 232, 238, 241 (top), 241 (bottom), 244, 245 (bottom)
Trans Globe : xvi, 140, 143, 177, 233, 260/261, 265
Western Australian Tourist Commission : 40, 258
The Image Bank/John William Banagan : 8, 120, 121, 149, 161, 164, 304/305, 310/311, 358
The Image Bank/Walter Bibikow : backcover (top right),108
The Image Bank/Ira Block : 82, 84 (bottom)
The Image Bank/P & G Bowater : 257, 265 (bottom)
The Image Bank/John Callanan : backcover (bottom), 61, 123, 126, 180/181, 200/201, 242
The Image Bank/Flip Chalfant : backcover (top left)
The Image Bank/Alain Choisnet : 246
The Image Bank/Giuliano Colliva : 118, 267
The Image Bank/Michael Coyne : 30, 86, 202, 336
The Image Bank/Gary Crallé : 41, 160, 245 (top)
The Image Bank/PS Grad : 122
The Image Bank/Peter Hendrie : 31, 59 (top), 135, 165, 218, 228/229, 240, 319, 320, 350/351, 356
The Image Bank/Jeff Hunter : 340
The Image Bank/Lionel Isy-Schwart : 101
The Image Bank/Marcel Isy-Schwart : 94, 132/133, 339
The Image Bank/Tad Janocinski : 46
The Image Bank/Philip Kretchmar : 344
The Image Bank/Thomas R Rampy III : 162/163, 252, 256
The Image Bank/Don King : 353
The Image Bank/Margarette Mead : 63
The Image Bank/Eric Meola : 4, 88/89
The Image Bank/Robbi Newman : xii (bottom), xv (top), 26, 44/45, 52, 90 (top), 111, 271
The Image Bank/Jean Pierre Pieuchot : 54, 324/325
The Image Bank/Marc Romanelli : 273
The Image Bank/Michael Salas : 91, 92
The Image Bank/Al Satterwhite : 321
The Image Bank/Michael Skott : 347
The Image Bank/Paul Slaughter : 348
The Image Bank/Charles Tyler : 306, 308
The Image Bank/Alvis Upitis : 37
The Image Bank/Wanda Warming : 354

INDEX

NOTES